# THE MODERN THEOLOGIANS

# The Modern Theologians

## An Introduction to Christian Theology in the Twentieth Century
## Volume II

Edited by David F. Ford

Basil Blackwell

Copyright © Basil Blackwell Ltd 1989

First published 1989

Basil Blackwell Ltd
108 Cowley Road, Oxford, OX4 1JF, UK

Basil Blackwell Inc.
432 Park Avenue South, Suite 1503
New York, NY 10016, USA

*British Library Cataloguing in Publication Data*
The Modern theologians
Vol. 2 1. Christian doctrine I. Ford, David 230
ISBN 0–631–16807–9
ISBN 0–631–16808–7 pbk

*Library of Congress Cataloging in Publication Data*
The Modern theologians.
Contents: v. 2. An introduction to Christian theology in the twentieth century.
Bibliography: p. Includes index. 1. Theology, Doctrinal – History – 20th century.
I. Ford, David, 1948–
BT28.M59 1989     230'.09'04     88–34396
ISBN 0–631–16807–9 (v. 2)
ISBN 0–631–16808–7 (bk. : v. 2)

Typeset in Palatino
by Hope Services, Abingdon
Printed in Great Britain by
Billing and Sons Ltd.,
Worcester

# Contents

Preface                                                              vii

Notes on Contributors                                                 ix

Editorial Note                                                       xii

**Part I   British Theologies**                                        1
 1 Theology through History               S. W. Sykes                  3
 2 Theology through Philosophy            Daniel W. Hardy              30

**Part II   Theologies in the United States**                         73
 3 Theology, Ethics, and Culture          Robin W. Lovin              75
 4 Revisionists and Liberals              James J. Buckley            89
 5 Process Theology                       Kenneth Surin              103
 6 Postliberal Theology                   William C. Placher         115

**Part III   Evangelical and Orthodox Theologies**                   129
 7 Evangelical Theology                   Ray S. Anderson            131
 8 Eastern Orthodox Theology              Rowan Williams             152

**Part IV   New Challenges in Theology**                             171
 9 Latin American Liberation Theology     Rebecca S. Chopp           173
10 Black Theology                         Patrick A. Kalilombe       193
11 Asian Theology                         Kosuke Koyama              217
12 Feminist Theology                      Ann Loades                 235

**Part V   Theology and Religious Diversity**                        253
13 Ecumenical Theology                    George Lindbeck            255
14 Theology of Religions                  Gavin D'Costa              274

Epilogue: Postmodernism and Postscript    David F. Ford              291

List of Dates                                                        298

Glossary                                                             300

Index                                                                319

# Preface

This second volume of *The Modern Theologians* has a wider diversity and geographical scope than the first. Volume I had a certain coherence through focusing largely on continental European theology. That tradition is of importance to most of the theologians discussed in this volume too, but there is also a wide variety of other influences, contexts, and orientations. The Introduction that appears in volume I is intended to cover this second volume as well. Here I give only a brief survey of contents and approach.

The attempt to do some justice to the range of theologies in this volume has led to different, overlapping ways of grouping them. Parts I and II, on theologies from Britain and the United States, are selected geographically, but with further divisions according to content. In part III, evangelical and Eastern Orthodox theologies are distinguished by their relationship to particular Christian traditions. The new challenges in theology in part IV are largely studied geographically but are linked together by the recurring themes of liberation from various forms of oppression, and, in that context, the Christian affirmation of fundamental aspects of human dignity – political, economic, racial, cultural, and sexual. Part V discusses theology and religious diversity through two flourishing twentieth-century developments, ecumenical theology and the theology of religions. Finally, there is some discussion of postmodern thought, which connects with the discussion of modern thought in the Introduction to volume I, and there is a concluding editorial reflection on both volumes.

This volume therefore portrays something of the global scope of modern Christian theology, its diversity amounting often to fragmentation, and the intellectual energy with which it has accompanied and been knitted into major Christian, interreligious, and secular movements.

As in volume I, the criteria for selecting theologians or types of theology have included the requirements that they cover a broad range of major Christian and modern issues and that they are widely studied at the third level (universities, colleges, seminaries). The overall purpose remains that of being a genuine introduction, encouraging readers above all to proceed to the study of the texts of theologians; yet it also aims to give some account of those theologies with which readers cannot engage first-hand. Even less than in volume I can the coverage claim to be comprehensive – the number both of the categories of theology and of the theologians discussed within each category could have been greatly increased. But within the limits of space, the coverage given attempts to be representative.

The contributors are all themselves practitioners of modern theology, and have been encouraged to engage in discussion that might further the debate about their topics. Most of them follow a common pattern: introduction, survey, treatment of selected representative theologians, the debate about their theology, assessment of its achievement and the agenda it sets for the future.

David F. Ford

# Notes on Contributors

**Ray S. Anderson** is Professor of Theology and Ministry, Fuller Theological Seminary, Pasadena, California. He was born in the United States and educated there and in the University of Edinburgh. His publications include *Historical Transcendence and the Reality of God* (London, Grand Rapids, Mich., 1976); *On Being Human* (Grand Rapids, Mich., 1982); *On Being Family* (Grand Rapids, Mich., 1986); and *Theology, Death and Dying* (Oxford, 1986).

**James J. Buckley** is Associate Professor of Theology in Loyola College, Baltimore, Maryland. He was born and educated in the United States. He has written articles on christology, anthropology, Karl Barth, Karl Rahner, and Austin Farrer.

**Rebecca S. Chopp** is Assistant Professor in Theology at the Candler School of Theology, Emory University, Atlanta, Georgia. She was born and educated in the United States. Her publications include *The Praxis of Suffering* (New York, 1986).

**Gavin D'Costa** is Lecturer in Religious Studies in the West London Institute of Higher Education. He was born in Kenya and educated in the Universities of Birmingham and Cambridge, England. His publications include *Theology and Religious Pluralism* (Oxford, New York, 1986) and *John Hick's Theology of Religions. A Critical Evaluation* (London, New York, 1987).

**David F. Ford** is a lecturer in theology in the University of Birmingham, England. He was born in Dublin, studied there and in the Universities of Cambridge, Yale and Tübingen. His publications include *Barth and God's Story. Biblical Narrative and the Theological Method of Karl Barth in the Church Dogmatics* (Frankfurt, Berne, New York, 1981; 2nd edn, 1985); *Jubilate. Theology in Praise*, with Daniel W. Hardy (London, 1984), US title *Praising and Knowing God*

(Philadelphia, 1985); and *Meaning and Truth in 2 Corinthians*, with Frances M. Young (London, 1987, Grand Rapids, Mich., 1988).

**Daniel W. Hardy** is Van Mildert Professor of Theology in the University of Durham, England. He was born in the United States and educated there and in the University of Oxford. His publications include *Jubilate. Theology in Praise* with David F. Ford (London, 1984), US title *Praising and Knowing God* (Philadelphia, 1985), and articles on creation, rationality, and theology and science.

**Patrick A. Kalilombe** WF, was Bishop of Lilongwe, Malawi, before becoming Lecturer in Third World Theologies, Selly Oak Colleges, Birmingham, and Co-Director of the Centre for Black and White Christian Partnership, Selly Oak Colleges. He was born in Malawi and educated there and in Rome, Graduate Theological Union, Berkeley, California, and the University of Birmingham. His publications include *Christ's Church in Lilongwe Today and Tomorrow* (Likuni, 1973) and *From Outstations to Small Christian Communities* (Eldoret, 1984).

**Kosuke Koyama** is John D. Rockefeller Jr Professor of Ecumenics and World Christianity in Union Theological Seminary, New York. He was born in Japan and educated there and in Drew University and Princeton Theological Seminary, USA and in Bossey, Switzerland. His publications include *Waterbuffalo Theology* (London, 1974), *No Handle on the Cross* (London, 1977), *Three Mile an Hour God* (London, 1978), and *Mount Fuji and Mount Sinai* (London, 1984).

**George Lindbeck** is Professor of Theology in Yale Divinity School, New Haven, Connecticut. He was born in China and educated in Gustavus Adolphus College, Minnesota, and Yale University. His publications include *The Future of Roman Catholic Theology* (London and Philadelphia, 1970), and *The Nature of Doctrine. Religion and Theology in a Postliberal Age* (Philadelphia, London, 1984).

**Ann Loades** is Senior Lecturer in Philosophy of Religion in the University of Durham. She was born in England and educated there and in McMaster University, Canada. Her publications include *Kant and Job's Comforters* (London, 1985) and *Searching for Lost Coins* (London, 1987).

**Robin W. Lovin** is Associate Professor of Ethics in the Divinity School, University of Chicago. He was born and educated in the United States. His publications include *Christian Faith and Public Choices* (Philadelphia, 1984).

**William C. Placher** is Professor of Philosophy and Religion in Wabash College, Indiana. He was born and educated in the United States. His publications include *A History of Christian Theology* (Philadelphia, 1983) and *Readings in the History of Christian Theology*, 2 vols (Philadelphia, 1987).

**Kenneth Surin** is Associate Professor in the Department of Religious Studies, Duke University, North Carolina. He was born in Malaysia and educated in the University of Birmingham. His publications include *Theology and the Problem of Evil* (Oxford, 1986), and *The Turnings of Darkness and Light: Essays in Philosophical and Systematic Theology* (Cambridge, 1988). He is editor of *Modern Theology*.

**S. W. Sykes** is Regius Professor of Divinity in the University of Cambridge. He was born in England and educated there and in Harvard University. His publications include *Christian Theology Today* (London, 1971, 1983), *The Integrity of Anglicanism* (London, 1978), *The Identity of Christianity* (London, 1984) and numerous edited volumes.

**Rowan Williams** is Lady Margaret Professor of Divinity, Christ Church, University of Oxford. He was born in Wales and educated in the universities of Cambridge and Oxford. His publications include *The Wound of Knowledge* (London, 1979), *Resurrection: Interpreting the Easter Gospel* (London, 1982) and *Arius: Heresy and Tradition* (London, 1987).

# Editorial Note

Where a book is referred to in the notes to a chapter and appears also in the bibliography, place and date of publication are given in the bibliography only.

A date of first publication refers to the first edition in the original language.

# Part I

# British Theologies

British theology differs greatly in history, character and institutional setting from most of the theologies discussed in volume I of *The Modern Theologians*, and the two chapters in this section are especially concerned to understand it in its context.

Stephen Sykes describes the institutional history of British theology as the background for a discussion of the untypical P. T. Forsyth, followed by analysis of three types of theology through history. In theology through New Testament studies, C. H. Dodd and C. F. D. Moule stand for the essential contribution of historical findings to an orthodox Christian faith, while Dennis Nineham is skeptical about the possibility of any such contribution. In the field of patristics, G. W. H. Lampe and Maurice Wiles are shown arriving through their historical studies at liberal positions on the Trinity and other classical Christian doctrines. In modern history, Norman Sykes recovers the value of the eighteenth century for contemporary ecclesiastical, ecumenical, and political practice; and Herbert Butterfield discerns through more recent centuries the involvement of God and the relevance of Christian faith. Also included is a brief discussion of the impact of the controversial volume *The Myth of God Incarnate*. The conclusion affiirms the value of this tradition and lists its current shortcomings, especially in the areas of ethics, politics, and social theology.

Daniel Hardy describes the distinctive features of British (especially English) theology as shaped by the effort of Anglicanism in the aftermath of the Reformation to be neither simply Protestant nor Roman Catholic, and to contribute to national as well as church life. He sees it rooted in common practice of life, thought, prayer, and politics, and committed to the public examination and development of that practice according to rational standards that are grounded in their author, God. He traces that tradition in modern times in its continuation and fragmentation, and in various departures from it. In particular, he discusses the theology of Donald MacKinnon, which continues the tradition, and those of John MacQuarrie, John Hick, and Don Cupitt, which represent different forms of divergence from it. He concludes with an affirmation of the potential for the future in recovering an approach to theology which accords so deeply with current emphases on common practice and particularity, on a balanced hermeneutics, on theology's concern for truth in the world, and on the well-being of the whole of society.

# 1

# Theology through History

## S. W. Sykes

### INTRODUCTION: THEOLOGY IN BRITISH UNIVERSITIES

It is a curious fact, worthy of some initial comment, that in a work devoted to modern theologians it has seemed appropriate to group the contribution of British writers into two sections, labelled respectively 'Theology through History' and 'Theology through Philosophy'. Why, looking at volume I of *The Modern Theologians*, should it be the case that whereas there is no shortage of German-speaking theologians of major stature, such as Karl Barth, Rudolf Bultmann or Karl Rahner, Britain can field only one such figure, Thomas Torrance?

One important explanation of this state of affairs has contrasted the favorable philosophical context in German intellectual life, with the situation in the British universities. In Germany, from the days of Immanuel Kant (d. 1804), philosophy was the indispensable and highly stimulating conversation-partner for successive generations of theologians. British theologians, who sometimes knew too little German to profit from this literature or who affected to despise it, enjoyed no comparable stimulus from their own context.

A further explanation – or rather excuse – has been frequently offered, namely that what is called 'the Anglo-Saxon mind' is inherently disinclined to engage in systematic reflection. For example, a well-known Scottish theologian, Hugh Ross Mackintosh, who wrote an account of *Types of Modern Theology* (posthumously published in 1937), whilst attributing greater numbers, freedom, and thoroughness to German theological scholarship, offered as a compensation the comforting thought that the 'Anglo-Saxon mind' very often displayed sounder judgment.[1] But it is necessary to be skeptical about the existence of national 'minds', if only for the reason that, in the past, theories which invoked these entities were often the vehicle of nationalistic prejudice. What these abstractions may amount to is the cumulative impact of a particular pattern of education upon the way in which generations of intellectuals have been taught to think. In the case of British education in theology there have been some very important differences from the way in which theology has been taught and studied on the European continent and in Scandinavia. To these we must give some attention.

Since the nineteenth century, theology of one kind or another has been taught in British universities. In England, the Church of England has been a strong influence upon the content of the syllabuses, and also, especially in Cambridge, Durham and Oxford, a very high proportion of the teachers of theology have been (until very recently) Anglicans in orders. From the late nineteenth century, however, the virtual Anglican monopoly on the ancient universities was broken, and syllabuses of theology were constructed which were (supposedly) denominationally neutral. That is to say, they were no longer conceived of as programs of study which prepared Anglicans for ordination in the Church of England, but courses which could properly be taken by any interested person. The Church of England from this time onwards developed its own independent theological colleges, or seminaries, in which specifically Anglican disciplines (liturgical and pastoral studies, for example) were taught. The Free Churches, which under Anglican persecution in the seventeenth century had developed their own sometimes distinguished Dissenting Academies, likewise trained their ministers in their own theological colleges from the late eighteenth century. The (supposed) neutrality of the new syllabuses in theology in both the ancient and the more recent civic universities enabled Methodists, Congregationalists, Baptists, and Presbyterians to participate as both students and teachers, and, subsequently, since the ecumenical developments of the 1960s, Roman Catholics have played an increasingly active role. Today both the staff and students of the theological departments of English universities are completely mixed denominationally, and, with the exception of certain professorial appointments reserved for Anglican priests in the Universities of Durham and Oxford, academic posts are without denominational (or indeed religious) tie or affiliation.

In this process the key development was the establishment by the Church of England of its own independent theological colleges. By contrast, the Church of Scotland has no such institutions, and the theological faculties of Scottish universities are considered to be ministerial training institutions, many of whose appointments committees have predominantly Church of Scotland representation. Although non-Presbyterians have been, and are, regularly appointed to university teaching posts in the theological faculties in Scotland, the Church of Scotland is obliged to preserve its influence in their syllabuses and staff if its pastoral needs are to be met.

The importance of university curricula to the formation of a national theological tradition will be obvious enough. In Europe and Scandinavia systematic or dogmatic theology is generally understood to be a church-related discipline. All the major theologians considered in volume I have taught in either Protestant or Roman Catholic institutions, and have been subject to the doctrinal norms (and in the case of one theologian, Hans Küng, the ecclesiastical discipline) of their respective denominations. In England, by contrast, the syllabus which is taught and examined is not conceived from the standpoint of the criteria of denominational orthodoxy.

From some points of view freedom from denominational control might well be seen as an advantage; but there have also been costs to be paid. An especially severe consequence has been the failure to promote the study of systematic theology in the university context. (We are speaking now of English and Welsh universities; an exception has to be made in the case of Scotland, where, for the reasons explained above, chairs of reformed dogmatic theology have existed from the sixteenth century. Thus it is no accident that Professor T. F. Torrance, the one British theologian to be included in Volume I of *The Modern Theologians* occupied such a chair at the University of Edinburgh.) In England it has not proved possible until very recently to conceive of a non-denominational way of approaching the subject-matter of systematic theology. The absence of this discipline has created a vacuum which has not gone unfilled; and a variety of substitutes for systematics can readily be identified. Among these have been 'biblical theology', 'dogmatic theology', 'modern theology' and 'philosophical theology'. By 'biblical theology' one should understand the attempt to construct a theological synthesis of biblical themes, an enterprise which became popular in the 1960s and 1970s and strongly influenced the teaching of New Testament theology. By 'dogmatic theology' is meant the study of the formally defined dogmas of the early church, an inquiry which syllabuses of Anglican origin generally terminated in the fifth century. Under 'modern theology' the syllabuses generally included the 'great names' of nineteenth- and twentieth-century European theology. 'Philosophical theology' was a specifically British development of the ancient discipline of 'apologetics', applied to the common eighteenth-century topics of God, freedom, and immortality, including such subjects as miracle, prayer, and providence, but generally abstracted from any consideration of the doctrines of creation, election, redemption or the last things. One major casualty of this more or less unconscious filling of the gap caused by a lack of denominational systematics has been the virtual absence of serious attention to the doctrines of the church and sacraments, which were generally avoided in universities as being either of secondary importance or else too controversial.

It now becomes apparent why it is necessary to treat the contribution of British theologians to modern theology indirectly through the attention given to history and philosophy. The main reason is that the institutional base for the study of systematic theology in the universities, outside Scotland, has been wanting. None the less, both the history and philosophy of theology have been lively disciplines and the contributions made by British theologians to both of these fields have contained some answers to the pressing questions of Christian doctrine.

In the sections that follow I propose to give attention to three doctrinal areas which have been characteristically treated in Britain by those whose training and habit of mind has been historical, rather than systematic. These are: christology, especially in the work of three historians of the New Testament period, C. H. Dodd, C. F. D. Moule and D. E. Nineham; trinitarian theology, in the writing of two patristic experts, G. W. H. Lampe and M. F. Wiles; and the doctrine of the church, in the work of two historians of the Reformation and modern eras, N. Sykes and H. Butterfield. But first we must consider the work of a man who, more than any other, deserves to be considered an exception to the account given above, a British systematician of wide influence and importance, Peter Taylor Forsyth.

## P. T. Forsyth (1848–1921)

It may come as some surprise that one should include as a modern theologian a man who died in 1921. The explanation lies in the publishing history of his major works. These, although for the most part written in the decade between 1907 and 1917, were all reissued in the 1950s, a period which also witnessed a flurry of studies of his theological achievement. One reason for the later revival of interest in Forsyth was the discovery that he had earlier articulated many of the themes of Karl Barth's protest against liberalism. Both Barth and Forsyth had reacted vigorously against the dominant Ritschlianism of the early years of the twentieth century, and both had expressed an early appreciation for the thought of Kierkegaard. But it makes no great sense of either Barth or Forsyth to designate the latter 'a Barthian before Barth'.

In the light of what we have said about the tradition of theology in Scotland, it will not come as a surprise to discover that P. T. Forsyth was a Scot, though a Congregationalist and not a member of the Church of Scotland. A classics graduate of the University of Aberdeen, his home town, he first worked as an assistant to the professor of Latin. Forsyth's interest in theology was greatly stimulated by friendship with a brilliant young orientalist, William Robertson Smith, who in 1870, at the age of 24, had become professor of oriental languages and Old Testament exegesis at the Free Church College, Aberdeen. It was at Robertson Smith's suggestion that Forsyth travelled to Göttingen to study theology under Albrecht Ritschl, returning to England to undertake ordination training for the Congregationalist ministry at New College, London. For twenty-five years, from 1876 to 1901, Forsyth worked in a series of pastorates, in Bradford, London, Manchester, Leicester, and Cambridge. In the light of this experience, it is perhaps unsurprising that in the opening sentence of his first major book, *Positive Preaching and the Modern Mind* (1907), he wrote: 'It is, perhaps, an overbold beginning, but I will venture to say that with its preaching Christianity stands or falls.' From 1901 until his death in 1921 Forsyth was Principal of Hackney College, a Congregationalist Theological College in London, one of seven (two Anglican, three Congregationalist, one Wesleyan and one Baptist) which in 1900 had combined to constitute a faculty of theology in the University of London. London University thus became a leading protagonist of the denominationally neutral syllabus of theological study, of which we have spoken. Students would study for the university degree in theology, while at the same time learning in their theological colleges the disciplines and outlook of their own denomination.

Although Forsyth was by every instinct a systematic theologian, rather than a practitioner of theology through history, as were the theologians we are to consider, it is none the less instructive to consider his view of the sort of historico-critical biblical study which had set the agenda for so much nineteenth- as also twentieth-century theology. Having whole-heartedly abandoned the doctrine of biblical infallibility, Forsyth insisted that the focus of the theologian's attention is on the gospel of God's grace, rather than the mere text of the Bible. It is the communication of the gospel which raises the Bible, he believed, above a mere chronicle of events to be dissected and discussed by scholarly pedants. A genuine historian is distinguished from an annalist by the fact that the former has a theory, hypothesis, or law to advance. In the case of Christian theology the place of theory is taken by an account of God's action, the gospel itself, which he speaks of as God's unique word to man, not man's hypothesis about God.

Forsyth adopted from a contemporary German theologian, Georg Wobbermin (1869–1943), a distinction between two German words, *Geschichte* and *Historie*. The latter he defined as 'history as it may be settled by the methods of historical science'; the former, as 'the evolving organism of mankind taken as a moral and spiritual unity'.[2] In the records of the events of the New Testament we have to do with both *Historie* and *Geschichte*. The act of God in Jesus Christ is an event conveyed in an inspired (but not infallible) apostolic interpretation emitting its own creative 'radiance'. Historical study of the life of Christ is not going to provide us with proofs of the propositions of christology, because it is *Geschichte* which supplies us with the tradition in which we stand and which is a larger thing than the sum of individually certain events as established by critical scholarship. The manifestation of the 'great fact' of Christ and its self-interpretation are indivisible from the active tradition and experience of the living Church and it is this integration of Christ, the Lord and the Holy Spirit which differentiates gospel history from all other history. It is the Holy Spirit who makes of Christ one who is our contemporary. Christian certainty has no foundation in reason or nature, but only points of contact. Religion, Forsyth roundly declared, is natural to man; faith is not. Christianity is not. The common origin of views of this kind, expressed by Forsyth and later by Karl Barth, is undoubtedly Martin Luther.

Biblical criticism is, therefore, no cause for panic for a faith which founds itself upon grace. Forsyth described how exposure to the historical research of biblical scholars had actually deepened his faith, turning it from 'ill-founded sentiment' and 'amiable religiosity' to the cross of Christ.

> What was needed before we discussed the evidence for the resurrection, was a revival of the sense of God's judgement – grace in the Cross, a renewal of the sense of holiness and so of sin, as the Cross set forth the one, and exposed the other.[3]

The unity of the Scripture is thus the unity given it by its being the history of redemption.

Forsyth wrote two books on the atonement, *The Cruciality of the Cross* (1909, consisting of revised and expanded papers from the years 1908–9) and *The Work of Christ* (1910). Although the interpretation of the cross was central to his thought, he is widely considered not to have given satisfactory expression to the profundity of what he had to say. Above all else Forsyth wanted to insist on the ethical force of the whole of Christian doctrine, and asserted the need for what he called 'the moralizing of dogma'. But unlike the Ritschlian school of his day this methodological proposal did not lead to what has been called the 'moral influence' theory of the atonement, the view that God draws humanity to himself by the power of Christ's example of loving self-sacrifice. On the contrary, Forsyth emphasized that God has *done* something for humanity, not merely demonstrated, shown, or said something. Here again we note the priority of the actual. What has been effected is a change of God's practical relation to humanity, carried out by God himself.

The reason for this emphasis lay in Forsyth's retention of the notion of holiness in every use of the idea of divine love. He accepted St Anselm's argument that it is impossible for a holy God to treat sin as though it were not sin. There is a moral necessity for divine judgment. Christ, as God in man, is humanity's representative, a form of anticipated solidarity with the whole of the human race, of which he is Head.

Although Forsyth did not with any clarity espouse any one of the so-called 'theories of atonement', one theme is predominant, that of sacrifice. The importance of this traditional idea is apparent in what for many is the most powerful and creative of Forsyth's works, *The Person and Place of Jesus Christ*, also produced in the astonishingly productive year, 1909. Here Forsyth explicitly defended a version of the so-called 'kenotic christology', which had flourished in German Protestantism in the second half of the nineteenth century. By 1909, however, this doctrine was, as Forsyth must have known, in eclipse in Germany, having been vigorously opposed by many writers, not least Albrecht Ritschl himself.

The central point of kenotic christology was to speak of the incarnation of the Second Person of the divine Trinity as his self-emptying. It was ostensibly based on Philippians 2: 5–11, especially on the description of Christ as one 'who, though he was in the form of God did not count equality with God a thing to be grasped, but emptied himself, taking the form of a servant, being born in the likeness of men'. Though the exegesis was disputed, and though the new theory plainly contradicted part of the christology of the authoritative Tome of Leo (AD 451), it proved irresistibly attractive to several

British theologians of the early twentieth century, among them a number of Anglicans.

There is no one standard form of kenotic theory, but many of the theories are linked by their receptivity to the idea of sacrifice. In Forsyth's case it is particularly striking that the whole theology of the self-offering of Christ is presented as the paradigm of what he called 'priestly religion'. The Christian faith, according to this remarkable Congregationalist, is priestly or it is nothing. 'It gathers about a priestly cross on earth and a great High Priest Eternal in the heavens.' Evangelical Christianity has, he believed, to choose between Christ as an inspiring social reformer and Christ as priestly redeemer. Forsyth laid his stress upon a collective, not merely individualistic priesthood of all believers, and declared:

> The greatest function of the Church in full communion with Him is priestly. It is to confess, to sacrifice, to intercede for the whole human race in Him. The Church, and those who speak in its name, have power and commandment to declare to the world being penitent the absolution and remission of their sins in Him.[4]

This priestly lay religion is founded upon the cross of Christ. Forsyth's program of the moralizing of dogma left him, he believed, with the alternative of conceiving of the incarnation either as the result of a progressive moral growth completed in Christ's sacrificial death, or as the outcome of a great and creative moral decision *before* he entered the world. The latter was Forsyth's preferred course. The act of incarnation, or coming into flesh, must itself, therefore, be a moral achievement on God's behalf. This is what, he insisted, the doctrine of kenosis, or divine self-emptying, was attempting to express:

> We face in Christ a Godhead self-reduced but real whose infinite power took effect in self-humiliation, whose strength was perfected in weakness, who consented not to know with an ignorance divinely wise, and who emptied himself in virtue of his divine fulness.[5]

Kenosis is matched by the plerosis, or self-fulfillment, of Christ. Two-nature christology is replaced, in Forsyth's theology, by a two-act christology, an act from the divine side and a corresponding one from the human side. The self-fulfillment he characterized as an appropriation and deepening of the man, Jesus, in a sinless life and holy work. Thus Forsyth allowed a 'progressive incarnation', so long as it is seen to have a kenotic basis. In order to explain what he had in mind he deployed the idea of a 'mode of being'. For one who is infinite omniscience the eternal mode of being will imply an intuitive and simultaneous knowledge of everything. The incarnate Lord, however, will have that mode of being which can have only a discursive and successive knowledge, enlarging itself to greater knowledge under the normal moral conditions of humanity. The entry of the infinite into the temporal and finite involved, therefore, a 'retraction' of the mode of being of the divine attributes from actual to potential; and the history of Christ's growth was, correspondingly, that of the recovery by gradual moral conquest of the mode of being from which he originally came.

The impact of Forsyth upon British theology, and not least of his espousal of a sacrificial-kenotic view of the incarnation and cross, has been considerable. His polemic against the ethical naïvety of sentimental Protestantism is still a delight to read. What the writings lack in analytic clarity they gain in rhetorical power, doubtless the result of his long apprenticeship in the pastoral ministry. His handling of the Bible was brilliantly intuitive and has survived the rise and fall of a number of critical fashions. But it must be said that the aphoristic style of writing which came so naturally to him leaves the student of Forsyth with a large number of puzzles. He was an excellent theologian, but his inheritance needed to be developed more fully and rigorously. Though in his day he had numerous admirers, Forsyth had no obvious successor. Lacking a tradition of systematicians to press further the issues which he so skilfully illuminated, British theology shows his abiding influence in the tradition of critical orthodoxy which has manifestly constituted the core of its theological life.

## NEW TESTMAMENT SCHOLARS

### C. H. Dodd (1844–1973)

We consider now the significance of a group of historians of the New Testament period who have made major contributions to British theology, notably in the area of christology. First among them is C. H. Dodd, a Welshman and Congregationalist. Dodd won a scholarship to Oxford where he took a first class degree in Classics in 1907. Like Forsyth he went to Germany for a semester, though in Dodd's case it was at Adolf von Harnack's feet that he sat in the University of Berlin, and the subject of his interest was Roman Imperial numismatics. After a period of training for the ministry at

Mansfield College, Oxford, he was for three years minister of a Congregational church in Warwick. He was called back to Oxford in 1915 to a tutorship in his old college, a post which he occupied until his election in 1930 to the Rylands Chair of Biblical Criticism and Exegesis in the University of Manchester. After five years in Manchester he was appointed Norris-Hulse Professor in the University of Cambridge, where he remained until his retirement in 1949. In 1950, however, he was made General Director of the ecumenical group which produced the *New English Bible* (New Testament first edition, 1961; second edition, 1970).

The bare recital of his career somewhat masks its significance in the institutional terms which we have emphasized. C. H. Dodd came up to Oxford a mere thirty years after Oxford and Cambridge had first opened their doors to those who could not in conscience subscribe to the Anglican Thirty-Nine Articles, and at a time when it was still impossible for non-Anglicans to receive higher degrees in divinity. Mansfield college had been founded specifically to enable non-conformists to train for the ministry in the setting of an ancient university and to provide a focus for Congregationalist undergraduates. The college quickly became a magnet for some of the outstanding non-Anglican scholars of the day, who were disbarred from promotion to chairs in Oxford, Cambridge, and London. Dodd's predecessor in the Rylands Chair in Manchester had been the first non-Anglican to become a professor of divinity in an English university, and Dodd's election to the newly-merged Norris-Hulse Chair of Divinity in Cambridge was the first occasion on which a dissenter had held a professorship of divinity in one of the ancient universities.[6]

All the more significant, therefore, is the fact that his sustained concern for the historical basis of the New Testament should closely accord with what one might call the critical-orthodox consensus of British theology as a whole. Dodd's writings concerned the central corpus of New Testament books, the letters of Paul, the Synoptic Gospels and the Fourth Evangelist. But the problem with which he was preoccupied throughout his life was one and the same, the relationship between the theological conviction that God is sovereign over history and the historical particularity of the events surrounding the life of Jesus and the early Christian communities. Dodd is chiefly celebrated as the originator of an influential theory about the character of the primitive preaching of the last things. This is generally known as 'realized eschatology', and by it he meant quite simply that the *eschaton* or Age to Come has already broken into history in the ministry, death, and resurrection of Jesus.

In 1905, in an essay devoted to the discussion of evolution, P. T. Forsyth had already insisted that human history does not bear the character of steady evolutionary progress, but rather of progress by crisis. From the standpoint of a Christian philosophy of history, there is a central and absolute crisis in the cross of Christ. In 1920, in Dodd's first complete book, *The Meaning of Paul for Today*, (published in a series with the Forsythian title *The Christian Revolution*), 'crisis' was the key concept in interpreting Paul's philosophy of history. The fundamental belief of all early Christians, according to Dodd, was their realization that they were living at the crisis of human history, that they were 'Children of the Day', and inhabitants of a new world. At first, according to Dodd, Paul had expected a visible return of Christ, but later the apocalyptic imagery with which this thought was clothed grew less central to his way of thinking, and he dwelt more explicitly upon the thought of what Dodd termed 'the Divine Commonwealth', a union of humankind deeper than the divisions of nationality, culture, sex or status.

'Crisis' remained a significant term in Dodd's first major book, *The Authority of the Bible* (1928), a work which contains the most complete statement of his constructive theological position. 'The death of Jesus', he affirmed, 'was the crisis of religion.' The reshaping of human history which was the outcome of the death and resurrection of Christ makes of Christianity a uniquely historical religion; 'for the Christian, things and events are a sacramental manifestation of God'.[7] This attitude towards history has a natural corollary in relation to research into the life and teaching of Jesus. Plainly such research must be pursued – as, indeed, Harnack had insisted. The difficulty was that Harnack's program had run into trouble from those, such as Albert Schweitzer and Johannes Weiss, who claimed that the New Testament demonstrated both that Jesus believed in the future, coming sovereignty of God, and that this expectation turned out to be unfilfilled. When scholars might arrive at such negative conclusions, was not commitment to historical research intolerably risky for the faith of a Christian?

Dodd's life-long defense of the necessity for Christian scholars to engage in historical research was of enormous importance for British theology. He maintained it on the grounds of principle, namely that there was no alternative to historical inquiry for a faith which based itself upon a revelation in history. But he did so in persistent and gentle dialogue with a number of prominent movements in biblical research which pointed in other directions. Mention has already been made of those who strongly emphasized

the eschatology of Jesus. Other schools of New Testament interpretation also had made an impact. The history-of-religion school,
for example, stressed the extent to which early Christianity borrowed
ideas from a variety of other religious sources; Dodd accepted many
of the school's suggestions, but insisted that, whatever the origins,
the assemblage of ideas and practices constituted something new.
Later, form criticism hoped to work out the tendencies guiding the
transmission of the independent gobbets of Jesus-tradition in the
pre-literary period; Dodd believed he could use the same methods
to reconstruct a considerable amount of authentic history. In
response to Barth's revolt against the dominance of a certain type of
theological liberalism which had invested strongly in historical
criticism, Dodd acknowledged the value of the idea of the unity of
revelation, but maintained that the historical questions needed
historical answers. When Rudolf Bultmann declared the impossibility
(and undesirability) of all attempts to write a life of the Jesus of
history, scholars in Britain taught or influenced by Dodd failed to be
impressed. In 1950 Dodd, in a revealing dialogue with Paul Tillich
precisely on the issue of the risk of historical research, maintained
his characteristic stance. The so-called 'New Quest' of the historical
Jesus, begun by Bultmann's pupils in the later 1950s, was greeted in
Britain with a certain (somewhat smug) satisfaction.

What we find in Dodd is a combination of 'crisis theology',
according to which the meaning of the whole of history is centered
upon the death and resurrection of Jesus, and a cautious and patient
commitment to historical research which provides the warrants for
relatively conservative conclusions about Jesus' life and teaching. At
the end of his career Dodd turned his attention to the Fourth Gospel
and argued, after an exhaustive treatment of its major themes in *The
Interpretation of the Fourth Gospel* (1953), for the independent
historical value of the traditions which it mediates (*Historical
Tradition in the Fourth Gospel*, 1963). In particular, and most
strikingly, he claimed that the Synoptic Gospels' portrait of Jesus is
fundamentally in agreement with that of John:

> The synoptic gospels, to sum up, in poetry, parable and vivid
> dialogue, yield a picture of Jesus as one whose impact on the
> situation brought men to judgement. Its finality is emphasized
> through the symbolism of doomsday, but in fact we see the
> judgement taking place before our eyes. John's method of
> presentation, in abstract general propositions, is widely different,
> but the picture lying behind it is essentially the same.[8]

## C. F. D. Moule (1908–)

Like C. H. Dodd, C. F. D. Moule was a classicist as a student, who received his theological education in theological college, though in Moule's case, in an Anglican institution. In a range of writing, Moule has continued the tradition of critical orthodoxy which we have examined, most notably in his *The Birth of the New Testament* (first edition, 1962; third edition, revised and rewritten, 1981), *The Phenomenon of the New Testament* (1967) and *The Origin of Christology* (1977). Like Dodd, Moule acknowledges the influence of German schools of interpretation, but retains a marked independence of mind and judgment. Over the long period of his tenure of the Lady Margaret Chair of Divinity in Cambridge from 1951 to 1975 he supervised large numbers of research students who have gone on to hold distinguished appointments themselves.

A major aspect of Moule's work has been the attempt to disprove what has seemed occasionally to be a kind of assumption among scholars, that a 'high' christology, which speaks of Jesus as Lord, evolved in the New Testament period out of a more primitive, 'low' christology, which treated him as prophet and teacher. Much of the problematic is determined by German scholarship on the significance of the titles used of Jesus in the New Testament. But Moule is centrally interested in the origins of the christology of Paul, for whom Christ is a corporate figure. He argues that from very early days Jesus was interpreted as 'one who, as no merely human individual, included persons and communities within him, and upon whom Christians found converging all the patterns of relationship between God and man with which they were familiar from their Scriptures'.[9] The purpose of the argument is quite plain. It is to press the apologetic question upon unbelievers how to account for the earliness of this phenomenon. The same strategy emerges in Moule's characteristic handling of evidence for the resurrection, in which he similarly argues that the story of the empty tomb is part of the earliest tradition, and likewise needs to be accounted for.

## D. E. Nineham (1921–)

It would be a mistake to suppose that British New Testament scholarship was committed to forms of 'critical orthodoxy' without dissent. The work of D. E. Nineham is an important indication that more skeptical positions, precisely on the historical issues, also received distinguished representation. Nineham has developed the stance of R. H. Lightfoot (1883–1953), whose early positive reception of form criticism had led to skepticism about the historicity of the Synoptic Gospels. In 1963 Nineham published a commentary on the Gospel of St Mark in which the text is treated as an interweaving of fact and interpretation, an amalgam on which it is simply impossible to deliver a confident historical verdict. A tentative historical outline of a reconstructed life of Jesus might be given, but it would be one which, Nineham increasingly began to feel, would be unacceptable to modern religious taste. In a critical review of C. H. Dodd's last book, *The Founder of Christianity* (1970), Nineham held that the latter's life-long struggle against the consistent eschatology of Weiss and Schweitzer had been unsuccessful. Nineham's subsequently published lectures, *The Use and Abuse of the Bible* (1976), in which he strongly emphasized the irretrievability of the New Testament past and its unavailability for contemporary Christian apologetic, can best be seen as a sharp reaction to the consensus which we have exhibited.

One of the reasons why the theologians we have discussed were so obdurate about the necessity of persisting with historical inquiry into Jesus' life and teaching may have to do with a fact about their education, namely that many of them were classicists before becoming theologians. A classicist is trained to believe in the possibility of reaching a relatively dispassionate conclusion on historical questions, and we may regard it as a considerable strength to British theology that it has scarely wavered from the conviction that the truth of certain key historical propositions about Jesus is logically entailed in the theological enterprise of christology. More challengeable, however, is the supposition that 'high' christology needs to be buttressed by a correspondingly large number of secure historical facts. A distinction was not carefully enough drawn between the verification of christological statements, and their falsification. It was not frequently enough perceived that the importance of historical research for christology lay in its ability to refute the negative or skeptical historical judgments which would have *falsified* Christian claims about Jesus (for example, that he never existed, that he was a bad man, that he suffered from delusions, and so forth). No facts of a historical kind (for example, that Jesus was crucified, that his disciples at a very early stage believed him to be the final divine intervention in the world) could possibly *verify* the claims of christology. Much of the antagonism which 'critical orthodoxy' provoked can be explained by the suspicion, which relatively conservative biblical historians aroused, that they were claiming too much for their conclusions.

## PATRISTIC SCHOLARS

### G. W. H. Lampe (1912–1980)

We turn now to two British theologians who have pursued their constructive theological interests by writing on the history of patristic theology. They are both Anglicans, and this fact itself is of significance. Anglican ordinands reared on the Thirty-Nine Articles of Religion, as most were until after the Second World War, would have read there the following affirmation:

VIII, Of the Three Creeds
The Three Creeds, *Nicene* Creed, *Athanasius's* Creed, and that which is commonly called the *Apostles'* Creed, ought thoroughly to be received and believed: for they may be proved by most certain warrants of holy Scripture.

Although similar propositions can be found in the writings of most of the continental reformers, and in many of the confessional documents of their churches, Anglicans have been particularly insistent that their reformed episcopalian form of Western Catholicism most closely approximates to the doctrine and order of the undivided church of the first five centuries. The famous words of the Anglican Bishop Lancelot Andrewes (1555–1626) encapsulate this claim with economy and precision: 'One canon reduced to writing by God himself, two testaments, three creeds, four general councils, five centuries, and the series of Fathers in that period . . . determine the boundary of our faith.' Such a view determined not just the faith of Anglicans; it also governed the implicit priorities of English syllabuses of theology, especially in the Anglican-dominated ancient universities. The supposed denominational neutrality of the syllabuses concealed the fact that they had been drawn up on Anglican assumptions.

It was, then, an Anglican presumption which determined the fact that the close, textual study of patristic theology (formerly and significantly known as 'dogmatic theology') was compulsory in most theological syllabuses, a state of affairs conditioning the theological formation of non-Anglicans as well as Anglicans and the atmosphere of the whole of British theology. G. W. H. Lampe was an Oxford-educated, patristic historian, whose main scholarly achievement was to oversee the completion of the massive Patristic Greek Lexicon (1961–8). In 1951 he wrote a notable work on the doctrine of baptism and confirmation in the New Testament and the fathers, entitled *The Seal of the Spirit*. In this book he challenged an opinion, which had grown popular in Anglican Anglo-Catholic circles, that baptism is no more than a prelude to the sacrament of confirmation. Since this had been argued by means of an appeal to the New Testament and patristic evidence, Lampe's riposte contained a substantial examination of the relevant patristic texts. The work stirred up a considerable discussion which has continued to the present. Lampe himself recognized that the issue in the end devolved upon a theology of baptism; and the sober author of the entry on 'confirmation' in the *Oxford Dictionary of the Christian Church* concluded: 'The complexity of the evidence is such as to suggest that a final solution will not be reached by an appeal to history.'

Lampe's theological pilgrimage took him from his student days when he was taught a brand of 'Barthian neo-orthodoxy', to his participation in a corporate statement of Anglican evangelical convictions, *The Fulness of Christ* (1950), to an increasingly outspoken theological liberalism in the 1960s. From the embracing of a broadly exemplarist theory of the atonement (in 'The Atonement: Law and Love', contributed to the controversial, collected work, edited by Alec Vidler, *Soundings*, 1964), he moved to an attack on the historicity of the narrative of the empty tomb. But it was in the 1970s that he mounted his most explicit and thorough reappraisal of orthodox trinitarian incarnationism, and this too was carried out by means of a reinvestigation of patristic texts.

Lampe, who had himself written the articles on 'only' or 'only-begotten' (*monogenes*) and 'son' (*huios*) in the *Patristic Greek Lexicon*, was in a formidable position to argue the case for the meaningless-ness of the trinitarian orthodoxy of the Athanasian Creed. Denying any distinction between dogmas and doctrines, he claimed that all doctrines are more or less tentative and provisional models constructed by Christians with a view to articulating their basic commitment or trust. What is distinctive about Christianity, according to Lampe, is not, therefore, its doctrines but the response to what has been experienced of God's love in the central and culminating point of Jesus Christ. In Jesus there is the perfect realization and embodiment of the union of the divine Spirit and the Spirit of humanity. The concept of divine Spirit reaching out to human personality and indwelling, inspiring, and motivating it, is Lampe's preferred doctrinal model, for the reason that, so he alleged, it makes possible a full and credible account of Jesus' humanity, a humanness whose autonomy is not violated. A powerful strain of Erasmian humanism thus permeates Lampe's whole approach to the trinitarian incarnationism of orthodoxy.

In his account of how that orthodoxy developed, he built on the fact that there co-existed in the early church's scriptures a variety of models by which Jesus' significance could be interpreted. Divine Spirit, God's son (as Adam, Israel, and the hoped-for Messiah were known), the Wisdom of God and the Word of God were all terms by means of which the experience of being touched, moved, and inspired by God could be rendered. Unhappily, under the influence of Platonic thought, another possibility arose, that of personifying the word or wisdom of God, which came to be seen as a subordinate agent of God and thus an intermediary between God and humanity. Confronted with the needs to interpret Jesus' own personal presence, early Christian theologians found it irresistible to develop a new interpretative model, that of a pre-existing divine being, God the Son. When the question was asked by Arius in the fourth century whether God the Son was not only distinct, but also different from God, the logic of the initial development compelled the answer given in the Creed of Nicaea. The Son is 'one in substance' with the Father, puzzlingly distinguished only by what was called his 'mode of subsistence'.

Matters were simply made worse, according to Lampe, by the subsequent developments in the theology of the Holy Spirit. Having already asserted the distinct 'personhood' of the Son, the Holy Spirit now had also to be seen as a 'Third Person', likewise only distinguished in 'mode of subsistence'. Having stated that the Father only was ingenerate, and that the Son only was begotten, the fathers now fixed on the word 'proceed' to describe the Spirit's uniqueness. Lampe regarded it as a sign that the models had somehow been misused that no one has ever ventured to suggest what the difference was between 'generation' and 'procession'. The fathers thus never asked themselves the question, which Lampe puts to their conclusions, whether the theological difficulty about specifying the unique mode of being of the 'person' of the Holy Spirit might not be an unreal one.

The importance of retracing the options open to the theologians of the early church lies in the fact that moderns, so Lampe believed, have no obligation to accept either the Platonist theology which undergirded the personification of the Logos or the literalistic exegesis of the proof texts with which they justified their conclusion. In Lampe's view modern theologians should not simply be content to accumulate fresh insights on the basis of those of the past; they must also be prepared to modify or abandon earlier conclusions. Much of the force of Lampe's position derived from his observation, which Friedrich Schleiermacher had made more than 150 years earlier, that Scripture lent itself as readily to a dynamic-monarchian interpretation of the divinity of Christ as to a trinitarian-incarnationalist one. Methodologically (and shockingly for an Anglican), what Lampe disputed was the authority of the orthodox creeds and fathers of the early church. The function of the creeds, he asserted, was less to give answers than to remind us of questions which we must keep on asking.

### M. F. Wiles (1929–)

That last opinion of Lampe's was expressed in an essay in a report produced by the Doctrine Commission of the Church of England in 1976. The chairman of that commission was Maurice Wiles, Regius Professor of Divinity in the University of Oxford, and, like Lampe, a historian of patristic thought. In essays published in the *Journal of Theological Studies* between 1957 and 1962, Wiles had already begun to submit the arguments of previous Anglican theologians for trinitarian orthodoxy to critical scrutiny. The last of these articles, 'In Defense of Arius', strove to demonstrate that Arius' teaching was no more logical and unspiritual than was that of Athanasius. Wiles's investigations proposed nothing less than the re-examination of the very heart of Nicene orthodoxy and the article gave rise to a vigorous debate which has lasted some twenty-five years.

At the time of the publication of the article on Arius, Wiles was a university lecturer in Cambridge, and from here he published a study of the principles of early doctrinal development, *The Making of Christian Doctrine* (1967). It was a brilliantly concise statement of a peculiarly Anglican problem, namely the status of the doctrines and creeds of patristic orthodoxy. Could they remain immune from the kind of critical inquiry which had already disposed of the infallibility of the Scriptures? Wiles held not. Just as it had not proved possible to place a 'cordon sanitaire' around the words of Jesus, whilst submitting the Old Testament and even the epistles of the New Testament to rigorous criticism, so it is impossible, Wiles argued, to protect the conciliar definitions from similar investigation. Modern theologians already hold that the work of the fathers proceeds by the normal fallible processes of argument, and because the official dogmas of the faith are so closely related to the whole pattern of patristic thought it follows that they, too, cannot be presumed to be free from the possibility of error. Wiles believed that the implications of critical inquiry in the area of patristic theology had not yet been faced with the necessary courage.

Wiles's account of how trinitarian theology developed in the early church anticipated Lampe's by several years, and, though it lays its stress differently, it is no less radical in implication. Wiles detects what he believes to be a contradiction between two stages in the development of trinitarian orthodoxy. In the first stage, the second and third centuries, theologians strove to demonstrate the distinctness of Father and Son in order to avoid teaching that the Father himself suffered (the heresy of patripassianism, otherwise known as modalist monarchianism). Having rejected the idea that there was a single divine monarchy in separate modes, by demonstrating the distinctness of Father and Son, Christian theologians in the next stage of the discussion, in the fourth century, promptly argued for the co-equality of Father and Son (and eventually of the Holy Spirit) by denying all the differences between the three persons, including the very differences which were the initial evidence for their distinctness.

The conclusion of this argument was necessarily negative. For Wiles, as for Lampe, the trinitarian model was in the end less satisfactory for the articulation of basic Christian experience than the unifying concept of God as Spirit. For Wiles, it is of particular importance to stress that trinitarian orthodoxy simply claims too much *knowledge* of God. Increasingly he has posed the issue epistemologically: what may be claimed for the Christian language of God acting? A philosophical argument to the effect that all our language about God is symbolic in character enables Wiles to claim that he is developing, not breaching or destroying the trinitarian tradition. It is important and instructive for us to note that within the approach to Christian doctrine via history certain philosophical issues constantly obtrude.

In 1977, with publication of a sensationally named work, *The Myth of God Incarnate* (edited by J. H. Hick), British theology erupted into a fever of activity which has still not abated.[10] But as many Continental and American critics have noted, the book concerned an intensely British preoccupation, and its authors were predominantly Scripture specialists or patristic scholars (two of the seven were philosophers; two were non-Anglicans). The approach to the question of doctrine was fundamentally to dispute that the evidence of Scripture and early tradition warranted the orthodox conclusion. The specifically philosophical inquiries concerned both the status of the Christian language of incarnation and its effects. The book, however, defies general description because of the contrariety of the viewpoints of its authors. Both Nineham and Wiles were contributors, and Lampe gave the book a warm welcome. Moule, on the other hand, was among its severest critics. One of the failings of the book lay in its unsubtle understanding of the subject-matter it purported to question, namely incarnational trinitarianism itself. It assumed that orthodoxy required one to defend the view that propositions about the Trinity had simply *replaced* the Scriptural narrative of God's dealings with humanity, as though, after the council of Nicaea, we had more knowledge of God than beforehand. Whether some orthodox defenders of the tradition have given that impression or not, this view is simply unintelligible in the light of century upon century of careful debate precisely about the knowledge of God. As we have seen, both Lampe and Wiles found it necessary to supplement their critical treatment of the history of the development of trinitarian orthodoxy with some views about the nature of religious language. In so far as this aspect of British theology has given rise to a more sophisticated and wide-ranging treatment of the status of talk about God acting, it will have served a useful purpose.

## MODERN HISTORIANS

### N. Sykes (1897–1961)

While it will be conceded that historians of the New Testament and patristic periods are likely to make important contributions to constructive theology, the case for so regarding historians of the later church appears at first sight more complex. The importance of the historical disciplines in English academic life has, however, ensured that a long succession of eminent church historians have made major contributions to theology, less by the direct fruit of their particular research than in some of the assumptions and instincts which have motivated and guided their work. The two historians considered here, however, have been chosen because, exceptionally, they have made explicit the connections between their academic labors and the life of the contemporary church.

Norman Sykes was an Anglican priest, who held chairs of history successively at Exeter and London before his appointment to the

Dixie Chair of Ecclesiastical History in Cambridge in 1944. He was a professional historian who, in a series of major works, *Edmund Gibson, Bishop of London 1669–1748* (1926), *Church and State in England in the Eighteenth Century* (1934) and *William Wake, Archbishop of Canterbury, 1657–1737*, 2 vols (1957), revolutionized the conventional dismissal of the eighteenth-century church. He held a high view of the significance for the church of the profession of ecclesiastical history. Because the Christian faith is based on unique historical events the challenge of historical inquiry could not be evaded. In one of the last of his works, *Man as Churchman* (1960), he made common cause with British New Testament scholars, including T. W. Manson and C. H. Dodd, against the skepticism of the continental form critics. He explicitly endorsed the view, expressed above, that the contribution of historical study to theology might well be limited to the refutation of hostile opinions, rather than the direct verification of Christian doctrines.

Two controversial cases in ecumenical theology exhibit his historical principles at work. A close study of Catholic arguments in favor of Petrine primacy show him ready to accord a providential status of preeminence to the Church of Rome, but unable on historical grounds to endorse the dogma of the First Vatican Council concerning the papal magisterium and infallibility. On the other hand, on the basis of the precise terms of the Council of Trent's decree on Scripture and Tradition which requires of authentic traditions a continuity of uninterrupted profession from the days of the Apostles, he claims the dubiety of the Dogma of the Bodily Assumption of the Virgin Mary. The impact of both of these arguments can be seen in the historical cautions and reservations of the documents of the Anglican-Roman Catholic International Commission relating to papal primacy and the Marian doctrines.

In no work is Sykes's major contribution to the instinctive sense of the English contribution to world Christianity plainer than in his brilliant summary work, *The English Religious Tradition* (1953, revised in 1961). Here there is an open celebration of 'the English genius for compromise', a phrase coined by Butterfield (see below) in *The Englishman and His History (1944)*. It was readiness to compromise which had made it possible for established churches both in England and Scotland to coexist with other churches enjoying complete religious liberty and civil equality. Sykes regarded the Butler Education Act of 1944 as an outstanding victory for the spirit of Christian unity and cooperation over denominational differences, an event of major importance because, as he elsewhere argued, educational policy is the central problem in the relations of the church and the modern state. Toleration and the spirit of liberty are, he held with Bishop Mandell Creighton (1843–1901), necessary to the life of the church, and through the contribution of English-speaking Christianity first to the missionary movement and then to the ecumenical movement of the twentieth century their influence can be seen on an international plane.

Though an Anglican, Sykes's view of English Christianity related not just to the episcopalian, but also to presbyterian and to independent churches, whose part in the English tradition he fully acknowledged. As a historian of the seventeenth and eighteenth centuries he had noted with approval the precise terms on which leading Anglican theologians of that period had simultaneously defended the episcopate but refused to deny the validity of the ministry and sacraments of the foreign reformed churches. In order to define what he deemed to be the central Anglican tradition he adopted a seventeenth-century distinction between the essence (*esse*) and the well-being (*bene esse*) of the church. An orthodox church with no episcopate may lose nothing of the essence of the church, but may miss something of its glory and perfection. Anglicanism, according to Sykes, has sustained a middle way on the matter of episcopacy. It has contented itself with asserting the historical grounds for its continuance of the threefold ministry. But it has nowhere officially formulated theological grounds for the exclusive dignity of the episcopate. Since the sixteenth century there has been a continuous succession of Anglican theologians who have interpreted the Prayer Book Ordinal and the relevant Articles and Canons specifically so as not to unchurch those who necessarily were deprived of the episcopate. He spoke of these writers as 'a great cloud of witnesses' and dismissed suggestions that they were anomalous voices or otherwise merely lax, opportunist or pragmatic in matters of church order.

Sykes's scholarly career coincided with the discussions which led to the successful launching of the united Church of South India in 1947, an event which he hailed as 'the boldest and most promising experiment in ecclesiastical union'. For him it reversed what he regarded as a major disaster of English church history, the failure to produce a comprehensive church at the Restoration of the monarchy in 1660, mitigated only by the fact that it led in 1689 to the Toleration Act which perforce recognized in a limited way the existence and right of Dissent. Of Catholicism he wrote in a way which was generous and open, but necessarily more distant, merely anticipating (in 1960!) the need for more unequivocal endorsement of the principle of freedom of conscience as a condition of any Christian discipleship whatsoever. That sound historical scholarship tended to charity in religion was one of his most cherished beliefs.[11]

### Sir Herbert Butterfield (1900–1979)

Butterfield, like Sykes, was a Yorkshireman; but his interest in the history of Christianity, unlike Sykes's, which was professional, was almost accidental, the consequence of childhood habits of piety which he never lost throughout his long and distinguished career. Born into a Methodist working-class family, he became a lay preacher at the age of seventeen, a ministry he continued as an undergraduate at, and later (from 1923) Fellow of, Peterhouse in Cambridge. In 1944 he was elected to a chair in modern history; he was Master of Peterhouse from 1955 to 1968, and Vice-Chancellor of the University from 1959 to 1961; he was promoted to the Regius Professorship of Modern History in 1963. From 1948 and for the rest of his active life, Butterfield, in addition to the production of major scholarly works of general history, regularly responded to requests for lectures on the relationship of Christianity and history. His was the outstanding contribution to the theme which we are considering in modern British intellectual history, a voice, somewhat like Dodd's, of maturity and moderation, the more authoritative and persuasive for being, in a certain sense, lay and indirect.

Butterfield's main scholarly works were on Napoleon, Machiavelli, George III and the origins of modern science. But a highly influential brief treatise on *The Whig Interpretation of History* (1931) made plain his critical interest in the role of presuppositions in the writing of history. The work is a sustained and effective attack on the Protestant and 'Whig' view which justified the Reformation on the grounds that it led to liberty. This Butterfield regarded as an illicit abridgment of the complexity of history, an opting for a comfortable distortion of the truth. The book was a plea for more detail, more impartiality, and more imaginative sympathy in a historian. It represented a viewpoint upon humanity which was recognizably post-liberal in the tradition of P. T. Forsyth, in that it focused not upon progress, but upon catastrophe and tragedy in human affairs. Though not itself an overtly theological work, it constantly turned to the interpretation of Luther for its examples, and implied a significant degree of scholarly detachment in its verdict on the religious fanaticisms of the sixteenth century.

It was many years later, in 1948, that Butterfield turned to an explicit treatment of Christianity as an historical religion, in a series of open lectures, published as *Christianity and History* (1949). He, like so many of the others we have treated, similarly insists that Christianity is rooted in the ordinary realm of investigation with which the technical student of history is concerned. By 'technical history' Butterfield meant a specific discipline of attending to what actually is the case. He linked its origins to the Christian origins of the study of natural science, namely the discovery of a better, because humbler way of studying the ways of Providence. None the less it was, Butterfield believed, a piece of willful forgetfulness when historians suggested that *all* that might be said about the historical process could be said on the basis of 'technical history'.

By way of explanation of this view Butterfield distinguished between three levels of historical analysis. The first is the biographical, in which human beings are taken as relatively free and responsible for their own decisions. The second is the analysis which seeks to identify deep processes, or even laws within the outworking of historical events. The third level is that of Providence embracing the whole of human history. Each one of these levels is important to the Christian. The Christian historian has to be emphatic about the reality of human freedom, for that is the precondition for seeing humanity in God's sight as sinners. The Christian should be no less responsive to the notion of historical process, which should elicit the response of charity and empathy. Butterfield regarded these apparently lower levels as consequences of the Providential view of history, so that each of them are in fact integral to each other.[12]

Butterfield, the Methodist lay preacher, instructively laid great emphasis upon the Old Testament. The people of Israel's contribution to human civilization was precisely the fact that they saw God as the God of history and regarded history as based on his promise. Despair is thus ruled out, despite the intervention of sin, catastrophe, and judgment. Indeed it is precisely catastrophe and judgment which is the setting for the greatest of those symbols or myths which Israel contributed to the Christian church, the ideas of the leaven that leavens the whole lump, the faithful remnant, and the suffering servant. This is the orthodox heart of Butterfield's interpretation of history, the more impressive for being expounded by a technical historian of brilliance:

> Ultimately our interpretation of the whole human drama depends on an intimately personal decision concerning the part we mean to play in it. It is as though we were to say to ourselves: 'There is dissonance in the universe, but if I strike the

right note it becomes harmony and reconciliation – and though they may kill me for it they cannot spoil that harmony.'[13]


## ACHIEVEMENT AND ASSESSMENT

The British theologians whose work we have surveyed do not readily fall into a group identifiable by shared theological convictions; none the less they constitute a tradition of theological scholarship which is recognizably British in character. As such they share certain concerns which are unquestionably those of their academic setting. The strong influence of a classical and historical training and the comparative degree of freedom from denominational control has inclined them to a certain impartiality and objectivity in their approach to theological conflicts of the past. It is perhaps fortuitous that each one has responded positively to a greater or lesser degree to the anti-liberalism of P. T. Forsyth, but one can sense a marked reserve, even in the absence of explicit discussion, towards the continental movements of existentialism and dialectical theology. There is evidence of a tradition of 'theology of crisis' in the work of such disparate figures as Forsyth, Dodd, and Butterfield, but it lacks the thorough-going anthropological perspective which existentialism and depth psychology gave to the continental movement. The overt celebration of the 'English [sic!] genius for compromise' in Butterfield and Sykes reflects not just an understandable nationalism in time of war, but also a quiet satisfaction specifically about certain cultural institutions embodying liberty and toleration, such as the education system, the universities and the BBC. Each of these reflect a particular settlement of the problem of church and state, with which the British had been wrestling since the sixteenth century. The context of the modern British university unquestionably offered a tolerant, academically serious and ecumenically significant environment for the work of a theologian.

But at the same time, its limitations are no less obvious to the present observer. Since the late 1960s it has shown no very marked ability to respond to the questions of justice and of peace which have risen to the forefront of the ecumenical agenda. Despite its history as a colonial power, Britain has been slow to evaluate its post-colonial responsibilities in moral terms and to allow the concerns and interests of its former dependencies to count in its national life. The universities have reflected all too faithfully a mood of national self-absorption. A major deficiency in philosophical ethics has left theologians simply untrained in certain crucial areas of the Christian tradition, moral theology and Christian social teaching. It is at this point that the tradition of theology which we have surveyed, an approach to theology through history, is capable of significant future development. There is every reason why, for example, liberation theologies of strongly ideological bent should be brought into contact with longstanding traditions of political history, of the history of international relations, and of colonial history. Britain, and more generally the English-speaking world, is still deeply involved in Asian and African affairs. Given the possibility of further growth in the range of imaginative sympathy and a willingness to admit a critical evaluation of past failures, there is a future as well as a past for a tradition of theology which is realistic about human beings.

## NOTES

1 H. R. Mackintosh, *Types of Modern Theology, Schleiermacher to Barth* (London, 1937), p. 4.
2 P. T. Forsyth, *The Principle of Authority*, pp. 112–16.
3 P. T. Forsyth, *Positive Preaching and the Modern Mind*, p. 284.
4 P. T. Forsyth, *The Person and Place of Jesus Christ*, p. 12. The last sentence of the quotation contains words drawn from the Absolution used at Morning and Evening Prayer in the (Anglican) Book of Common Prayer.
5 Ibid., p. 294.
6 See F. W. Dillistone's biography, *C. H. Dodd: Interpreter of the New Testament*.
7 C. H. Dodd, *The Authority of the Bible* pp. 282, 260.
8 From 'The Portrait of Jesus in John and in the Synoptics', in W. R. Farmer, C. F. D. Moule and R. R. Niebuhr (eds), *Christian History and Interpretation: Studies Presented to John Knox* (Cambridge, 1967), pp. 183–198; here pp. 191 ff.
9 C. F. D. Moule, *The Origin of Christology*, p. 136.
10 See the review of responses by G. M. Newlands in S. Sykes and D. Holmes (eds) *New Studies in Theology* (London, 1980), pp. 181–92.
11 See the Preface by G. V. Bennett, in G. V. Bennett and J. D. Walsh, *Essays in Modern English Church History: In Memory of Norman Sykes* (London, 1966). pp. v–viii.
12 See the essay 'God in History' (1952), reprinted in C. T. McIntyre (ed.), *Herbert Butterfield Writings on Christianity and History*, pp. 3–16.
13 H. Butterfield, *Christianity and History*, p. 86.

## BIBLIOGRAPHY

### Primary

Butterfield, H., *Christianity and History* (London, 1950).
—, *Man on His Past* (Cambridge, 1969).
Dodd, C. H., *The Meaning of Paul for Today* (London, 1920).
—, *The Authority of the Bible* (London, 1947).
—, *Historical Tradition and the Fourth Gospel* (Cambridge, 1963).
—, *The Interpretation of the Fourth Gospel* (Cambridge, 1968).
—, *The Founder of Christianity* (London, 1970).
Forsyth, P. T., *Positive Preaching and the Modern Mind* (London, 1901).
—, *The Cruciality of the Cross* (London, 1909).
—, *The Person and Place of Jesus Christ* (London, 1909).
—, *The Work of Christ* (London, 1910).
—, *The Principle of Authority* (London, 1952).
Hick, J. H. (ed.), *The Myth of God Incarnate* (London, 1977).
Lampe, G. W. H., *The Fulness of Christ* (London, 1950).
—, *The Seal of the Spirit* (London, 1951).
—, *God as Spirit* (Oxford, 1976).
McIntyre, C. T. (ed.), *Herbert Butterfield, Writings on Christianity and History* (Oxford, New York, 1979).
Moule, C. F. D., *The Phenomenon of the New Testament* (London, 1967).
—, *The Origin of Christology* (Cambridge, 1977).
—, *The Birth of the New Testament* (London, 1981).
Nineham, D. E., *The Gospel of Mark* (London, 1963).
—, *The Use and Abuse of the Bible* (London, 1976).
Sykes, N., *Man as Churchman* (Cambridge, 1960).
—, *The English Religious Tradition* (London, 1961).
Wiles, M. F., *The Making of Christian Doctrine* (Cambridge, 1967).
—, *The Remaking of Christian Doctrine* (London, 1974).
—, *Faith and the Mystery of God* (London, 1982).
—, *God's Action in the World* (London, 1986).

### Secondary

Anderson, Marvin A., (ed.), *The Gospel an Authority*, A P. T. Forsyth Reader (Minneapolis, 1971).
Bennett, G. V. and Walsh, J. D., (eds), *Essays in Modern English Church History*, in Memory of Norman Sykes (London, 1966).
Bradley, W. L., *P. T. Forsyth: The Man and His Work* (London, 1952).
Brown, R. M., *P. T. Forsyth, Prophet for Today* (Philadelphia, 1952).
Dillstone, F. W., *C. H. Dodd: Interpreter of the New Testament* (London, 1977).
Mozley, J. K., 'The Theology of Dr. Forsyth', in *The Heart of the Gospel* (London, 1925).
Moule, C. F. D., (ed.), *G. W. H. Lampe* (London, 1982).

# 2

# Theology through Philosophy

## Daniel W. Hardy

### THE VISION OF ENGLISH THEOLOGY

There is a remarkable statement in Richard Hooker's *Laws of Ecclesiastical Polity* (1594) which sums up the characteristic vision of English theology:

> Behold therefore we offer the lawes whereby we live unto the generall triall and judgement of the whole world, hartely beseeching Almightie God, whome wee desire to serve according to his owne will, that both we and others (all kinde of partiall affection being cleane laide aside) may have eyes to see, and harts to embrace the things that in his sight are most acceptable. And because the point about which wee strive is the qualitie of our laws, our first entrance hereinto cannot better be made, then with consideration of the nature of lawe in generall, and of that lawe which giveth life unto all the rest, which are commendable just and good, namely the lawe whereby the Eternall himselfe doth worke.[1]

The implications of Hooker's words need careful consideration.

When the proponents of the national Church of England attempted to bring together the conflicting claims of the Reformers and Catholicism, the two principal 'simple' possibilities for doing so were not available to them. A direct appeal to Scripture would have followed the Reformed principle of *sola scriptura*, but alienated those of Catholic persuasion; a direct appeal to 'the laws of the Church' would have alienated those of a Reformed disposition. This feature of their approach is in itself quite important; for them there was not a single authority by which the life of the church was constituted. It was their answer to an enduring question, whether there is, or should be, a single source or authority for the life of Christian people. In place of such authorities they took 'the thinges that are established', in other words *present organized practice*, which was to be taken as trustworthy – at least for the moment. Equally significant is the fact that Scripture and church laws are considered through the *medium* of current church practice – as mediated in the practical reason by which people lived together in the church.

Given this, a whole series of issues arose which required considered attention of the appropriate kind. One was about the *quality* of current practice. The simple fact that things *were* was not an argument that they should remain as they were, for there was a question about their quality. If authorities were mediated through current practice, current practice itself might be taken as authoritative, as an 'historical given', thereby making it inviolate. But if it was so, it was removed from rational inquiry.

In the situation we have been examining, that was unacceptable. It was not supposed that things could remain as they were. The simple fact that there was no single authority by which Christian life is guided, and that therefore there was disagreement about the quality of current practice, made this kind of historical complacency impossible. The quality of present practice, though historical, required *scrutiny*. The given of historical practice was to be opened to judgment. If current church practice was the medium through which the church's life was to be considered, and through it Scripture and church laws, it was to be considered *rationally*, but in a fashion suitable to its subject-matter – *faithfully* as we might say. Implicitly, this suggests a necessary complementarity between 'history' and 'philosophy' or 'rationality'.

And how was scrutiny to be carried out? How was the value of current practice to be resolved? The issue was to be settled in *open trial*, impartially, with clarity of vision and willingness to accept what was good – without interference by prejudice or prior inclination. That too was potentially a difficult issue. For what was this 'public'? It was presumed that it was those who were already involved in this national church, and parties interested in the question of the quality of its life. This was potentially a difficult issue for a society becoming increasingly complex.

Given the necessity of open trial, two other issues followed. One was the question of what *standard* was to be employed. The issue as it was conceived in the period we have been discussing was how to recall things – in this case the common practices of the church – to their own proper nature, to the 'laws' by which they should work.[2] In other words, practically-mediated theology had to be recalled to its truth. The other was the question of what *rational judgment* was to be used. Those who judged were not to be self-important; their reason was to be recalled to its truth. By being recalled to its truth, it could be proportioned to its object, which was the discovery of the truth of church practices. Those who judged were to be bound by 'the law of reason which bindeth creatures reasonable in this world, and with which by reason they may most plainly perceive themselves bound'.[3]

In order to recall them to their truth, both practically-mediated theology and the rational judgment appropriate to it required reference to things more ultimate, their *author*. For both the laws by which things should work and the law of reason binding those who judged were, through 'nature's' law, set down by God. God is lawful himself and the worker of the laws of nature: 'only the workes and operation of God have him both for their worker, and for the lawe whereby they are wrought'.[4] Hence, the rational task to be performed in open trial was quite specific, that of judging current practices by referring their 'working laws' to their author, where the judges also needed to refer the practice of their reason to its divine source. Not only nature but human beings are to be 'according to [God's] owne will', if they are to fulfill what is proper to their nature. In more formal terms, there needs to be a *correspondence of agency*. The agency of human beings is to coincide with the agency of God; what seems a 'double agency' (natural and divine) is actually to be a 'single agency'. Not, by the way, that this involved homogenizing the rich variety of opinions available: this God was the author of this abundance and variety. As unity, he afforded to each one 'something peculiar and proper'; as Triune, he shows 'his most glorious and abundant vertue . . . in varietie'.[5]

The agenda of issues which emerges from Hooker's words is apparent now, with one exception. That is the importance which is given to what could be called the two goals. There is a goal of *agreement* whose own goal is *societal*. The purpose of open trial of current church practice is for human beings to agree on the organization of their life together, for that gives life to their life together. In theological terms, it is the means by which the people of England participate in the life-giving of the Holy Spirit. In Hooker's words, they are to agree on 'the manner of their union in living together', for that is 'the very soule of a politique body'.[6]

### Engaging with Common Practice

By now, it is clear that the 'focus' of English theology is common practice, in which is mediated such authorities as Scripture and tradition. That 'common practice' is itself a rich composite of life, thought, and prayer, each comprised of the habitual or institutional and the creative. Its distinctive character can be seen by comparing it with the most common alternative. It is commonplace for theology to be seen as a free-standing triumvirate of 'Scripture', tradition, and interpretation in mutual correction. When suitably developed, such a free-standing 'theology' is then applied to common practice, telling it what it should be.[7] But properly speaking, English theology operates in a different way, beginning from practice and correcting it through historical and rational consideration referred to divine truth.

In English theology, common practice is seen to mediate divine authorship, though obviously not as fully as might be. While it is 'natural' and as such divinely authored, at the same time it requires closer affinity with its divine author; it has not yet achieved its full nature under God. And this is to be achieved by subjecting it to common scrutiny and judgment, the judgment of those who recognize the laws of reason and their divine author. To undertake study of common practice, which mediates not only Scripture and tradition but also its divine author, and to enable it to achieve its full nature under God, requires the utmost sensitivity to its *character and possibility*, and the development of appropriate methods.

The task of theology, then, is to begin from common practice and examine its quality in open trial by the use of natural reason in order to discover the truth of this practice, by a truth-directed reason; and the fulfillment of this purpose requires reference to the author of practice and practical reason. And the outcome of the trial should be an agreement on the proper organization of common life which would actually promote the practice of society. It is notable that throughout the concern is *public*, theology mediated in public practice, the use of public reason, open trial of the truth and the achievement of truly social existence.

But how does one engage with such a thing? There is a sense in which theology in the English milieu is so much a public matter that it is the responsibility of anyone skilled to attempt it; and its purpose is closely bound up with the functioning of society. And there is an honorable tradition of people in public life who make theology their concern, for the sake of public life. Equally, if one follows this avenue, there is a sense in which academic theology is the concern of a whole university, not simply that of a faculty of theology.

There are, none the less, two '*master concerns*' which run through all the rest, those which focus on common practice as it has been and is, and those which focus on the trial of this practice by reference to truth. In this sense, as distinct from the accepted meaning of the terms, *history* and *philosophy* are the presiding 'metadisciplines' of English theology; but their 'agendas' are established by the vision which we have attempted to describe. To call them 'master concerns' or 'metadisciplines', however, is not to make their significance only epistemological or methodological, for they are also closely related to what is the case, and hence to ontology. Common practice is as it is through having come to be in the realities of history, and needs to be understood historically. At the same time, common practice is as it is through the rationally purposive life of humankind as bound by the creative and redemptive activity of God, and needs to be understood philosophically. If there is a division to be made between them – which is very difficult – history has as its task the public study of common practice as it has been and is, while philosophy has as its task the trial of practice for its truth.

### Persistence and Change in the Vision of English Theology

The vision, both of the 'object' of theology and of the 'master concerns' by which one engages with it, survives in the twentieth century, and survives in much that is done in the name of theology in England. But there is an uneasy tension between what one could call vision and realization. For a variety of influences have come into play, particularly in the nineteenth and twentieth centuries, which both contribute to and obstruct the achieving of the vision. It is worthwhile mentioning at least some of the major issues which have intruded themselves for better or for worse.

The wish for a theology grounded in common practice remains, and so does the concern for this to be served by studies appropriate to it. Significantly, theology remains in the public arena as an accepted subject in universities funded from secular sources; and this theology is not simply another title for that which is studied – for example, in American universities – as 'religion'. Neither is it 'confessional' theology. This theology is thought to be related to a significant portion of society, and therefore to justify its position in the university. But equally significantly, with the fragmentation of universities into more sharply differentiated faculties, the notion of common practice has fragmented also. Correspondingly, the position of a theology faculty *vis-à-vis* others has changed; each is supposed to relate to common practice in its own way, which is distinct from that of others. That means also that the skills appropriate to common practice in theology are not thought necessarily to be similar to those found in other faculties. Even so, there is an uneasy feeling that the origins of all, as well as their methods, should be common so far as can be. And this encourages theologians, if not others, to seek rootedness in common practice and commonness of skills.

The search for roots in *common practice* has, most frequently, employed the technique of generalization. This is no accident. For many years a distinction has been drawn between general and specific starting-points, the assumption being that the general is neutral and the specific is not. This could be traced to the emphasis laid on general truths by the Deists and those influenced by them, as distinct from the 'symbolic' character of the particular truths seen by particular groups such as the Christians. If this view were not already strong in English theology through its Platonic heritage and the prominence of the notion of 'natural religion', it was made so through the influence of German idealism, following G. E. Lessing and Immanuel Kant. Accordingly, it has come to be thought that, in order to retain its roots in common practice, theology should concentrate more and more on the general. And so it has.

Dwelling on the general features which are supposed to be neutral, two kinds of starting-points have come to be used. One begins from the general features of reality in which philosophy and theology converge – God, truth, goodness, transcendence, and the like. The large-scale systems of realist philosophy to be found in English philosophy and theology between 1920 and 1935 were of this kind, including those of Samuel Alexander, A. N. Whitehead, William Temple, and F. R. Tennant;[8] frequently, they are particularly interesting for their reconsideration of these issues in the light of modern scientific understanding. The other begins from general ethical and religious practices; many examples are to be found in the 1930s, amongst them those of A. E. Taylor, John Oman and the 'encounter' theologian H. H. Farmer.[9] These are supposed by those who use them to be inclusive, concrete summations of the historically 'given' practices of religious people, which capture the heart of concrete religion. (It is puzzling to those who use such generalizations for religious people to question their reliability, and they may accuse them of 'confessional' special pleading.[10]) Considerable effort is sometimes given to demonstrating their reliability.[11] Several means are used. One is to intersperse discussion of general features of theology with the discussion of historical figures and movements. Another is to justify the generalizations which are used by providing histories of thought. A third, used by those who begin from general religious practices, is to justify the use of certain categories for the explanation of religion by summarizing samples of religious behavior which exemplify the categories. But all in fact are generalist, subsuming the particular and specific under the general.

The use of generalizations in place of the specific, with the supposition that it roots theology in common practice, raises a considerable problem for those whose understanding of religious life arises differently. This is particularly so for those whose view of religious life is actually formed through participation in the common practice in which English theology is rooted. To them, these general accounts – despite the supposition that they include the common practice of all people – are highly abstractive, the products of 'academic' intellectualization which omit the salient issues. So for them there is a question about whether what those who use such generalizations are in touch with is common experience at all. And that raises a fundamental issue about the approach to common practice of those who use such a general, 'neutral' starting-point. It is roughly indicated by the response of the farmer to 'city-folk' asking directions back to the city: 'If I were going there, I wouldn't start from here.'

There is a genuine issue between the two which is not easily resolved. It is the issue of the nature of the object which is common to history and philosophy. At the risk of oversimplification, the difference between the two is similar to that between Platonist and Hebrew understanding, the one pleading for the primacy of general forms, the other pleading for the primacy of the particular. While pretending to be 'neutral', each in fact tends to legislate for the other in an ideological fashion.

Interlocked with rooting common practice in general forms was the development of a theory of common rationality. As we saw, reason was once thought to be the natural means of finding and trying the laws by which things are organized, and itself bound by 'the law of reason which bindeth creatures reasonable in this world, and with which by reason they may most plainly perceive themselves bound'.[12] As a 'natural endowment', however, whose development was not only the province of religious people but also in the hands of the wider community, it was quickly affected by whatever were the practices of the wider community, thereby following the vicissitudes of the development of philosophy and the sciences. At first, this did not mean that it lost its usefulness for common religious practice; but later, particularly where reason was tied to the sensible world (Locke) or to its own intrinsic patterns (Kant), it was detached from practically-mediated theology and came to be seen simply as natural and autonomous. Being natural and the instrument of a wider community, it was subject to its fragmentations; in the end, reason could be seen as relative to human cultures and their history or to individuals. Two very important discussions through which the issue of reason has been carried on in England from the mid-1930s to the present day have been those concerned with language (the 'linguistic turn') and with historical and social relativity. The first occupied many thinkers from Moore, Russell, Ayer, and Wittgenstein onwards; the second has been more recent, and is to be seen in the impact of sociology of knowledge, leading frequently to the supposition that reason itself is historically contingent and fragmented in hypothetical units – paradigms or models.[13]

According to the English vision of theology, from common practice, and employing methods of historical and rational judgment, it was thought to be the task of human beings to judge the *quality* of common practice, the common practice of the nation, in order to correct it by reference to its own truth. Here again, however, considerable changes have taken place.

In this connection, the first matter of note is the replacement of the wider issue by a narrower one. With rare exceptions, discussion is confined to the beliefs and practices of avowedly religious people, and those which concern the basis of the common life of the nation as a whole are set aside.[14] The second is to note problems in the practice of historical inquiry and rational judgment.

In historical inquiry, the goal of 'neutral' understanding often replaces that of judgment, in a desire to rest in 'what is the case'. This can be seen in two examples. (1) There are some theologians who begin from 'neutral generalizations' and make it their concern simply to engage in the analysis of their meaning; such people include highly sophisticated analysts and logicians. At certain times, this was considered the best form of defense against those who claimed that religious assertions lacked all meaning.[15] (2) And there are some theologians who begin from historical data (biblical, historical or doctrinal) and make it their concern simply to understand the meaning of what is or has been; they include highly qualified specialists in history and languages. And they too consider their work the best way of maintaining the value of the given. In both cases, the goal of understanding replaces that of the judgment of quality, and such understanding is considered conducive to the maintenance of value. In one sense, this is profoundly constructive. But it has the effect of legitimating the 'given of historical practice', without opening it to judgment by reference to the truth: 'what is' becomes 'what should be' without first being judged. Such strategies are inherently 'conservative', as distinct from the search for the truth of common practice.

In the use of rational judgment, problems also appear. There is frequently a direct attempt to judge what is good, sometimes in the disguise of a mere attempt to understand either generalizations or historical data,[16] sometimes in more obviously prescriptive form.[17] This conceals a very serious matter. For it is easily possible for philosophers or theologians concerned with the consideration of a general object or method to move from 'neutral' ones to providing autonomous objects and methods which then become religious surrogates. By that means, what starts as a discussion of the general issues in which theology and philosophy converge, or the rationality in which they are both interested, becomes the construction of metaphysical or spiritual 'objects' on the one hand, or the advocacy of rational or spiritual possibilities on the other hand, whose relationship to historical or present-day common practice, or the truth which such practice mediates, is very questionable. But then, of course, those who engage in construction of this sort can rationalize history to bring it into accordance with the position advocated; and only the most careful understanding of philosophical truth and historical fact can show the rationalizations for what they are. In fact, most theology and philosophy verges on this at times, not only the work of those who consciously advocate the development of such surrogates.

The major problem which this raises has to do with the *kind of quality* which common practice has and should have. In earlier times, as we saw, common practice was thought to have had its true nature given it by God, and the intent of judging its quality was to recall it to that. Though the presumption that common practice received its true quality from God is by no means lost, as the writing of Austin Farrer and E. L. Mascall shows,[18] it is now widely assumed that these religious practices are much more accidental, 'practical symbols' which are more likely the result of cultural influences. And this has the effect of freeing those who judge them to declare that they are, in effect, a 'mistake' or culturally-introduced 'myth'. In other words, the realism upon which earlier analysis was based is now counted as idealism, in which ideas are superimposed on reality; and it is thought that such idealism needs to be supplanted by a new kind of realism. The new realism allows no such easy 'givenness' by God; it is more a question of human beings interpreting things in relation to God, if indeed there is a God at all. Even if the conclusions arrived at are not radical, the effect of this new realism is to rest theology on human experience and reason.

A further problem concerns the position of those *by whom* judgment is undertaken. In its earlier form, judgment was to be by and for the national community. Whatever it was that was mediated in the historical community of Christians was to be tried by those who were already participants in that community, in order to achieve a fuller life for the community. But then, as society changed and became more complex, those who judged also became more various. On the one hand, those by whom judgment was conducted might not be concerned with religious beliefs and practices, or likely to become so; they might in fact be hostile to such issues. On the other hand, those by whom it was conducted might still be members of the historical community of religious believers, but they might feel themselves obliged to operate by what they saw as 'public standards', the standards of those who did not care. Whether there could ever be a *common* public standard, whether amongst the 'outsiders', or between them and the 'insiders' (participants), or indeed amongst 'insiders', is debatable. Furthermore, the lines between 'insiders' and 'outsiders' could not be clearly drawn. In the complex world of competing loyalties, they might run through an individual, torn between 'common faith' and commitment to 'public' standards of judgment. And there are many cases amongst those concerned with historical and rational inquiry in theology who face the anxiety of competing loyalties.

Another problem is the *purpose* of judgment. Traditionally, its purpose was the achievement of agreement, in order to enable people to agree on the organization of their life together, and thereby give life to their common life, since agreement is 'the very soule of a politique body'. There is a vestige of this remaining in the wish to meet 'public standards' of credibility, by submitting faith to trial by 'the whole world'. But there are two things which interfere. One is the importance which is given to private judgment. Common agreement is often considered secondary to a more primary purpose, that of 'judging for oneself'. The other is the difficulty of achieving wide acceptance. The task of judging has tended increasingly to marginalize those by whom judgment is undertaken, as lone individuals mediating between complex and competing demands. To be acceptable to anyone, they must win acceptance. If they appeal to the wider community, they are likely to lose the acceptance of the historical community of religious believers; if they remain credible to the historical community, they are likely to lose credibility with the wider community. The result, where there is no agreed religious basis of life, is marginality. Either way, whether it is because of the importance given to private judgment, or because winning acceptance from conflicting groups marginalizes, the result is that judgment has lost its earlier purpose. It is now not so much for the common good as for something much more preliminary – simple acceptance of views.

## The Present Institutional Shape of English Theology

The influences which have come to bear on English theology have deeply affected it, for better and for worse. Both the original vision and these influences are to be seen in the shape of English theology as it is in academic institutions today. As one might expect, while theology still has an accepted place in public institutions, it is sharply differentiated from other academic disciplines. And the study of theology is now pursued through a number of different, largely autonomous subjects; and each of these has legitimated itself by strategies which identify its distinct subject-matter and method.

Like all academic subjects, the tendency in the study of theology has been to drift away from its original concern with common practice through the development of special subjects and techniques which are considered informative for common practice. In other words, the starting-points are subject-determined, rather than determined by common practice; and the studies are pursued for their informative value, not to bring common practice to its truth. In these respects, the study of theology in England has become more similar to the pattern found in Scottish universities, while still retaining its concentration on 'history' and 'philosophy' and Scripture. The origins of theology in Scotland are more in the characteristics of a confession-based tradition; and this has produced, not a common-practice-mediated object for theology, but a series of independent subjects which are considered in their own right and for their educative value: Old Testament, New Testament, Dogmatics, Church History, and Practical Theology.

Each of the subjects pursued within theology in English universities is justified by its own 'formative' importance and special agenda. For *history*: (1) particular periods of history are identified as 'formative'. For example, it is supposed that history should be centered on early Christian history; this may be supplemented in some (relatively few) more adventurous places by reformation studies and modern history and theology. (2) A further way of focusing what is to be.done in these historical periods is to set a specific agenda of concerns, requiring that certain themes be discussed, e.g. 'the doctrine of the atonement to 1900'. For *philosophy*: (1) a particular object is singled out, sometimes called 'religion', and defended as formative for culture; in practice 'religion' is usually taken as meaning Christianity because of the 'formative' influence of Christianity on English religion. The tendency to move to 'neutral generalizations' is evident in two ways: Christianity is taken in a very general sense, or religion is taken to mean 'religion in general' (phenomenology of religion) or 'all religions'. (2) Additionally, a very common way of focusing the distinctive character of philosophy taught in a faculty of theology is to operate from a standard 'general' agenda for Christianity: the nature of faith, God, freedom and immortality, miracle, prayer, providence, the problem of evil and later the problem of religious language; or where the emphasis is on 'religion in general', the agenda concentrates on general issues (such as 'religion', symbols, beliefs and the like). *Scripture* as a whole is justified as 'formative', and within that there is: (1) a focus on the main course of historical events and tradition leading to Christianity, and (2) it too is defined by an agenda of concerns, concentrating on such main personages as Jesus and Paul, and the study of beliefs associated with them. In practice, it is historical skills which predominate.

There is no question that the benefits of these procedures have been very great, benefits very like those of other forms of academic study which have been developed through fragmentation and concentration – the typical pattern of modern academic study. In the case of theology, a vast amount of historical material, accompanied by advanced explanations, has been the result. But it is noticeable that concentrating attention on 'historical' and 'philosophical' subjects in theology, serves (*a*) to detach them from common practice and (*b*) to displace them from their proper position as 'master concerns'. This can be seen in the fact that each confines itself to establishing what is the case and what is true in its own field. History becomes the province of historians, and philosophy the province of philosophers; and both leave aside the objective of trying common practice by reference to the truth.

The procedures are strongly embedded in modern English theology, and perpetuate themselves institutionally, but they are not without their critics. For there are those who realize, instinctively, that these subjects (history, philosophy and Scripture) have lost touch with the common practice in which they were mediated and with the question of achieving public agreement as to its truth. Their reaction has usually been to allow existing institutionalized forms to continue, but to add something else which will restore concern for the basis of English theology in common practice. For example, the strong emphasis given today to such subjects as systematic theology and ethics may – at least in part – be a response to what are perceived to be the problems of 'alienated theologies' of the sort we have been considering. In effect, they may each be a protest at what is considered a false abstraction from common practice. But the establishment of such subjects is no guarantee whatever that they will not themselves fall prey to the same problems which beset their predecessors; and there is strong evidence that they have. Under the pressures of the same self-consciously-developed subjects and methods as those of 'history' and 'philosophy', they may have little alternative.

### TWENTIETH-CENTURY THEOLOGY THROUGH PHILOSOPHY: FOUR CASES

The question which confronts us now is the response of twentieth-century theologians, operating within these institutions, to the vision of English theology.

If we look back over those who have enaged in the philosophical task in twentieth-century English theology, we will find them amongst systematic theologians and philosophers of religion as well as others. But we must focus our attention more directly now on a small number of philosophers and systematic theologians, leaving aside those whose concern is more directly historical and who do not usually engage in philosophical judgment as to the truth of common practice, as well as many others.[19] We shall concentrate on four who have been important figures in English theology: Donald M. MacKinnon (b. 1913), John Macquarrie (b. 1919), John H. Hick (b. 1922) and Don Cupitt (b. 1934).

### Donald M. MacKinnon

Donald M. MacKinnon was born in Oban, a fishing port on the west coast of Scotland, in 1913. He was educated at Winchester College and at New College, Oxford University, and served for a year as an Assistant in Moral Philosophy at Edinburgh University (to A. E. Taylor) before becoming Fellow and Tutor at Keble College, Oxford, for some ten years, lecturing also at Balliol College in the later years. In 1947, he was appointed Regius Professor of Moral Philosophy at the University of Aberdeen, and afterward (in 1960) became Norris-Hulse Professor of Divinity at the University of

Cambridge until his retirement. An Anglican, he is a member of the Scottish Episcopal Church, and now lives in Scotland. He is also active politically as a member of the Labour Party.

MacKinnon's chief influence has probably been through his impact on the generations of those who have studied or worked with him, who have benefited so much from the intensity of his engagement with them and the breadth and sensitivity of his learning. He has a wide interest, spanning literature, philosophy, politics and theology, and his writings are largely comprised of intensive essays on particular topics; their unity is at times difficult to identify. But there are, none the less, major concerns which run through his writing.

Despite the intensity which characterizes his work, there is a sense in which MacKinnon – as a self-declared moral philosopher – begins in, and remains with, the common practice which we have previously attempted to describe, and sees himself as serving the process of public judgment by which the quality of this practice may be improved. If common practice means the way people live, think and pray together as mediating the work of God, the practical as mediating the transcendent, this seems to be at the heart of MacKinnon's concerns. And even when he goes on to discuss the issues which emerge there, he does not lose sight of the 'moral location' of the issues, and the moral implications of positions taken. Furthermore, this 'moral location' is not the exclusive province of religious people, or theologians or philosophers; it is a public domain, where political philosophies are important and public judgment operates.

Common practice or ethics is unquestionably a very serious matter for MacKinnon, precisely because it mediates transcendent claims. Speaking of Bishop Butler, he says:

> Butler's empiricism is shown in his insistence that we look at the particular elements of our nature, one by one, turning aside from none of them. But it is just when he is doing this that he is most insistently defending the transcendent claims of morality; as if he is sure that only when we see morality as a coming to terms with our actual nature will we esteem it for what it is, something at once quite simple and authoritative, and yet as rich and diverse in content as human life itself.[20]

But the content of common practice is not vacuous, as if human beings had been given permission to engage in do-it-yourself life. Unlike those who stress autonomous human freedom, for MacKinnon common practice is grounded ultimately in 'what is the case':

the way in which we live our lives, even the sharpness with which the question how we should do so presses on us, imposes a veto on any sort of light-hearted disregard of questions concerning the ways in which things are. Morality is not a matter of arbitrary choice; it is in some sense expressive, at the level of human action, of the order of the world.[21]

And that requires consideration of what *is* the order of the world. So there is 'some kind of analogy between our commerce with the transcendent, and our commerce with the world around us'.[22]

So far as MacKinnon is concerned, the mediation of the transcendent in the practical (this 'commerce with the transcendent') is not properly dealt with, either by those who rely on some form of ethical naturalism (the utilitarians or Bentham, for example) or by avant-garde theologians (under the influence of the logical positivists and empiricists) who dispense with the metaphysical and replace it with 'the free play of undisciplined inventiveness'. On the one hand, the deep moral insight which is found in the difficulties and tragedies of life (often as expressed in literature) is beyond what can be explained in terms of any form of ethical naturalism.[23] On the other hand, MacKinnon insists on the human 'receptivity' of faith 'elicited, though not compelled, by external occurrence, and always orientated upon that which lies outside the interior life of the believing subject'.[24]

One further aspect of common practice requires to be noted, its 'factual' aspect. The mediation of the transcendent in the practical does not divorce it from the realm of facts. As MacKinnon suggests, illuminatingly, a concern for the metaphysical (the transcendent) requires a concern for the anti-metaphysical (the simply factual); concern for that which is beyond observation requires concern for observation. On the one hand, then, there is no easy appeal to the transcendent: 'such propositions remain completely vulnerable to refutation by what, in the last resort, our senses reveal to us.'[25] On the other hand, there is no such thing as a simple appeal to facts and observation, as the 'less sophisticated empiricists' suggest; Kant showed how complex was the use of sense-observation in the process of arriving at knowledge. So, on the one side, there is the possibility of reference to the transcendent from the practical, but on the other side it is always vulnerable to refutation, but not by reference to an oversimplified notion of fact: 'our notion of fact requires liberalisation; but still, of course, it must remain fact.'[26]

Common practice also mediates theological content. And this is not the same as the metaphysical, while 'the very concept of metaphysics, that besets the consciousness of those concerned with its possibility, is one that owes something to the interplay of religion and metaphysics in the Christian tradition'.[27]

> There is of necessity a continual shift and interplay between what we call metaphysics, and religion and theology. The laws governing the languages of religion and theology are not quite like those, if such there be, which govern impulses of metaphysical speculation.[28]

In metaphysics, it is the purpose of ontology 'to give as satisfactory and complete an account as possible of our ultimate conceptual scheme', but in theology this is 'bent to new purposes . . . enlarged and stretched in its use'.[29] But this 'arcane' of the transcendent is no less the inner reality on which the order of the world is founded, and the most basic point of reference for our moral practice – the depth which is responsible for those profound moral insights evident in great literature.

That makes it a matter of the presence of the transcendent in the factual, of God in the empirical realm, not only in the moral life of people but in *history*. Above all, the theological issue which exercizes an 'almost obsessive sovereignty' over MacKinnon is the *mysterium Christi*, the presence of God in the historical person Jesus. That raises again the question of fact, not only as a general philosophical question, but as a question which also requires attention to the actual practice of historians, the philosopher freeing the historian from imposing 'a restricted inflexible paradigm of what it is to be a fact'.[30] There are different sorts of facts, but a genuine difference between what is and what is not factual, and the truth of Christianity rests on the factual.

> Christianity faces men with the paradox that certain events which could have been otherwise are of infinite, transcendent import; and this without losing their character as contingent events. . . . We cannot allow any seriousness to Christianity's claim to truth unless we can also claim factual truth in a simple, ordinary sense, for propositions concerning the way [Jesus] . . . approached his end.[31]

And the question of the factuality of the incarnation and resurrection of Jesus Christ is one in which history and faith condition each other, and meet their limits in a mystery which 'involves and encompasses them'.[32] Human understanding reaches its limits in an ontological mystery, the mystery of the conformity of God to the limitations of human particularity, which is precisely where God most fully meets, and discloses himself, to mankind.[33]

It is already evident that for MacKinnon common practice is rich and deep, and its full quality not altogether fathomable; and the transcendent and religious which it mediates not capable of full explication which is not contingent, and therefore vulnerable. But beyond such contingencies (and incompleteness, because MacKinnon recognizes the need to do justice to the world-religions), common practice is problematic and disputable. More than that, it is deeply enmeshed in evil, for which in a genuine sense there is no solution. And one cannot turn a blind eye to these problems, which are empirical, social, metaphysical, and religious in scope, not least because avoiding them is to remain in thrall to them, while at the same time impoverishing human understanding of the fundamental conditions of life.[34] In practical failure, therefore, there is philosophical and theological failure. In a particularly telling comment on current theology, MacKinnon remarks:

> On occasions one notices that a readiness to jettison much that might be thought central to traditional Christian belief goes hand in hand with a tired institutional conservatism. Indeed the former is sometimes invoked to buttress the latter, as if the irreformability of the structures alone provided security against the volatility of faith. But it is by their faithful witness to the *Mysterium Christi*, through word and teaching, through worship and sacrament, that those very structures must be judged, and if found wanting, swiftly rejected.[35]

By what means are things to be improved, then? Implicitly, MacKinnon puts forward the importance of the 'master concerns', philosophy and history, to guide public judgment. His work is primarily in philosophy, and is distinguished not only by its deep (but sharply analytical) assimilation of the influence of Immanuel Kant, but also by the deep respect it shows for past and present British philosophy. But his work in philosophy is finely balanced; respect for historical fact disallows full-blown idealism, just as respect for the work of Lenin prevents Christianity from 'withdrawing into the securities of metaphysical idealism',[36] while respect for the transcendent disallows a simple appeal to observation. And the balance is frequently maintained through careful attention to literature and the issues raised there.[37]

It is possible to summarize MacKinnon's philosophy as a combination of self-consciousness, openness and ethical realism. Fundamentally, he (like Kant) employs philosophy with the greatest self-consciousness about its assumptions and limits; reason is not to be self-important. He is always preoccupied with the limits of human awareness. At the same time (following his own description of the philosophy of history), philosophy is to operate with 'a certain openness of texture or porosity', having 'no fixed horizons'.[38] If that is so, in his case, such openness is combined with a profound realism, since it is a search for the truth of things, contingently and ultimately; and it is directed to bringing about a correspondence between things and their truth.[39]

The ultimate truth to which things are to correspond is the loving will of God. How can one even talk about such a thing, never mind enable human beings to correspond to it? For, as MacKinnon stresses so strongly, theological truth lies at the limits of philosophy, in 'the abyss of the unknown, never precisely to be measured but discernibly not altogether fathomless, an infinite resistant to, yet not ultimately alien to, the reach of understanding'.[40] After one clears away all the images improperly applied to him, God is inexpressible, to be thought of 'only within the context of the most rigorous discipline of silence'.[41]

In that silence, however, MacKinnon finds the possibility of speaking of God, but not through a triumphalist understanding of revelation. God can be spoken of because he himself, in *limiting himself to the finite* in Jesus Christ, has disclosed the basis of his relation to the world. That is why, despite its necessary incompleteness, the doctrine of the incarnation

> still represents a tremendous effort to do justice to the belief that in Jesus Christ we have to reckon before all else with a quite unique movement from God to man . . . the reality of divine . . . self-limitation, even . . . a wholly unique act of such divine self-limitation that discloses in a way altogether without parallel God's relation to the world he has created. It discloses that relation in a way without parallel because this act of self-limitation is itself the ground of that relationship.[42]

What so many have failed to appreciate is that for God to be accessible to humanity required not only his coming to humanity, but his self-transformation in order to come. The relation of God to the world which is shown in the incarnation is one of loving self-giving, in which are involved Father, Son and Holy Spirit; and it is that – a factual occurrence in Jesus Christ – upon which all human relation to God depends. It is by that means alone that humanity may be brought into correspondence with the truth of God.

Humanity may correspond to the loving will of God because of the self-limitation of God. But MacKinnon's view is more radical and realistic than than that: 'If the Christian faith is true . . . its truth is constituted by the correspondence of its credenda with harsh, human reality, and with the divine reality that met that human reality and was broken by it, only in that breaking to achieve its healing.'[43] So Christianity does not 'deal with the problem of evil by encouraging the believer to view it from a cosmic perspective':

> Rather Christianity takes the history of Jesus and urges the believer to find, in the endurance of the ultimate contradictions of human existence that belongs to its very substance, the assurance that in the worst that can befall his creatures, the creative Word keeps company with those he has called his own.[44]

The fact is that human beings still find such a God with them in the tragedies and tests of their lives. That is why they still believe – despite all opposition and all the alternatives which clever people provide. The presence of God in the perplexities of common practice is the basis of his relationship with them and for the truth by which they are to live. In the end, therefore, the content of Christian faith, and the possibility which it affords for the common practice of life, arises from the activity of God in sharing the conditions and suffering of human life.

### John Macquarrie

John Macquarrie was born in Renfrew, Scotland in 1919, and educated at the University of Glasgow in mental philosophy and divinity. After ordination in the Church of Scotland, he served as an army chaplain and then a parish minister (during which he began postgraduate study on Heidegger and Bultmann) before becoming a lecturer in systematic theology at the University of Glasgow in 1953. He went to the Union Theological Seminary in New York in 1962 as Professor of Systematic Theology and was soon ordained a priest in the American Episcopal Church. In 1970, he was appointed Lady Margaret Professor of Divinity at Oxford, and Canon of Christ Church, and remained there until his retirement in 1986.

Macquarrie's interests and influence have been international. Though there were phases in his work when he was attracted to the English idealists, particularly F. H. Bradley, and to the existentialists Bultmann and Heidegger, he consciously broadened the base of his theology through his examination of the range of modern religious thought,[45] and through the influence of such people as Karl Rahner and Hans Urs von Balthasar. This broadening base, which gave particular consideration to the interface of philosophy and theology, was very important in the evolution of his Christian theology. In turn, through his very extensive writing,[46] and particularly his one-volume systematic theology *Principles of Christian Theology*,[47] he has himself attracted interest around the world, well beyond the two countries in which he has taught.

His work also shows steady development, but within certain parameters which remain unchanged. There is an identifiable tension in his theology, that between a general religious faith and the particular claims of Christian faith. He attempts to sustain both in their interrelation by philosophical means which are appropriate to the modern era. But he also does so in conscious response to catholic Christianity. Just as his move to a broadly-based philosophy is significant, so also is his shift to Anglicanism.

The continuing importance of general religious faith in Macquarrie's work is unmistakable. Looked at from the point of view of the English vision we discussed earlier, it is interesting to note the starting-point for Macquarrie's theology in religious awareness.

> I had a naturally religious temperament . . . By 'religion' I mean an awareness of the holy, of the depth and mystery of existence. It can be a sense of presence, or, paradoxically, a sense of absence . . . I thought of this mystery in terms of immanence rather than transcendence. It was this kind of religious experience that drew me away from the rather dreary evangelical Protestantism in which I had been reared towards what may be broadly called the 'catholic' tradition'.[48]

In this case, the mediation of the transcendent in the immanent is still present, as it was in the case of the common practice we discussed, but the mediation is in present religious *awareness* rather than in practice as such. And in religious awareness, it has a noticeably *general* character, of the sort we found to be characteristic of post-Enlightenment thought; in itself it lacks the specificity of the formulation which might be given it through conceptions of God or of the 'eternal laws' whereby God operates (of the sort to be found in early English theology). That perhaps is why, in his earliest thought, Macquarrie found a natural kinship with F. H. Bradley's notion of a supra-rational Absolute present for human life, and also agreed that anything more specific was only a symbol of this higher truth.

But such a position creates an interesting difficulty. On the one hand, it is possible to be aware of the Absolute, and therefore to be 'religious'; but, even if this is universal in human awareness, it is neither practical nor public in the sense of having ethical and social content. On the other hand, Christian belief (as well as its supposed historical basis) is left in a very weak state, alienated from eternal truth. And Christian doctrines are only pre-rational 'symbols'; attempts to treat them as more, such as those of Calvin and Barth, must be 'systematic superstition'.[49]

Macquarrie meets these difficulties in several ways. Chronologically, his first important move was through sharing and refining the position of Rudolf Bultmann. With that, the 'mighty acts' of which Christians speak, but which general religious awareness leaves as optional symbols, are given 'practical' import but of a very confined kind: they are seen as a summons to decision through which a new possibility of existence is provided. But while they do provide this new possibility of existence, and in that sense are objective, they do so for those individuals whose existence is transformed by response to the summons. So the objectivity of the new possibility is conditional on its actualization in the existential response of the believer. And the historical record, the New Testament, is to be understood in this way:

> it intends to bring the reader into an understanding of his own being. Its essential meaning, therefore, lies not in any record of historical facts which it may contain, not in any world-view which it may reflect, but in that possibility of existence, that self-understanding, that way of life which it presents to the reader.[50]

And, of course, understanding its meaning requires the appropriation of that possibility of existence which is presented.

Correspondingly, the call of Jesus Christ, when preached, mediates God's justification to those in whose existence it is actualized. But speaking of this in historical terms, and preaching of the possibility which is available, both 'objectifies' and 'symbolizes' it, as we might say, by employing cosmic and cultural notions; this is what occurred in the New Testament. Such 'myths' need to be translated, together with the vocabulary in which their significance is stated by writers such as Paul, in such a way as to draw out their fundamental message about human possibilities, a process which requires the use of 'viable philosophical concepts' such as those of Heidegger.[51]

Understood in one way, this is not so far from Macquarrie's concern with general religious awareness as it first seems, for Bultmann's position suggests how general religious awareness becomes salvific through a particular call responded to in particular existential decisions. How its mediation in the life, death, and resurrection of this man Jesus occurs, and why that is important, and what are the particular consequences for those who respond, are left unclear. Like some of those to whom Macquarrie is attracted, Karl Rahner for example, it seems that the actuality of the human existence of Jesus, and that of those who respond to the call, are of secondary importance. To put it differently, mediation in materiality seems to make little difference; existential response has taken its place.

It is interesting to see how Macquarrie develops both aspects, the general religious awareness and its concrete mediation. There is clearly a problem about both which he recognizes. In the one case, can this notion of religion be sustained against secularist views? Bultmann's unclarity about the status of such statements as 'God speaks' and other accounts of divine activity 'from outside us' – concentrating instead on existential appropriation of the events in which God is active – conceals a problem, when 'in a secular age one may not assume that language about God affords a universally intelligible starting point for an interpretation of the Christian faith'.[52] In the other case, while Macquarrie remains convinced that 'the best approach to many of the problems of theology and philosophy is through the study of our humanity',[53] the understanding of humanity must be redeveloped to avoid the 'subjectivism' and narrow individualism of pure existentialism. For example, the nature and activity of human beings must be understood more fully than old, rationalist thinking allowed:

> There is a broader understanding than that which belongs to the purely theoretical reason, and it is this broader understanding, arising out of the whole range of our existence in the world, that alone can help us to penetrate into the meaning of religious faith.[54]

So Macquarrie continues to expand his view of both God and humanity; and these concerns remain central for him throughout his theological work.

The method by which Macquarrie proceeds is that of an 'existential ontological theism'; this is to be a philosophical theology (or 'new style natural theology') to replace traditional 'metaphysical theism'. It is to be both more fundamental, tracing the convictions underlying old arguments, and more descriptive (as opposed to deductive); it is a 'let us see' approach, for that 'brings out into the light the basic situation in which faith is rooted, so that we can then see what its claims are'.[55] This avoids the twin temptations of reducing Christianity to the categories of any one individual, culture or philosophy, and of exalting Christianity to a position above all such. But it is to begin from humanity.

> The starting point of philosophical theology is man himself, the common humanity that is known to each of us men existing in the world. This analysis of our own existence will draw attention especially to those structures and experiences which lie at the root of religion and of the life of faith.[56]

Such a method investigates the universal conditions for the possibility of any religion or theology, including those for 'God-talk' or particular revelations, as a preparation for the special symbolic theology of Christian faith. So it continues as general, providing for an analytic description of the general conditions for religion and its mediation in particularities. In other words, there is still a question about the importance of mediation in particularities.

Macquarrie employs this philosophical method to discuss human existence, revelation, being and God, the language of theology and religion. He then moves to an interpretative method (hermeneutics) to discuss the coherent verbal expression of faith in symbolic theology, and considers the major loci of Christian theology, the Trinity, creation, God's relation to the world and evil, the person and work of Christ, the Holy Spirit and salvation and the last things. Afterward, he takes up the expression of faith as guided by reflection in a 'quality of life': church, ministry and mission, word and sacraments, worship and ethics. The result is an illuminating defense of Christian faith by description and interpretation, in which material is so used as to give a fair account of modern discussions while also providing a distinctive rationale for theism and for Christianity. In other words, it provides a sophisticated account – at least for those prepared to use this existential-ontological method – of the intelligibility of the claims which Christians make.

The same combination which we have previously noted, that of generalism with the claim that it is particularized for those who respond to it, features throughout Macquarrie's account. For example, he allies the question of being and the question of God very closely; and that raises problems about the adequacy of his notion of transcendence. So far as Macquarrie is concerned, the experience of being (the experience that anything can be at all) as present for human beings and the experience of God refer to the same thing. 'Being is the *transcendens*, it is already thought with every being, it is the condition that there may be any beings whatsoever.'[57] The difference between this general experience of being – which is the business of ontology – is that it may be a matter of indifference or alienation ('this might not have been, but it is'), while the particular experience of being as 'holy being' – which is the province of philosophical theology – includes an attitude of acceptance and commitment appropriate to an *'incomparable* that *lets-be* and is *present-and-manifest*, . . . strikingly parallel to the analysis of the numinous as *mysterium tremendum et fascinans'*.[58] The difference of the one from the other, the general from the particular, is that between neutrality and positive assent or trust. And Macquarrie suggests that this is not simply a difference of experience, but also a difference in the being which is experienced.

This positivity, as we may call it, comes to concrete theological expression in symbolic theology. Here, where 'holy being' is named 'God', 'primordial Being' is seen as the Father (the 'ultimate act or energy of letting be'), 'expressive Being' is the Son and 'unitive Being' is the Holy Spirit. Likewise, the very nature of 'holy being' to 'let be' brings it to be present and manifest in created beings, without which it would be indistinguishable from nothing; but it does not lose its nature as holy being by being present in this way. (This is a position which Macquarrie later described as panentheism.) In one of these beings, Jesus, there is a manifest growth towards christhood which is finally achieved in his death. Jesus is therefore God in the sense that he finally manifests the full possibilities of creaturely beings; and there is a continuity of what he achieves and that which is achieved by Being in other beings.

This positivity also comes to expression in a quality of life which is to be seen in the church. Macquarrie's consideration of humanity emphasizes, much more than do the existentialists, the roots and expression of faith in common humanity. As being is manifest in common humanity, so 'holy being' as responded to by Christians is manifest in the common life of Christians; faith must be practiced corporately, brought to expression through the sacramental life of the church: 'Prayer and worship lie at the center of Christian existence, and . . . they build up selfhood, authentic community, and ultimately (such is the Christian hope) the kingdom of God.'[59]

By these means, Macquarrie moves away from the difficulties we noted in his early theology, though how completely must remain a question. The lack of specificity in his early account of religion is met by the analysis of 'holy being', and the problem about its seriousness about particularities is met, on the one hand, by its analysis of humanity and the 'dynamic character' of the incarnation, and on the other hand, by its consideration of the common life of

Christians in the church. Throughout, it is dialogical, in the sense that it is controlled both by sources and by its own description and interpretation: it discusses being through its existential-ontological method; it discusses symbolical theology through an interpretation of Christian doctrine; it discusses the common life of Christians, by reflecting on Protestant and Roman Catholic church practice.

But there is a marked difference between Macquarrie's achievement, whose quality of its kind is undoubted, and the typical English vision in theology, which is much more focused on the judgment and improvement of the quality of current practice, by reference to the particular will of its author, not only through philosophy but also through historical inquiry. By comparison with this, Macquarrie's work is both more grounded in general religion interpreted through particular symbols and common life, which are examined philosophically more than historically, and less directed to the judgment and improvement of current practice.

## *John H. Hick*

John Harwood Hick was born in Scarborough, Yorkshire in 1922, and in 1940 entered the Presbyterian Church in England. He first studied law at Hull University, and after a period of service in an ambulance unit during the Second World War, went to Edinburgh University to study philosophy and afterwards to complete a doctorate of philosophy at Oxford with H. H. Price. He then trained for ordination and served as a minister for three years. Two appointments in the United States followed, first at Cornell University, then at Princeton Theological Seminary, before he became a lecturer in the Faculty of Divinity at Cambridge; in 1967 he was appointed professor at Birmingham University, an appointment which he later shared with one at Claremont Graduate School in California, to which he went full-time in 1982.

Unlike MacKinnon and Macquarrie, the starting-point of his development was in a personal conversion and conservative evangelical Christianity. And this included whole-hearted acceptance of:

> the entire evangelical package of theology – the verbal inspiration of the Bible; creation and fall; Jesus as God the Son incarnate, born of a virgin, conscious of his divine nature and performing miracles of divine power; redemption by his blood from sin and guilt; his bodily resurrection and ascension and future return in glory; heaven and hell.[60]

And his subsequent study of philosophy, during which (as afterward) he engaged primarily with the heritage of Kant and the philosophy of the Anglo-Saxon tradition, brought him to be dissatisfied with what he considered a simple faith too readily impatient with questioning.

What did not seem to change for Hick, however, was his conviction of the reality of encounter with the transcendent. This, rather than the common practice we saw to be characteristic of the English vision of theology, has remained the center of his theology. His understanding of the encounter develops in accordance with his philosophical views, and this gradually modifies his theology from one which is christocentric to one which is theocentric. His view of the encounter is at first controlled by Christian doctrine – in a sense it mediates the truth of Christian doctrine. Later that also shifts, as these doctrines are glossed with particular interpretations of them.

Mediation of the transcendent in experience – in accordance with his own beginnings and with the tradition of Schleiermacher, but unlike Kant – is fundamental for Hick; but his particular interest is mediation in knowledge. There is a common epistemological pattern in which religious knowledge partakes, and it has to do with the establishment of significance:

> By significance I mean that fundamental and all-pervasive characteristic of our conscious experience which *de facto* constitutes for us the experience of a 'world' and not of a mere empty void or churning chaos. We find ourselves in a relatively stable and ordered environment in which we have come to feel, so to say, 'at home'.[61]

And that is not only correlated with the structure of our own consciousness, but also provides appropriate kinds of action. In theistic religion, 'the primary locus of religious significance is the believer's experience as a whole . . . a uniquely "total interpretation"'; therefore, relating oneself to the divine entails a way of being in the world, a way of 'directing ourselves within the natural and ethical spheres'.[62]

But such an interpretation is 'not given to us as a compulsory perception, but is achieved as a voluntary act of interpretation'. Such cognitive freedom varies according to whether it operates in sense perception, where it is minimal, or occurs in matters of aesthetic and ethical significance, or in religious cognition of our environment, where it is maximal.[63] Faith is, therefore, a 'fundamental expression of human freedom'.[64] This explains why people can take such different views in Christianity: these partake of the freedom which characterizes faith.

To suggest that faith is a matter of freedom is ironically to imply that the kinds of faith should be subject to a kind of 'quality-control'. This is often seen in Hick's writing in the form of polarities, after the fashion of some Calvinism. In Hick's case, a contrast is drawn between 'two Christianities', that of established orthodoxy which is devotionally strong and confessional but simplistic, objectivistic, and wrongly realistic, and that of truth-seeking liberals who are more cautious, experimental, subjective, and rightly realistic. Later, a similar contrast appears between adherents of 'Ptolemaic' and 'Copernican' views, those who center their views of other religions on their own and those who are fully theocentric and universalistic. The technique of polarizing serves to sharpen the issue of quality which features prominently in Hick's thought. The choices which he highlights are choices of 'quality', for he is concerned above all with the quality of human response to the transcendent. For example, the 'orthodox' are wrong in what Hick considers is their kind of realism – the supposition that their faith is simply 'given', to be accepted unquestioningly and confessed. The 'truth-seekers' are right in their kind of realism, because faith is an interpretative element within religious experience, arising in freedom.

If quality is to be judged both philosophically and historically, by those 'master concerns' we noted before, there is a worrisome issue in such polarizing of alternatives. Those included in the alternative groupings are frequently strange partners to each other, alike perhaps only in one feature. The wish to build a case through historical examples leads away from close attention to historical detail and explanation.

Hick's view of faith has profound implications for the question of God, for the position of Christ and Christianity and for the conception of human life in and beyond this world. Even in Hick's early writing, it was clear that for human beings to be so free, God

> must, so to speak, stand back, hiding himself behind his creation, and leaving to us the freedom to recognize or fail to recognize his dealings with us. Therefore God does not manipulate our minds or override our wills, but seeks unforced recognition of his presence and our free allegiance to his purposes. He desires, not a compelled obedience, but our uncoerced growth towards the humanity revealed in Christ, a humanity which both knows God as Lord and trusts him as Father.[65]

So the preservation of what Hick calls an 'epistemic distance' on the part of God is necessary for human beings to have full freedom. The only choices are coercive presence (the option espoused by 'orthodoxy') or absence for the sake of human freedom (Hick's view).

How then are human beings actually to be free? For Hick, like Kant, the issue emerges in connection with the achievement of good in the face of evil, and the question of the span within which good is to be achieved.[66] It is unacceptable that evil should be used in such a way as to provide an insuperable obstacle to the freedom of human beings to achieve goodness through a lived faith, and so he turns away from what he styled the 'Augustinian' theodicy with its emphasis on radical evil in humanity which required direct redemption, to his 'Irenean' theodicy, in which evil played its place in the human growth into the likeness of God. So far as the span of life is concerned, he argues for an eternal life through reincarnation in many worlds, as an ascent to goodness comparable with the Christian's growth to the likeness of God. The choice in both issues is between, on the one side, evil and life reckoned as issues of insoluble difficulty and, on the other side, the maximization of the conditions of human freedom by incorporating evil and life in a perspective in which human beings can achieve goodness. The question is intimately related to the issue of God and his actions, and of course, Hick's view of the epistemic distance required of God limits the possibility that God's action actually changes the human situation; God, as he put it, acts by being believed in.

Hick's concern for religious language, provoked by logical positivist criticisms of the meaning of theistic language (the theology and falsification debate) at the time, reflects much the same strategy. For Hick, it is necessary to accept the empiricist point that for something 'to exist' must make an observable difference, lest religious language become non-cognitivist, a 'protected discourse, no longer under obligation to show its compatibility with established conclusions in other spheres'.[67] And for the transcendent theist, the existence of God does make a difference. Equally, for the humanist, human beings are produced by natural causes, and there is no God to make a difference. Given the freedom of faith, and the ambiguity of the world, each view must be tenable. The issue between these views can only be decided eschatologically, through 'our participation in an eschatological situation in which the reality of God's loving purpose for us is confirmed by its fulfillment in a heavenly world'.[68] That is not for the believer to beg the question, because – as Hick shows – belief in such a 'heavenly world' is at least intelligible.

Such views do not necessitate, but open the way for, a change in the understanding of human relatedness to God, as well as a progressive limitation of the centrality of Christ. Hick's view of God distances him from particular action in the world, and his views of faith and evil are implicitly universalistic, and the problem is how to reconcile these with the notion of there being one, and only one, true religion. The answer which Hick adopts is to assimilate the notion of the Christ-event to his notion of faith:

> There has to be both divine action in the world and man's appreciation of the occurrence *as* divine action; both God's self-revealing activity and the human response which we call faith. And the Christ-event has these two sides to it. God was acting in human history but acting, as always, in such a way that man remained free to see or fail to see what was happening *as* God's doing. For religious faith, in its most basic sense, is the cognitive choice whereby we experience events and situations as mediating divine activity.[69]

Correspondingly, the New Testament and subsequent doctrinal formulations of the incarnation are 'interpretations of the meaning of the Christ-event, and not part of the event itself'.[70] While cognitive, these are interpretations, whereby the Christians *experience* Jesus *as* the Christ, finding salvation in him. And modern biblical and philosophical views show that they are not to be read literally, but as metaphorical or mythological expressions of such interpretations; what is more, they vary widely historically.[71] Like the 'Ptolemaic' view of the universe, they are extended to explain divergent views (including those of other faiths) by the addition of 'epicycles' but without thereby allowing sufficient recognition to other views. Also like the Ptolemaic view, they are historically relative.

Recognizing that such Ptolemaic views can be operated by any religion, Hick calls for a 'Copernican revolution', in which there is a shift to a theocentric understand of the religions. In such a case, one begins with the recognition, universal to the religions, that the 'ultimate divine reality is infinite and as such transcends the grasp of the human mind':

> From this it follows that the different encounters with the transcendent within the different religious traditions may all be encounters with the one infinite reality, though with partially different and overlapping aspects of that reality. This is a very familiar thought in Indian religious literature . . . in the Bhagavad Gita the Lord Krishna, the personal God of love, says,

'Howsoever men approach me, even so do I accept them; for, on all sides, whatever path they may choose is mine.'[72]

With this, we may look forward to a future 'in which what we now call the different religions will constitute the past history of different emphases and variations within a global religious life'.[73] And the person of Christ will be seen to be a 'temporal cross-section of God's Agapéing, . . . not the entirety of that of which it is a cross-section'.[74]

Hick's encounter-centered theology, with its subordination of Christianity (as well as other religions) to a universal realism, forms a contrast of another kind to the English vision discussed earlier. Where that sought an improved quality for common practice through finding the correspondence between the laws of nature and reason and the regularity of their divine Author, Hick has replaced this by the freedom of human encounter with a transcendent reality whose nature remains ambiguous. Whether this accords with the truth of the religions as they conceive themselves, or indeed provides for their future in a secular world, remains a question.

## Don Cupitt

Don Cupitt was born in the northwest of England, in Lancashire, in 1934. An Anglican, he studied biology and the history and philosophy of science as an undergraduate at Cambridge; he was supervised by N. R. Hanson, and learned from him both the philosophy of Karl Popper and Hanson's own constructivist position. Afterward, preparing for ordination at an Anglican theological college, he took Part III of the Theology Tripos at Cambridge before going in 1959 as a curate to Salford, an industrial area in Manchester. Three years later, he returned to the same theological college as vice-principal, and then became Fellow and Dean of Chapel at Emmanuel College, Cambridge in 1966. He has remained there since then, first as Assistant Lecturer, then Lecturer in Philosophy of Religion in the Faculty of Divinity.

His influence in Britain has been wide. This is no doubt partly because in some ways his own progress in religious faith mirrors a sequence of widely-held positions with which he has been in dialogue. But Cupitt is also notorious for his very public defense of unorthodox views. He has written a series of short books in which he has chronicled the development of his views; and two television series *Who Was Jesus?* and *The Sea of Faith*. These have shown his development – leaps might be a better word – from the religious conservatism with which he began adult life to a variety of 'unorthodox' views, eventually dispensing with the objectivity of God and the possibility of grace-given goodness in favor of spiritual development unencumbered by such 'controls', and moving even beyond that to a view of faith as creative response to contingency.

After a period as a conventional Christian in which he seems to have followed the typical path of English public school religion, where Christian beliefs are used as support for traditional English social order, Cupitt was 'rather abruptly' converted at 18, and became a member of what he described as 'a conservative and pietistic Protestant group'.

> The curiously powerful tyranny which that group exercised over its members depended upon an uncritically literal use of religious language. You had to say you 'knew the Lord', but you were not allowed to question precisely what could be *meant* by a claim to 'know' the Lord. Ever since, I have equated anthropomorphism with bondage to idols, and the negative way with spiritual freedom.[75]

Correspondingly, his early theological work shows three features: a conviction of the importance of objectivity in theology, the conviction that it is in principle unattainable, not simply that it has not yet been achieved, and a certain restlessness bound up with the freedom of the human being. Thus it shows a 'restless iconoclasm' which 'strives after intelligible content, and yet must by its own inner dialectic always negate any proposed specific content'.[76] To a large extent, Cupitt's subsequent development is traceable to an uncompromising outworking of these three features.

For Cupitt, the notion of God seems to be built up by a process of removal whereby God is removed from the images through which human beings must think God; monotheism is therefore inseparable from the polemic against idols. While that produces a high notion of God, it is also an abstractive, remote one of the sort to be found in Deism. And by the nature of the case, theories of analogy or incarnation which justify knowledge of this God must fail. In effect, they only repeat the problem of how something so far away as God can also seem near. Jesus 'supremely exhibits what it is to have to do with God . . . the epitome of the universal situation before God, the Yes and the No, the nearness and the farness'.[77] 'To see Jesus as the crux for belief in God, the fulfilment of Israel's history, one who "must" suffer, "must" be Christ, is to perceive something like a dramatic necessity.'[78]

None the less, while the transcendent is entirely beyond human knowing, it is present in human practice; it 'enters into the moral realm as that unknowing and unknown through which and from which supreme goodness is alone attainable'.[79] So far as this emphasizes the mediation of the divine in human practice, Cupitt's view accords with the English vision which we considered earlier; but his view leaves the divine presence as what might be called the 'fact' of a free gift which is beyond what we could create for ourselves and which expresses itself in the moral life as

> spontaneous, unselfconscious, and disinterested love, generosity, and sympathy: everything embraced by the word *dilectio*, delight. Theistic ethics [as distinct from nontheistic] is under a moral necessity to ascribe such qualities to the transcendent, and so (within its programme) to speak of him as personal and as the final good.[80]

It is noticeable that these qualities in which the divine manifests itself are those appertaining to the individual; those 'laws' by which the divine manifests itself in the formation of social life are left aside.

Such mediations of God in human practice, however, are particular to cultural frameworks: '"God" exists, not as a universal essence, but only in his various particular specifications, whether religious or metaphysical.'[81] There is a wide diversity of such worldviews in today's world, though there is some analogy between them, and programs of action rest on different specifications shared by people within communities.[82]

Interestingly, the difference between programs of action in a pluralistic world raises the issue of their moral quality. This is not far distant from the question about the quality of common practice which was raised in Hooker's day by those who disagreed about which authority (Bible or established practice) was to determine common practice. It was then an issue about truth which manifested itself as an issue about common practice, realism in ethical form. Cupitt makes the same connection between truth and morality, and examines the implications of bad moral consequences for the Christian truth which sponsors them, though later (in a Preface to the second edition of his *Crisis of Moral Authority*) he sees this connection as implying that 'we cannot in fact be realists, for we all of us treat a serious moral objection to a dogma as a weighty reason for doubting its *truth*. This in turn implies that our real view of religious truth must be ethical'.[83] Originally, however, Cupitt argues that a serious consideration of the moral consequences of Christian views reveals the harm to which Christian theology has led, and that not only the content, but also the function, of theology should therefore be altered. Correspondingly, the anthropomorphisms of religion, much of its asceticism and sexual views, its physical and psychological terrorism, its authoritarian imagery and its attempt to provide a unified backing for moral principles, and its obscurantism in general, should be discarded in favor of something more honest and pluriform. And the function of religion should now be seen as that of a practical witness to moral values.[84] This conclusion is consistent with his earlier view of the divine presence as functioning in practice, but here religion is seen as the mediation of that divine presence.

It is clear that by 1980 Cupitt was preoccupied with the practical medium of religion and its importance for the symbolization and enactment of human values; the importance of religious *thought* was much attenuated, and with it the possibility of discerning the effects of the divine presence for human practice. Furthermore, much of his moral critique had been directed at the restrictive and harmful effects of developed Christian thought for a healthy human morality, and the corrections he suggested served to attenuate the notion of the divine still further. It may also be that he had discovered that the 'restless iconoclasm' by which he was proceeding, which he also identified with the success of modern science, was in fact an expression of human freedom.

> These were the days of positivism and the verification principle, a time when theology was under sharp attack. My idea was that theology might follow natural science by giving up the idea that it is in possession of any fixed deposit of truths, and instead becoming consistently self-critical, revisionist and iconoclastic.[85]

Of course, the archetypal fixity was God, or the truth itself. As we have seen, Cupitt had struggled to free humanity of the improper restrictions associated with religious images, while still supposing that beyond these there was the possibility of a healthy life of spontaneous love lived from the goodness given by the transcendent God. But in *Taking Leave of God*, the argument changes: there is no goodness without radical freedom, and radical freedom requires that there be no extrinsically imposed rules, only self-made and self-imposed rules intrinsically authoritative for me, joined to the freedom of action by which I may follow them.[86] In the face of this, Cupitt's (largely vestigial) supposition that God mediates goodness disappears. What he later called his earlier 'obediential realism' is gone, and in its place is rational autonomy:

For a morality that deserves to be adopted must be rational, consistent and impartial. That being so, we begin to see how a society of autonomous persons might be possible. Each chooses his own ethic, but in so far as they each recognize that morality has to be consistent and impartial, a public socially-agreed morality will tend to emerge as a product of their separate choices. Hence the possibility of a fully free society, a liberal democratic republic, the best kind of society.[87]

There is a sense in which Cupitt speaks with a different voice than previously in *Taking Leave of God* and the books which follow – its companion volume *The World to Come*, *Only Human*, *The Sea of Faith* and *Life Lines*. Why? One answer is that he has moved beyond a 'dualistic' vision to a singular one. There had been an unresolved problem in his thought, and it had to do with the limitation imposed on him by his sharp division of the transcendent from the world, which takes the form of an insistence on 'hiddenness' as the defining characteristic of God, which in turn makes the presence of God always indirect and relative.[88] He could therefore only draw out the implications of this position. But the position itself is problematic; it is not much different from maintaining a fact without meaning, in this case maintaining the fact of a transcendent with no interpretation of its presence – except perhaps in very formal and programmatic terms. And Cupitt moves decisively away from the position and the problems with which it had provided him. Though the move away from God is presented in *Taking Leave of God* as necessary for moral – as well as psychological – autonomy, the move is actually required by Cupitt's own position about the transcendent. Perhaps this is why a transcendent whose position was so much reduced in Cupitt's earlier thought suddenly reappears as the 'supernatural control' which must be discarded in the name of freedom.

It is not that he jettisons religion or Christianity. Morality in so far as it seriously concerns a change in our relation to existence is inevitably led toward religion. Cupitt therefore redevelops Christianity as autonomous spiritual practice, ostensibly maintaining Christian content, spirituality, and values in a Buddhist form. In all those forms of Christianity cataloged in *Life Lines* which emphasize a real God upon whom human beings are dependent for their reality, the 'reality' is beyond: 'an objective God "out there" would be spiritually oppressive and would block man's attainment of full self-consciousness. To liberate man, God must be internalized.'[89] But the religious claim must now be interiorized as an a priori practical principle, like the Buddhist's Way. It will then be seen that 'God is a unifying symbol that eloquently personifies and represents to us everything that spirituality requires of us' – in effect a surrogate for the Spiritual Way by which the human consciousness is fully unified. Jesus, however, embodies and teaches this Way. While God had to become 'objectively thinner and thinner in order to allow subjective religiousness to expand . . . [he] is still the *deus absconditus*, the hidden God who is found at last to hide himself in the depths of the heart.'[90] And, as in Cupitt's old view of the transcendent, this God is present through the willing of the good.

As Cupitt's position evolves from this point, its ethical content unfolds following what he says is the only path accepted in our culture:

> There is not much real truth, and it is only provisional; but it is all we have, and it is found by the rigorous testing of theories against evidence not under their control, by free critical reason operating independently of social authority. That alone is truth, and everything else is the product of power, fashion, custom and choice.[91]

But the effect of this is to diminish the possibility of an a priori practical principle of the sort for which he wished, together with the possibility of the personification of the Spiritual Way as God. The pattern of his earlier thought therefore repeats itself, with the Way becoming ever more hidden, or – in the face of postmodernist thought – ever more contingent:

> This new ultra-naturalism or immanentism has become a very strong intellectual imperative. It refuses any kind of jump to a higher level, to a reality behind the appearances. We have to say Yes to what is before us, in all its contingency. Such is, I believe, the final message of an incarnational religion. The Eternal descends into the contingent world and is diffused through it.[92]

And the proper response is creative and innovative religious action. He sums up the course of his work as follows:

> So the labours of twenty-odd years have changed not just my 'position', and not just 'me': more profoundly, my conception of what sort of change it is that I have been undergoing has been changing. The literary project takes on a Chinese-box quality: as I change, the project changes – and the change changes, too.[93]

We have now seen that, while Cupitt has in a sense followed the main lines of the English vision, he has also departed from it in significant respects. The practical element, as mediating the divine, has loomed large in his views, even if the practice with which he is concerned is insufficiently social and organized. That which is mediated there is much less well-developed; his use of iconoclasm prevents any full discussion of the divine, long before he 'takes leave of God'. And he has employed history and philosophy to test and correct the quality of common practice in religion. But his trust for post-Enlightenment modes of thought (a certain way of trusting the historical 'given'), such as the Kantian or later the Nietzschean, has led him first to a dualism, then increasingly to an immanentist and highly contingent spirituality, with little attempt to criticize the underlying assumptions of these views. It remains a question whether he has not drastically oversimplified both the implications of modernity for religion and the religious response to modernity.

## THE FUTURE OF THE ENGLISH VISION

We saw earlier that English theology was thought (1) to begin in present common practice, through which were mediated such authorities as Scripture and tradition, (2) to proceed by examining the nature of this common practice – its quality – in open trial (*a*) by rational judgment, (*b*) suited to the subject-matter. This rational judgment, with the help of those skilled in the mutually complementary master disciplines – history and philosophy – and its purpose, was (3) to find the higher truth of common practice through reference to the author or agency of nature and reason. And the outcome of the trial was to be an agreement on the proper organization of common life which was conducive to the good of society. Throughout the concern was public – theology mediated in public practice, the use of public reason, open trial of the truth and the achievement of truly social existence.

Yet we have seen remarkable variations in the ways by which theologians using philosophy have proceeded with their task, as if there were no common vision shared by English theology. None the less, it is not antiquarianism which recalls this vision and uses it to question English theologians. It is also an awareness of major areas of theological concern today in the late 1980s, which coincide remarkably with the major elements of the earlier vision. What are these? They can be briefly listed:

1 Concern for common practice in its particularity, and the search for its truth in ways which are less abstractive than many of the past (sometimes called postmodernism).

2 The need to balance historical, scientific, and philosophical disciplines in finding not only what has been but what is true and good in the present (hermeneutics).

3 The need to find the nature of the truth which is in the world and its people, and not alien to them (the issue of realism in theology).

4 The need to bring about the well-being of society itself.

All of these interpenetrate each other in current discussions. And all of them are the standard by which English theologians of the past and present will be judged for their adequacy.

## NOTES

1 Richard Hooker, *Of the Lawes of Ecclesiasticall Politie*, Bk 1, ch. 1, p. 58.

2 'That which doth assigne unto each thing the kinde, that which doth moderate the force and power, that which doth appoint the forme and measure of working, the same we tearme a lawe: all other things according to a *Lawe*. . . All things therefore do worke after a sort according to a lawe, whereof some superiours, unto whome they are subject, is author; only the workes and operations of God have him both for their worker, and for the lawe whereby they are wrought. The being of God is a kinde of lawe to his working: for that perfection which God is giveth perfection to that he doth' (Hooker, *Lawes*, Bk 1, ch. 1, pp. 58 ff).

3 Ibid., ch. 3, p. 63.

4 Ibid., ch. 2, p. 59.

5 Ibid., ch. 2, p. 61.

6 Ibid., ch. 10, p. 96.

7 This makes English theology very vulnerable to those, whether institutions or individuals, who formulate a philosophy of history or practice and seek to impose it. Some well-intentioned churches and theologians wish to 'save' the English by imposing a *magisterium* or spirituality.

8 S. Alexander, *Space, Time and Deity* (1920); A. N. Whitehead, *Process and Reality* (1929); W. Temple, *Nature, Man and God* (1934); F. R. Tennant, *Philosophical Theology*, 2 vols (1928, 1930).

9 A. E. Taylor, *The Faith of a Moralist*, 2 vols (1930); J. Oman, *Grace and Personality* (1917); H. H. Farmer, *Experience of God* (1929).

10 The supposition of an opposition between 'neutral' and 'confessional' may be one underlying cause for the practice, which became common in England in the 1970s, of splitting faculties of theology into theology and religious studies. The practice also owes something to the importation of the 'study of religion' from American universities, where its separation from 'confessional theology' had been used to legitimate the presence of religion in public institutions obliged to observe the Constitutional separation of state and church.

11 Interesting examples of historical accounts are those by John Hick (*Evil and the God of Love*) and Don Cupitt (*The Sea of Faith* and *Life Lines*) and of phenomenological accounts, Ninian Smart's *The Religious Experience of Mankind*.

12 Hooker, *Lawes*, Bk 1, ch. 3, p. 63.

13 There have been too many people involved in the debate about religious language to list here, but A. Jeffner, *The Study of Religious Language* provides a useful systematic statement of positions taken. Examples of the work of sociologists of knowledge are P. Berger and T. Luckmann, *The Social Construction of Reality* (London, 1967) and M. Berger in *The Social Reality of Religion* (London, 1969). The philosophers of science T. S. Kuhn (*The Structure of Scientific Revolutions*, Chicago, 1970) and Ian Barbour (*Myths, Models and Paradigms*, New York, 1976) have been much quoted by those concerned with the use of reason in religion.

14 One important exception is Basil Mitchell, in *Morality Religious and Secular* and *The Justification of Religious Belief*.

15 See A. Flew and A. MacIntyre (ed.), *New Essays in Philosophical Theology* (London, 1955). A useful consideration of the debate about religious language is Jeffner, *The Study of Religious Language*.

16 Cf. M. Wiles, *The Making of Christian Doctrine* (London, 1967).

17 Cf. Cupitt, *Life Lines*.

18 A. Farrer, *Finite and Infinite* (London, 1943); E. L. Mascall, *He Who Is*.

19 There are not a few of these. One thinks, for example, of F. C. Copleston and G. C. Stead, notable historians of philosophy.

20 D. M. MacKinnon, *A Study in Ethical Theory*, p. 178.

21 D. M. MacKinnon, *The Problem of Metaphysics*, p. 38.

22 Ibid., p. 39.

23 'It may well be, as I would be prepared to argue, that if we take seriously the sort of moral insight contained in such a work as Shakespeare's *Julius Caesar*, we have already advanced beyond the frontiers of, e.g., a thorough-going Benthamite ethical naturalism; indeed to take such an insight seriously is one way of advancing beyond such frontiers; to do it *is* so to advance.' Ibid., p. 44 ff.

24 Ibid., p. 44.

25 D. M. MacKinnon, *Themes in Theology*, p. 14.

26 MacKinnon, *Problem of Metaphysics*, p. 43.

27 D. M. MacKinnon, *Borderlands of Theology*, p. 217.

28 Ibid., p. 220.

29 Ibid., p. 27 ff.

30 Ibid., p. 76.

31 Ibid., p. 87.

32 Ibid., p. 79.

33 Ibid.

34 'It may well be thought that [as regards the significance and role of power in human life] the Churches have all in one way or another failed, either by accepting uncritically the attitudes and standards of the society around them, or of certain strata within it, or else by a kind of half-

deliberate aversion from the problems raised, and decisions become necessary, by means of their own involvement with the power-structures around them . . . in my own personal judgement, we have to reckon with a continuing impoverishment of fundamental theological thought springing from excess reverence for the powers that be as ordained of God.' MacKinnon, *Themes in Theology*, p. 4.

35 Ibid., p. 6.
36 D. M. MacKinnon, *Explorations in Theology*, p. 22.
37 See, for example, MacKinnon, 'On the Notion of a Philosophy of History' in *Borderlands of Theology*, pp. 152–68.
38 Ibid., p. 153.
39 MacKinnon, *Problem of Metaphysics*, p. 30.
40 MacKinnon, *Themes in Theology*, p. 1.
41 Ibid., p. 19.
42 Ibid., p. 140.
43 MacKinnon, *Explorations in Theology*, p. 21 ff.
44 MacKinnon, *Borderlands of Theology*, p. 93.
45 J. Macquarrie, *Twentieth Century Religious Thought: The Frontiers of Philosophy and Theology, 1900–1960*.
46 A bibliography of his writing to 1984 is included in the volume of essays dedicated to him, *Being and Truth*, eds A. Kee and E. T. Long (London, 1986).
47 First published in 1966, and revised and enlarged in 1977.
48 'Pilgrimage in Theology', in *Being and Truth*, p. xi.
49 Ibid., p. xii.
50 J. Macquarrie, *Studies in Christian Existentialism*, p. 104.
51 Ibid., p. 110 ff.
52 Ibid., p. 4.
53 J. Macquarrie, *In Search of Humanity* (London, 1982), Preface.
54 J. Macquarrie, *Principles of Christian Theology*, p. 50.
55 Ibid., p. 50.
56 Ibid., p. 51.
57 Ibid., p. 194.
58 Ibid., p. 105.
59 Ibid., p. 443.
60 J. H. Hick, *God Has Many Names*, p. 2.
61 J. H. Hick, *Faith and Knowledge*, p. 98.
62 Ibid., pp. 113, 107.
63 Ibid., pp. 123–8.
64 Hick, *God Has Many Names*, p. 4.
65 Ibid., p. 135.
66 The one is dealt with in *Evil and the God of Love* and the other more specifically in the context of Hick's concern with world religions, in *Death and Eternal Life*.
67 J. H. Hick, *God and the Universe of Faiths*, p. 9.
68 Hick, *Faith and Knowledge*, p. 199.
69 Hick, *God and the Universe of Faiths*, pp. 111 ff.

70 Ibid., p. 114.
71 See J. H. Hick, (ed.), *The Myth of God Incarnate* and M. Goulder (ed.), *Incarnation and Myth: The Debate Continued* (London, 1979).
72 Hick, *God and the Universe of Faiths*, pp. 139 ff.
73 Ibid., p. 146.
74 Ibid., p. 159.
75 Don Cupitt, *Explorations in Theology*, 6 (London, 1979), p. viii.
76 Don Cupitt, *Christ and the Hiddenness of God*, p. 8. There is also, however, a curious sense in which all his movement is under the influence of his Cambridge teacher N. R. Hanson, who emphasized the 'unsettled, dynamic research sciences' in 'the interplay between facts and the notations in which they are expressed [and] the "theory-laden" character of causal talk'. See N. R. Hanson, *Patterns of Discovery* (London, 1958), pp. 1 ff.
77 Ibid., p. 213.
78 Ibid., p. 9.
79 Don Cupitt, *The Leap of Reason*, p. 91.
80 Ibid., p. 92.
81 Ibid., p. 109.
82 It is not that Cupitt wishes at this point to move to pure religious relativism. With the possibility of neither a wholly adequate temporal image of God, nor an absolute historical incarnation of God, 'for me, Jesus's finality lies not in himself but (as he himself says) in what he proclaims, and in the way he bears witness to it. Jesus is final, not as an absolute icon of God – there cannot be such a thing – but because of the way he bears witness to what is final and unsurpassable. His finality is relative to man's spiritual aspirations . . . Jesus's life is a final paradigm of man's relation to God, for he dramatically exemplifies the triumph and tragedy of faith', *The Leap of Reason*, p. 129.
83 Cupitt, *Crisis of Moral Authority* (2nd edn., 1985), p. 8.
84 Or, as Cupitt put it later in retrospect, to 'symbolize, celebrate, enact and make effective our values, but we should not look to religious thought to justify our views', ibid.
85 Ibid., p. 10.
86 Don Cupitt, *Taking Leave of God*, p. ix.
87 Ibid., p. x.
88 See Cupitt, *The Leap of Reason*, pp. 101 ff.
89 Cupitt, *Taking Leave of God*, p. 8.
90 Ibid., p. 13.
91 Don Cupitt, *The World to Come*, p. 143.
92 Don Cupitt, *The Long-Legged Fly*, p. 8.
93 S., Cowdell, *Atheist Priest? Don Cupitt and Christianity*, Foreword by Don Cupitt, p. x.

## BIBLIOGRAPHY

### Primary

Cupitt, Don, *Christ and the Hiddenness of God* (London, 1971 and 1985).
—, *Crisis of Moral Authority* (London, 1972 and 1985)
—, *The Leap of Reason* (London, 1976 and 1985).
—, *Taking Leave of God* (London, 1980).
—, *The World to Come* (London, 1982).
—, *The Sea of Faith* (London, 1984).
—, *Life Lines* (London, 1986).
—, *The Long-Legged Fly* (London, 1987).
Hick, J. H., *Faith and Knowledge* (2nd edn, London, 1967).
—, *God and the Universe of Faiths* (London, 1973).
—, *Death and Eternal Life* (London, 1976).
—, (ed.), *The Myth of God Incarnate* (London, 1977).
—, *Evil and the God of Love* (London, 1979).
—, *God Has Many Names* (London, 1980).
MacKinnon, D. M., *A Study in Ethical Theory* (London, 1957).
—, *Borderlands of Theology and Other Essays* (London, 1968).
—, *The Problem of Metaphysics* (Cambridge, 1974).
—, Explorations in Theology 5: Donald MacKinnon (London, 1979).
—, *Themes in Theology* (Edinburgh, 1987).
Macquarrie, J., *An Existentialist Theology: A Comparison of Heidegger and Bultmann* (London, 1955, 1965, 1972).
—, *The Scope of Demythologizing* (London, 1960).
—, *Twentieth Century Religious Thought: The Frontiers of Philosophy and Theology, 1900–1960* (London, 1963, 1971, 1981).
—, *Studies in Christian Existentialism* (London, 1966).
—, *Principles of Christian Theology* (London, 1966, 1977).
—, *God-Talk: An Examination of the Logic and Language of Theology* (London, 1967).
—, *In Search of Deity* (London, 1984).

### Secondary

Cowdell, S., *Atheist Priest? Don Cupitt and Christianity* (London, 1988).
D'Costa, G., *John Hick's Theology of Religions* (Lanham, 1987).
—, *Finite and Infinite* (London, 1943).
—, *The Glass of Vision* (London, 1948).
—, *Faith and Speculation* (London, 1967).
Farrer, A., *Reflective Faith*, ed., Charles Conti (London, 1972).
Hooker, R., *Of the Lawes of Ecclesiasticalle Politie* (Cambridge, 1977).
Jeffner, A., *The Study of Religious Language* (London, 1972).
Mascall, E. L., *He Who Is* (London, 1943).

Mitchell, B., *The Justification of Religious Belief* (London, 1973).
—, *Morality Religious and Secular* (Oxford, 1980).
Sell, A. P. F., *The Philosophy of Religion 1875–1980* (London, 1988).
Smart, R. N., *The Religious Experience of Mankind* (London, 1971).
Whitehead, A. N., *Process and Reality* (London, 1929).

# Part II

# Theologies in the United States

The United States of America now shares continental Europe's leading role in modern theology, if measured by numbers of academic posts, students and publications, and the variety and vigor of the debates. It is helped by its inheritance from many groups of immigrants, its accompanying inner diversity, its vast third level educational network, and its global involvement, aided by economic and political power and the English language. It is also likely that more Christian theologians from other parts of the world who study or teach abroad do so in the United States than anywhere else. Theology in the United States is covered more widely in this volume than in the present section: Carl Henry in evangelical theology, the American black and feminist theologians, ecumenical theologians and theologians of religions.

In this part the four types of theology discussed are highly diverse. From earlier this century Robin Lovin selects Reinhold Niebuhr and H. Richard Niebuhr as 'theological realists' who did much of their theology through politics and ethics. He portrays their grappling as Christians with public issues, their liberal roots joined with a sober pessimism about the limits of social and political transformation, and the striking project of H. Richard Niebuhr – to understand Troeltsch's 'historical relativism' in the light of 'theological and theo-centric relativism'. He also suggests where their continuing relevance lies and outlines current developments.

James Buckley brings Edward Farley, Gordon Kaufman, Schubert Ogden, and David Tracy into a fascinating debate with each other and, in conclusion, with their outside critics. He sets them clearly in the context of nineteenth- and twentieth-century European theologies, and shows how lively and sophisticated their theologies are.

Schubert Ogden also appears in the following chapter (chapter 4) on process theology, which Kenneth Surin identifies as liberal in character. He outlines the complex philosophy of Whitehead and Hartshorne, and deals with the theologies of Ogden and Cobb. He concludes with a discussion of process theology in which the main critical standpoint is that of postmodernism.

Finally, the most recent group to emerge (although it had been developing for many years before its naming) has been the postliberals. William Placher introduces them through their main *alma mater*, Yale, and describes their distinctive approach to religion in its particularity and communality, and the nature of their concern for narrative. He then treats Hans Frei, George Lindbeck, Stanley Hauerwas, and Ronald Thiemann, before entering into debate and raising the central question of truth.

# 3

# Theology, Ethics, and Culture
## Robin W. Lovin

### BACKGROUND TO THEOLOGICAL REALISM

Reflection on society and culture has an important place in American Protestantism. Indeed, for many European observers, it has seemed that American Protestant theology and preaching consists of little else. No doubt this grows in part from the close historical identification between American culture and Protestant faith. Well into the nineteenth century, Protestant writers viewed American growth and prosperity as a divine endorsement of American virtue, and that theme still has an important place in popular religion.

More critical observers thought that American advantages called for a more rigorous Christian judgment. By the turn of the twentieth century, the Social Gospel movement had developed an exegesis that discerned in the teaching of Jesus a divine concern for human welfare and a rational commitment to human unity and equality. This 'pure ethic of Jesus' stood in judgment not only over the intervening centuries of superstitious dogmatism, but over the inequalities and class divisions of modern America. The combined progress of historical scholarship, rational religion, and industrial productivity creates a situation in which this gospel ethic can for the first time become a social reality.

> The sadness of the failure hitherto is turned into brightest hope if we note that all the causes which have hitherto neutralized the social efficiency of Christianity have strangely disappeared or weakened in modern life. Christianity has shed them as an insect sheds its old casing in passing through its metamorphosis, and with the disappearance of each of these causes, Christianity has become fitter to take up its regenerative work.[1]

The subject of this chapter is a movement which succeeded the Social Gospel and, in the wake of widespread disillusionment following the First World War, brought to Protestant theology in America a sobering awareness of the limits on human power and the distance that inevitably separates a biblical ideal from social reality. We shall give this movement the name 'theological realism', or occasionally just 'realism'. This nomenclature recognizes the important role in the movement of a form of religious social ethics generally known as 'Christian realism', but it also calls attention to the fact that the leaders of Christian realism emerged out of a broader group of religious thinkers who called for 'realism' in theology or for a 'realistic theology'. Walter Marshall Horton expressed their aspirations in this way:

> The word 'realism' suggests to me, above all, a resolute determination to face all the facts of life candidly, beginning preferably with the most stubborn, perplexing, and disheartening ones, so that any lingering romantic illusions may be dispelled at the start; and then, *through* these stubborn facts and not *in spite of them*, to pierce as deep as one may into the solid structure of reality, until one finds whatever ground of courage, hope, and faith is *actually* there, independent of human preferences and desires, and so casts anchor in that ground.[2]

The young realists of the 1920s retained a keen interest in the 'ethics of Jesus', but, from the realistic perspective, Jesus' insistence on the absolute power of love becomes an 'impossible ideal' that points to the limits of even our best efforts at love and justice. The theological realists had no illusions about the early achievement of a social order that approximates the gospel ethic, and so they gave more attention to the immediate political choices that defined the real options for social change. Particularly in the ethics of 'Christian Realism', the realist impulse expressed itself in a new concern with social analysis and the details of policy in business, government and international relations.

A distinctive realistic theology received explicit formulation only later, and then apart from or even in opposition to the ethics of Christian Realism. None the less, the theology and the ethics are united by their roots in American Protestant liberalism and by their cautious relationship to the European forms of 'crisis theology' and religious socialism. From our present vantage point, about a quarter-century beyond the era of Christian Realism in ethics, it makes sense to look again at the connections between Protestant theology and Protestant ethics in that era, and to rediscover the search for theologican realism that linked the men who became the leaders of that generation during the earliest years of their careers.

## SURVEY OF THEOLOGICAL REALISM

The first formulations of theological realism came from a small group of theologians that included D. C. Macintosh, H. Richard Niebuhr, Robert Lowrie Calhoun, and Walter Marshall Horton. The realist criticism of society and culture was, however, chiefly developed by H. Richard Niebuhr's elder brother Reinhold, a professor of ethics at Union Theological Seminary. Reinhold Niebuhr's social insights had been honed by extensive travels in Western Europe and thirteen years as a pastor in Detroit.

In 1932, Reinhold Niebuhr's *Moral Man and Immoral Society* offered a powerful criticism of the hope that society could be transformed by the moral intentions of individuals. Persons may be responsive to ideals, Niebuhr argued, but institutions and nations are shaped by power.

> The selfishness of human communities must be regarded as an inevitability. Where it is inordinate, it can be checked only by competing assertions of interest; and these can be effective only if coercive methods are added to moral and rational persuasion. Moral factors may qualify, but they will not eliminate, the resulting social contest and conflict.'[3]

This stark realism rested on a theological assessment of human nature which we will examine more closely in the next section of this essay, but it also drew on forms of social criticism which explain moral and religious ideals in terms of economic interests and point to the ways in which a group's moral commitments can be distorted by pride or resentment over their place in society. That line of criticism was familiar in Marxist formulations, but Niebuhr extended it to the proletariat as well, pointing out that their egalitarian ideals are compounded of both a genuine demand for justice and a resentment of the more comfortable position of others. While this evenhanded criticism precluded a real identification with proletarian revolutionaries, the early Christian Realists inclined toward some form of religious socialism. This tendency was reinforced by the arrival in America of Paul Tillich and other European religious socialists who fled the rise of Nazism. American religious socialism was, however, never so theoretically consistent as the theological interpretation of Marxism presented by Tillich, and the Christian

Realists had in practical terms more in common with the British reformers led by Archbishop William Temple and J. H. Oldham. Both Reinhold Niebuhr and his younger colleague John C. Bennett were active participants in the Oxford Conference on Church, Community, and State in 1937, and the understanding of the churches' role in social change which emerged from those discussions played an important part in Christian Realism's approach to policy issues for some decades afterwards.

During the Second World War, the chief social problem for theological realism shifted from economic inequities to the conflict between freedom and totalitarianism, with the result that during the war against Nazi Germany and again during the postwar conflict with Soviet Communism, the realists found themselves closer to the mainstream of American political and social thought. Reinhold Niebuhr's wartime book, *The Children of Light and the Children of Darkness*, offered a measured defense of democracy, denouncing its sometimes exaggerated confidence in political reason, but affirming democracy in the end as the form of government best suited to the ambiguous possibilities inherent in human nature. 'Man's capacity for justice makes democracy possible' Niebuhr wrote, in an aphorism that has become justly famous; 'but man's inclination to injustice makes democracy necessary.'[4]

This convergence between American democratic ideals and the social aims of Christian Realism led to a shift in attention from general social criticism to a concentration on the details of public policy. While the most thoughtful and systematic authors always upheld a biblical ideal that was at least one step beyond present social achievements, realist writings after World War II often do not differ substantially from policy analysis and proposals by non-theological authors. John Bennett developed from the materials of the Oxford Conference and from his own earlier work on church and society a method of approaching policy questions through 'middle axioms', rather than theological principles. Middle axioms stress broadly shared points of consensus about the·directions in which society must now move – toward universal health care, or a guaranteed employment policy, for example. Middle axioms do not claim universal validity, nor do they require that everyone who agrees on the axiom agree upon an ultimate theological justification for it. They indicate points of action on which Christians and others can unite to change society in ways that will improve it in present terms.

Given the early social criticism and the eventual emphasis on policy consensus, it is not surprising that the theological questions that initiated the realist movement were sometimes lost to view. The Christian convictions shaping theological realism were powerful, but often they were not fully articulated. Realists tended at first to identify themselves theologically in terms of what they were not. They rejected the sentimental optimism of the Social Gospel and poured scorn on any who dared to hope for social transformation on moral grounds alone; and though they recognized in Karl Barth's crisis theology a parallel attempt to respond to the disillusionments of the twentieth century, they found his radical condemnation of all human achievements and values too extreme.

Probably the theological realists' eagerness to avoid identification with the Social Gospel obscured their vision of the links that still connected them to American Protestant liberalism, with its reliance on personal religious experience and its almost Pelagian emphasis on works of charity. As a result, the American realists were often unable to find ways of expressing their differences with Barth and other European Protestant contemporaries, and theological realism often lacked precisely what should have distinguished it, namely an adequate and explicit theology. The 'theocentric relativism' that H. Richard Niebuhr developed in his later theology seems to express the theological orientation of many of the American Christian Realists, but a complete assessment of the theology of the realist movement must await a more careful analysis of the themes that link it to American Protestant liberalism, as well as the important points of difference on which the early theological realists insisted.

## REINHOLD NIEBUHR

Reinhold Niebuhr's importance should already be clear from our survey of the realist movement. The task of this section is to develop some of the main points of the theological account of human nature on which his various essays in social analysis and criticism rest.

The perspective of *Moral Man and Immoral Society*, while it marks an important break with the moral idealism of the Protestant liberalism, seems at first to yield entirely negative results. Even the victims of economic exploitation and racist domination, who have no stake in the hypocrisies of bourgeois culture, are subject to their own fanatic illusions, so that in the end the revolutionaries are as dangerous as the oppressors. What is needed, therefore, is not a new ideology, but a perspective on human aspirations and limitations that accepts the inevitable clash of divergent interests without destroying the hope for greater justice.

The needed insight is, according to Niebuhr, uniquely expressed in the biblical narratives that present the human being as both a finite, limited creature and as the image of God. As a result, each person and group is bound to a definite point in history and troubled by anxiety over the fragility of life and achievements; but each person and group is also capable of an 'indefinite transcendence' of these limitations. Any plan that ignores the human as creature will be wrecked by the unexpected resurgence of selfish interests and anxieties that make a purely rational reconciliation of human differences impractical, but any plan that assumes that selfish interests are the only forces at work in society will miss the possibilities for the genuine increases in justice that human imagination can provide.

Niebuhr developed this theological anthropology most completely in his Gifford Lectures of 1939, later published as *The Nature and Destiny of Man*. Here he develops the paradoxes of the biblical view in specific contrasts to its ancient and modern rivals. In the assessments of Stoicism, Romanticism, naturalism, and other perspectives, we see Niebuhr's complete confidence in the biblical faith, but we also learn something about his theological method. He is not a craftsman of precise and timeless formulations. His theological point becomes vivid in contrast to other possible ways of understanding human problems, and it is the adequacy of the biblical view relative to those understandings, not its absolute truth, that he aims to demonstrate. For all Niebuhr's sharp criticisms of John Dewey and the community of rational inquiry Dewey thought he could create by education, Niebuhr's own implicit understandings of truth and meaning remain squarely within the traditions of American pragmatism. What verifies Christianity, is the power of Christian faith to motivate further action. 'By its confidence in an eternal ground of existence which is, nevertheless, involved in man's historical striving to the very point of suffering with and for him, this faith can prompt men to accept their historical responsibilities gladly.'[5]

Niebuhr's theology thus provides a strong motivation for responsible political action, but it also offers a substantive account of what responsible action is. The limitations of every individual and group perspective suggest the importance of democratic checks and balances, reminding all parties that even their best efforts to act for the good of the society will be tainted by self-interest. Moreover, the pragmatism that avoids claims to absolute truth in theology obviously extends to truth-claims in politics. When political regimes are characterized as democratic, totalitarian, oligarchical, etc., the labels must be understood to cover dynamic, changing historical situations. Niebuhr treats even the central normative concept of justice as an equilibrium between demands for liberty and demands for equality, so that what counts as justice depends in large part on the historical forces at work in a situation. Where a regime has maintained rigid constraints on wealth and initiative, giving greater liberty to individual enterprise may be a move toward greater justice, while the same measures in a system that already allows considerable inequality might count against the justice of that regime. No theory of justice can establish a precise balance between liberty and equality against which all historical arrangements could be measured. It is not merely that moral suasion alone cannot establish justice without the assistance of coercive power. There is no absolute measure of what justice is that stands above the conflict of particular, historic claims.

Niebuhr's stress on human finitude yields a political realism that gives an important place to interests, conflict, and balances of power. He rejects what he calls the 'too consistent' realism of Augustine, Luther, and Hobbes, who virtually eliminate any independent role for moral ideas in political life. As the political units become larger, however, it becomes more difficult to see the difference between Niebuhr's vision and Hobbes' state of nature. A Niebuhrian realist is dismayed, but not surprised, by the realities of global conflict, and when Reinhold Niebuhr assessed the super-power competition after the Second World War, he regarded the rough parity of strength between them as a far better guarantee of peace than any system of world law could be.

## H. RICHARD NIEBUHR

H. Richard Niebuhr perhaps felt the tragedy of human conflict more keenly than his elder brother. Where Reinhold found in Christian faith a motivation for the people of the Western democracies to shoulder their historical responsibilities, H. Richard experienced war as a kind of 'crucifixion'.[6] H. Richard Niebuhr's writings, moreover, tended toward broader reflections on faith and culture, rather than analysis of particular social issues. He was at best tangentially related to the movement that is generally known as Christian Realism, but his theological realism leads to an understanding of God and human values which is essential to a complete account of theology and culture.

Niebuhr begins with a realistic assessment of social influences on religious commitments and affiliations. In an early work, *The Social Sources of Denominationalism*, he argues that the differences between confessional groups in American religious life are determined not by historic creeds, but by the class position of the membership today. The key distinction is between 'the churches of the middle class', the typical Protestant, and 'the churches of the disinherited', groups whose poverty, race, or ethnicity forces them to the margins of society. Niebuhr draws on Ernst Troeltsch and Max Weber for his understanding of the social role of these sectarian forms of Christianity, but his point in the American context is to stress the rapid transformation of the churches of the disinherited into the denominations of the middle class, and the compromise with the radical moral demands of Jesus that inevitably attends this new respectability. Like other critics of the Social Gospel, Niebuhr no longer regards the original ethics of Jesus as a real, historical possibility. What is theologically interesting are the patterns of compromise that social reality imposes on Christian communities.

Niebuhr by no means intends this sociological realism to imply a determinism that would make religion merely the product of economic and cultural forces. Social factors certainly influence religious ideas, but religious ideas also help shape social reality. Niebuhr attempted to demonstrate this in *The Kingdom of God in America*. Here again, he sees not a single religious idea, but a variety of perspectives on it, shaped by historical experience, but also lending different interpretations to that experience.

Like Reinhold Niebuhr's *Nature and Destiny of Man*, then, H. Richard Niebuhr's principal works reflect on the diversity of competing perspectives on human problems. H. Richard Niebuhr is, however, more aware of the diversity *within* the Christian tradition, and he does not speak so readily as Reinhold about 'the Christian view of man'. While this pluralism might imply for some either the dissolution of the idea of Christian theology or a necessary choice between the alternatives, Niebuhr eventually develops a theological account of such differences that allows us to incorporate them into a realistic appreciation of human faith and its limits.

In *Christ and Culture*, Niebuhr attempts on the scale of global Christian history the same identification of basic types of belief that he developed in *The Kingdom of God in America*. At the beginning of *Christ and Culture*, Niebuhr acknowledges a debt to Ernst Troltesch's historical studies that extends back to his earliest work on religion and society. His own project, he explains with disarming directness, has been simply to understand Troltesch's 'historical relativism' in light of 'theological and theocentric relativism'.[7]

Theocentric relativism moves beyond the pragmatic assessment of religious truth claims in terms of their ability to motivate and sustain further action. It makes explicit a theological premiss which is already contained in the appreciation of diversity, but which must be articulated if the realistic emphasis on human finitude and the social determinants of belief is not to lead us into relativism, pure and simple. That premiss is what Niebuhr calls 'radical monotheism'. Radical monotheism is the insistence that despite all contrary appearances, the diverse communities, values, and principles of human.life do relate to a single center of value. To believe in One God is finally to insist that all things can be related to one another because they are already related to the common source of their being.

> For radical monotheism the value center is neither closed society nor the principle of such a society but the principle of being itself; its reference is to no one reality among the many but to the One beyond all the many, whence all the many derive their being, and by participation in which they exist. As faith, it is reliance on the source of all being for the significance of the self and of all that exists.[8]

From the perspective of radical monotheism, the claim of relativism that systems of value and principles of morals differ so completely that their claims are simply meaningless across the barriers of history and culture makes no sense. Everything that is, including all genuine values, must in the end be related. But precisely because the center to which all things relate is not identical with the principle that organizes my values and my community, I must expect divergences from every particular form of value that I hold, up to and including the values by which I understand my relationship to the One center of value.

Radical monotheism makes sense of the appreciation for different forms of Christian belief and community that characterized H. Richard Niebuhr's work from the beginning. The idea of One God to whom all things must be related precludes any absolutizing of my own values, but it also suggests that other values, however different, must be in some way related to mine. We need not set up one form of Christianity as the yardstick against which all others are to be measured in order to understand how the different forms are related.

More important, radical monotheism supplies the missing premiss required for pragmatic defenses of Christian truth like the one in *The Nature and Destiny of Man*. Unless there is some commonality to the human problem that competing systems of belief claim to solve, the realist claim that Christian belief is more adequate than its rivals makes no sense. If Stoicism, naturalism, Romanticism, Marxism and the rest were just different solutions to different problems, it would be impossible to evaluate them in comparison to Christianity. Radical monotheism does not insure the triumph of the Christian faith, but it is a theological perspective from which the question of its relative adequacy makes sense.

### DEBATE

The theological realists were often adept controversialists who entered readily into the politics and policy debates of their time. John Bennett, Reinhold Niebuhr, Robert Lowrie Calhoun, and others developed a concern for economic justice and peace that continues to influence the social ethics of mainstream Protestantism. The persistent debates about theological realism, however, revolved more around the theological and ethical method that determined how these issues were approached than around the constantly changing agenda of social problems themselves.

Perhaps the sharpest division within Protestant theology was between the American realists and the European 'crisis theology' formulated under the leadership of Karl Barth. We have already noted that the influence of Protestant liberalism remained strong among the early theological realists, despite the fact that both they and their Barthian counterparts recognized the need to make a break with the excessive optimism of nineteenth-century theology. These theological differences had immediate implications for social ethics. Barth's radical judgment on all human values and projects led him to declare that no social change or movement of reform could be regarded as even a first step toward the Kingdom of God. Reinhold Niebuhr insisted that while the Kingdom of God remains an ideal beyond all human action, specific achievements of mutuality and increments of justice could be related to God's purposes and had to be understood as central tasks in the Christian life. During the Second World War this theological controversy was largely set aside, but it reappeared in 1948 in a famous exchange between Karl Barth and Reinhold Niebuhr during the assembly of the World Council of Churches in Amsterdam. Niebuhr praised the role that crisis theology had played in sustaining Christian resistance to tyranny during the war, but he questioned its value as a social ethic for more ordinary times.

Perhaps this theology is constructed too much for the great crises of history . . . It can fight the devil if he shows both horns and both cloven feet. But it refuses to make discriminatory judgments about good and evil if the evil shows only one horn or the half of a cloven foot.[9]

As Christians have attended to the ambiguous, and often technically complex, social issues of recent decades, Niebuhr's concern for a system capable of specific moral guidance has largely prevailed, but the debate with crisis theology over the relationship between discriminating human judgments to the ultimate Judgment of God raises theological questions of continuing importance.

While the theological realists argued that the crisis theologians failed to make specific moral choices, they regarded the natural law tradition in Roman Catholicism as too absolute and unchanging to provide a realistic basis for addressing contemporary problems. Moreover, the realists' critical awareness of how self-interest can distort moral arguments led them to suspect that much of what the tradition regarded as 'natural' in relationships between men and women, or in political and social authority, was a legitimation of privileges that were in fact merely contingent historical developments.

The realist arguments against natural law raise important issues, but they seem in retrospect to be part of a Protestant–Catholic polemic that our present, more ecumenical era has largely set aside. Few of the Christian Realists show any extensive acquaintance with the literature of Catholic moral theology, and their attacks on natural law are largely based on a textbook reading of Thomas Aquinas. Perhaps most important, the realist position itself clearly rests on a specific understanding of human nature, and so is in its own way a kind of 'natural law' argument, however much its reading of human nature may differ from the ideas the realists find in the Catholic tradition of natural law. In recent years, a new Protestant appreciation for the moral importance of natural orders and limits has met with Catholic efforts to formulate an idea of human nature that includes a larger place for human freedom. The simple opposition between Protestant rejections and Catholic affirmations of natural law has been largely left behind.

## ACHIEVEMENT AND AGENDA

The theological realists sought to address the modern world in its own terms from a perspective formed by faithful attention to the biblical understanding of persons and their relationships to God. Realism sought to be relentlessly self-critical without losing confidence in its commitments to justice and democracy. It stressed the importance of quite specific moral achievements while attempting to avoid moral absolutism. Theirs was a complex theology that combined many disparate elements, and we should not be surprised that subsequent writers have emphasized different elements of the theological realism and developed the realists' legacy in different directions.

Realism's early concern for an adequate grasp of the facts of modern life continues in contemporary sociology of religion and, more generally, in the efforts of social ethicists to master the technical details of problems in economics, medicine, genetics, and other areas where new developments have raised significant moral issues. In theological ethics, James Gustafson has articulated a theocentric perspective that makes scientific accounts of the origins, biological limits, and probable end of the human species important data for theological reflection.

Protestant theological ethics today tends to be divided between those who seek to locate their religious ethics among the varieties of contemporary moral philosophy, and those who argue for strict attention to the formation of character and moral discernment within the Christian community. Paul Ramsey's insistence that Christian moral principles must be formulated with more clarity and philosophical rigor than his realist predecessors had applied initiated the movement toward moral philosophy. Stanley Hauerwas (discussed in chapter 6 below) has become the most important American voice for the moral uniqueness of the Christian community.

Third World, minority, and feminist theologians who have examined Christian Realism have appreciated its early concerns for racial equality and its critical awareness of the way that power has shaped moral arrangements as diverse as economic relationships between nations and personal relationships between the sexes. For the most part, however, these new voices in Protestant theology have also criticized the realists' readiness to compromise with existing systems and their concern to maintain social order, even at the cost of justice. Those who speak for the disinherited say that the realist tendency to treat moral ideals as merely useful illusions underestimates the motive power of revolutionary hopes among those who are cut off from all other sources of power.

The post-realist developments in Protestant theological ethics have no doubt marked substantial gains in philosophical rigor and historical accuracy. While few have attempted a work with the scope of Niebuhr's *Nature and Destiny of Man*, Niebuhr himself might regard the relationship between scope and rigor as one of those equilibria, like the balance between liberty and equality, in which something must be given up on one side to secure a gain on the other. What may be more important to recover, however, is the early realists' understanding of the relationship between critical rigor and social change. The Niebuhrs, Bennett, Horton, Calhoun and the rest pursued a more self-critical, realistic assessment of human nature and its possibilities, not for the sake of analytical rigor, but because they, no less than their Social Gospel predecessors, were committed to a more humane social order. They sought, as Horton put it, 'to pierce as deep as one may into the solid structure of reality' because they were confident that a more enduring structure of justice could be built on that foundation. They were prepared to undertake the investigation even if it led them beyond the recognized boundaries of Christian truth and even if it called into question their own virtues and the virtues of the people they sought to help. At a time when Christians are often tempted to identify truth with their own formulations of it and to fear the encounter with forms of knowledge and methods of investigation that challenge their traditions, we could use more of the self-criticism and self-confidence that marked the early years of theological realism.

## NOTES

1 Walter Rauschenbusch, *Christianity and the Social Crisis* (New York, 1910), p. 201.
2 Walter Marshall Horton, *Realistic Theology* (New York, 1934).
3 Reinhold Niebuhr, *Moral Man and Immoral Society*, p. 272.
4 Reinhold Niebuhr, *The Children of Light and the Children of Darkness*, p. xiii.
5 Reinhold Niebuhr, *The Nature and Destiny of Man*, II, p. 321.
6 H. Richard Niebuhr, 'War as Crucifixion', *Christian Century*, 60 (1943), pp. 513–15.
7 H. Richard Niebuhr, *Christ and Culture*, p. xii.
8 H. Richard Niebuhr, *Radical Monotheism and Western Culture*, p. 32.
9 Reinhold Niebuhr, 'We Are Men and Not God', *Christian Century*, 65 (1948), p. 1139.

### BIBLIOGRAPHY

#### Primary

Bennett, John, *Christian Realism* (New York, 1941).
—, *Christian Ethics and Social Policy* (New York, 1946).
Niebuhr, H. Richard, *The Kingdom of God in America* (New York, 1937).
—, *Christ and Culture* (New York, 1951).
—, *The Social Sources of Denominationalism* (Cleveland, 1965).
—, *Radical Monotheism and Western Culture* (New York, 1970).
Niebuhr, Reinhold, *The Children of Light and the Children of Darkness* (New York, 1944).
—, *Moral Man and Immoral Society* (New York, 1960).
—, *The Nature and Destiny of Man*, 2 vols (New York, 1964).


#### Secondary

Brown, Robert M. (ed.), *The Essential Reinhold Niebuhr* (New Haven, Conn., 1986).
Cooper, John W., *The Theology of Freedom: The Legacy of Jacques Maritain and Reinhold Niebuhr* (Macon, Ga, 1985).
Diefenthaler, Jon, *H. Richard Niebuhr: A Lifetime of Reflections on the Church and the World* (Macon, Ga, 1986).
Fowler, James W., *To See the Kingdom: The Theological Vision of H. Richard Niebuhr* (Nashville, Tenn., 1974).
Fox, Richard, *Reinhold Niebuhr* (New York, 1985).
Grant, C. David, *God the Center of Value: Value Theory in the Theology of H. Richard Niebuhr* (Fort Worth, Texas, 1984).
Harries, Richard (ed.), *Reinhold Niebuhr and the Issues of Our Time* (Grand Rapids, Mich., 1986).
Kegley, Charles W. (ed.), *Reinhold Niebuhr: His Religious, Social, and Political Thought* (New York, 1984).

# 4

# Revisionists and Liberals

## James J. Buckley

### INTRODUCTION: HISTORY AND INFLUENCES

On the one hand, 'revisionists' and 'liberals' are a tradition of theologians devoted to shaping Christian practices and teachings in dialogue with (revisionists) or on the basis of (liberals) modern philosophies, cultures, and social practices. On the other hand, the labels 'revisionist' and 'liberal' (like all theological labels) are only useful for some sharply circumscribed purposes. This essay will concentrate less on the labels than on the stands four representative theologians (Edward Farley, Gordon Kaufman, Schubert Ogden, and David Tracy) take on four particular issues (truth, God, human beings, and Jesus Christ). But a brief account of historical context will suggest why revisionists and liberals do indeed form a distinctive tradition.

Challenged by the rise of modern philosophies, sciences, and histories in the eighteenth and nineteenth centuries, Christian theologians were pressed to give a new account of the hope that was in them. Philosophers, scientists, and historians challenged the truth of Christian teachings and/or the human authenticity of Christian affections and actions. From one side, orthodox fundamentalists and pietists perceived modernity as a massive threat; from the other side, Christians variously called liberal or modernist endeavored to show that Christian teachings and/or practices were the fulfillment of autonomous humanity. 'Mediating theologians' positioned themselves on the boundary of such extremes, arguing Christian faith and modernity can and should live together in peace.[1] Such mediators – this is crucial – were not of one sort. For example, Friedrich Schleiermacher and his followers could suggest that a faith focused on the unique figure of Jesus Christ 'does not contradict' modern science, while some followers of Hegel could argue that the former was 'a demonstrable part' of the latter.[2]

Such arguments among mediators were largely overshadowed around the turn of the century. In the face of cultures largely post-theistic, several novel (neo-) reaffirmations of classic Christianity ('-orthodoxy') were constructed. Precisely because twentieth-century mediating theologians take this ('neo-orthodox') stage seriously, it would be false to suggest that they always (or even usually) continue a nineteenth-century mediating movement. The label 'revisionist' or 'revisionary' theology nicely sets them apart from their predecessors. But it is true that today's revisionaries and liberals aim to resolve problems left by the second stage precisely by creating a third stage which sublates the first two. On this reading, neo-Marxisms, existential phenomenologists, liberation theologians and others in the 1970s and 1980s 'resume the immanentist, humanist trend of nineteenth century theology, after its interruption by the Barthian period in Protestantism and the Thomist revival in Catholicism'.[3]

Bultmann, Lonergan, Rahner, Schillebeeckx, and Tillich – to restrict ourselves to samples from volume I of *The Modern Theologians* – could each be plausibly taken to continue the tradition of 'mediating theology' in the twentieth century. Edward Farley, Gordon Kaufmann, Schubert Ogden, and David Tracy are leaders among those who have pressed something like the mediating option in North America. These representatives suggest revisionist and liberal theology is a dominant form of doing theology in North America. But the nexus of influences on these theologians is quite different and will constantly jeopardize efforts to embrace them under a single label. All are Christian theologians, but Kaufman a Mennonite, Ogden a Methodist, and Tracy a Roman Catholic. All are committed to mediating Christian practices and teachings to modern culture, but they focus on different features of modernity. All are committed to critical revisions of this Christian fact and this modern culture, but each locates the key items up for revision in different ways. The following effort to sketch their proposals is made even more complicated by the fact that each will publish still other works over the next decades. All this suggests just a few of the limits of this effort to essay their proposals. The central claim will be that, despite differences among and between these theologians, revisionist (or revisionary or mediating) theology is a *sui generis* style of theology, irreducible to any other; by its nature, it can only be appraised piecemeal. My primary aim is to raise some questions that readers of these pages can use when they turn to the texts of these theologians themselves.

SURVEY

What revisionists and liberals share in common is a desire to 'mediate' between Christianity and culture on a range of teachings and practices. This section will suggest how four common themes are dealt with in different ways by our four representatives.

First, all four theologians agree that Christian theology makes truth-claims and provides reasons for its claims. Thus, all reject the notion that Christian theology makes no truth-claims as well as simple appeals to 'the house of authority' (Farley) to back up such claims. But how can *Christian* theology make *truth*-claims? Here they begin to diverge. Ogden and Tracy espouse versions of a 'method of correlation'. The central task of theology, says Ogden, is correlating 'the Christian witness of faith and human existence', assessed by criteria of 'appropriateness' (Is *x* normatively Christian?) and 'credibility' (Is *x* logically consistent and experientially significant?).[4] Tracy has become more cautious about speaking of correlation (better, mutually critical correlations), but he insists that the main theological constants are the 'disclosive' engagement of our interpretation of a particular religious tradition and a reading of our contemporary situation.[5]

Farley and Kaufman (for reasons we shall see) resist such methods of correlation but share with Ogden and Tracy a concern with showing that Christian teachings are not only 'Christian' but also 'true'. Farley proposes that the problem of truth is at once 'the problem of reality' ('how reality comes forth, occurs, is manifest') and 'the problem of criteria' ('how the reality-manifesting grounding rises into the judgment'). Because the former is a faith-apprehension of reality, Farley insists that judgments about the latter are 'not members of a more general class'; he calls the latter 'ecclesial universals' to highlight the way they are different from and similar to more generic universals.[6] For Kaufman, 'only criteria of coherence and pragmatic usefulness to human life are relevant and applicable' to large concepts like 'world' and 'God'.[7]

The technicalities in which all eventually couch the issue of truth ought not distract from a second common ground: all four are concerned with human beings as free *subjects* embedded in a physical and social and historical world, radically threatened by ambiguity and suffering and evil, and seeking ways to overcome this situation. For Tracy, the self is 'radical agapic self-transcendence'. There are 'real and perhaps even irreconcilable ideals of the self', but the self is subject-in-process, 'never substance but subject, affected by and affecting both God and the world'.[8] For Farley, faith-apprehensions 'occur pre-reflectively and by means of an enduring participation in a form of corporate historical existence which we are calling ecclesia'. Our subjectivity is always a 'determinate inter-subjectivity' expressed in stories and images, myths and doctrines.[9] Ogden weaves together the diverse construals of subjectivity (Tracy) and intersubjectivity (Farley) in Wesley, Bultmann, and even liberation theology under a kind of process philosophy for which the self is aware of and responsible for itself as continually becoming, internally related to time and others, an essential fragment of 'the integral whole of reality'.[10] For Kaufman, human beings are individual, social, and historical beings – but also and particularly, human beings struggle to overcome those evils which threaten 'our most foundational value configurations'.[11]

Third, all agree that the monarchical God of classic theism (who acts in history in ways that jeopardize or destroy human subjectivity in nature and history) must be replaced by a God (or other ultimate reality) related to human, religious, or specifically Christian experience. Ogden and Tracy argue on behalf of the God whom we meet in the limit-questions of our experience and who, as soul of the world, is both in and beyond that world.[12] Farley argues for faith's indirect apprehension of God – not a God 'represented mythically as thinking, willing, reflecting, and accomplishing in the mode of an in-the-world-being who intervenes selectively in world process' nor simply a general religious 'transcendent' but a God for whom 'ecclesial process as such *is* the salvific work of God in history'.[13] Kaufman argues that 'the image/concept of God serves as a focus or center for devotion and orientation' – a focus which must be represented 'on a continuum running from highly mythical and symbolical images – God as a personal being who loves and cares – to the more abstract notion of the cosmic ground of all humanity'.[14]

Fourth, all agree that life and thought in relationship to the specific figure of Jesus is shaped by the previous issues, although they diverge on exactly how. Of our four figures, Farley is most sympathetic to a kind of 'primacy of christology'. Jesus of Nazareth is 'appresented' as historical redeemer in ecclesial existence. One of the tasks, 'perhaps the central one', of what Farley calls theological portraiture, is inquiry into the Jesus of Nazareth 'proclaimed as the redemption-effecting person' – 'not simply the past Jesus but the present Christ'.[15] For Tracy, the event and person of Jesus Christ – in the immediacy of experience mediated by the tradition (which is normed by the expressions of Scripture), developed and corrected by historical and literary and social criticisms, and correlated with our present situation – is the prime analog for theological imagination.[16] For Ogden, Jesus Christ is the decisive re-presentation of God for us – mediately not immediately necessary to our authenticity.[17] Of our four figures, Kaufman is most critical of traditional christology – although he insists that 'the picture and story of Jesus' provides 'qualities and potentialities' 'normative for human life'. The category of Christ qualifies 'in a definitive way' other theological concepts; 'Christ crucified' is an appropriate image for a God who 'suffers crucifixion in the hope of the resurrection of a new community called to non-violence'.[18]

### REPRESENTATIVES: FARLEY, KAUFMAN, OGDEN, TRACY

Describing our representatives individually will suggest the differences that accompany their common ground on select issues. After works analyzing the collapse of neo-orthodox theology and piety,[19] Farley has written two volumes which constitute prolegomena to a planned multi-volume interpretation of the major themes of the Christian mythos. *Ecclesial Man. A Social Phenomenology of Faith and Reality* is an analysis of faith's given apprehensions of reality. Farley argues that 'faith's apprehensions occur pre-reflectively and by means of an enduring participation in a form of corporate, historical existence which we are calling ecclesia'. Some of these realities are 'directly present' and others are 'appresented' (Jesus, creation, God). *Ecclesial Man* not only appropriates a social phenomenology but transforms it, for the intersubjectivity of faith is a determinate intersubjectivity, a positivity irreducible to any universal scheme. *Ecclesial Reflection. An Anatomy of Theological Method* internally deconstructs various levels of the 'house of authority'. Ecclesial reflection is (roughly) an inquiry with three moments: historical and biblical ('theological portraiture'), philosophical and systematic, and practical. We find them applied to theological education in Farley's *Theologia*, where theology is described as a particular sort of *habitus* in the context of ecclesiality.[20]

Gordon Kaufman's *Systematic Theology. An Historicist Perspective* sought to meet the problem of the irrelevance of Christian faith to our ordinary secular history 'by giving at every point a radically *historicist* view of the Christian perspective and its major doctrines'.[21] The collection of essays in *God the Problem* deconstructed the concept of God partly begun and partly presupposed in earlier writing, leading Kaufman to later propose a notion of theological method as the 'activity of *construction* (and reconstruction) not of description or exposition'. The 'order of construction' moves from experience through construction of a concept of the world and a concept of God which limits and relativizes the concept of the world – and back to reconceiving experience and the world in the light of this concept of God. Kaufman's recent essays develop and apply this new method to a range of topics. The centerpiece is a proposal that the 'basic task of Christian theology' is uncovering 'the Christian categorial scheme' – humanity, the world, God, and Christ – beneath the multiplicity of Christian images and stories, liturgical and other practices. In *Nonresistence and Responsibility, and Other Mennonite Essays*, Kaufman displays the ways he has over the years sought 'an understanding of Christian faith which is Mennonite but not authoritarian' – which, for all its technical changes, has remained 'concerned primarily with forming persons and communities devoted to redemptive love'.[22]

Schubert Ogden's own work reflects his description of theology as a correlation of Christian faith and human existence (see above). *Christ without Myth. A Study based on the Thought of Rudolph Bultmann* criticizes the internal inconsistency of Bultmann's claims that Jesus Christ is the act of God and his demand for existential demythologization. *The Reality of God and Other Essays* pursues this proposal, particularly by using linguistic analysis (Toulmin) and process philosophy (Whitehead and Hartshorne) to support Christian claims about divine agency. *Faith and Freedom. Toward a Theology of Liberation* is, on the one hand, a move from the issues raised by existentialism, process thought, and linguistic analysis to the challenge of liberation theologies on issues of 'justice and action'. There is, Ogden implies, a kind of liberation theology which calls for a 'method of correlation'.[23] On the other hand, liberation theology provides the political analog to Bultmann's existentialism – or the Pauline 'faith without works' balanced with the Pauline 'faith works by love' – and thus returns Ogden to the issues with which he began. *The Point of Christology* gathers up these themes in 'a christology of liberation'. Behind the New Testament's mythical and ideological formulations, the Jesus-kerygma expresses a God of boundless love calling us to boundless love.[24]

After *The Achievement of Bernard Lonergan*,[25] David Tracy began a project which will eventually yield a trilogy on fundamental, systematic, and practical theology. The first volume, *Blessed Rage for Order*, applies a method of correlation (very much like Schubert Ogden) to issues of religion, God, and life. *The Analogical Imagination* turns to systematic theology. Tracy proposes that the complexity and ambiguity of theology's publics (society, academy, church) calls for a division of theological labor using 'distinct models for truth'. Systematic theology is hermeneutical, i.e., the interpretation (not repetition) of a tradition given us by our historicity and finitude. The key example of hermeneutics are 'classics', 'i.e., expressions of the human spirit which disclose a truth about our lives so compelling that we cannot deny them 'some kind of normative status'. A religious classic is 'an event of disclosure, expressive of the "limit-of," "horizon to," "ground to" side of "religion"'. The *Christian* classic is 'the event and person of Jesus Christ' disclosed in a correlation of the various genres of Scripture with contemporary experiences of homelessness and transforming our situation. This is a paradigm of the analogical imagination which works by picking a primary analog, showing the unity-in-difference within and between analogs (their order, perhaps harmony, their variety and intensity, including dialectical negations), and risks the self-exposure of putting these similarities and differences in the public forum.[26]

## DEBATE

A full description of the debates over revisionary and liberal theologies would require locating these theologians in relationship to all the other chapters of these volumes. Here we must be satisfied with more modest remarks.

The internal debate is shaped by a sense that the differences (suggested by the discussion of the four representatives above) override the common ground (cf. Survey above). This accounts for the fragmentary and even sometimes polemical nature of the debate (e.g., Tracy accusing Kaufman of an uncritical acceptance of modernity, Farley accusing Tracy of pre-revisionary conservativism, and Kaufman accusing both of not carrying through their revisionary proposals to their practical conclusions). But these discussions offer clues to the larger debate. Take, for example, the debate over the possibility and actuality of Christian truth-claims. One way to understand this debate is to range their positions on a spectrum *from* Farley's claim that faith-apprehension yields ecclesial universals *through* Tracy's and Ogden's methods of correlation *to* Kaufman's ultimately pragmatic and humanistic test for truth. This spectrum suggests a logic behind the remarks each has made about the others. Thus, Kaufman thinks that Farley's faith-apprehension retains too many vestiges of 'objectivist thinking', while Farley wonders how Kaufman's critique of traditional correspondence theories of truth can lead us beyond subjectivism. Farley, let us say, uses a *general* phenomenological framework to show that Christian truth-claims are *specific* to particular communities – while Kaufman requires that specifically Christian claims conform to his pragmatic framework. Tracy and Ogden propose subtle correlations of generality and specificity (and hence belong in the middle of the spectrum). However, both Farley and Kaufman are suspicious of methods of correlation – because they can threaten Christian particularity (Farley), because they leave Christian particularity 'substantially unquestioned' (Kaufman), or because it is hard to tell whether their revisionary force is central or marginal.[27] The spectrum places Tracy closer to Farley because Farley's 'theological portraiture' and Tracy's hermeneutical conversation are more analogous to each other than either is to Ogden or Kaufman. Also, Farley and Kaufman seem less suspicious of Ogden's method of correlation than of Tracy's locating of the correlational task in a philosophically eclectic 'hermeneutical' context; along with Ogden, Farley and Kaufman worry that Tracy's hermeneutical disclosure experiences avoid rather than confront hard questions about truth (as Farley, Kaufman, and Ogden variously define it). Tracy in turn worries that Ogden does not take into account the 'poetic' character of the religious conversation, that Kaufman is too uncritical of modernity, and Farley only implicitly critical.[28]

The external debate is shaped by a sense that the common ground among revisionists and liberals overrides the differences they perceive among each other. For example, there are both theological and philosophical challenges to revisionist and liberal notions of truth. Thus, Ronald Thiemann proposes a notion of revelation which enables him to criticize Kaufman (for simply exchanging a divine foundation for a human one) as well as Tracy and Ogden (for steering an unstable middle course between revelation and human imagination).[29] A philosophical challenge comes from those philosophers of religion less interested in making or justifying Christian truth-claims than in studying them as doctrines of religious communities. Thus, William Christian has argued that there are fewer problems with a community taking its authentic doctrines to be true (Farley) than taking every truth to be a doctrine of their community (Kaufman) – or than 'correlating' their own and other truth-claims (Tracy and Ogden). Christian's stand is more like Farley's than Kaufman's or Ogden's or Tracy's, but his appeal is to the practices and teachings of *particular* communities rather than to Farley's *general* phenomenology (even though Farley's is a phenomenology which centers on faith's positivity and particularity).[30]

## ACHIEVEMENT AND QUESTIONS FOR THE FUTURE

The key achievement of revisionists and liberals has been to challenge our received practices and teachings about truth, human beings, God, and Christ. The key (if not only) questions for the future have less to do with the challenge than with the alternatives revisionists and liberals propose. On this score, certainly revisionists and liberals ought continue to address the issues raised by the debate over 'truth' (e.g., is truth correspondence to reality, pragmatic effectiveness, disclosure? Do we need a theory of truth?). But both internal and external critics ought not to permit this issue to dominate the future agenda; settling issues of truth will not settle issues of who we are, who God is, or who Christ is. Indeed, there are signs that the key questions for the future will have less to do with a theory of what truth is and a theory of how we know or test for the truth than with the other features of the internal and external debate.

For example, a major achievement of revisionary and liberal visions of humanity (our own and others) is the insistence on the way we are *free* subjects embedded in a physical, social, and historical world. Yet a major challenge comes from those who affirm human freedom but doubt that the turn to the subject resolves how the subject's self-constitution does justice to the material bases of human life – or aptly describes our identity before God not only as passive subjects but also agents. Perhaps, the argument goes, we need a 'turn to the agent' rather than 'turn to the subject' – or, if not a turn to a general theory of agency, then a piecemeal discussion of the particular activities that constitute our identities (e.g., reading Scriptures, celebrating liturgies, forming communities, working and talking with other religions and the modern world more generally).[31]

Another achievement of revisionary and liberal theologies is their insistence that our claims about God be related to the broader world of human religiosity. However, they have thus far paid more attention to the general features of the religious world than to its particularities. For example, all share a great deal if we focus on Kaufman's 'formal' notion of God, Ogden's early use of God in a 'completely general sense', or Tracy's most recent case for Ultimate Reality. Yet when it comes to identifying this God, Farley appeals to determinate divine activity, Ogden and Tracy to process theism, and Kaufman to a non-agential cosmic ground. These are the makings of different religions rather than of a common revisionary or liberal theological project.[32]

Finally, a key achievement of revisionists and liberals (with the possible exception of Kaufman) is the continuation of a broadly christocentric tradition. 'Broadly' is important, for a central challenge to revisionist christologies comes from those like Karl Barth who insist that 'there is no question of placing Christ within some allegedly more comprehensive context. Christ *is* the adequate context of Christian theology.'[33] Our representatives disagree over what the context ought be: faith-apprehensions, conversations over texts, the modern world in its historicist-pragmatic complexity, etc. And it is more accurate to describe the revisionary (in contrast to liberal) task as one of correlating 'context' and 'Christ' rather than giving absolute priority to the 'event' or 'person' (the 'context' or 'Christ') of Jesus Christ. But *that* the particular figure Jesus requires some prior context to be applicable or intelligible all agree. From this point of view, while revisionists and liberals have made considerable advances over the anthropologies and cosmologies of their mediating predecessors, the christological issue remains much the same.

The comprehensiveness of revisionist and liberal agenda assures that it will be subject to piecemeal critiques on each issue – and that it will withstand them for some time to come. Then again, it may be that the mistake of revisionists and liberals is less in the detailed stand they take on the four topics (truth, human beings, God, and Jesus Christ) than in the order in which they take up these topics. The central challenge to their achievement may come from those who take up issues of truth in the context of attending to divine and human agency in particular narratives, centered on the narratives of Jesus Christ. But then it could be that the next chapter will show substantive problems with this option too.

## NOTES

1 For different uses of the label, see R. Baumer, 'Vermittlungstheologie', *Lexikon für Theologie und Kirche*, eds Josef Hofer and Karl Rahner, 2nd edn (Freiburg, 1965), vol. 10, p. 721; John P. Clayton, *The Concept of Correlation. Paul Tillich and the Possibility of a Mediating Theology* (Berlin and New York, 1980), pp. 7–9.

2 Hans Frei, 'David Friedrich Strauss', in *Nineteenth Century Religious Thought in the West*, vol. 1, ed. Ninian Smart, John Clayton, Steven Katz, and Patrick Sherry (Cambridge, 1985), p. 221.

3 John Macquarrie, *Twentieth Century Religious Thought. The Frontiers of Philosophy and Theology, 1900–1980*, pp. 380, 410. In the discussion of Farley, Kaufman, Ogden, and Tracy below, note how their early writings

include a critique of the internal inconsistency of some phase of neo-orthodoxy.

4 Schubert M. Ogden, *On Theology*, pp. 3, 89.

5 David, Tracy, *The Analogical Imagination. Christian Theology and the Culture of Pluralism*, pp. 59–62, 88 n. 44.

6 Edward Farley, *Ecclesial Reflection. An Anatomy of Theological Method*, pp. xiii, 304–5, 310, 338, 343.

7 G. D. Kaufman, *An Essay on Theological Method*, p. 75; *Relativism, Knowledge, and Faith* (Chicago, 1960), p. 94.

8 Tracy, *The Analogical Imagination*, pp. 435–6.

9 Edward Farley, *Ecclesial Man. A Social Phenomenology of Faith and Reality*, pp. 127, xiii, 86, 93, 150, 158.

10 Schubert M. Ogden, 'Process Theology and the Wesleyan Witness', *The Perkins School of Theology Journal*, 37 (1984), pp. 18–33.

11 G. D. Kaufman, *The Theological Imagination. Constructing the Concept of God*, pp. 113, 164, 166.

12 Schubert M. Ogden, *The Reality of God and Other Essays*, David Tracy, *Blessed Rage for Order. The New Pluralism in Theology*.

13 Edward Farley and Peter C. Hodgson, 'Scripture and Tradition', in *Christian Theology. An Introduction to Its Traditions and Tasks*, ch. 2. Cf. Farley, *Ecclesial Man*, pp. 13, 224, 226; *Ecclesial Reflection*, pp. 156–7.

14 Kaufman, *The Theological Imagination*, pp. 32, 51; *Theology for a Nuclear Age*, ch. III; 'The Historicity of Religions and the Importance of Religious Dialogue', *Buddhist–Christian Studies*, 4 (1984), pp. 5–15.

15 Farley, *Ecclesial Man*, pp. 217–19; *Ecclesial Reflection*, pp. xvii, 209, 225.

16 Tracy, *The Analogical Imagination*, pp. 233–41.

17 Ogden, *On Theology*, pp. 39, 41.

18 Kaufman, *Theology for a Nuclear Age*, ch. IV; *The Theological Imagination*, pp. 116, 189–90.

19 Edward Farley, *The Transcendence of God. A Study in Contemporary Philosophical Theology* (Philadelphia, 1960), a study of Reinhold Niebuhr, Paul Tillich, Karl Heim, Charles Hartshorne, and Henry Nelson Wieman; *Requiem for a Lost Piety. The Contemporary Search for the Christian Life* (Philadelphia, 1966).

20 Farley, *Ecclesial Man*, pp. 127, 29, 57; *Ecclesial Reflection*, p. 190; *Theologia: The Fragmentation and Unity of Theological Education*.

21 G. D. Kaufman, *Systematic Theology. An Historicist Perspective*, p. ix. For background, see his *Relativism, Knowledge and Faith*, arising out of a dissertation on Dilthey, Collingwood, and Tillich, and *The Context of Decision. A Theological Analysis* (New York, 1961) (Menno Simons Lectures, 1959).

22 G. D. Kaufman, *God the Problem* (Cambridge, Mass., 1972); *An Essay on Theological Method*, pp. x, 46; *The Theological Imagination*, p. 102; *Non-resistance and Responsibility, and Other Mennonite Essays*, pp. 9–10.

23 Not all kinds of 'liberation theologies' are focused on the mediating task, though some are. For a mediating theology focused on 'praxis,' see

Matthew Lamb, *Solidarity with Victims. Toward a Theology of Social Transformation* (New York, 1982), ch. 3.

24 Schubert Ogden, *Christ without Myth. A Study based on the Thought of Rudolph Bultmann* (London, 1962; 2nd edn, Dallas, 1979); *The Reality of God and Other Essays*, pp. 34, 138, 57; *Faith and Freedom. Toward a Theology of Liberation; The Point of Christology*, particularly the move to a thoroughly 'transcendental' (rather than 'categorial') metaphysics in ch. 7. For a self-analysis, see the second editions of the first two works cited above as well as Ogden's 'Faith and Freedom', in *Theologians in Transition. The Christian Century 'How My Mind Has Changed' Series*, ed. James M. Wall (New York, 1981).

25 New York, 1970. For a self-analysis, see Tracy's 'Defending the Public Character of Theology', in *Theologians in Transition*, ed. Wall, pp. 113–24.

26 *The Analogical Imagination*, pp. 62, 99–100, 103, 108, 163, 358, 374–6. For re-descriptions of the central claims of this difficult volume, see Tracy's 'Theological Method' in Peter Hodgson and Robert King, *Christian Theology. An Introduction to Its Tasks and Traditions*, 2nd edn, pp. 35–60 and Tracy, *Plurality and Ambiguity. Hermeneutics, Religion, Hope*, ch. 1. For self-criticism of *The Analogical Imagination*, see *Plurality and Ambiguity*, pp. 97, 120 n. 57, 129–30 n. 2, 134 n. 40, 139 n. 46.

27 For a defense of methods of correlation which disputes their normal use, see Peter L. Berger, 'Secular Theology and the Supernatural', *Theological Studies*, 38 (1977), pp. 39–56; and the response by Langdon Gilkey, Schubert M. Ogden, and David Tracy, 'Responses to Peter Berger', *Theological Studies*, 39 (1978), pp. 486–507.

28 This paragraph is a summary of discussions and (more often) allusions our representatives make to each other in the texts cited above (see name indices as well as subject indices under key words like 'hermeneutics', etc.), reviews, and a set of unpublished responses of Farley and Kaufman and Tracy to each others' work at a 1982 meeting of the American Academy of Religion. The reviews include Edward Farley, 'A Revisionist Model [on Tracy], *Christian Century*, XCIII (1976), pp. 371–3; Gordon D. Kaufman, [Review of Farley's *Ecclesial Man* and Tracy's *Blessed Rage for Order*], *Religious Studies Review*, 2 (1976), pp. 7–12 and 'Conceptualizing Diversity Theologically [A review of Tracy's *The Analogical Imagination*]', *Journal of Religion*, 62 (1982), pp. 392–401.

29 R. Thiemann, *Revelation and Theology. The Gospel as Narrated Promise* (Notre Dame, Ind., 1985). Note how Thiemann's criticisms of Kaufman are similar to Farley's and Tracy's – and his criticisms of Tracy are similar to Farley's and Kaufman's.

30 William A. Christian, Sr, *Doctrines of Religious Communities. A Philosophical Study* (New Haven, Conn., 1987), especially ch. 4.

31 David Kelsey, 'Human Being', in *Christian Theology. An Introduction to Its Traditions and Tasks*, ch. 6; see also Fergus Kerr's critique of turns to the subject (particularly Ogden and Kaufman) in *Theology After Wittgenstein* (Oxford, 1986), ch. 1.

32 Kaufman, *Theology for a Nuclear Age*, p. 32; Ogden, *The Reality of God*,

2nd edn, p. 10; Tracy, *Plurality and Ambiguity*, ch. 5. For a critique, see Thomas F. Tracy, 'Enacting History: Ogden and Kaufman on God's Mighty Acts', *Journal of Religion*, 64 (1984), pp. 20–36.

33 Walter Lowe, 'Christ and Salvation', in Peter Hodgson and Robert King (eds), *Christian Theology*, ch. 8.

## BIBLIOGRAPHY

### Primary

Baum, Gregory, *Religion and Alienation. A Theological Reading of Sociology* (New York, 1974).

Davis, Charles, *What is Living, What is Dead in Christianity Today. Breaking the Liberal–Conservative Deadlock* (San Francisco, 1986).

Evans, Donald, *Faith, Authenticity, and Morality* (Toronto, 1980).

Farley, Edward, *Ecclesial Man: A Social Phenomenology of Faith and Reality* (Philadelphia, 1975).

—, *Ecclesial Reflection: An Anatomy of Theological Method* (Philadelphia, 1982).

—, *Theologia: The Fragmentation and Unity of Theological Education* (Philadelphia, 1983).

—, *The Fragility of Knowledge. Theological Education in the Church and the University* (Philadelphia, 1988).

Gilkey, Langdon, *Naming the Whirlwind. The Renewal of God-Language* (Indianapolis, 1969).

Kaufman, Gordon D., *Systematic Theology. An Historicist Perspective* (New York, 1968; with a new preface, 1978).

—, *An Essay on Theological Method* (Missoula, Montana, 1975; rev. edn, 1979).

—, *Nonresistance and Responsibility, and Other Mennonite Essays* (Newton, Kansas, 1979).

—, *The Theological Imagination: Constructing the Concept of God* (Philadelphia, 1981).

—, *Theology for a Nuclear Age* (Manchester, Philadelphia, 1985).

Ogden, Schubert M., *The Reality of God and Other Essays* (New York, 1966; London, 1967; 2nd edn, New York, 1977).

—, *Faith and Freedom. Toward a Theology of Liberation* (Nashville, Tenn., 1979).

—, *The Point of Christology* (San Francisco, London, 1982).

—, *On Theology* (San Francisco, 1986).

Tracy, David, *Blessed Rage for Order. The New Pluralism in Theology* (New York, 1975).

—, *The Analogical Imagination. Christian Theology and the Culture of Pluralism* (New York, 1981).

—, *Plurality and Ambiguity. Hermeneutics, Religion, Hope* (San Francisco, 1987).

*Secondary*

See the ongoing reviews of the above authors in *Religious Studies Review, Journal of Religion*, and *Theological Studies*.

Macquarrie, John, *Twentieth-Century Religious Thought. The Frontiers of Philosophy and Theology, 1900–1980* (New York, 1981).
Hodgson, Peter, and King, Robert (eds), *Christian Theology. An Introduction to Its Traditions and Tasks*, 2nd edn, revised and enlarged (Philadelphia, 1985).

# 5

# Process Theology

## Kenneth Surin

### INTRODUCTION: THREE TENDENCIES

'Process theology' designates more than one theological movement or school. Most of its adherents are based in the United States, where it has taken three main directions, all of which have as their starting-point the metaphysical system adumbrated by Alfred North Whitehead. The philosophico-theological movements or tendencies constitutive of process theology came to real prominence in the 1960s.

The first tendency owes its inspiration to Charles Hartshorne, and is associated primarily with the formulation of a 'neoclassical theism'. The second tendency takes Whitehead's work in a more empirical direction, and has Henry Nelson Wieman and Bernard M. Loomer as its luminaries. The third tendency, which has taken Whitehead's system in a more overtly *Christian* theological direction, is associated in the main with the work of John B. Cobb, Jr. In this chapter attention will be focused on the first and the third of these tendencies.

### SURVEY

#### Whitehead's Philosophy in Relation in God

Alfred North Whitehead (1861–1947) was a logician, a metaphysician and a philosopher of science. He was not a theologian. But he did have an abiding interest in religion, and he made proposals which have profound implications for those interested in the availability of a 'philosophically' adequate doctrine of God.

Whitehead saw all 'actual entities' or 'actual occasions' (his terms) as being, in some measure, self-creative. God, however, is the eminent or unsurpassably superior form of self-creation. Whitehead harnesses to this principle the insight that a self-creative being must in some way be creative of divine reality. God is conscious of all entities, and since each entity manifests in an inferior way the self-creativity which God manifests supremely, all entities are co-creators of the divine reality. At least, they are creative of that aspect of divinity which is consequent upon the world. (This, 'Consequent Nature' of God is distinguished by Whitehead from the 'abstract' or 'Primordial Nature' of the divinity. It should also be noted that for Whitehead God is an 'actual entity', but since he is a nontemporal being, God is not an 'actual occasion'.[1]) It is a corollary of these Whiteheadian principles that every finite entity is essentially God-related, that God is the presupposition of the world, and the world the presupposition of God. A properly-constituted philosophical theology would therefore be one which sought to understand God in terms of the self-same conceptuality by which all other entities are understood. It would in no way make God an exception to this conceptuality. These insights are given succinct expression by Whitehead in a famous series of antitheses:

> It is as true to say that God is permanent and the World fluent, as that the World is permanent and God is fluent.
> It is as true to say that God is one and the World many, as that the World is one and God many.
> It is as true to say that, in comparison with the world, God is actual eminently, as that, in comparison with God, the World is actual eminently.
> It is as true to say that the World is immanent in God, as that God is immanent in the World.
> It is as true to say that God transcends the World, as that the world transcends God.
> It is as true to say that God creates the World, as that the World creates God.[2]

The theistic metaphysics which ensues in these antitheses is used by process theologians to underpin what they regard as a new and philosophically adequate doctrine of God.

At the heart of process theology (in all its strands), therefore, is an attempt to dispense with, or at least to reconstruct, what its adherents take to be the God of 'classical theism'. This critique is usually accompanied by the formulation of an alternative theism. Process theology thus accords a decisive centrality to the doctrine of God.

The divinity of process theism is a synthesis of concrete and abstract aspects: the latter comprising God's 'abstract' or 'necessary' attributes (the 'Primordial Nature' of deity, in Whitehead's terminology); the former God's 'concrete' or 'accidental' attributes (the 'Consequent Nature' of deity, in Whitehead's words). Its proponents hold neoclassical theism to part company with its classical counterpart precisely by virtue of its ascription to God of 'accidental' attributes – such attributes, it is held, cannot in principle be ascribed to God by orthodox Christian theism. Classical or 'monopolar' theism thus holds God to be devoid of relativity and becoming, whereas process or 'dipolar' theism predicates of God a supreme relativity and becoming (in respect of the 'concrete' pole of deity), *as well as* the attributes of eternity, absoluteness, necessity and independence (these being assigned to the 'abstract' pole of deity). Again, it is possible to use a set of antitheses – necessarily selective in this case – to indicate the nature of the relation between these two modes of deity:

| ABSTRACT POLE | CONCRETE POLE |
|---|---|
| conceptual | objectual |
| objective | subjective |
| potential | actual |
| universal | particular |
| existent | actual |
| essential | accidental |

These essentially complementary poles represent *dual* aspects of the *one* deity. Classical theism is said to be riven with contradictions precisely because it cannot countenance a 'dipolar' conception of deity. Several such contradictions are alleged to bedevil orthodox or 'monopolar' theism. Thus process theists charge that orthodox theists want to affirm that everything in God is necessary, including the divine will, although the world willed by God is contingent. Orthodox theists are also accused of maintaining that God knows and loves the creaturely realm, while denying that God is affected by that which is known and loved in this unsurpassable divine way. Again, orthodox theists are said to uphold an absolute divine omnipotence, which gives God an unqualified monopoly over all power. But if this is so, say process theists, how can creatures be said to have a real freedom which they can use or abuse? Classical theism is vitiated by such contradictions because it makes the mistake of thinking that the divine perfection entails a corresponding absoluteness. This assumption, however, is untenable. On the contrary, the more perfect something is, the more intimately it is related to other entities. Likewise, the more perfect a being is, the more it can be expected to register and to be impressed by the changes which take place in other beings. God is enriched and changed by the world. But God in turn changes and enriches the world by perfecting and passing back to it the actuality which had transformed his consequent nature. God perfects the world, and while the world changes God, it can never hope to surpass God in perfection. God alone is infinite. Process theism, therefore, is not a 'pantheism' but a *'panentheism'*: it asserts that God 'includes' the world but does not go on to say that the divine reality is reducible to the reality of the universe (if process theism made this reduction it would indeed be a pantheism).

### Charles Hartshorne (1897–)

Whitehead's metaphysical and cosmological insights were developed by Charles Hartshorne into a full theory of God's nature and activity. This theory differs from Whitehead's, though process theologians have not always been in agreement about the exact nature of these differences. The main difference seems to be that whereas Whitehead saw God as a single actual entity, Hartshorne regards God as an ordered personal series of actual occasions, i.e., as a divine person enjoying a concrete existence. The outcome is that Hartshorne tends to ascribe to God as a whole those qualities and operations, e.g., providing initial aims for finite entities, which Whitehead tends to confine to the Primordial Nature of divinity.[3]

Hartshorne's doctrine of God has several distinctive features. Of these, two are especially noteworthy: (1) Hartshorne's reconceptualization of divine perfection; and (2) his belief that the assertion 'God exists' is an a priori or necessary truth.

As Hartshorne sees it, divine perfection is compatible with the assertion that God depends on creaturely reality, that creatures can change and alter the shape of divine experience. He defines divine perfection in a way which allows God to be influenced by external forces:

> let us define perfection as excellence such that rivalry or superiority on the part of other individuals is impossible, but self-superiority is not impossible . . . the perfect is the 'self-surpassing surpasser of all.'[4]

God does not necessarily have to be self-surpassing. But God is self-surpassing because it is divinity's sovereign prerogative to do so.

God is self-surpassing, according to Hartshorne, because the divine perfection entails that God be receptive to change, that God change with change. God remains super-eminent and unrivalled because, even in changing, the divinity is surpassed by no reality except itself.

This doctrine of the divine super-eminence has important implications for the so-called metaphysical attributes of deity. Thus, as Hartshorne sees it, God's being dependent on creatures is compatible with the divinity's aseity or self-existence; God has a real relation to finite beings, but this real relation is compatible with the divine infinity; the ineluctable *harmony* that exists within the divine nature is precisely what constitutes God's unity; God includes the temporal dimension of the world within the divine experience, but is eternal because this temporal dimension is not exhaustive of the divine reality; God's aim and experience can change, but the *character* of the divine aim and the *perfection* of divine experience are immutable; the divine willing and knowing can be affected by complexity to the extent that their objects are complex, but God is simple because there is no duality between the divine knowing and willing, and so on.[5]

Even process theologians acknowledge that Whitehead's formulations never entirely dispel the impression that he is on the verge of countenancing two separate divine principles ('ditheism').[6] Hartshorne, however, steers clear of any lurking 'ditheism' by making it plain that the relation between the abstract (or absolute) and the concrete (or relative) poles in divinity is not a relation between two conjoined entities; it is, instead, a relation of 'inclusiveness'. But, significantly, it is the concrete/relative which is inclusive of the abstract/absolute, and not vice versa. Hartshorne's is thus a theism which, unusually, manages to conform broadly to the principles of a reconstructed metaphysical monism while eschewing pantheism.

Hartshorne is renowned for his advocacy of the ontological argument for the existence of God.[7] He uses this argument to sustain the principle that the assertion 'God exists' is an a priori or necessary truth. It follows from this that God's existence is either logically necessary or logically impossible, and that 'empirical' evidence, such as that furnished by the existence and magnitude of evil, has no bearing whatever on the question of God's existence or nonexistence. If it is possible for God to exist, then necessarily God exists. Hartshorne, however, is not claiming that all truths about God belong to the nonfactual domain: as he sees it, only the affirmation of the divine existence is purely formal or necessary, whereas propositions about the divine actuality are of course contingent or factual.[8]

Hartshorne is emphatic in his claim that the 'dipolar' God of neoclassical theism is the only adequate object of religious faith and worship. This claim has been taken up by other process theologians, most notably Schubert Ogden and John Cobb.[9]


### Schubert M. Ogden (1928–)

Schubert Ogden has sought to extend Hartshorne's philosophy of religion in a more explicitly theological direction, but without making this philosophy into a narrow scholasticism (which is what it has tended to become in the hands of some of process theology's less distinguished practitioners).[10]

Ogden believes that the norms of meaning and truth are universal and given in human experience. The availability of such norms therefore awaits a theory of human experience, i.e., a metaphysics – in this case a specifically theistic metaphysics. As Ogden puts it: 'Thus not only is it evident that Christian faith alone is an insufficient ground for theology's assertions, but it is also clear that such assertions cannot even be established as meaningful except by establishing a theistic metaphysics which is true independently of specifically Christian faith.'[11] And, as Ogden sees it, Hartshorne's system is the most suitable candidate for this requisite theistic hermeneutic: for him Christian theology is grounded in common human experience via Hartshorne's theistic metaphysics. The upshot is that Hartshorne's metaphysics becomes the *sine qua non* of any vindication of a Christian theology.


### John B. Cobb (1925–)

John Cobb's is arguably the most comprehensive and systematic theological appropriation of Whitehead's neoclassical metaphysics. His early *A Christian Natural Theology* (1965) is the most explicitly 'Whiteheadian' of his books. Subsequent works have retained a Whiteheadian conceptual framework, but the technical vocabulary of neoclassical metaphysics has been less in evidence. Cobb's theological concerns are wide-ranging. *A Christian Natural Theology* deals primarily with the doctrine of God. *The Structure of Christian Existence* (1967) adumbrates a theological anthropology. *Christ in a Pluralistic Age* (1975) concerns itself with christology. *Process*

*Theology as Political Theology* (1982) confronts process theology with the works of Johann Baptist Metz, Jürgen Moltmann, and Dorothee Soelle, and provides the rudiments of a process ecological theology. *Beyond Dialogue* (1982) addresses the question of the relationship between Christianity and Buddhism.

The governing motif in Cobb's writings is the notion of 'creative transformation'.[12] Creative transformation – whether it be in morality, political action, personal relationships, art, etc. – comes about through the introduction of novelty. The source of novelty is the divine Logos, as incarnate in Christ. The presence of Christ is thus essential to the existence of creative transformation. Christ's presence, which is the presence of God's love, makes creative human love possible, and this love in turn is a condition of creative transformation. With this transformation, human beings are freed to love in a way that is generative of more love, a love that is a Spirit-filled response to a Christ-generated creative love. The notion of 'creative transformation' is thus an amalgam of christological, pneumatological and cosmological elements, and it is precisely for this reason that Cobb's is the most comprehensive of the several process theologies.

### DEBATE

The debates surrounding process theology take two forms. Some debates are conducted entirely from within the paradigm espoused by the process theologians. Other debates are undertaken from an extra-paradigmatic perspective.

Perhaps the most significant of the intra-paradigmatic issues posed by process theology concerns its waiving of the so-called 'axiom of *apatheia*', that is, the axiom which holds that God can have no experience of pain or sorrow because God cannot be 'affected' by an external reality. A central thrust of the process-theological paradigm is that a God who cannot be a 'co-sufferer' with creaturely sufferers, who does not 'depend' in any way on creaturely beings, is not a God who is an adequate object of religious faith and worship. However, it is not entirely clear whether process theologians have a warrant for believing that God's putative inability to suffer emotionally with creaturely beings *necessarily* implies that God is not capable of a 'redemptive' involvement with the sufferings of such creatures. Contrary to this belief, it may be possible to affirm that God is 'involved' with the sufferings of creatures *without* having to jettison the 'axiom of *apatheia*'.[13]

The process theist who grants that his or her concept of God is internally consistent, and that all intra-paradigmatic problems are resolvable in principle, is still left with a cluster of extra-paradigmatic difficulties to address. Foremost among these must be the question: how essential is neoclassical metaphysics to the dipolar conception of deity, and vice versa? Three answers provided so far to this question have intriguing implications. Donald Sherburne has argued, persuasively, that deity is a *dispensable* category in the process categorial scheme.[14] Keith Ward has argued, again persuasively, that it is possible to retain the dipolar conception of deity while discarding the baggage of process metaphysics.[15] Michael Welker has argued, yet again persuasively, that the Whiteheadian cosmology provides, not a plausible doctrine of God, but a theory of the relation between heaven and earth.[16] If the arguments of Sherburne, Ward and Welker are accepted they would sanction the view that neither dipolar theism nor neoclassical metaphysics are essential to each other (Sherburne and Ward), and that, in any case, neoclassical metaphysics has nothing terribly important and satisfactory to say about God (Welker).

Another extra-paradigmatic issue that can be raised concerns the attempts of process theologians to develop an adequate 'theism', albeit one of a neoclassical cast. Most process theologians concerned with the delineation of such a theism do so by setting their doctrines over against those sponsored by so-called 'classical theists' (and in particular St Thomas Aquinas). However, it is now fairly widely acknowledged that (philosophical) 'theisms' of any kind have their provenance in a set of canonical notions and principles put in place, whether directly or indirectly, by the 'theories of knowledge' of Descartes and Locke. 'Theism', on this view, is a *seventeenth- and eighteenth-century* philosophico-theological *construction*.[17] If 'theism' is a theoretical construction, then its neoclassical counterpart must also be deemed to be a product of a historically-contingent, post-Enlightenment intellectual world. This post-Enlightenment intellectual horizon – 'modernity' – thus provides process theology with its operating conditions. The person who is concerned to view theology from a 'postmodern' perspective will therefore be disinclined to accept without question the operating conditions of process theology. Such a person will inevitable not share the estimation that process theologians have of their own accomplishments.

## ACHIEVEMENT AND AGENDA

The understanding that one has of process theology's achievement will depend crucially on whether or not one happens to be a proponent of 'classical theism', or whether or not one eschews the very idea of any kind of 'theism'. Proponents of 'classical theism' who criticize process theology tend invariably to raise the questions of its internal consistency and of its capacity to furnish a conception of God adequate to Christian faith and worship (here glossed in terms of the specifications of a certain kind of 'philosophical theism').[18] However, if one is disposed to reject 'theism' as a construction grounded in a not irremovable post-Enlightenment intellectual horizon, then the question of process theology's internal consistency becomes largely irrelevant and any consideration of the God of Christian faith and worship then ceases to be a problem for 'metaphysics'. Instead it becomes a matter for a historical and interpretative analysis of the discourses which have this God as their focus. In other words, the really important question concerning process theology is not that of its coherence or plausibility, but the matter of what it means for process theism to have appeared when and where it did. The agenda created and addressed by process theology is an agenda set by a characteristic post-Enlightenment mode of reflection. An assessment of its achievement will therefore hinge on an understanding of the structures of intelligibility and plausibility which give rise to these modes of reflection. Suffice it to say that exponents of 'liberal' or 'revisionist' theologies tend to accept at face value those structures of intelligibility and plausibility constitutive of 'modernity'. Such individuals may view process theology in a favorable light. But those not disposed to make an accommodation of 'modernity' – and this precisely in the name of 'postmodernity' – will almost certainly be less inclined to form too positive an estimation of the achievement of process theology. Or any 'liberal' theology for that matter.[19]

### NOTES

1 On the 'nontemporality' of Whitehead's God, see Lewis S. Ford, 'The Non-Temporality of Whitehead's God', passim.

2 A. N. Whitehead, *Process and Reality*, p. 528.

3 On the relation between Whitehead and Hartshorne, see Lewis S. Ford (ed.), *Two Process Philosophers*, passim; Gene Reeves, 'Whitehead and

Hartshorne', pp. 125–37; and Charles Hartshorne, *Whitehead's Philosophy*, passim.

4  Charles Hartshorne, *The Divine Relativity*, p. 20.

5  This conceptualization of God is in accord with Hartshorne's well-known 'principle of dual transcendence'. For this principle, see his 'The God of Religion and the God of Philosophy', passim.

6  For this acknowledgment, see J. B. Cobb, Jr and D. R. Griffin, *Process Theology*, p. 62.

7  For Hartshorne's version of the ontological argument, see his *The Logic of Perfection*, passim, and *Anselm's Discovery*, passim.

8  For this caveat, see Hartshorne's 'Response to Smith,' in J. B. Cobb Jr, and F. I. Gamwell (eds), *Existence and Actuality: Conversations with Charles Hartshorne*, pp. 109–10.

9  For another attempt to transpose Hartshorne's work in a more explicitly theological, and in this case christological, context, see Thomas W. Ogletree, 'A Christological Assessment of Dipolar Theism', passim.

10  See Schubert Ogden's *The Reality of God* for this theological elaboration of Hartshorne's metaphysical theism. For more on Ogden see above, chapter 4.

11  Schubert Ogden, 'The Task of Philosophical Theology', p. 80.

12  Cobb's most substantial treatment of 'creative transformation' is to be found in his *Christ in a Pluralistic Age*.

13  This is the gist of the argument advanced in Herbert McCabe, *God Matters* (London, 1987), pp. 39–51; and Richard E. Creel, *Divine Impassibility*, pp. 140–58.

14  Donald W. Sherburne, 'Whitehead Without God,' pp. 305–28.

15  Keith Ward, *The Concept of God* (Oxford, 1974), p. 156.

16  Michael Welker, *Universalität Gottes und Relavität der Welt*, pp. 201 ff.

17  For this view see Walter Kasper, *The God of Jesus Christ* (London, 1984), pp. 249 ff.; Nicholas Lash, 'Considering the Trinity', *Modern Theology*, 2 (1986), pp. 183–94; Denys Turner, 'De-Centering Theology', *Modern Theology*, 2 (1986), pp. 125–43; and Theodore W. Jennings, *Beyond Theism* (New York, 1985). See also the brilliant critique of the Cartesian 'project' to be found in Eberhard Jüngel, *God as the Mystery of the World* (Edinburgh, 1983).

18  For an example of this kind of critique, see H. P. Owen, *Concepts of Deity* (London, 1971), pp. 75–89. The difficulty here is that process theologians take 'classical theism' to be a rubric which encompasses theologians of such contrasting views as say, St Thomas and Kierkegaard, or Calvin and David Burrell. An unavoidable element of artificiality therefore surrounds any designation of this or that theologian as a 'classical theist'.

19  The reader is referred to the chapters in the present volume by James Buckley (Revisionists and Liberals, ch. 4) and William Placher (Post-liberals, ch. 6) for maps of the terrain covered by my concluding remarks.

## BIBLIOGRAPHY

This list is restricted to items dealing specifically (though not necessarily solely) with neoclassical metaphysics and process theology. More extensive bibliographies are to be found in the works by Brown et al., Cobb and Griffin, Cousins, and Sia cited below.

### *Primary*

Brown, Delwin, James, Ralph E., Jr, and Reeves, Gene (eds), *Process Philosophy and Christian Thought* (New York, 1971).

Cobb, John B., Jr, *A Christian Natural Theology* (London, 1966).

—, *The Structure of Christian Existence* (London, 1968).

—, *Christ in a Pluralistic Age* (Philadelphia, 1975).

—, *Beyond Dialogue: Toward a Mutual Transformation of Christianity and Buddhism* (Philadelphia, 1982).

—, *Process Theology as Political Theology* (Philadelphia, 1982).

—, and Gamwell, Franklin I. (eds), *Existence and Actuality: Conversations with Charles Hartshorne* (Chicago, 1984).

—, and Griffin, David Ray, *Process Theology: An Introductory Exposition* (Belfast, 1977).

Cousins, Ewart H., (ed.), *Process Theology: Basic Writings* (New York, 1971).

Creel, Richard E., *Divine Impassibility: An Essay in Philosophical Theology* (Cambridge, 1986).

Ford, Lewis S., 'The Non-Temporality of Whitehead's God', *International Philosophical Quarterly*, 13 (1973), pp. 347–76.

—, (ed.), *Two Process Philosophers: Hartshorne's Encounter with Whitehead* (Chico, Ca., 1973).

Griffin, David R., *Power and Evil: A Process Theodicy* (Philadelphia, 1976).

Hartshorne, Charles, *The Logic of Perfection* (La Salle, Ill., 1962).

—, *Man's Vision of God* (Hampden, Conn., 1964).

—, *Anselm's Discovery* (La Salle, Ill., 1965).

—, *A Natural Theology for our Time* (La Salle, Ill., 1967).

—, 'The God of Religion and the God of Philosophy', in G. N. A. Vesey (ed.), *Talk of God* (London, 1969), pp. 152–67.

—, *The Divine Relativity: A Social Conception of God* (New Haven, Conn., 1972).

—, *Whitehead's Philosophy: Selected Essays, 1935–1970* (Lincoln and London, 1972).

Ogden, Schubert M., *The Reality of God and Other Essays* (London, 1967).

Ogden, Schubert M., 'The Task of Philosophical Theology', in Robert H. Evans (ed.), *The Future of Philosophical Theology* (Philadelphia, 1971), pp. 55–84.

Whitehead, Alfred North, *Religion in the Making* (Cambridge, 1926).

—, *Process and Reality* (New York, 1929).

—, *Adventures of Ideas* (Cambridge, 1933).

*Process Studies* is a journal devoted exclusively to articles in process theology.

## Secondary

Creel, Richard E., *Divine Impassibility: An Essay in Philosophical Theology* (Cambridge, 1986).

Ogletree, Thomas W., 'A Christological Assessment of Dipolar Theism', *The Journal of Religion*, 47 (1967), pp. 87–99.

Reeves, Gene, 'Whitehead and Hartshorne', *The Journal of Religion*, 55 (1975), pp. 125–37.

Sherburne, Donald W., 'Whitehead without God', with Delwin Brown, Ralph E. James and Gene Reeves (eds), *Process Philosophy and Christian Thought* (New York, 1971), pp. 305–28.

Sia, Santiago, *God in Process Thought* (Dordrecht, 1985).

Welker, Michael, *Universalität Gottes und Relativität der Welt: Theologische Cosmologie im Dialog mit dem amerikanischen Theologie*, vol. 1 (Neukirchen-Vluyn, 1981).

# 6

# Postliberal Theology

## William C. Placher

### INTRODUCTION: THE STUDY OF RELIGION AT YALE

George Lindbeck's *The Nature of Doctrine*, published in 1984, brought the work of a number of theologians who share at least a 'family resemblance' into focus as a new theological option. The last chapter of the book was entitled 'Toward a Postliberal Theology', and within a year or two of its publication references to 'postliberal theology' regularly appeared. Still, reception has not been unanimously favorable. An account of 'postliberalism' in a popular journal like *The Christian Century* drew an astonishingly virulent round of letters denouncing it as arrogant nonsense and 'theological imperialism' whose adherents demand 'an oath of loyalty to the "Yale school"' and have much in common with Jerry Falwell, Pontius Pilate, and the Athenians who killed Socrates.[1] Other charges include 'fideism', 'sectarianism', and even 'tribalism'. So just what is 'postliberal theology'? Because of the newness of this still emerging theological approach (given even a name only a few years ago), this chapter will provide more basic exposition than critical analysis and emphasize common themes even at the risk of ignoring the differences among theologians sufficiently diverse that they may not form a 'school' at all.

A list of the intellectual influences on postliberal theology seems something of a mish-mash: the theology of Karl Barth, Thomas Kuhn's philosophy of science, analytic philosophers like Wittgenstein and Gilbert Ryle, sociologists like Peter Berger, anthropologists like Clifford Geertz, and literary theorists like Erich Auerbach. Nearly all the postliberal theologians have had some connection with Yale (many of the movement's roots lie in the work of the Yale theologian H. Richard Niebuhr), and some comments about the teaching of religion at that university may help explain how these pieces fit together.

In the tradition of scholars like Mircea Eliade of the University of Chicago, many religious studies departments in the United States teach 'religion', particularly in an introductory course, as a universal phenomenon whose themes and symbols manifest the experience of the sacred in different but related ways in different cultures. Christian theology then takes its place as one set of answers to those universal human questions – a way of thinking about theology Paul Tillich stated in classic form.

At Yale the pattern has been different, with an emphasis on the study of particular religious traditions, each in its own historical and cultural context. Students working in non-Christian fields specialize in Judaica or Buddhist studies, but not 'the history of religions'. The Yale philosopher of religion William Christian has noted the implausibility of claims that all religions are really 'saying the same thing' and warned his readers, 'in response to the generous impulse which often prompts people to harmonize the doctrines of the world religions, that understanding one another does not always lead to agreement and that respect for one another does not depend on agreement'.[2]

By the late 1970s, new styles in biblical studies had emerged at Yale. The New Testament scholar Wayne Meeks sought to 'describe the first Christian group in ways that a sociologist or an anthropologist might', seeking 'in social history an antidote to the abstractions of the history of ideas and to the subjective individualism of existentialist hermeneutics.'[3] Following a quite different line of thought, Brevard Childs proposed a 'canonical' approach to the Old Testament, which would pay attention to the shape of the text as we have it, not just probe for the sources which lie behind it. Moreover, Childs believes that understanding a text involves at least in part noting how it has functioned, and he reminds us that *this* text has functioned primarily in the context of 'the community which treasured it as Scripture', not the community of historical-critical scholars.[4]

Childs's colleague David Kelsey, indeed, has argued that the authority of scriptures lies precisely in the way a community uses them, not in some feature of the texts themselves. 'To call a set of texts "scripture"', he has written, 'is, in part, to say that they ought so to be used in the common life of the church as to nurture and preserve her self-identity.' Thus, Scripture is not the starting-point for theology. Indeed, a theological system does not consist of 'one long over-arching argument' resting on *any* starting-point, whether religious experience or scriptural text, but rather 'is a set of several different families of argument' which 'taken as a whole might be looked at in a quasi-aesthetic way as a solicitation of mind and imagination to look at Christianity in a certain way'.[5]

## SURVEY

The writers mentioned so far might not agree with each other on many issues or want to sign on as 'postliberal theologians', but they have helped shape a milieu where people studied religious traditions as communal practices more than as the expressions of individual experience, and studied religious texts as they have functioned in their communities more than as historical sources or symbols of universal myths. Hans Frei had been thinking about theology in related terms for many years, and Lindbeck gave such an approach a name: 'postliberal theology'. That name, incidentally, seems unfortunate: in the late 1960s, when Frei and Lindbeck were developing these ideas, 'postliberal' implied a radical challenge to existing society, but by the time Lindbeck's book appeared in 1984, in an age of Reagan and Thatcher, it sounded as if it meant 'conservative'.

To attempt a brief statement of basic concerns: postliberal theology attends to the biblical narratives as narratives rather than simply as historical sources or as symbolic expressions of truths which could be expressed non-narratively. But unlike some other theologians interested in narrative, postliberals do not let the stories of *our* lives set the primary context for theology. They insist that the *biblical* narratives provide the framework within which Christians understand the world. Christian theology describes how the world looks as seen from that standpoint; it does not claim to argue from some 'neutral' or 'objective' position and indeed denies the possibility of such a position. It pursues apologetics, therefore, only on an *ad hoc* basis, looking for common ground with a given conversation partner but not assuming some universally acceptable standard of rationality.[6]

## *Hans Frei*

Everyone associated with postliberal theology owes a great debt to Hans Frei. In *The Eclipse of Biblical Narrative* (1974) he showed how, until at least the seventeenth century, most Christians read the Bible as one grand story, making sense of their own lives as they fit into the world of that story. The question of the correspondence of that narrated world to the 'real world' never arose, since it *was* the real world. But by the eighteenth century, 'It is no exaggeration to say that all across the theological spectrum the great reversal had taken place; interpretation was a matter of fitting the biblical story into another world with another story rather than incorporating that world into the biblical story.'[7] The world of people's daily experience came to seem primary, and theologians felt they had to establish the biblical world's reality by fitting *it* into *that* world – in one of two ways. (1) For John Locke and many others, 'The meaning of the stories is their ostensive reference or their failure to refer to certain events.'[8] The world of the biblical narratives refers to the 'real world' by making historical claims. (2) Alternatively, the narratives refer to some eternal truth which they symbolize. The meaning of the story is not the story but some moral lesson or religious truth it illustrates.

These two options have dominated the theological scene since the eighteenth century – Wolfhart Pannenberg and Schubert Ogden still represent them in fairly pure form. A third option – simply reading the story as a story, which means what it says, in the way that a realistic novel does – has virtually disappeared from the scene. Frei claims that that third option is most faithful to the character of these texts, which often do not seem to claim historical accuracy but whose narrative character seems essential to their meaning. But if the work of critical historians or the agenda of contemporary existential concerns defines 'reality', then that third option leaves the Bible as 'fiction'. Frei therefore argues that a theology which wants to be hermeneutically faithful to the character of the biblical texts must eschew systematic efforts at apologetics (which let the historian or philosopher set the rules of the game) and, like Karl Barth, simply describe the biblical world as 'a world with its own linguistic integrity, much as a literary art work is a consistent world in its own right', while insisting 'that unlike any other depicted world it is the one common world in which we all live and move and have our being'.[9]

Similarly, in *The Identity of Jesus Christ*, Frei considers the concepts of Jesus' *identity* and *presence* and maintains that the logic of Christian faith requires that we begin with identity, not presence. Beginning with 'the often nagging and worrisome questions of *how* Christ is present to us and *how* we can believe in his presence' is again a way of letting *our* experience set the agenda. It leads either to trying to establish on the historical evidence that Jesus was raised from the dead or else to trying to find Jesus present as the eternal symbol of universal human concerns.[10] Both approaches are unfaithful to the gospel narratives, which do not claim to be accurate history but are also not the stuff of myth. Unlike the timeless, universal symbols provided by myths, they offer the portrait of an unsubstitutable person. We know who he is, as we learn about a character in a novel, by hearing stories about him.

Drawing on the philosophy of Gilbert Ryle, Frei argues that a person ordinarily *is* what he or she says and does, not some mysterious 'ghost in a machine'. In any life story, there are trivial events and anomalies but also moments when one's identity takes focus, and Frei argues that in the gospel narratives Jesus is most himself in his resurrection. Beginning with questions about Jesus' presence led to a dead end, but in this one unique case beginning with identity leads to presence, for the story tells us that he is the resurrected one and therefore his identity, properly understood, implies that he is present with us. 'He *is* the resurrection and the life. How can he be conceived as not resurrected?'[11] Frei's argument here is analogous to Anselm's ontological argument for the existence of God, where a proper understanding of who God is – God's identity – implies that God must exist.

Now obviously, this is not an argument to persuade the non-believer, and Frei after all is committed to avoiding systematic apologetics. Believers will recognize that, yes, this is the Christ in whom they believe, and Frei thinks it best not to worry overmuch about how nonbelievers become believers, for such concerns lead back to apologetic strategies which inevitably fall into one or another distortion of the biblical text. Theology must stick primarily to its descriptive task of laying out the internal logic of Christian faith.

### George Lindbeck

George Lindbeck has also described a theology which works descriptively and begins with the world of canonical texts: 'for those who are steeped in them, no world is more real than the ones they create. A scriptural world is thus able to absorb the universe. It supplies the interpretive framework within which believers seek to live their lives and understand reality.'[12] What does such an 'intratextual' approach imply about the function of doctrines? Lindbeck considers three models of how doctrines work (with the inevitable danger that such models oversimplify his opponents' positions): (1) the *propositionalist* 'emphasizes the cognitive aspects of religion and stresses the ways in which church doctrines function as informative propositions or truth-claims about objective realities'; (2) the *experiential-expressivist* 'interprets doctrines as noninformative and nondiscursive symbols of inner feelings, attitudes, or existential orientations'; (3) on Lindbeck's own *cultural-linguistic* or *regulative* view, 'the function of church doctrines that becomes most prominent . . . is their use, not as expressive symbols or as truth-claims, but as communally authoritative rules of discourse, attitude, and action.'[13]

Consider the assertion, 'We are saved by grace alone'. The propositionalist will take this as a *factual* claim about the mechanism of salvation. The experiential-expressivist will understand it as the *symbolic expression of an experience* of the power of God in salvation. On Lindbeck's view, the meaning of the doctrine can be expressed in a *rule* like, 'Christians should always speak and act about their salvation in a way that expresses gratitude to God, not pride in their own accomplishment.'

From his long experience as a Lutheran participant in ecumenical discussions, Lindbeck notes one problem with the propositionalist model: it cannot explain the cases where participants in ecumenical discussions find that their communities can now agree on a point where they formerly disagreed, without either side sensing that it has changed its position. On the propositionalist model, if Lutheran and Catholic doctrines were in contradiction in 1541, then they still are. But on a regulative model, rules could apply in one circumstance but not another. They could still disagree about what it was essential to the health of the church to say in 1541, while agreeing on what needs saying now.[14]

Lindbeck devotes most of his argument, however, to defending the superiority of his model over experiential-expressivism. He argues the implausibility of claiming that all Christians – much less all religious people – share some common experience which religious language seeks to articulate. Indeed, he denies that we can have pre-linguistic 'religious experience'. Cases like Helen Keller and 'supposed wolf children . . . illustrate, that unless we acquire language of some kind we cannot actualize our specifically human capacities for thought, action, and feeling.'[15] In particular, we cannot have the kind of experience Christians or Buddhists have, or see the world in the way they do, unless we have the linguistic framework to structure and articulate that experience. One simply could not have an 'experience' of 'being saved by faith in Christ' without a language that included ideas like 'salvation', 'faith', and 'Christ'.

Therefore we cannot judge a religious language by measuring it for faithfulness against some pre-linguistic experience. Nor can we judge it primarily as to factual accuracy. Lindbeck turns to the standard of 'categorial adequacy'. Doctrinal systems are in this respect like languages. We do not judge a language 'true' or 'false'. 'But one language may in the long run open up all the riches of human history . . . while the other, the better a child learns it, imprisons him more tightly in his little tribe or village.'[16] People who grow up in the language of a tribe unaware of modern science do not. say false things about particle physics – they lack the vocabulary to talk about it at all. Similarly, a religious system may lack the grammar and vocabulary that enable us to lead richer lives more faithful to the nature of things. Thus,

> As actually lived, a religion may be pictured as a single gigantic proposition. It is a true proposition to the extent that its objectivities are interiorized and exercised by groups and individuals in such a way as to conform them in some measure in the various dimensions of their existence to the ultimate reality and goodness that lies at the heart of things.[17]

Lindbeck acknowledges, to be sure, that some religious utterances will make truth-claims or even express experiences.[18] But if the fundamental function of doctrines is to establish the framework of language for a community's conversation, then the adherents of a religion should not concentrate on searching for universal human experiences but rather on perfecting their own 'language' from within. Lindbeck is not optimistic that Christianity will take this path, for he sees much in contemporary Western culture that encourages 'experiential-expressivism' and discourages the cultivation of the discipline of language and community invited by the cultural-linguistic model. Both university teachers of religion and their students often tend to value individual experience more highly than communal discipline, and they only reflect the attitudes of their societies. Yet perhaps only through disciplined communities will religions exert their greatest influence. So thinks the next theologian we consider.

### Stanley Hauerwas

Stanley Hauerwas did his graduate work at Yale and taught for a number of years at the University of Notre Dame, Indiana before taking his present position at Duke University, North Carolina. He believes that most contemporary Christian ethics fits Lindbeck's experiential-expressivist model, assuming that 'there is some universal experience that all people have that can be characterized as religious. The particular religions and their doctrines are but manifestations of that experience.' In contrast, Hauerwas holds that 'by our becoming members of a particular community, formed by Christian convictions, an experience not otherwise available is made possible. From this perspective Christian ethics does not simply confirm what all people of good will know, but requires a transformation both personally and socially if we are to be true to the nature of our convictions.'[19]

Frei talks about 'narratives'; Hauerwas tends to discuss 'stories', but the idea is roughly the same, and the category is central to his thought in at least two ways. First, he thinks that too much contemporary ethics takes the form of 'quandary ethics'. It discusses difficult moral choices in isolation from what goes before or after them and assumes that either some universal moral principle can be brought to bear or else we face moral chaos.[20] Hauerwas believes that we receive moral guidance from stories more than from principles. Stories help us imagine what sorts of persons we think we ought to be. They point to the importance of virtue and character in ethics, for these are formed, not in an isolated moral decision, but in the shape of a life. If we see someone who needs help, the story of the Good Samaritan may be more use to us than any abstract ethical principle, and we lose part of the helpfulness of the story if we try to reduce it to an abstract principle.

Stories also function in shaping our communities. A nation, a tribe, a school, or any social group defines itself in part by telling a common story. Yet in Hauerwas's view too much contemporary ethics seeks to free us from tradition, so that we can guide ourselves by some universal standard of rational ethics. 'The story that liberalism teaches us is that we have no story.'[21] Hauerwas insists that it is the stories we tell that provide us with options, with different models of the virtuous life. They create possibilities rather than limiting freedom.

The task of Christian ethics, then, is not to establish universal moral principles on the basis of natural law or some general anthropological claim, but to call Christians to preserve a community that tells the stories that make Christian virtues possible:

> The church's social task is first of all its willingness to be a community formed by a language the world does not share . . . the church's social ethics is not first of all to be found in the statements by which it tries to influence the ethos of those in

power, but rather . . . is first and foremost found in its ability to sustain a people who are not at home in the liberal presumptions of our civilization and society.[22]

As a pacifist, Hauerwas has been particularly concerned to call the church to offer 'a political alternative to every nation, witnessing to the kind of social life possible for those that have been formed by the story of Christ'.[23]

### Ronald Thiemann

Ronald Thiemann, who went from graduate work at Yale to teaching at Haverford College, Pennsylvania and is now Dean of Harvard Divinity School, has brought similar concerns about narrative and community to bear on the doctrine of revelation. A good many theologians, he argues, have gone wrong by associating revelation with a foundationalist epistemology, the conviction 'that knowledge is grounded in a set of non-inferential, self-evident beliefs'.[24] Revelation then becomes the certain starting-point from which one could derive the rest of Christian beliefs. Philosophers like Wilfred Sellars and Richard Rorty have traced the philosophical objections to foundationalism; Thiemann shows how it has led a long line of theologians on a doomed quest for some absolutely certain starting-point for theology, some miraculous evidence or religious intuition so unambiguous that it just could not be questioned.

Confronted with the resulting problems, some contemporary theologians have proposed giving up the doctrine of revelation altogether. But Thiemann shows how talking about revelation safeguards God's *prevenience*, the conviction that a divine initiative precedes all our speaking and acting and responding. Given his own principles, Thiemann cannot begin with some indisputable starting-point, whether the authority of Scripture or religious experience, that would 'prove' divine prevenience. Instead, he offers a 'holist justification' as an example of the kind of argument he thinks theologians ought to make.[25] He shows how much of Christian life and liturgy would have to be sacrificed if we abandoned prevenience, if we said that our speaking and acting about God comes before any divine initiative. If prevenience seems so central to Christian life and thought, and revelation protects prevenience, then a Christian theologian has good reasons for wanting to rescue a doctrine of revelation. Thiemann thinks we can do so if we free it from its association with foundationalism.

He proposes an understanding of revelation as 'narrated promise'. The idea of 'promise' preserves the priority of God's initiative, for one can respond to a promise only after it has been made. For Thiemann, we learn of the promise through Scripture's narration of the identity of God as the one who promises. In a careful reading of the Gospel of Matthew, Thiemann does not try to penetrate behind the narrative to some moral or experience but shows how the shape of the narrative itself begins with divine initiative and opens up to invite our response. He refuses to try to 'found' theology either on religious intuition or on revelation itself but treats revelation as a part of the doctrine of God, one implication of God's narrated identity, to be defended by showing its coherence with other aspects of Christian life and teaching.

### DEBATE AND AGENDA

Thiemann's emphasis on divine prevenience implies that religious language refers to a God who exists independently of human speech and belief, and Hans Frei's theology involves both ontological and historical truth-claims. Frei emphasizes the difficulty of *any* positive description of what happened at Jesus' resurrection, for instance, but he admits, 'About certain events reported in the Gospels we are almost bound to ask, Did they actually take place?'[26]

On the other hand, Hauerwas, David Kelsey, and Charles Wood sometimes write as if Christian language refers *only* to the speech and 'forms of life' of the Christian community, and does not make either historical or ontological claims beyond the description of communal practice – a way of understanding religious language that owes much to one way of reading some of Wittgenstein's remarks. Lindbeck seems an ambiguous case. In the body of his book *The Nature of Doctrine*, he makes careful qualifications and supports a 'modest cognitivism' such as he finds in St Thomas Aquinas. Yet the polemic edge of the book seems to depend, among other things, on a contrast between the 'propositionalists', who hold that doctrines make truth-claims about matters of fact, and his own 'regulative' view, in which doctrines (*only?*) describe the rules of discourse within a community. So – does Christian theology simply lay out the rules for how Christians talk and behave, or does it make assertions about some kind of objective truth? Such questions about the nature of Christian truth-claims surely stand at the top of the agenda for postliberal theologians.

'Narrative' is an important category for postliberal theology, and here too some questions arise. Many new approaches in biblical scholarship, from feminism to deconstructionism, have shown how there are many different, sometimes conflicting, narratives within Scripture. Modern novelists at least since James Joyce, and contemporary literary critics, sometimes undercut the whole idea of a clear coherent narrative as something that no longer fits the chaos of our experience. A theology that appeals confidently to the biblical narrative (in the singular) has some explaining to do.

The relation of church and society raises another set of problems. Frei has not addressed such issues directly, while Thiemann has begun to explore the question of church and wider society from a number of perspectives. But Hauerwas acknowledges his great debt to the admittedly 'sectarian' ethics of the Mennonite John Howard Yoder, and Lindbeck has suggested that the church may have to establish a kind of 'sociological sectarianism',[27] developing the kind of 'close-knit groups . . . needed to sustain an alien faith'.[28] Postliberalism's opponents too quickly dismiss the possible social impact of the witness of a disciplined community that knows what it believes. Sectarian communities of Christian pacifists, socialists, or the early Quaker opponents of slavery, after all, have helped shape the consciences of their societies. Yet Christianity as a whole is not yet, anyway, quite a sectarian community. National leaders and ordinary citizens still widely claim allegiance to Christian faith. That implies, it would seem, some social responsibilities for the direction of society as a whole that the sectarian model does not fit.[29]

## ACHIEVEMENT

Nevertheless, its critics often too hastily charge postliberal theology with retreat from the arena of general intellectual debate. Philosophers as diverse as Richard Rorty, Hans-Georg Gadamer, Jacques Derrida, and Michel Foucault have recently raised varyingly radical challenges to the Enlightenment dream of a universal rationality. Alasdair MacIntyre has redirected ethical thinking among philosophers away from the search for universal moral principles and toward the importance of community and tradition. In such a radically pluralistic, post-Enlightenment context, postliberalism just might provide the kind of theology best suited to join the general conversation.

More importantly, postliberalism has challenged a kind of functionalism to which much of the preaching and teaching of Christianity has fallen victim.[30] Too often, as Lindbeck has noted, 'religions are seen as multiple suppliers of different forms of a single commodity needed for transcendent self-expression and self-realization'.[31] College teachers present them as therapeutically interesting answers to late adolescent identity crises. In the churches, 'prophetic' voices for social change too often seem to see Christianity principally as a support for their political agendas. At least as often, their conservative opponents appeal to 'old-time religion' as a means to the end of attacking social changes they dislike or defending 'democratic capitalism' or the 'American way of life'. Postliberal theology proposes that one might take Christianity as the central vision of one's life, not as a means to some other end, and adopt ethical values because they follow from Christian faith rather than adopting Christian faith because it lends support to one's ethical values. As good theology always does, it raises hard questions not only about the views of other theologians but also about the life of the Christian community.

## NOTES

1 'A Challenge to Willimon's Postliberalism', *The Christian Century*, 104 (1987), pp. 306–10.
2 William A. Christian, *Oppositions of Religious Doctrines* (New York, 1972), p. 5. Paul Holmer's studies of Kierkegaard and Wittgenstein certainly influenced his colleagues and students at Yale, but most of them did not follow him into what has come to be called 'Wittgensteinian fideism,' and Christian has been the deeper philosophical influence.
3 Wayne A. Meeks, *The First Urban Christians* (New Haven, Conn., 1983), p. 2.
4 Brevard S. Childs, *Introduction to the Old Testament as Scripture* (Philadelphia, 1979), pp. 40–1. For Childs's cautious response to 'the new Yale theology', see his *The New Testament as Canon: An Introduction* (Philadelphia, 1984), pp. 541–6.
5 David H. Kelsey, *The Uses of Scripture in Recent Theology*, p. 150, pp. 136–7.
6 Hans Frei developed the idea of 'ad hoc apologetics'. See William Werpehowski, 'Ad Hoc Apologetics', *The Journal of Religion*, 66 (1986), pp. 282–301.
7 Hans W. Frei, *The Eclipse of Biblical Narrative*, p. 130.
8 Ibid., p. 99.
9 Hans W. Frei, 'An Afterword: Eberhard Busch's Biography of Karl Barth', in *Karl Barth in Re-View*, ed. H.-Martin Rumscheidt (Pittsburgh, 1981), p. 114.
10 Hans W. Frei, *The Identity of Jesus Christ*, p. 4.
11 Ibid., p. 146.

12  George A. Lindbeck, *The Nature of Doctrine*, p. 117.
13  Ibid., pp. 16–18.
14  Ibid., p. 15.
15  Ibid., p. 34.
16  Ibid., p. 60.
17  Ibid., p. 51.
18  Ibid., pp. 68–9.
19  Stanley Hauerwas, *Against the Nations*, p. 2.
20  Stanley Hauerwas, *A Community of Character*, p. 134.
21  Ibid., p. 84.
22  Hauerwas, *Against the Nations*, pp. 11–12.
23  Hauerwas, *Community of Character*, p. 12.
24  Ronald F. Thiemann, *Revelation and Theology: The Gospel as Narrated Promise*, p. 158 n. 20.
25  Ibid., pp. 171–2, n. 2.
26  Frei, *Identity of Jesus Christ*, p. 132.
27  George A. Lindbeck, 'The Sectarian Future of the Church', in Joseph P. Whelan (ed.), *The God Experience* (New York, 1971), pp. 226–43.
28  Lindbeck, *Nature of Doctrine*, p. 78.
29  Lindbeck addresses such issues in ibid., p. 133.
30  This analysis rests on George Hunsinger, 'Where the Battle Rages: Confessing Christ in America Today', *dialog*, 26 (Fall 1987), pp. 264–74.
31  Lindbeck, *Nature of Doctrine*, p. 22.

## BIBLIOGRAPHY

### Primary

Frei, Hans W., *The Eclipse of Biblical Narrative* (New Haven, Conn., 1974).
—, *The Identity of Jesus Christ* (Philadelphia, 1975).
Hauerwas, Stanley, *A Community of Character* (Notre Dame, Ind., 1981).
—, *Against the Nations* (Minneapolis, 1985).
Kelsey, David H., *The Uses of Scripture in Recent Theology* (Philadelphia, 1979).
Lindbeck, George A., *The Nature of Doctrine* (Philadelphia, 1984).
Thiemann, Ronald F., *Revelation and Theology: The Gospel as Narrated Promise* (Notre Dame, Ind., 1985).
Wood, Charles M., *The Formation of Christian Understanding* (Philadelphia, 1981).

### Secondary

Christian, William A., *Doctrines of Religious Communities* (New Haven, Conn., 1987).
Green, Garrett, *Scriptural Authority and Narrative Interpretation* (Philadelphia, 1987).
Gustafson, James M., 'The Sectarian Temptation: Reflections on Theology,

the Church, and the University', *Proceedings of the Catholic Theological Society*, 40 (1985), pp. 83–94.

*Modern Theology 4* (January, 1988), pp. 107–209. Special issue on *The Nature of Doctrine*. Articles by Gordon E. Michalson, Jr, Geoffrey Wainwright, D. Z. Phillips, Lee Barrett, Stephen Williams, and Kenneth Surin.

*The Thomist 49* (July, 1985), pp. 392–472. Symposium on *The Nature of Doctrine*. Articles by William C. Placher, Colman O'Neill OP, James J. Buckley, and David Tracy.

# Part III

# Evangelical and Orthodox Theologies

Evangelical and Orthodox theologies are best understood first of all in relation to their respective church traditions. Ray Anderson carefully defines what is meant by evangelical theology and how it relates to the evangelical movement in contemporary Protestantism. He discusses three diverse examples of its theology in G. C. Berkouwer, Helmut Thielicke and Carl F. H. Henry. He shows how they dealt with the core evangelical concerns of Reformation orthodoxy, biblical authority, and personal experience of salvation, and also how they have responded variously to the challenges of modernity. The revival in the United States during and after the 1950s of an evangelical theology which is not fundamentalist and is concerned for high academic standards is given special attention, the achievement of the whole tradition is assessed, and an agenda for the future suggested.

Rowan Williams offers a pioneering account of twentieth-century Orthodox thought. He begins with the nineteenth-century Russian background, including the major figures of Kireevsky, Soloviev, and Khomyakov. He then discusses three theologians: S. N. Bulgakov, the Marxist economist turned philosopher and theologian, whose unified theological metaphysic and thoroughgoing kenotic approach to God are described; V. N. Lossky, with his more hermeneutical, patristic approach and influential 'negative theology'; and G. V. Florovsky, who was likewise oriented to patristics, and pursued a program of 're-Hellenizing' Christianity in reaction against much modern thought. The conclusion is a brief, original survey of recent Orthodox thought in many places – Greece, the United States, France, and Eastern Europe, with a glance at India – accompanied by suggestions about its agenda and encouragement to Western theologians to engage more fully with it.

Both evangelical and Orthodox theologians have been more at

home in churches and their seminaries than in universities (like Congar and Balthasar in volume I), and are in close relationship with traditions representing many millions of Christians. They have not yet been done justice to by academic theologians, and Anderson and Williams open the way for this to happen with benefit to all sides.

# 7

# Evangelical Theology

## Ray S. Anderson

### INTRODUCTION: THE MEANING OF 'EVANGELICAL'

No Christian theologian has a proprietary claim on the phrase 'evangelical theology'. As it pertains to the gospel of God's act of saving grace through Jesus Christ, the word 'evangelical' is rooted in the earliest traditions of the church's theology including, most certainly, the Pauline and Johannine theology of the New Testament itself. A theology which is not 'evangelical' in this fundamental sense may have betrayed both the formal and material reality of its claim to be a 'Christian' theology.

It would be naive, however, to ignore the history of theology which has invariably witnessed a polarity of one form or another between theologians who view the 'evangel' from quite different perspectives. As a result, theologians of the early Christian era who sought to defend the historical and philosophical truth of the gospel as located in the person and work of Jesus Christ constructed an orthodox formulation of the 'evangel' as opposed to what they considered to be a heterodox, or even heretical theology. Thus began the association of the word 'evangelical' with 'orthodox', and later, with 'reformed,' 'conservative', or even 'fundamentalistic', as opposed to 'modern' or 'liberal'.

Theology in the Protestant tradition, by its very nature, sought to define its stance over and against other theological traditions. In so doing, it has given rise to a variety of nuances to the word 'evangelical' which provide a broad context for the specific purpose of this chapter. While the Reformed (Calvinistic) theological tradition assumed an implicit evangelical and christological orientation, the European Lutheran tradition often carried an explicit evangelical confessional designation. In this way, both attempted to overcome what was perceived as a 'non-evangelical' theory and experience in their medieval theological and ecclesial antecedents. In Latin America, more recently, the term 'evangelical' is often taken as equivalent to Protestant in distinction from Roman Catholic.

The focus of this chapter is narrower and more selective than this broad and general use of the term 'evangelical'. We are using the phrase 'evangelical theology' in a way that is more contemporary than historical. Rather than thinking of 'evangelical' as descriptive of a specific denomination or theological tradition, we intend here by the phrase to depict more a theological ethos than a school of thought. In this way, the representative theologians presented here transcend denominational, geographical, and confessional boundaries. On the other hand, it will be shown that there is an identifiable cluster of concerns and commitments which are common to the ethos of evangelical theology as a contemporary phenomenon.

### SURVEY

The American historian George Marsden has identified three overlapping spheres which may be used to identify evangelicalism, as a religious and theological phenomenon.[1] In the first sense, evangelicalism may be seen as a conceptual unity of those who typically emphasize (1) the Reformation doctrine of the final authority of Scripture; (2) the real, historical character of God's saving work recorded in Scripture; (3) eternal salvation only through personal trust in Christ; (4) the importance of evangelism and missions; and (5) the importance of a spiritually transformed life.

A second means of identifying evangelicalism, he suggests, is to see it as a dynamic movement, with common heritages, common tendencies, and an organic character. This 'mosaic' is made up of some denominations, so-called parachurch organizations, and evangelistically oriented movements. Widely-common hymnody, techniques of evangelism, styles of prayer and Bible study, worship and behavior mores demonstrate the informal unity of the movement.

In a third sense, Marsden suggests, there is a more narrowly-defined grouping of those who merge a common heritage and interests into a self-conscious, though loosely-structured, community. In this respect, evangelicalism is more like a denomination. It is a religious fellowship or coalition of which people feel a part. Evangelicalism in this more specific sense is essentially a trans-denominational assemblage of independent agencies and their supporters. During the first half of the nineteenth century, evangelicals from Britain and the United States founded scores of 'voluntary societies' for revivals, missions, Bible and tract publication, education, charity, and social and moral reform. The Evangelical Alliance, founded in 1846, was the most formal expression of this international evangelical community. In North America, evangelical denominations and organizations formed the National Association of Evangelicals in 1942, as a self-conscious alternative to the more ecumenical and inclusive National Council of Churches.

Two things are quite clear in surveying the emergence of contemporary evangelicalism as both a conceptual unity and a dynamic movement. First, any attempt to define the movement must be content with the concept of a 'mosaic' which resists reduction into a single pattern with clearly structured boundaries. Second, viewing evangelicalism as a movement reveals little by way of systematic theological reflection and, with the exception of biblical commentaries, a singular lack of a scholarly theological tradition. Only when one looks at evangelicalism from the perspective of conceptual unity (Marsden's first sphere), does a coherent basis for a theological structure to evangelical theology emerge. While the relation between evangelical theology and evangelicalism as a movement is an uneasy alliance at best, both need each other.

The distinctive features which set contemporary Protestant evangelical theology apart from other theologies can be expressed by three concerns. There is a concern for orthodoxy in doctrine which is rooted in the Reformation confession of *sola scriptura* and *sola gratia*; a concern for biblical authority as an infallible guide to faith and practice; and a concern for a personal experience of salvation through Jesus Christ as proclaimed in the gospel and received by faith through the power of the Holy spirit.

Christian theology is a broad continuum where these same concerns might be found in diverse forms and differing degrees. What marks evangelical theology as unique is not an exclusive claim to orthodoxy, biblical authority, or Christian experience. Rather, what evangelical theologies hold in common is an expressed concern for these as essential elements of the gospel of Jesus Christ as a confession of faith, a standard for teaching, and a mandate for evangelization and mission to the world.

Evangelical theologies of this sort tend to be developed as movements within or between ecclesial traditions rather than out of a particular confessional or scholarly community. Thus, while representative evangelical theologians may themselves be strongly identified with a tradition or confessional statement, their students and followers form a constituency which cuts across sectarian and denominational boundaries.

Three theologians will be presented in this chapter as representative of three significant and contrasting evangelical theologies. From continental Europe, two theologians will be considered as representative of contemporary evangelical theory. G. C. Berkouwer, Professor of Dogmatic Theology at the Free University of Amsterdam, stands within the Dutch tradition of Bavinck and Kuyper. His fourteen volumes in the series *Studies in Dogmatics* offer one of the most comprehensive and systematic expositions of theology from an evangelical perspective available in the English language. Helmut Thielicke, a distinguished Lutheran pastor and Professor of Theology at the University of Hamburg has produced more than 50 books. Many of these are now available in English, including several volumes of published sermons, theological explorations of contemporary issues, a multi-volume work on *Theological Ethics*, and a three-volume theological dogmatics, *The Evangelical Faith*.

In North America, the development of a distinctively evangelical theology in the twentieth century followed a period of conservative fundamentalism which was noted for its vigorous apologetic for orthodoxy in the face of a liberal theology which was perceived as capturing the major centers of theological training and denominational leadership. This 'new evangelicalism' was marked by a vision for scholarship combined with evangelical zeal with the express purpose of re-capturing the intellectual and ecclesial leadership for the future of the church. As a product of this movement, and as one of its most distinguished scholars, Carl F. H. Henry has made the most systematic attempt to write an evangelical theology in his six-volume work *God, Revelation and Authority*. In presenting the work of Carl Henry, discussion will also include mention of other evangelical theologians with somewhat different emphases, but each within this distinctive movement.

Each of these three theologians shares the three concerns which have been used to identify the distinctive ethos and characteristics of a contemporary evangelical theology. At the same time, it will be shown that each represents a contrasting emphasis and approach to theology from within the broader context of the evangelical movement. It should also be noted that the criteria for the selection of representative evangelical theologians are quite arbitrary. The chief criterion is publication of significant scholarly theological works which make accessible to the larger theological and ecclesial community a systematic formulation of what has been defined above as evangelical theology. Within the various evangelical movements and constituencies there are other significant theologians and leaders who represent their own movement's theology and distinctives.

### Gerrit Cornelis Berkouwer (1903–)

G. C. Berkouwer has served as pastor and theologian in the *Gereformeerde Kerken* in Holland for his entire life. He received his theological education at the Free University of Amsterdam. After serving as a pastor for 18 years he was appointed to the chair of dogmatics at the Free University in 1945, where he spent the remainder of his career.

Berkouwer's theological orientation continues in the tradition established by the Dutch Calvinists Abraham Kuyper and Herman Bavinck. Kuyper (1837–1920) was the founder of the Free University in 1880 and its first professor of theology. Bavinck (1854–1921) was professor of theology at the small seminary of the *Christelijke Gereformeerde Kerk* in Kampen from 1883 to 1902, and then succeeded Kuyper at the Free University in 1902, serving there until his death. Kuyper's main emphasis was the common grace which made possible the organic connection between knowledge of the empirical world and knowledge of God. True knowledge of God is only possible through the Holy Spirit and regeneration, and yet, knowledge of God leads to a knowledge of the world and human society as an integrated whole. It is Bavinck, however, to whom Berkouwer refers most often in his own dogmatic studies, though he never studied under him or met him personally. Bavinck rejected both idealism and empiricism, and held that there is a correspondence between an object and its representation in the experiencing subject. God's creative wisdom, the *Logos* has been implanted in the human mind as the divine image. All knowledge is ultimately revealed knowledge, and not ascertainable through direct empirical observation nor through independent mental activity. Thus, for Bavinck, all knowledge rests on faith.

When Berkouwer began his theological studies, the same issues as preoccupied Kuyper and Bavinck prompted his attention. Modernistic theology, influenced not only by Jacob Arminius but by Descartes, who lived in Holland for twenty years (1629–49), continued to set the agenda with regard to the relation of theology to science and culture. Under the Cartesian influence, the Reformation in Holland began to stress more the rational autonomy of the human mind rather than the response of the believer. Reformed theology appeared to capitulate the truth of divine revelation to the critical and rational human mind. Pietists retreated to the safe world of religious experience and religious values with largely a negative response to the effect of the Enlightenment. Berkouwer speaks approvingly of Bavinck's response: 'Bavinck became a model of how theology could be done with commitment to the truth combined with openness to problems, and carefulness in judgments against others.'[2] In the end, however, Berkouwer did not follow Kuyper and Bavinck in two ways. Kuyper's 'organic relationship' between human understanding and the physical world, and Bavinck's 'Logos theory' both pointed toward the fact that God must himself provide the necessary connection between the human mind and natural knowledge as well as the human mind and religious knowledge. Berkouwer did not employ this analogy and reacted strongly against the parallel between natural faith and Christian faith. Secondly, Kuyper and Bavinck both stressed the corporate aspect of the witness of the Holy Spirit. In his book *Holy Scripture* Berkouwer did not pick up this emphasis. He laid great stress on the relation of the Spirit to the words of Scripture, but not on the witness of the Spirit to the corporate church body. On the matter of the nature of biblical authority, however, Berkouwer clearly follows the pathway of Kuyper and Bavinck in stressing the saving purpose of Scripture. The authority of Scripture is affirmed by the inward testimony of the Holy Spirit rather than by the principle of external evidences. Thus, Berkouwer is open to the full humanity of Scripture and accommodation to its historical context. Textual problems do not present a contradiction to the truth of the Word of God as received through the witness of the Spirit in the text itself.

Berkouwer began his theological career with the same concern which was to remain with him throughout his life: the relationship between faith and revelation. The liberal theologians, concluded Berkouwer, had moved toward the subjective side of this issue, with the experiencing human subject the criterion for divine revelation. Orthodox theology, on the other hand, he saw as moving toward the objectivity of revelation as an abstract construct of doctrinal formulations or, as in the case of Barth, a concept of divine relevation as 'divine objectivity' and 'totally other' than human experience. It is the very nature of divine revelation as Word of God spoken and heard in Holy Scripture, argued Berkouwer, which provides true correlation, or co-relation, between faith and knowledge, between faith-subject, and revelation-object.

Berkouwer carried through this theme of correlation in the titles of his first three volumes in his *Studies in dogmatics: Faith and Justification; Faith and Sanctification;* and *Faith and Perseverance.* Faith has no value in and of itself. The value of faith comes entirely from its object, and it is only in correlation with its object – salvation in Jesus Christ – that faith has reality. Faith is not only response to the Word of God which is revealed to us through Holy Scripture, but faith has epistemological significance in that it is only through faith that true knowledge of God and his revelation comes to us.

Berkouwer acknowledged the ambiguity of this concept of 'correlation'. The concept is open to abuse, he admits, where the subjective axis of faith could be construed as determinative at the expense of the sovereignty of divine grace. On the other hand, he will not surrender the decisive character of personal faith in the act of correlation by which the objective knowledge of God is apprehended. He puts it this way:

> Faith in the correlation bespeaks the working of the Holy Spirit directing man to God's grace . . . it is faith, true faith, which honors the sovereignty of grace. And this is what the reformers and the confessions meant by speaking of faith as an instrument, as well as by the emptiness, the vacuity, the passivity of faith. Such concepts in no way deny the activity of faith, its grasp of its object, or its working itself out in love. Faith is still a human act.[3]

The human act of faith is never merely a human act, however, it is always a gift of God, a result of the working of the Holy Spirit.

Three components of Berkouwer's theology demonstrate his standing as an evangelical theologian. First there is his commitment to the absolute authority of Scripture as the source of divine revelation which faith grasps in a knowing way. The Bible serves as the 'boundary' which qualifies both existential faith and rational knowledge. Second, there is a salvific content of Scripture which summons one to faith and personal involvement. Without this correlation between faith and revelation, revelation would either have a purely external authority subject to critical reason, or a purely inward authority subject to human experience alone. Third, the Word of God is decisive as a criterion by which all of humanity is to be seen as under condemnation due to sin and through which the gospel of salvation in Christ is offered to all. Thus, the mission of the church is bound up in its own hearing of the gospel, for the salvation of Christ is not for the sake of the church but for the world.

Through the correlation of faith and revelation, with Scripture as the boundary, Berkouwer attempted to avoid the speculations which plagued scholastic theology. Speculation, argued Berkouwer, attempts to pierce through into the shades of eternity. This is why true faith is content to confess God's revealed truth as the content of his eternal nature and purpose. His concern was for a theology which spoke directly to the need for faith as a personal experience which had practical results in human lives. 'For my way of thinking,' he once wrote, 'theology never seeks a knowledge of the things of faith that transcends the faith of the common people. Theology never seeks to unravel mysteries.'[4] Theology must serve revelation and faith, not theology itself as an independent discipline of study. Berkouwer summons the church to listen to the Word of God, to subject its creeds and confessions to the normative criterion of Scripture, and to be the church of the living Word in its worship and its mission to the world.

## Helmut Thielicke (1908–1986)

Helmut Thielicke studied philosophy and theology at Greifswald, Marburg, Erlangen, and Bonn. Upon ordination, he spent the first years of his ministry as a pastor and theological teacher in Württemberg. As a Lutheran pastor in Nazi Germany during the church struggle and resistance movement to Hitler, Thielicke was one of the few men in the church who clearly saw the fateful consequences of the merging of romantic nationalism with a theology of the glory of the human spirit under the guise of a 'German Christian Theology'. In the theological and political chaos of post-war Germany, Thielicke stood with one foot in the pulpit and one in the classroom, and sought to reconstruct the theological foundations for faith, hope and ethics, grounded in the free and yet historically relevant Word of God. Following a post-war faculty appointment at the University of Tübingen in systematic theology, in 1954 he assumed the chair of systematic theology at Hamburg, where he served until his retirement in 1974. There he began to reconstruct an evangelical theology which was both a return to the essentials of Reformation theology based on 'Christ alone', as well as a way forward into the future based on the 'Spirit with us'. In his sermons, many given during the terrible days of the collapse of Germany, he proclaimed a message of God's creative and liberating Word. So powerful were these in setting forth a theology of God's creative judgment and grace, that several volumes were translated into English as some of the first exposure of Thielicke's theology outside of Germany.

Thielicke firmly believed that proclamation must precede theology.

The gospel is the answer to the crises of life as well as the critique of human attempts toward self-justification. The final confidence for the theologian as well as for the believer is the self-evident truth of the message of Christ as the Holy Spirit speaks and applies it to the hearer. The ethical task for the theologian begins with the light of the gospel and the primary relationship with God to which the problems of life ultimately must answer. Ethics, therefore, forms the primary link between proclamation and theology proper.

His *Theologische Ethik* (1958–64) builds upon a theological foundation carefully laid in the primacy of Jesus Christ over all areas of Christian thought and life. A monumental four-volume work in German, it has been translated into English in the form of three volumes, *Theological Ethics* (1966). This work stands as a landmark in theological ethics from a self-conscious evangelical commitment to the christological and spiritual priority of God in human affairs as the only way out of the nihilism and fatalism which pervades contemporary society. As with Karl Barth, who clearly has exercized some influence on Thielicke, the foundation for his ethics is a trinitarian structure where the being of God 'for us' is identical with the being of God in and of himself. Because he views the trinitarian being of God as personal, relational, and historically relevant, his ethics assume that same orientation. The human person, as a psychological, social and historical self, is an authentic locus of personal responsibility whose justification in Christ provides the basis for responsible life in the world for and with others.

Publishing his first volume of dogmatic theology in 1968 (*Der evangelische Glaube*, translated into English as *The Evangelical Faith*, three volumes, 1974–7), Thielicke began with a radical critique of the theological task itself. Using the Cartesian principle of the priority of the human subject, he divided contemporary theological approaches into two categories. Theology A he termed 'Cartesian theology'. Under this category he placed all theologies which took in some form the priority of the human person as a criterion to which the Word of God must be 'appropriated'. He linked in this way, not only the older liberal theology of Schleiermacher and Ritschl with the primacy of self-consciousness as the criterion for revelation, but the more recent existential theology of Rudolf Bultmann with the primacy of the existing self as criterion. In the category of Cartesian theology, to the consternation of many, he placed the conservative orthodox theologian for whom the objective truth of revelation was determined by the criterion of human rationality. All such approaches to theology, argued Thielicke, are Cartesian in that they seek to appropriate the Word of God to the primacy of the human subject, whether through an intuitive principle, an ethical principle, an existential principle, or a rational principle.

Theology B, countered Thielicke, is a theology which is directed by the Holy Spirit through which the human subject is appropriated to the Word of God. This is evangelical theology, for it preserves the sovereignty and freedom of God in creating faith as response, both experientially and rationally. In taking this approach, Thielicke is clearly following in the Lutheran tradition of 'justification by faith alone'. In this case, however, this does not become a 'principle' or distinctive by which a dialectic is maintained between law and gospel as a soteriological structure. Rather, in Thielicke's approach, justification by faith is a Christological structure of reality by which the structures of human thought and action are radically judged as inevitably idolatrous and nihilistic and in need of redemption through grace. For Thielicke, one cannot separate justification and sanctification nor theology and ethics. The Word of God reaches into every nook and cranny of human life and exposes the stubborn and perverse spirit of resistance to God, often concealed in a system of religious, political, and ethical structures viewed as essentially good and valuable in and of themselves.

God's incarnational work is viewed as the solution to the separation between God and the world, with the continuing ministry of the Holy Spirit the source of fellowship with God as well as the criterion for a theological interpretation of moral, social, and political structures of human life. The incarnation means solidarity between God and humanity. The ministry of the Holy Spirit means the use of human instruments and encounter with the problems, struggles, and aspirations of human life.

Unlike Barth, Thielicke does not eschew apologetics, but rather seeks to address the contemporary person in his or her own cultural and existential situation with the ethically relevant message of the gospel. While Thielicke takes with full seriousness the contemporary situation, he none the less brings it radically under the judgement and then the transforming grace of God. His theology is evangelical in the sense that he sees in the Bible God's authentic Word, focusing his attention on *the* Word incarnate, Jesus Christ, in whom God makes our existence his, and in whom he is crucified and raised for our salvation. The cruciality of Christ for faith is not only a theme for his sermons, but is the evangelical foundation of his ethics and theology.

## Carl F. H. Henry (1913–)

In 1978, the American theologian Carl Henry was named by *Time Magazine* as evangelicalism's 'leading theologian'. Henry, the son of a Roman Catholic mother and a Lutheran father, was baptized and confirmed in the Episcopal church. At an early age he began a career in journalism, but at the age of 20 experienced a radical conversion experience through the witness of a friend. Enrolling in Wheaton College, a Christian liberal arts college in Illinois, he completed his college work in 1938 and promptly enrolled in Northern Baptist Seminary in Chicago, where he graduated and was subsequently ordained as a Baptist minister. After some parish experience, he completed a PhD at Boston University in 1949, having already accepted in 1947 an appointment to the faculty of the newly founded Fuller Theological Seminary in Pasadena, California.

The academic setting for Henry whetted his appetite for scholarly work, and with his strong journalistic skills, he completed nine books during his career of nine years at Fuller Seminary. In 1956, he became the first editor of the newly created evangelical fortnightly journal, *Christianity Today*, where he served until 1968. Through his leadership, the journal, devoted to scholarly articulation of evangelical theology, grew to a circulation of more than 160,000. Leaving the journal after twelve years of service, he became 'professor at large' at Eastern Baptist theological seminary, and began a career of teaching, writing, and speaking on some of the United States's most prestigious campuses and in countries on every continent. He has written twenty-seven books (some translated into Korean, Norwegian, German, and Spanish), and has contributed numerous articles to a variety of publications. His most ambitious project in systematic theology was the publication of a six-volume work titled *God, Revelation and Authority* (1976–83). His most recent book is the story of his own life, *Confessions of a Theologian – An Autobiography* (1986).

The theological career of Carl Henry must be placed within the context of the collision between theological fundamentalism and liberalism during the early part of this century, and particularly in its second quarter. In reaction to the inroads of what some perceived to be a liberal influence in theological schools and church mission endeavors, a series of pamphlets was published between 1910 and 1915 called *The Fundamentals: A Testament to the Truth*. The word 'fundamentalism' became a pejorative term in the minds of many, suggesting an obscurantist and separatist mentality which split off the more militant defenders of orthodoxy, both culturally and theologically, from those who wished to work as evangelicals within the mainstream Protestant church in North America.

In the early 1940s a remarkable phenomenon occurred. A group of young scholars, many of whom were graduates of Wheaton or Gordon College, began to distinguish themselves from the separatist mentality of the fundamentalists and sought to prepare themselves to recover the vitality of evangelical theology within the mainline church. Carl Henry, along with many others, during this period pursued doctoral studies at prestigious universities for the express purpose of giving theological and scholarly credibility to the movement. Such men as Edward John Carnell, George E. Ladd, Kenneth Kantzer, and Merrill Tenney, to mention but a few, should be noted. Of these, perhaps Carnell held the greatest promise as a shaper of the new evangelical theology through his brilliant early works on philosophy of the Christian religion and Christian apologetics. His most significant book, in the minds of many, was his critical, but largely misunderstood, study of epistemology, *Christian Commitment* (1957). In this book he sought to bring faith as a structure of knowing and love as a criterion for truth into the epistemological task. His premature death while a professor at Fuller Seminary in the late 1960s cut short his academic and scholarly career. Even so, he left an indelible mark on the lives of many students, and, with unerring instinct, forged a pathway for others to follow in steering conservative theology away from the backwaters of fundamentalism into the fresh and turbulent waters of evangelical theology.

Under the stimulus of Harold J. Okenga, pastor of historic Park Street Church in Boston, this movement began to assume national attention. Okenga became the first president of the National Association of Evangelicals in 1942 and, in 1947, the first president of Fuller Theological Seminary, an institution founded to provide the evangelical movement with first rate scholarship and theological integrity for the training of pastors, missionaries, and evangelists.

Through his gifts of scholarship, an insightful theological mind, and his ability to articulate the new agenda for these evangelical leaders, Henry soon rose to the forefront of the movement. Positively, Henry and the 'new evangelicals' sought to affirm traditional evangelical theology (Protestant orthodoxy linked with American revivalism) and negatively to reject fundamentalism with its provincial, separatist, and often obscurantist approach to biblical and theological scholarship. Years later, looking back on the origins of this movement, Henry would write:

What distressed the growing evangelical mainstream about the fundamentalist far right were its personal legalisms, a suspicion of advanced education, disdain for biblical criticism per se, polemical orientation of theological discussion, judgmental attitudes toward those in ecumenically related denominations, and an uncritical political conservatism often defined as 'Christian anticommunism' and 'Christian capitalism' that, while politicizing the gospel on the right, deplored politicizing it on the left.[5]

In a way that was typical of Henry's theological insight and critical analysis, his book published in 1947, *The Uneasy Conscience of Modern Fundamentalism*, set the agenda for the new evangelical theology. Here he called for a renewed concern for social issues, serious interaction with science and culture, and above all, a renewed commitment to biblical theism as the basis for an apologetic which focused on the theological essentials on which evangelicals could unite, not on secondary issues on which they tended to divide.

The distinctive motif of Carl Henry's approach to evangelical theology is clearly seen in what he calls 'evangelical theism'.

The strength of evangelical theism lies in its offer of religious realities that human unregeneracy desperately needs and cannot otherwise provide. In a time of spiritual rootlessness Christianity proclaims God the self-revealed heavenly Redeemer. In a time of intellectual skepticism, it adduces fixed truths about God's holy purpose for man and the world. In a time of ethical permissiveness, it offers moral absolutes and specific divine imperatives. In a time of frightful fear of the future, it presents a sure and final hope. In a time when daily life has turned bitter and sour for multitudes of humans, it offers life-transforming dynamic.[6]

This concept of biblical, or evangelical theism, constitutes the formative basis for Henry's most substantial work, *God, Revelation and Authority*. Far from being a comprehensive systematic theology, with equal treatment of the basic loci of theology, this work is based on two major theological themes – the nature of revelation as truth, and the nature of God as the foundation for theological reflection upon creation, human life, and ethics. With his strong commitment to philosophical and analytical method, Henry is basically an apologist, not a biblical scholar. His analysis of the contemporary situation is that the 'modern mind' has succumbed to relativism with a loss of absolutes in moral values and of certainty with regard to truth. Christian faith must be rationally defensible in terms of the criteria by which all truth is verified. Otherwise, Henry argues, claims for faith fall back on the slippery slope of existential and subjective experience, with no basis for certainty. Strongly dependent upon his chief intellectual mentor, Gordon Clark, philosopher and theologian, Henry sees the theological task as one of defining and defending faith in terms of truth rather than in personal relationship to God. Influenced also by Edgar Brightman, a personalist philosopher with whom he did doctoral studies at Boston University, Henry argues that faith has its own ontology which is grounded in the objective reality of personal being open to but also critically interacting with nonrevelational worldviews.

Henry is basically a presuppositionalist with regard to the foundations of theology. Philosophically, his presupposition is the Aristotelian principle of the law of noncontradiction. Both Christians and non-Christians use logic as a test for truth. Theologically, his presupposition is the principle of biblical theism. 'From a certain vantage point, the concept of God is determinative for all other concepts; it is the Archimedean lever with which one can fashion an entire worldview.'[7] The basis for biblical theism is the assumption that God has revealed the truths which determine all rational knowledge and make it certain. 'Divine revelation is the source of all truth, the truth of Christianity included; reason is the instrument for recognizing it; Scripture is its verifying principle; logical consistency is a negative test for truth and coherence a subordinate test. The task of Christian theology is to exhibit the content of biblical revelation as an orderly whole.'[8]

The structure of Henry's six-volume work is thus organized around two fundamental principles. First, revelation is the ground and authority for faith, and second, the existence and being of God is the answer to the contemporary concern for stability and certainty as the ground for faith and hope. Volume I consists of preliminary considerations, setting forth the basic assumptions for true knowledge of God. Volumes II, III, and IV deal broadly with the subject of revelation and religious epistemology under the heading, *God Who Speaks and Shows*. Volumes V and VI set forth a Christian doctrine of God under the heading, *God Who Stands and Stays*. In each of the volumes, Henry deals with a broad range of contemporary theologians and issues, critically examining each by the epistemological and theological criteria which he has established.

For Henry, the question of authority is the key issue for evangelical theology. Authority must be grounded in absolute certainty. The means of knowing this certainty must be logically verifiable and rationally accessible to every person, otherwise, the commitment of faith which constitutes a saving relation to God will be liable to doubt and question. Divine revelation is given to us in Holy Scripture in propositional form. This means that the truth which grounds Christian belief in certainty must be univocally related to the human mind, not merely analogical or certainly not equivocal. The finite and the infinite are comprehended in one and the same logicality, Henry has stated.[9]

God is the proper subject of a Christian theology, Henry argues, and from this axis flow all discussions of soteriology and eschatology, as well as social ethics. Christ is the means by which God has provided for salvation through his atonement. The Holy Spirit is the means by which God continues to regenerate and renew individuals on the basis of the revelation given in the Bible and communicated to us in propositions which can stand the test for truth. Human logic and reason has been created as a basis for knowing and testing the truth of divine revelation. Henry's theology is evangelical not only in that it attempts to restate the tenets of orthodoxy as an apologetic, but in that it seeks the conversion of the individual through a personal relationship with Jesus Christ. At the heart of his theology is the passion of his own conversion experience, and the aim of his theology is to authenticate Christian conversion and the Christian life as a viable and intellectually credible alternative to modern secularism and humanism with its inevitable existential despair.

## DEBATE

The differences between the three evangelical theologians presented above are quite obvious, despite their common commitment to the tenets of Protestant orthodoxy, their appeal to biblical authority as a source of divine revelation, and their concern for a personal experience of salvation through Jesus Christ. Berkouwer would sharply disagree with Henry's insistence that human reason can grasp and even validate divine revelation apart from the work of the Holy Spirit and the presence of faith. Thielicke has already, in principle, placed Henry's 'rational theism' in the category of Cartesian theology with its claim that the human mind is on the same continuum as the Logos of God. For his part, Henry is suspicious of the 'correlation' between revelation and faith which Berkouwer espouses, fearing that it undermines the objective reality of revelation itself as a cognitive construct. Thielicke, as well, comes under the critical eye of Henry as compromising the authority of

Scripture in favor of a 'spiritual hermeneutic' which shifts the criterion for truth from revelation to faith itself.

At the same time, Bernard Ramm, perhaps the most significant American evangelical theologian alongside of Henry, and a colleague in the development of the new evangelical front in the United States, faults Henry for failing to provide a paradigm of evangelical theology which does not 'gloss over' the critical perspectives gained through the Enlightenment. He rates Berkouwer and Thielicke as offering better options for evangelical theology in its interaction with the Enlightenment.[10]

Some conservative Lutheran theologians, however, wonder if Thielicke has not 'abandoned the orthodox theology of the ancient church as well as of the Reformation'. They are concerned that he has taken a psychological approach to christology, and also to his hermeneutic which, they argue, is closer to Schleiermacher than to Luther. In the end, these critics say, his personalistic approach abandons the objective reality of God as an object of faith, and makes faith itself more of a feeling than a fact.[11] From this perspective, some would not call Thielicke an evangelical theologian. It is true that Thielicke regards the classic creedal formulations (such as Chalcedon) as too abstract and impersonal to 'capture' the person of Christ himself. Yet, it is clearly the reality and the person of Christ of whom these formulations speak that Thielicke holds to be the criterion of faith. What makes faith evangelical, says Thielicke, is not faith as an object of reason, but Christ as the Lord of reason, bringing it into captivity to his own true order of reality.

The lines of the debate within evangelical theology, as might be expected, are more sharply drawn between American evangelical theologians. We have already mentioned Bernard Ramm as one who now has called for a new paradigm for evangelical theology, and suggests that the theological approach of Karl Barth, or even Berkouwer or Thielicke, will serve better than that of Carl Henry. Harold Lindsell, a former colleague of Carl Henry at Fuller Seminary, and the editor of the journal *Christianity Today* following Carl Henry, is charged by Ramm with providing a polemical rallying point for fundamentalists and evangelicals with his book on biblical inerrancy (*The Battle for the Bible*, 1976).[12] Ramm's own view is that evangelical theology must be grounded on a solid biblical theology rather than biblical theism. He is concerned that evangelical theology, if it follows the lead of Carl Henry, will fail precisely at the point where he wishes it to make its mark – that is, its rational system of apologetics will appeal only to those who accept the philosophical epistemology on which it is built. If this is true, as many critics of

Henry feel it is, then orthodox doctrine rather than a vital and compelling experience of God himself will become the bastion of evangelical theology's defense, and a further retreat from creative encounter with contemporary society.

Donald Bloesch, who has himself made a significant contribution to the literature of contemporary evangelical theology, echoes these concerns. 'The method of Gordon Clark and Carl Henry is deductive, deriving conclusions from given rational principles' writes Bloesch. Revelation remains mysterious even in its openness to us through the living Word of God. 'We *intend* the truth in our theological statements, but we do not *possess* the truth, since reason is always the servant and never the master or determiner of revelation.'[13]

To the credit of Carl Henry, in surveying the evangelical scene from the perspective of more than forty years of involvement as one of its key leaders, he pleads for a new spirit of openness and unity among evangelical theologians: 'just when the world-press publicly conceded "the year of the evangelical",' Henry wrote, the evangelical dialogue became focused on 'epistemological differences that depicted evangelicals as openly at odds with each other'.

> An opportunity existed of rallying the whole evangelical enterprise to socio-cultural engagement in which even a crippled soldier might somehow serve the cause of faith. Instead, exulting in their evident public gains, evangelicals indulged in the luxury of internal conflict and channeled theological energies into the controversy over biblical inerrancy. . . . While scriptural authority must be part of any authentic evangelical renewal, evangelicals will affirm it to their own reproof apart from the cry, 'Let my heart be broken' and filled with the truth and grace of God.[14]

## ACHIEVEMENT AND AGENDA

The achievements of evangelical theology are modest when viewed from the perspective of academic theology. The work of Berkouwer will certainly survive and be read by future generations of students as part of the Dutch Neo-Calvinist tradition begun so ably as Kuyper and Bavinck. Despite a certain provincialism in Berkouwer's interaction with other theologians and movements, his work has provided and will continue to provide a substantial resource for theological students and pastors who especially appreciate the distinctives of the Reformed tradition. Thielicke will perhaps be read more for his profound contribution to ethics than for his systematic theology. His wide-ranging and penetrating commentary on contemporary issues provides a refreshing challenge to be contemporary in both theological preaching and practical theology. Henry's work will more than likely be viewed as a mandatory research assignment for anyone wishing to evaluate the finest attempt by twentieth-century evangelicalism to argue its case before the bar of modern reason. It will less likely to be found on the pastor's study shelf and even less satisfactory as a programmatic exercize on which future evangelical theologians can build.

From the perspective of the evangelical movement as whole, however, evangelical theology has made significant achievements. Not least of these has been its success in breaking free from the theological tragedy of fundamentalism without capitulating to the theological fads of post-liberal radicalism. The heavy investment, often at great cost, personally and financially, in establishing first rate evangelical schools, is already beginning to pay rich dividends. The major main-line Protestant denominations are beginning to experience spiritual and theological reinvigoration through a flood of pastors and leaders trained under the influence of these evangelical faculties. Theologians with evangelical commitments as defined above are finding their way into university faculties and denominational schools, where they are creating a new dialogue between the Scripture as a relevant and revealed Word of God and the contemporary issues and needs of modern society.

If these contributions are to be conserved and expanded, however, issues currently on the agenda of evangelical theology need to be addressed and contructively resolved. The issue of biblical authority and the nature of biblical revelation, particularly with regard to the relation of the text of Scripture to the Word of God, cannot be avoided. There yet remain to be established the grounds for a theological consensus among evangelical theologians on this vital issue.

Evangelical theology has not yet answered effectively the challenge from the larger theological community, not to mention society at large, that it is more concerned for the spiritual and intellectual aspects of salvation than for the social and physical needs of people. With evangelization of the world and the intended conversion of every person to Jesus Christ as a fundamental imperative, evangelical theology has yet to articulate a theology of mission and evangelism which does not tend to be culturally and ethnically imperialistic. The 'particularism' of Jesus Christ as the driving force for evangelical mission to the world has not yet dealt with the theological pluralism which pervades the contemporary Christian culture. In the face of rising challenges to this christological particularism inherent in the theological paradigm of evangelicalism, theologians have yet to restate the case for conversion to Christ in compelling and convincing terms.

Where liberation is the code word as well as the creative force behind much of the most vigorous and exciting theology coming out of the 'two-thirds world', evangelical theology has tended to retreat from a praxis-oriented theology into a theory-laden defense of orthodoxy. Contextualization is largely an unknown and basically untried theological method for evangelical theologians. The viability of evangelical theology rests with its willingness to venture into the future, rather than to reside in the present and to take comfort from the past. In a generation, there will be new names in the books written about evangelical theologians. That is as it should be, for evangelical theology is a living and creative continuum, leaving behind its theologians, with gratitude and respect.

## NOTES

1 George Marsden, 'The Evangelical Denomination', in *Evangelicalism and Modern America*, ed. George Marsden (Grand Rapids, Mich., 1984), pp. ix ff. For other attempts to define evangelicalism as a contemporary phenomenon, see: George Marsden, *Reforming Fundamentalism – Fuller Seminary and the New Evangelicalism* (Grand Rapids, Mich., 1987), James Davison Hunter, *American Evangelicalism* (New Brunswick, NJ, 1983); George Marsden, *Fundamentalism and American Culture – The Shaping of Twentieth-Century Evangelicalism: 1870–1925* (New York and Oxford, 1980); John D. Woodbridge, Mark A. Noll, and Nathan O. Hatch (eds), *The Gospel in America: Themes in the Story of America's Evangelicals* (Grand Rapids, Mich., 1979); Robert E. Webber, *Common Roots – A Call to Evangelical Maturity* (Grand Rapids, Mich., 1978), pp. 25–35; Kenneth S. Kantzer (ed.), *Evangelical Roots* (New York, 1978); David F. Wells and John D. Woodbridge (eds), *The Evangelicals – What They Believe, Who They Are, Where They Are Changing* (New York and Nashville, Tenn., 1975); Richard Quebedeaux, *The Young Evangelicals* (New York and London, 1974); Bernard L. Ramm, *The Evangelical Heritage* (Waco, Texas, 1973), pp. 11–22; Donald G. Bloesch, *The Evangelical Renaissance* (Grand Rapids, Mich., 1973); Ronald H. Nash, *The New Evangelicalism* (Grand Rapids, Mich., 1963).
2 G. C. Berkouwer, *A Half Century of Theology*, p. 11.
3 G. C. Berkouwer, *Faith and Justification*, (Grand Rapids, Mich., 1954), p. 178.

4  G. C. Berkouwer, 'Review of Current Religious Thought', in *Christianity Today*, December 22, 1961, p. 39.
5  Carl F. H. Henry, *Evangelicals in Search of Identity*, pp. 30–1.
6  Carl Henry, *Confessions of a Theologian*, p. 389.
7  Carl Henry, *Remaking the Modern Mind* (Grand Rapids, Mich., 1946), pp. 232, 171.
8  Carl Henry, *God, Revelation and Authority*, vol. I, p. 215.
9  Carl Henry, *God, Revelation and Authority*, vol. III, pp. 221–2.
10  Bernard Ramm, *After Fundamentalism – The Future of Evangelical Theology* (San Francisco, 1983), pp. 26–7. Other books by Ramm include: *Offense to Reason: A Theology of Sin* (San Francisco, 1985); *An Evangelical Christology: Ecumenic and Historic* (Nashville, Tenn., 1985); *The Evangelical Heritage* (Waco, Texas, 1973).
11  As an example of such criticism, see, Richard Klann, 'Helmut Thielicke Appraised – A Review Essay', in *The Concordia Journal*, 6 (July 1980), pp. 155–63.
12  Ramm, *After Fundamentalism*, p. 45.
13  Donald Bloesch, *Essentials of Evangelical Theology*, vol. II (San Francisco, 1979), p. 268. In addition to his two-volume *Essentials of Evangelical Theology*, other publications by Bloesch include, *Freedom for Obedience: Evangelical Ethics for Contemporary Times* (San Francisco, 1987); *The Future of Evangelical Christianity: A Call for Unity amid Diversity* (Garden City, NY, 1983).
14  Carl Henry, *Confessions of a Theologian*, p. 389.

## BIBLIOGRAPHY

### Primary

Berkouwer, G. C., *Studies in Dogmatics*, 14 vols (Grand Rapids, Mich., 1952/ 1976).
—, *Modern Uncertainty and Christian Faith* (Grand Rapids, Mich., 1953).
—, *The Triumph of Grace in the Theology of Karl Barth* (Grand Rapids, Mich., 1965).
—, *A Half Century of Theology* (Grand Rapids, Mich., 1977).
Henry, Carl F. H., *Christian Personal Ethics* (Grand Rapids, Mich., 1957).
—, *Evangelicals at the Brink of Crisis: Significance of the World Congress on Evangelism* (Waco, Texas, 1967).
—, *Evangelicals in Search of Identity* (Waco, Texas, 1976).
—, *God, Revelation and Authority*, 6 vols (Waco, Texas, 1976–1983).
—, *The Christian Mindset in a Secular Society: Promoting Evangelical Renewal and National Righteousness* (Portland, Oreg., 1984).
—, *Confessions of a Theologian: An Autobiography* (Waco, Texas, 1986).
Thielicke, Helmut, *Nihilism, its Origin and Nature, with a Christian Answer* (New York, 1961).

—, *The Freedom of the Christian Man: A Christian Confrontation with the Secular Gods* (New York, 1963).

—, *Theological Ethics*, 3 vols (an abridgment and translation of *Theologische Ethik*) ed. William H. Lazareth (Philadelphia, 1966).

—, *The Evangelical Faith*, 3 vols (Grand Rapids, Mich., 1974–1977).

—, *Living with Death* (Grand Rapids, Mich., 1983).

—, *Being Human – Becoming Human: An Essay in Christian Anthropology* (New York, 1984).

## Secondary

Baker, Alvin, *Berkouwer's Doctrine of Election* (Phillipsburg, NJ, 1964).

Bromiley, Geoffrey, 'Helmut Thielicke', in *A Handbook of Christian Theologians*, enlarged edn, ed. Dean G. Peerman and Martin E. Marty (Nashville, Tenn., 1984).

De Moore, J. C., *Towards a Biblically Theo-Logical Method – A Structural Analysis and a Further Elaboration of Dr. C. G. Berkouwer's Hermeneutic-Dogmatic Method* (Kampen, Holland, 1980).

Fackre, Gabriel, 'Carl F. H. Henry', in *A Handbook of Christian Theologians*, enlarged edn, ed. Dean G. Peerman and Martin E. Marty (Nashville, Tenn., 1984).

Higginson, Richard, 'Thielicke: Preacher and Theologian', in *The Churchman*, 90, (July/September 1976), pp. 178–92.

Klann, Richard, 'Helmut Thielicke Appraised – A Review Essay', in *The Concordia Journal*, 6 (July 1980), pp. 155–63.

Patterson, Bob E., *Makers of the Modern Theological Mind – Carl F. H. Henry* (Waco, Texas, 1983).

Rogers, Jack B., 'A Third Alternative: Scripture, Tradition and Interpretation in the Theology of G. C. Berkouwer', in *Scripture Tradition and Interpretation*, eds Ward Gasque and William LaSor (Grand Rapids, Mich., 1978), pp. 70–91.

Smedes, Lewis B., 'G. C. Berkouwer', in *Creative Minds in Contemporary Theology*, 2nd edn, ed. Philip Edgcumbe Hughes (Grand Rapids, Mich., 1969), pp. 63–98.

Timmer, John, 'G. C. Berkouwer, Theologian of Confrontation and Correlation', in *Reformed Journal*, 19 (1969), pp. 17–22.

# 8

# Eastern Orthodox Theology

## Rowan Williams

### INTRODUCTION: BACKGROUND

For most of the twentieth century, the story of Orthodox theology is the story of Russian theology, both in Russia itself before 1917 and in the emigration afterwards (especially in Paris). The exceptional vitality of Russian intellectual life in the later nineteenth century was without parallel in any other historically Orthodox society – partly for the simple reason that no other such society had enjoyed real cultural independence for centuries. Even when Greece finally emerged as a nation after throwing off the Ottoman yoke, it was to be many years before it could begin to boast an intellectual ethos of its own. But Russia, accustomed to be the standard-bearer of the Orthodox world, was the setting for the first serious encounters between traditional Eastern theology and Enlightenment and post-Enlightenment thought; and it is as if three centuries of development in Western Christian thinking had to be telescoped in Russia into a few decades. If Russian religious thought appears at times bizarre, naive and extravagant to Western eyes, we should remember that it is a response to an unprecedented intensity of new impressions, social and intellectual stimuli crowding in over a relatively brief period.

One crucial factor in understanding modern Russian religious thought is the role of Hegel and, even more, of Schelling in the formation of systems. Hegel's work became known in Russia first by way of the theological schools of the Ukraine; it has been very plausibly suggested that Hegel's interest in the late Neopolatonism of Proclus resonated with a theology that accorded great authorty to the Pseudo-Dionysius's writings, also deeply marked by the influence of Proclus. But two other factors should be borne in mind as well. German idealism arrived in Russia in close connection with

German mysticism – both the Catholic mysticism of the mediaeval and post-mediaeval Rhineland and the quasi-hermetic Protestantism of Jakob Böhme. In the early decades of the nineteenth century, the new philosophical ideas coming from Germany appeared as simply another form of the new images of religious interiority offered by German hermetism and eclectic pietism. In other words, idealism was, from the first, received in Russia as a religious philosophy, which, though ambivalent from the point of view of Orthodoxy, might yet be put to work for the traditional faith. The combination of Böhme with Schelling and Hegel seemed to open the way towards a metaphysic of the world as organism, a participatory and intuitive account of knowledge and a certain relativization of the ideas of an automomous and finite ego. It is fair to say that one problem that has *not* beset Russian religious thought is an excess of dualism.

In addition to this, however, it may be that Russian history itself helped to make Hegel attractive. It had been a history of violent alternations – from the Byzantine and European civilization of the Kievan period to the increasing cultural isolation of the Mongol and Muscovite centuries to the Francophile and Francophone culture of the governing class in the eighteenth century; and the war against Napoleon had involved a deep emotional retrieval of the Muscovite ideal of 'Holy Russia'. Culturally and politically, Russia was eager to find an identity that would resolve the contradictory heritage of the past and heal the injuries caused by the massive disruptions of that history. Thus much of Russia's intellectual history up to 1917 (and since) has to do with the variety of conflicting 'bids' to define the nation. Was its destiny to resolve its tensions by joining the history of the European 'mainstream', or was there a quite different kind of polity and politics to which it could witness? Nehru or Gandhi? One of the most striking things about revolutionary Marxism in Russia is that it succeeded in blending these two opposing impulses. But for a society with this kind of agenda in the early decades of the nineteenth century, the appeal of a historically-oriented metaphysic is obvious. Hegel confirmed the characteristic Russian tendency to fuse together the religious, the philosophical and the political, and the whole of the enterprise of Russian religious philosophy reflects this fusion.

There were those, however, who, accepting this program, still believed that Hegel was to be left behind. Ivan Vasilievich Kireevsky (1806–56) published, in the year of his death, an essay on 'The Need for New Foundations in Philosophy', which argued that Hegel represented the decisive end of one particular style of philosophy, that originating with Bacon and Descartes – i.e. a philosophy whose fundamental problematic was 'What is it to *think*?', and which dealt with this in terms of analysing the processes of observation and argumentation. Kireevsky turned instead to the alternative tradition represented by Pascal (and was also impressed by Schleiermacher), and to the anthropology of the Eastern fathers, especially the monastic writers, searching for a perspective neither intellectualist nor voluntarist, for a doctrine of the formation of historical persons in action and relation, an integral view of the human. Reasoning, in such a perspective, is concrete and committed, not ahistorical, and we are delivered from the absolute dominance of a 'tragic' vision of the relation between spirit and nature. Kireevsky's literary remains are fragmentary and slight, but the reader will catch startling glimpses of something like Kierkegaard as well as something like Heidegger, hermeneutics set against a logos-metaphysic.

Vladimir Sergeevich Soloviev (1853–1900) represents most dramatically the opposite approach, a passion for metaphysical construction and systematization. His importance is chiefly in his elaboration of a quasi-mythological cosmology centered upon the figure of 'Sophia', the divine Wisdom, the Eternal Feminine. For Soloviev, the Absolute exists both as being and as becoming, as a transcendent unity and as the totality of modes in which that unity can express itself and relate to itself; and this latter form of the Absolute, in so far as it always preserves a movement towards unity, is an organic whole. This is 'Sophia' – fragmented in the empirical universe, but still at one in God. In this perspective, the incarnation of the divine Word is the central act of *reintegration* in the cosmos; in the Church, in which the fruits of the incarnation are realized, human personality is united to the cosmic whole (*vseedinstvo*, 'total unity'), and delivered from its finite limitations, its alienation from matter and from other subjects. The Orthodox Church does not operate by external and legalistic systems of authority, as does the Roman communion, nor does it countenance the individualism of the Protestant; it is therefore uniquely qualified to be the bearer of the promise of 'sophianic' humanity, of *bogochelovechestvo*, 'divine humanity' (or 'Godmanhood', as it is often rendered). In Orthodox societies, the aim should be a 'free theocracy', not legally imposed but organically evolving, which will draw other nations into a universal Christian communion, both church and state.

Soloviev develops some of the ideas of the earlier writer Alexei Stepanovich Khomyakov (1804–60), especially in the use of organic models for the church and in the elaboration of the concept of *sobornost*, the Russian word for 'catholicity', as a special designation for the supra-individual consciousness of the (Orthodox, especially

Slavic) Church. But the vision of Sophia is new, as is the passionate insistence on a universal perspective. Soloviev is without doubt the single most influential Russian religious writer of the age (his impact upon Dostoevsky is clear), and nearly all major Orthodox thinkers up to the Revolution are in one way or another in dialogue with him. However, his system gives very sharp focus to the problems hinted at by Kireevsky: what is the role of history in this, real, *contingent* history? And what can be said about individual identity and liberty in so comprehensive and near-deterministic a scheme? Soloviev's last works include a strange piece of apocalyptic fiction ('A Story of Antichrist') suggesting that he recognized the presence of irresoluble tensions in his metaphysics, and the possibility of tragic revolt and discontinuity. His legacy proved to be as controversial and many-sided as that of Origen; much of the work of his admirers is an attempt to restate a 'sophiology' without the elements of pantheism and determinism that pervade a great deal of his writing.

The history of Russian theology in the twentieth century is largely one of debate between those who have, broadly speaking, felt comfortable with the legacy of Soloviev and those who have repudiated it in favour of a more consciously traditional and Church-focused style, seeking to derive general principles for a theological anthropology from the interpretation of the Fathers of the early centuries. Generally, the rejection of Soloviev has been accompanied by a suspicion of Khomyakov's theology as well. The appeal to a distinctive kind of corporate consciousness in the church, analogous to that typical of premodern, especially Slavic, societies has been seen as a naturalistic reduction of the supernatural reality of communion in the Holy Spirit. Twentieth-century Russian theology is thus, in its most creative period (c. 1925–55) deeply marked by polemic. The rejection of Soloviev and others by a younger generation has some parallels with the rejection of liberal Protestant conventions by the new theologies of the Word in Germany. In both, there is an attempt to shed the legacy of idealism in philosophy, and to break free from what was seen as a psychologizing or moralizing or 'naturalizing' of faith, so as to recover a sense of the givenness, the historical and punctiliar character, of a revelation that reconstructs the whole of human knowing and relating. What is different of course is the persistent Orthodox attempt to pursue a theology of the historical *mediation* of revelation, a theology of tradition. For many students of the field, this remains one of the most abidingly interesting and fruitful contributions of the Orthodox vision in contemporary theological discussion.

In what follows, three theologians, Bulgakov, Lossky, and Florovsky, will be discussed in some detail, before surveying and assessing the wider field of Orthodox theology today.

## THREE ORTHODOX THEOLOGIANS

### S. N. Bulgakov

Foremost among those who sought to rework Soloviev's themes in more acceptable form was Sergei Nikolaevich Bulgakov (1871–1944). Alienated from the Orthodox Church as a student, he had become a Marxist teacher of economics, with a considerable international reputation, before drifting away from dialectical materialism, first towards a Kantian moralism, then towards Hegel. He finally made his peace with the church in the early years of this century, and was ordained a priest in 1917; after expulsion from Russia in 1923, he spent most of his remaining years in Paris, as Dean of the newly-formed Institut Saint-Serge, a seminary for *émigré* Russians – and also as a deeply-loved pastor and director of souls. He was a prolific writer, whose dense and florid style conceals a surprising conceptual boldness which sets him apart from most of his fellow-Orthodox theologians, and occasioned a minor ecclesiastical *cause célèbre* in the Russian emigration when, in 1935, he was denounced to the Patriarchate of Moscow as a heretic, and his theology was condemned by the Patriarchal *locum tenens*, Metropolitan Sergii. He was, however, supported by his own ecclesiastical superiors (whose relations with Moscow at this time were hostile anyway). His work attracted some interest outside the Orthodox world partly because he had become a well-known figure in the ecumenical movement, but a great deal of his writing remains available in Russian only.

Bulgakov's rejection of Marxism had a great deal to do with a theme that he explores in several essays between 1903 and 1911 – the inadequacy of *homo economicus* as a basis for social and political ethics. An account of human needs in terms of economically-determinable factors leads – paradoxically – to an alienation from the historical and the material, since it seeks a way out of *personal* struggle and growth, out of the risks of creativity. It sets up a mechanical opposition of economic interests, to be settled either by the logic of history (Marxism) or by the laws of the market (capitalism); but both resolutions sidestep the specifically human task of transfiguring the material world in and through the creation of community. Artistic and economic activity are equally indispensable in this – art as the gratuitous expression of an 'eschatological' change in things, matter charged with meaning, economics as the functional harnessing of the world to human need. Either of these in isolation is destructive.

It is Bulgakov's interest in the *work* of humanizing the world that sets him apart from Soloviev, as well as from pure Hegelianism (he remarked once that no one who had ever taken Marxism seriously could accept abstract or passivist versions of idealist dialectic). Hence his assimilation of the Sophia myth represents a considerable qualification of Soloviev's version (and in this he was much influenced by the work of his spiritual mentor, Fr Pavel Florensky, a brilliant and eccentric polymath who finally disappeared in the Gulag), and is continually being revised and refined throughout the whole of Bulgakov's work. Sophia *is* the divine nature, God's own life considered under the aspect of God's freedom to live the divine life in what is not God. God as Trinity is an eternal movement of 'giving-away', displacement, so that God's very Godhead presupposes the possibility of there being an object of love and gift beyond itself. Bulgakov is careful to clarify (especially between 1917 and 1925) the point that Sophia is not an 'hypostasis' (correcting both Florensky and his own earlier work), and to purge out any residual pantheism: divine Sophia is not an objectified World-Soul, but the impulse in things towards harmony and order, towards complex unity of organization. Bulgakov speaks of this impulse as the world's 'eros'; and such language should remind us that Bulgakov's sophiology is far more a sustained metaphor than a theory.

Bulgakov rejects a matter–spirit dualism; but the nature-hypostasis dualism with which he often works introduces some of the dangers he wishes to avoid. When he says that the hypostasis of a human subject, the uncategorizable core of personal identity, is 'uncreated' or 'absolute', his concern is chiefly to deny that personal identity is an observable determinate *thing*; but the language is redolent of the Germanic hermetism which Bulgakov found both intensely attractive and theologically unsatisfactory. He constantly seems to be implying that there is in human psychology a level or dimension of direct *natural* participation in God – a view which Orthodox theological tradition has normally regarded with hostility. Thus his account of human liberty oscillates between an impressive seriousness about freedom as constituted in historical relation and creativity, and a more monistic notion of a universal divine *Urgrund* of liberty, the image of God residing in a mysterious hinterland of transcendence common to all personal beings.

However, when he addresses the question of the divine image in his later and explicitly theological work, it is more often the *active* role of the human subject that is to the fore. Human being is the agent of meaning in the universe; when distorted self-love breaks the 'sophianic' whole into mutually excluding fragments, the redemptive work of God as Word and Spirit is to enable us to be once again capable of revealing the wholeness of things, in work, art, and sacrament. This cannot be simply a matter of injunctions to be obeyed, programs to be followed: redemption actually effects a change in spiritual self-awareness, so that we know we can exist as selves *only* in communion with other selves. Here the nineteenth-century theme of 'catholic' consciousness, *sobornost'*, reappears: the church, Bulgakov was fond of saying, is the fact of human 'consubstantiality', not merely a society; it is 'Sophia in the process of becoming'. The language used about the church as ideal form of creation can, however, mislead. Bulgakov is quite clear that the empirical church is flawed, its work incomplete, its decisions provisional and risky, its existing limits 'pragmatic not absolute' – which explains why he has little on the theology of ministerial or hierarchical authority, and was an enthusiastic advocate of inter-communion in certain circumstances. The church is essentially the fellowship of the Spirit, held together by the ontological bond of God's love as figured in the eucharist; the rest is a matter of conditioned historical decisions and policies.

Not surprisingly, perhaps, he is critical of certain kinds of christocentrism in ecclesiology. If the identity of the church is made to reside solely in its relation to Christ rather than in the quality of its consubstantial and catholic life in the Spirit, the church will tend to look for Christ-substitutes – an infallible Pope, an inerrant Bible – or to encourage people to concentrate on an *individual* relation to the Savior. But the work of the Trinity is fundamentally characterized by *kenosis*, a central theme in all Bulgakov's work, but especially in the theological writings of the 1920s and 1930s: Christ therefore acts in the church not as an omnipresent individual, focusing attention on himself, but through the Spirit's formation of the new consciousness – which in turn works 'kenotically', directing us to the Father and working always with and never against created freedom. Thus Bulgakov's suspicion of christocentrism does not mean that christo-logy does not have a central and normative place: here, in the life and death of Jesus, the kenotic pattern is spelled out. The divine self of the Word, unchanged as such, is the subject for which the human self of Jesus now becomes an object: the Word is the 'I', the consciousness, for which the humanity of Jesus is the 'me', the material of self-consciousness. This is a complex idea, which

Bulgakov fails to work out in full detail, but which shows signs of rather more conceptual sophistication than some forms of English kenoticism. Here his doctrine of the 'uncreated' hypostasis in all human beings serves him well: he can identify the ultimate subjectivity of Christ with the Word of God while avoiding downright Apollinarianism. But this whole area of his thinking is abstruse and unclear. His main concern in christology, however, is to show how Christ is the place where uncreated and created Sophia are united: the divine life of unconditional self-forgetting generates a created, historical life of the same quality, in which the mutual isolation and refusal of fallen creation is overcome. The incarnate Word as incarnate selflessness is open to *universal* relation, universal accessibility: as that relation becomes ours in the Spirit, our isolation is ended, and the *sobornost'* of the new creation is established.

Bulgakov's achievement is remarkable. His work is sprawling, repetitive, unsystematic, and often appallingly obscure, but it is a rare attempt at a unified theological metaphysic. Many of his insights on the nature of the church became the common currency of the ecumenical movement, and were specially influential for Anglican writers of a certain generation. But other aspects of his work have remained almost unknown. He is one of the first theologians to use and develop the term 'panentheism', to distinguish his doctrine of the world's ideality in God from pantheism; he is clearly fascinated by feminine imagery for the Godhead, although he works with an uncritical male/active, female/passive-or-receptive disjunction; he is certainly the only theologian of the century to use kenosis as a pivotal and normative concept for *all* language about God, in creation as in redemption; and in this as in other ways, his use of Jewish Cabbalistic imagery (the myth of *zimzum*, God's self-withdrawal in the creative act) is deeply suggestive. He has yet to be taken fully seriously by Western theology, and yet, of all the major Orthodox thinkers of the century, he is probably the one most consciously and extensively engaged with post-Enlightenment thought (and Western biblical scholarship). Among non-Orthodox writers, it is probably Hans Urs von Balthasar who stands closest to him – in the themes touched upon, but also in densely metaphorical idiom.

## V. N. Lossky

The fierce debate over Bulgakov's work in 1935 and 1936 brought into prominence a young historian, Vladimir Nikolaevich Lossky

(1903–58), son of a well-known (vaguely idealist) philosopher. Lossky had already begun work on Meister Eckhart (work which was to occupy him intermittently for the rest of his life), and had been instrumental in establishing the 'Brotherhood of Saint Photius' in Paris, a group highly critical of Slavophil particularism and the mystique of Holy Russia, but also loyal to the canonical authority of the Patriarchate of Moscow, in contrast to the more aggressively anti-Soviet elements in the emigration and the liberal group (including philosophers like Nikolai Berdyaev and philosophical theologians like Bulgakov), gathered around Metropolitan Evlogii and linked to the Patriarch of Constantinople. The Brotherhood had been active in the denunciation of Bulgakov, and Lossky wrote a substantial (ninety-page) pamphlet on the whole issue in 1936. In this, he attacked Bulgakov's eclecticism and identified various errors and imbalances in his theology: he criticizes the crypto-Apollinarian strand in Bulgakov's christology, his failure to get rid of the determinist or monist heritage of Soloviev, and above all his confusion of person, will, and nature. Kenosis cannot be 'natural', cannot *be* the nature of God, since it is always a free act, in God and in us. If love is nature, it is not innovative or creative, it does not belong to the realm of the personal.

The distinction between person and nature is central in the whole of Lossky's work; but the important point to notice in the 1936 essay is Lossky's strong commitment to an 'authentic', patristically based Orthodoxy, freed from the philosophical dilettantism, as he saw it, of the Russian tradition (he had a deep aversion for Dostoevsky). The rest of his sadly brief career as a theologian was devoted to the building-up of a patristic synthesis – classically expressed in his vastly influential little book of 1944, *Essai sur la théologie mystique de l'église d'Orient* (translated into English as *The Mystical Theology of the Eastern Church* in 1957). Digests of the lectures he gave in the last years of his life were published posthumously, edited by his pupil, Olivier Clément. Throughout his work, Lossky's major impulse is hermeneutical – in the tradition of Kireevsky rather than Soloviev. His project is to uncover in patristic tradition the kind of central and normative strand that can allow Orthodoxy to offer a resolution to the tensions of Western Christianity. This leads him into some slightly questionable historical judgments, and to what appears in his earlier work as a persistent unfairness to the Thomist approach (though his mature writing, especially the great book on Eckhart, goes far towards redressing this balance), and to many aspects of Western spirituality. Yet his unpublished wartime journal shows how deep was his affection for French Catholic culture, medieval and modern, and he was on friendly terms both with Thomist scholars like de Gandillac and Gilson and with the great names of the *nouvelle théologie*, de Lubac and Daniélou. His influence on Bouyer and Congar is manifest; and he also enjoyed warm relations with Anglican scholars of the day, notably E. L. Mascall. His polemical vigor was not exercized in the cause of Byzantine, let alone Slavophil, particularism, but in defense of deeply-held convictions about what was authentically *Christian*.

His earliest theological work, prior to the controversy with Bulgakov, dealt with the theme of 'negative theology' in Pseudo-Dionysius, and this forms the basis for much of the 1944 *Essai*. Negative theology is not, for Lossky, primarily a verbal technique, a dialectical move to qualify positive affirmations about God en route for a developed theory of analogy; it is the *primordial* theological moment, the moment of stripping and renunciation. Theology begins in a kind of shock to, a paralysing of, the intellect – not by propositions that offend the intellect, but by an encounter with what cannot be mastered. The dialectical imagery of 'light' and 'darkness', as used by both Dionysius and his precursors, the Cappadocian Fathers, is designed to take us beyond both agnosticism (the being of God is ultimately inaccessible) and intellectualism (the being of God is akin to the finite mind and so its proper and natural object): the reality underpinning apophatic theology is 'ecstasy' – not a particular brand of individual mystical experience, but the sober acknowledgement that we must let go of the control of conceptual analysis when we are touched by God and advance to a stage beyond the life of conscious 'natural' individuality, closed upon itself. It is in this encounter, this recognition, that *personal* being is brought to birth. The life of an individual of a certain nature is not in itself the life of a person: individuality is a particular configuration of *repeatable* natural features. The person, on the other hand, emerges in and only in the act of spiritual creativity which is response to the self-gift of God – in *ekstasis* and *kenosis*, self-transcending and self-forgetting, the overcoming of the boundaries of mutual exclusion that define individuals over against each other.

It is in this context that Lossky claims that the doctrine of the Trinity is the cardinal point of 'negative theology'. It is a 'cross for the intellect' not in merely providing a logical conundrum but in presenting to us an image of the source of all reality that overturns our understanding of individuality as the most basic category. God is neither an individual nor three individuals: God is the supreme paradigm of the personal, a life wholly lived in *ekstasis* and *kenosis*, since the divine hypostases which are God are wholly defined by relations of love, gift, response. It is from the paradigm of the divine hypostases that we come to grasp our own vocation to personal being.

Thus Lossky attacks all theologies that concentrate on the level of 'nature' – what can be grasped and objectified. His fierce criticisms of Western scholasticism are motivated by a conviction that the Western theological tradition separates the divine essence from the divine persons (and so elevates an abstract divinity over the living God), and operates a juridical and external morality based on an artificial concept of human nature, to which grace is added as an extra *thing*. His critique of the *filioque* in the Western creed assumes that post-Augustinian trinitarian theology makes the source of the Spirit's life not the person of the Father but the abstract nature shared by Father and Son (in this critique, he goes further than most of his Orthodox predecessors, but has a special debt to the work of V. Bolotov on the *filioque* at the turn of the century, and to the patristic and medieval studies of L. P. Karsavin, one of his teachers). However, Lossky also insists that the reaction against scholastic Catholicism is just as unbalanced: here is 'person' without 'nature', voluntarism and subjectivism. The Protestant error is to turn away from the real ontological transformation effected by encounter with God. So, as Christian trinitarianism mediates between two misguided forms of monotheism, Hellenic abstract monism and Hebraic anthropomorphism and voluntarism, Orthodoxy mediates between Catholic essentialism and Protestant existentialism.

The critique of the West also draws in Lossky's interest in the speculations of the fourteenth-century theologian and mystic Gregory Palamas. Palamas had distinguished between the 'essence' and the 'energies' or 'activities' of God, so as to insist that God was authentically known and 'participated' through his activities while remaining incomprehensible in essence. Lossky believes that the absence of this distinction leads back to the unacceptable choice of intellectualism or agnosticism; either God is known in essence, in *definitions*, or he is not known at all. The doctrine of the 'energies' allows both real and ultimate unknowing and a real share in the divine life. Lossky was not the first to revive interest in Palamas: Bulgakov had used him, and, in the 1930s, the Russian Basil Krivoshein and the Romanian Dumitru Staniloae had both published important scholarly studies. Lossky's work, however, established Palamas as a focal figure in Byzantine theology, and did much to stimulate the striking development of Palamas scholarship in Europe and the United States in the past thirty years.

There is a Kierkegaardian streak in Lossky (it is not surprising that he thought highly of the French Kierkegaardian scholar Jean Wahl), but it is balanced by a carefully worked out ecclesiology. The church exists at *both* 'natural' and 'personal' levels, human nature objectively restored in Christ, human persons each uniquely transformed by the Spirit. Thus institutional and canonical regularities matter (Lossky's stubborn loyalty to the canonical authority of the weak and almost discredited Patriarchate of Moscow through many difficult decades expresses this eloquently); but they are not there to impose centralized despotism or unified models of spiritual growth. The institutional and the charismatic are bound together as inseparably as the Word and the Spirit in the Trinity. 'Tradition' in the Church is not just a process of narrowly doctrinal transmission, but the *whole* of the Spirit's ecclesial work, realizing in each, in a unique way, the heritage of all, by way of Scripture, ministry, sacraments, iconography and the disciplines of holiness. And catholicity is more than a sentimental *sobornost'*, a deep and emotional sense of solidarity: it is the capacity in each believer and each congregation to receive and live the fullness of God's gifts.

Lossky remains probably the best known and most influential of all modern Orthodox writers. His polemic can be wide of the mark at times, and he remains more firmly within the nineteenth-century Russian tradition than he might have cared to admit, but his originality and imagination in interpreting the Eastern fathers should secure him a firm place among twentieth-century theologians, and practically all Eastern Orthodox ecclesiology in the past few decades has taken his scheme as a starting-point.

## G. V. Florovsky

Lossky was not alone in combating the influence of Slavophil mystique in Russian theology, and in trying to rescue the doctrine of the church's catholicity from edifying rhetoric about Slavic *sobornost'*. Georgii Vasilievich Florovsky (1893–1979) pursued the same course in search of a 'neo-patristic synthesis', though he did so in more direct and conscious engagement with philosophical questions: his earliest essays (after he had abandoned studies in the natural sciences) addressed fundamental issues of metaphysics and epistemology. In these pieces, he repudiates absolute idealism, insists on the impossibility of affirming or denying anything about objects of cognition in themselves, since they enjoy an inaccessible presence to themselves, and argues on this basis for a radical causal underdetermination in the universe, a kind of 'free will' in the material order. He saw very clearly the connection between idealist epistemology (each particular proposition entailing and being entailed by the ensemble of true propositions) and a certain sort of determinism, and his later opposition to Bulgakov's sophiology has its roots in these essays of the pre-war period and the early 1920s. In the 1920s, he was also involved in the 'Eurasian' controversy among the Russian *émigrés*, a debate (once again) about where Russia was to be culturally 'located'; his anti-Slavophil stance in this was pronounced and he was already looking to the ideal of a 'Christian Hellenism', with patristic and Byzantine roots.

In the early 1930s, Florovsky worked for a while alongside Bulgakov in Paris (he was ordained in 1932), but his disagreements became sharper – and may have been further sharpened by contact with Barth in 1931. His theological papers in these years show both an aggressive insistence on the priority of revelation, and a growing use of patristic categories and argument. In 1931 and 1933, he published his two magisterial surveys of Eastern theology up to the eighth century, and, in two important papers in 1936 and 1938, he castigated the bondage of Russian theology to post-Enlightenment philosophy and announced his program of 're-Hellenizing' the Christian faith, arguing that Christian theology could only recover itself by deepening its commitment to the baptized Hellenism of the fathers and the Byzantine world. He never wavered in this loyalty to the Greek character of theology, in opposition both to Western religious and secular thought and to the ethnic religiosity of many Russians. In 1937 he published *Ways of Russian Theology*, a brilliant and encyclopedic history of Christian thought in Russia that elaborated a relentlessly hostile account of Slavophil Christianity and concluded with a clarion call to return to the Fathers.

As much of his work shows, Florovsky's patristic enthusiasm was not as naive or as positivist as might appear (though one Russian reviewer in 1931 described an essay of Florovsky's on the atonement as 'talmudic' in its use of the fathers). Florovsky's radical indeterminism disposed him to emphasize the central significance of *history* in knowledge – the encounter with a complex of contingent acts in which we encounter persons. In historical knowledge, above all, we must recognize the impossibility of 'objective' mastery: historical inquiry brings a personal, a committed, agenda, and looks for personal records, unique points of view. There is no historical source that is not a point of view, and no historical research that is not done from a point of view. Historical 'events' are acts, mediated by further acts of interpretation (Collingwood and Dilthey are invoked on this); and the meaning of history is an eschatological projection. As against pre-emptive efforts to settle the issue of meaning (Hegel, Marx, Nietzsche), Christianity takes seriously the unfinished and unfinishable character of historical activity, and thus the unique and unfathomable character of the acting *person*. But this also means that Christianity is irreversibly committed to what has as a matter of contingent fact been constructed in its history: we cannot pretend that we can free ourselves of 'Hellenism', or that the kerygma is directed from and to a timeless interiority. Hence the priority of patristic methods and themes – though this does not mean that we can do no more than parrot slogans or imitate the style of a distant culture; simply that *these* are our starting-point, *this* is how Christian language has concretely taken shape. If we wish to go on speaking a Christian language at all, we cannot ignore or try to dismantle this set of determinations.

As some Russian critics more sympathetic to Bulgakov noted, Florovsky did less than justice to the turbulently dialectical nature of patristic theology, and tended to treat as a finished whole what could only be part of a conversation (comparison with some recent theological uses of Gadamer is instructive). But Florovsky's sophisticated discussion of historical knowledge (most accessibly set out in an article for the 1959 Tillich Festschrift) is of great interest, the most detailed exposition of what we have been calling the 'hermeneutical' alternative voice in Russian religious thought, suspicious of metaphysics divorced from doctrinal and ascetical tradition. The emphasis on historical creativity, history as a pattern of free acts, leads naturally to a critique of all theologies that undervalue the historical Jesus: for Florovsky, the category of *podvig* (roughly equivalent to 'achievement', even 'exploit', and common in speaking of ascetic saints) is central in understanding Christ, as in understanding all human action. Jesus' *whole* existence must be the triumph of freedom in the world if we are to be liberated for proper historical action. Thus his death must be, in some sense, his *act* – and not only contingently so. Florovsky startlingly revives the late patristic notion that Jesus, as possessing a sinless and unfallen humanity, did not *have* to die. And in that Jesus thus brings death itself within the scope of created freedom, the possibility of incorruptible life is implanted in humanity. Necessity, in the form of mortality and disintegration, is shown to be conquerable by freedom – the fusion of divine and human freedom in Christ. We shall die, but we know now that our human nature is still 'free' beyond death, as it has been taken through death into resurrection by the man Jesus, whose glorified humanity is given to us in the eucharist.

The eucharist is thus also the foundation of true, ecclesial *sobornost'*. In it, we come to share fellowship not only with one another, but with the whole company of heaven and the entire cosmos; we do so because we here make contact with a humanity free from the limits of ordinary individuality, a humanity belonging to our history yet not sealed off in the past by death. And in the eucharistic fellowship, as 'human impermeability and exclusivity' are overcome, human community becomes the image of the divine: the Church (not the individual) is *imago Trinitatis*. Florovsky makes much in this context of the Farewell Discourses in the Fourth Gospel, though patristic evidence is harder to come by; following the lead of a very different kind of theologian, Antonii Khrapovitsky (Metropolitan of Kiev before the Revolution), author of treatises on the 'moral idea' of various dogmas, he alludes to Cyril of Alexandria and Hilary of Poitiers. But the notion of the church as imaging the plurality-in-unity of the divine life owes more directly to the nineteenth-century Russian ethos than to the fathers. It may be a legitimate development of patristic themes, but Florovsky, as much as Lossky, cannot but read the Fathers through spectacles faintly tinged with Slavophil interests.

Florovsky's range of skills and erudition is impressive, though the work overall is more uneven than Lossky's much slighter *oeuvre*. Considerable philosophical sophistication and originality stand side by side with what can sometimes be an archaizing and inflexible theological idiom. His insistence on freedom gives a rather voluntaristic flavor to some of his writings, and there is no clear category unifying the work of divine and human love to compare with the striking use of kenosis in both Bulgakov and Lossky. Methodologically, however, he is much the most lucid and systematic, and his work in this area deserves far more serious attention.

## SURVEY AND ASSESSMENT OF CURRENT ORTHODOX THEOLOGY

The Russian emigration produced many other significant figures, not least Nikolai Afanasiev, author of a major work on ecclesiology that developed many of the themes emerging in Lossky and Florovsky (the *imago Trinitatis*, the centrality of the eucharist), and Pavel Evdokimov, a prolific and eloquent writer of books on the interrelation of liturgy, theology, and spirituality, indebted equally to Lossky and to Bulgakov, as well as to Jung and Eliade. But as the first generation of *émigrés* died, the impact of the Russian theological revival spread beyond Slavic Orthodoxy. Greek-speaking theologians increasingly took up the challenge; until the 1950s, Greek theology had tended to be cast in a rather scholastic mode – doctrinal *capita* with patristic catenae added – but the impact of Lossky and Florovsky has transformed this situation in some areas at least of the Greek Church. John Romanides has developed a fiercely anti-Augustinian theology, and has been an important presence in ecumenical discussions. Christos Yannaras studied Heidegger in Germany and produced a remarkable series of books uniting Lossky's theology with Heidegger's metaphysics. He must be counted as one of the most outstandingly creative voices in Orthodoxy today; his reworking of the essence–energies distinction in terms of *ousia* as *parousia*, 'being' as 'presence', and his elaboration of the category of *eros* as fundamental in understanding the personal represent an important assimilation of major European philosophical concerns into a consciously but critically traditionalist theology. Yannaras has also made a considerable name as a writer on ethics, politics, and ecology. John Zizioulas' work on ecclesiology links Afanasiev's themes (not without some criticism and refinement) to a whole metaphysic of relation, centered on the trinitarian image of being as *essentially* relational: the great philosophical error is to look for isolated ahistorical substances, since the source of all reality is not 'a' substance but a relational system. Zizioulas' doctoral thesis, on eucharist, episcopate, and unity, has been seminally important in ecumenical theology.

In the United States Alexander Schmemann and John Meyendorff transmitted the Russian *émigré* heritage to new generations, Schmemann with a number of works on liturgical and sacramental theology (above all that small classic, *The World as Sacrament*), Meyendorff with several books on Palamism and Byzantine Christianity in general, and essays on ecclesiology. Both the major Orthodox seminaries in the United States, St Vladimir's and Holy Cross, produce substantial periodicals. The Institut Saint-Serge continues in Paris, and several Orthodox groups there publish theological journals. Orthodoxy in France is now overwhelmingly Francophone, and its leading constructive theologian, Olivier Clément, is of French birth. A friend and pupil of Lossky, he has developed Lossky's critique of the abstract foundations of Western theism, and written of the dialectical necessity of European atheism as a step to recovering the vision of a living God. He has succeeded in constructing an Orthodox theology very deeply engaged with the mainstream of Western European culture, and free from either Byzantinist or Slavophil nostalgia. The role of converts like Clément is of increasing importance in Orthodox intellectual life; one other distinguished instance is (Bishop) Kallistos Ware in England, author of several works on Byzantine spirituality, and an important interpreter of the Orthodox theological style to British academic theology.

In Eastern Europe, theological production is limited largely to historical scholarship; though Romania has nurtured a major dogmatic and ascetical theologian in Dumitru Staniloae (very much in the tradition of Lossky), and 'dissident' religious writing in Russia has rediscovered many of the themes of the great Russian writers of the pre-Revolutionary era (and Bulgakov is widely, if clandestinely, read).

The constraints and tensions of modern ecumenical dialogue have not, on the whole, encouraged exploratory or creative theology in the Orthodox world in the past couple of decades (with some outstanding exceptions); but there are many encouraging signs, in the Third World as well as in Europe and the United States. Orthodox theology has lately had a considerable impact on Western theology (Congar on tradition and the Holy Spirit, Moltmann on the Trinity, various writers on the church), and is increasingly studied with academic seriousness. Many connections – historical and systematic – wait to be made. Zizioulas's recent work suggests the possibility of useful interaction between this kind of ecclesiology and various Western attempts at 'postmodern' or 'postliberal' schemes, in its critique of a metaphysic of unrelated substances and an epistemology based on the myth of a detached or neutral subjectivity. Orthodox theologians have shown some willingness to engage with Heidegger, but it is perhaps time for a comparable engagement with Gadamer on the one hand and Wittgenstein on the other (the Romanian novelist Petru Dumitriu has testified eloquently to the importance of Wittgenstein in his own recovery of Christian commitment, but his is not a voice heard at all clearly within 'mainstream' Orthodox theology).

For this sort of development to go forward, Orthodox theology at large has to overcome a certain suspicion of (at worst, contempt for) the world of Western philosophy, a suspicion that is part of the inheritance of the debates in the Russian emigration earlier in this century. The impressive examples of Clément and Yannaras, and (from the non-Chalcedonian world) Metropolitan Paulos Mar Gregorios of New Delhi, have shown what can be achieved by confronting the mainstream of European intellectual life, scientific and political as well as philosophical, with perspectives formed, but not restricted, by the Greek patristic vision. And it may be that, if this is to flourish, there needs also to be a new appreciation – however critical it may still be – of the contribution of the Russian religio-philosophical tradition, a reclaiming and reworking of some of the themes of Soloviev and Bulgakov. There are relatively few signs of this as yet (though it is worth noting a recent surge of interest in Florensky, Bulgakov's mentor); but Orthodox thought in the past hundred years has repeatedly surprised Western observers by its self-renewing energy.

## BIBLIOGRAPHY

### Primary

Bulgakov, S. N., *The Wisdom of God* (London, 1937).
—, *Du verbe incarné* (Paris, 1943).
—, *Le Paraclet* (Paris, 1946).
Florovsky, Georges, *The Collected Works of Georges Florovsky* (Belmont, Mass., 1972–9).
Lossky, V. N., *The Mystical Theology of the Eastern Church* (Cambridge, 1957).
—, *Orthodox Theology: An Introduction* (Clément's digest of Lossky's lectures) (Crestwood, NY).
Pain, James, and Zernov Nicholas (eds), *A Bulgakov Anthology* (London, 1976). (A further selection, with critical introduction and notes is in preparation for the Collins series, *The Making of Modern Theology*.)

### Secondary

Clément, O., *Questions sur l'homme* (Paris, 1972).
Dumitriu, P., *To the Unknown God* (London, 1982).
Evdokimov, P., *L'orthodoxie* (Neuchâtel, 1965).
Gregorios, Paulos Mar, *The Human Presence* (Geneva, 1978).
Lelouvier, Y. N., *Perspectives russes sur L'Église. Un theologien contemporain: Georges Florovsky* (Paris, 1968).
Read, C., *Religion, Revolution and the Russian Intelligentsia, 1900–1912* (London, 1979).
Schmemann, A., *The World as Sacrament* (London, 1966).
Staniloae, D., *Theology and the Church* (Crestwood, NY, 1980).
Ware, K., *The Orthodox Way* (London, 1979).
Williams, G. H., Georges Vasilievich Florovsky, *Greek Orthodox Theological Review*, (1965), pp. 7–107.
Williams, R., 'The Via Negativa and the Foundations of Theology. An Introduction to the Thought of V. N. Lossky' in *New Studies in Theology* I, ed. Stephen Sykes and Derek Holmes (London, 1980), pp. 95–117.

Yannaras, C., *The Freedom of Morality* (Crestwood, NY, 1984).

Zernov, N., *The Russian Religious Renaissance of the Twentieth Century* (London, 1963).

Zizioulas, J., *Being as Communion. Studies in Personhood and the Church* (Crestwood, NY; London, 1985).

# Part IV

# New Challenges in Theology

Many of the theologies discussed under this heading express the 'suppressed knowledge' of communities and groups that have suffered and continue to suffer terribly. These theologians are identified with the poor of Latin America, blacks in the United States, Africa and elsewhere, Asians, and women: the vast majority of the world's population. They represent a powerful new development in twentieth-century Christianity which has happened quite quickly and has already had profound effects.

Comprehensiveness is even less possible in this than in other sections, but the aim is to give a sense of what sort of challenges these are, to introduce a very few leading representatives and to point the way to further reading.

Rebecca Chopp describes the ways in which Latin American liberation theology was influenced by Vatican II, political theology, and Marxism, and she defines clearly what is meant by praxis and liberation. She portrays a vigorous new genre of theology that expresses a fresh transformation of the Christian faith itself. She offers an original interpretation of the development of the theology of Gustavo Gutierrez, from a primary focus on the transformation of history through the praxis of the poor to a new 'more radical and constructive' centering on the God of faithfulness and love, who is manifested also in captivity, suffering, and exile. She then outlines the theology of José Miguez Bonino, before entering into the controversies about liberation theology and finally suggesting how it calls most modern theologies fundamentally into question and threatens them with rupture. In addition, at the opening and conclusion of her chapter she faces the problem of how those who are not poor might genuinely listen to this theology.

The other three contributors are themselves participants in the types of theology they discuss. Patrick Kalilombe describes black theology in North America, black Africa, and South Africa, with the representative figures being James Cone, John Pobee, and Allan Boesak. He traces the momentous and rapid developments, the differences, the growing cooperation and the outstanding issues and problems.

Out of the immensity of Asia, Kosuke Koyama selects three theologians for discussion and the editor has selected (and written the section on) Koyama himself. Stanley Samartha explores Christianity and its relation to other faiths in Indian terms; Choan-Seng Song's method of transposition grapples with the relationship of Israel's history to Asia's; Hyun Younghak identifies with the most oppressed and marginalized of his people; and Koyama works out a practical, dialogical theology centered on the suffering of God.

Finally comes perhaps the most pervasive movement of all, that of feminism. It challenges the identity of Christianity fundamentally, and the first representative thinker illustrates this: Mary Daly is no longer a Christian. Ann Loades makes clear in other ways too the profundity of the crisis that this movement has provoked in only twenty years, and describes the critical and constructive theologies of Phyllis Trible, Elizabeth Schüssler Fiorenza and Rosemary Radford Ruether. Must Christianity be 'a male-identified project of redemption'?

# 9

# Latin American Liberation Theology

## Rebecca S. Chopp

### INTRODUCTION: CHARACTER, ORIGINS, AND INFLUENCES

Latin American liberation theology is a reflection on God's activity and God's transforming grace amongst those who are the victims of modern history. To read and really hear this logos of the theos, if one is not a member of the despised masses of the poor, one must begin with an attitude of respect and care in order to be open to the voice of the others of history. In this attitude of respectful care Latin American liberation theology will not be received as an interpretation, a second-level reflection on common human experience, but rather an interruption, an irruption of how God is active, life is lived, and Christianity is practiced amongst the poor. This chapter assumes that its readers are not the poor, the subjects of Latin American liberation theology, and hence attempts to let Latin American liberation theology speak in its voice, but to do so with an interpreter who stands ever ready to say again and again that this knowledge of God is not directly equitable, or commensurable with the modern theology of the First World bourgeoisie. We must hear the voice of Latin American liberation theology, and we must try to listen closely before we can understand; but we must also accept, at the beginning, the integrity of a different voice, a different experience, a different genre of theology that belongs to the same God, the same church, the same Christ of which we speak.

Latin American liberation theology speaks of God as manifest in the poor of history. It must speak of this, for it arises out of the poor's experience of God, an experience that is dependent, as Gustavo Gutierrez has insisted, upon God's choosing to reveal God's self in the poor.[1] Like many other theologies, this one grows out of and reflects back upon faith itself; it is not laid upon faith by well meaning theologians, nor is it arrived at by a few radical revolutionaries. Liberation theology seeks to speak of this faith and thus to speak of God; in so doing it seeks to give voice to liberation, which involves not only freedom from oppression but also freedom to become new subjects in history. Liberation theology and the faith upon which it reflects does not try to make the poor the rich, or the rich the poor, or some intermediary in between: rather the experience of and reflection of God and the poor seek to guide the transformation of all human beings into new ways of being human, ways not dependent upon structures of division between rich and poor, the common and the despised, the persons and the nonpersons of history.[2]

Many factors contribute to the distinctive voice of Latin American liberation theology. The first, and most important factor, is the context of Latin American liberation theology in the concrete situation of massive poverty, a context that can only be hinted at by terms such as poverty, starvation and oppression. The masses of Latin America struggle to survive in severe poverty, severe enough that two-thirds of the population of Latin America live with hunger as their constant companion. Most of the land and nearly all of the business are in the hands of a wealthy minority. The masses suffer frequent unemployment, and when they do find work, the wages are not enough to provide what we in the First World might call a decent standard of living. The poor see their children starve and often watch them die from the lack of food, health care, and proper sanitation. In the midst of this massive poverty, many of the poor live under repressive regimes and have few, if any, political rights.

This present context grows out of the 'modern' history of Latin America, a history which, since the 'discovery of the New World' has been marked by oppression and colonization.[3] Spain and Portugal settled the New World through the devastation of native cultures in order to make slaves for the conquerors and to Christianize the 'heathens' *en masse*. Even with the emergence of many Latin American nations in the beginning of the nineteenth century, neo-colonialism, a system of economic dependency and exploitation, existed between nations and First World countries, first with Great Britain and later with the United States. The 1950s and 1960s saw international commitments to develop dependent countries to be like First World nations such as the United States, but this movement created more and more dependent relations, this time through military oligarchies and multi-national corporations.[4] The 'modern' history of Latin America, the modern history we know as named by terms such as progress, science, freedom, has been best characterized in words such as exploitation, poverty, and oppression.

A major factor in the development of Latin American liberation theology was the positions on justice and peace that Roman Catholicism and Protestantism began to take in the 1950s and 1960s. Most important among the stances taken was the social teachings of Vatican II concerning human dignity and the need for structural change. Latin American bishops met in Medellin, Colombia in 1968 to discuss the impact of Vatican II for Latin America; the papers adopted by the bishops became the founding documents of liberation theology.[5] At this conference the struggle for change that would guide liberation theology was invoked, a struggle against the institutionalized violence of the rich against the poor. A new vision of faith was articulated in the view of the poor as human subjects active in history. This vision was located in small grass-roots communities where the poor could determine their own destiny and express their faith as they participated in conscientization, or consciousness-raising.

Besides these historical events and contexts, two other influences must be noted: the first that of political theology and the second, of Marxism. Political theology arose in West Germany as a critique of modern Christianity's concern for the ahistorical authenticity of the bourgeois subject and a reformulation of Christian theology in light of events of massive suffering, such as the Holocaust, in progressive, modern nations. The works of political theologians such as Jürgen Moltmann and Johann Baptist Metz suggested new theological terms such as privatization, oppression, ideology, and liberation.[6] Metz, to take one example, criticized the consciousness and subjectivity of the bourgeoisie from a theological position that took seriously the relation of God and those who suffer in history. Beginning with the full corporality of the human subject in nature and history, Metz constructed a theological anthropology that was social and political. As Metz pursued his commitment to take seriously the social and political constitution of life, he started to advocate a 'practical' theology that abandoned the foundations of German Idealism to begin in the historical relation between reason and society. At the same time, Metz began to unfold a new vision of Christianity as a critical witness in society, a witness using symbols such as eschatology and apocalyptic to oppose the destructive consciousness of modernity by being in solidarity through the dangerous memory of Jesus Christ with those who suffer. Political theology also hinted at a vision of salvation and liberation that had to do with political conditions in a society, following its vision of faith as a witness to liberation and transformation in history, in the present, toward a new future for all people.

As both a theoretical tool of social analysis and as a philosophy of history, Marxism has influenced liberation theology.[7] As a tool of social analysis, Marxism has supplied a dialectical analysis rather than a functional one, an analysis focusing on the relations of power and force in a society instead of covering such forces up in an ideology of society as an organism needing balance. As a philosophy of history, Marxism has contributed, along with other philosophies, toward a view of the human subject as socially or historically constituted, history as open to change and transformation, and oppression and alienation structured through the productive relations of society. Marxism and political theology are both discourses that take seriously the many dimensions of histories and discourses that underscore the priority of transformation and change. Latin American liberation theologians, especially in the early years, critically adopted some of the language and insights from Marxism and political theology; but they did so only by transforming these insights and language into their own theological reflections.

## SURVEY

Latin American liberation theology is not primarily academic discourse for academic debate; it is, rather, church theology coming out of and aimed toward its ecclesial context in basic Christian communities. Basic communities are grass-roots communities among the masses, in which Christians seek to form and live out their Christian witness in their historical situation. Thus the locus of Latin American liberation theology is the church, not the academy, and its genre of liberation theology can be characterized as a reflection on and guide to piety rather than a second-level hermeneutical reflection on the theoretical meaning of Christianity. Thus Latin American liberation theology is first a practical, theological discourse on the faith of the poor. But the poor do not just happen, they are created by structures and institutions, and, thus, liberation theology is a critique of the structures and institutions that create the poor, including modern Christianity which has identified with the rich.[8] In order to do this, liberation theology engages in dialogue with not only philosophy but also with the social sciences. As a theological discourse of critique and transformation in solidarity with the poor, liberation theology offers a theological anthropology that is political, an interpretation of Christianity that may be characterized through the term liberation, and a vision of Christianity as a praxis of love and solidarity with the oppressed.

The image of human existence, and theological anthropology is always guided by an image; in Latin American liberation theology it is the poor. The bishops of Latin America meeting at Puebla in 1979 identified the faces of the poor, the subjects of liberation theology:

> the faces of young children, struck down by poverty before they are born . . .; – the faces of indigenous peoples, and frequently that of the Afro-Americans as well, living marginalized lives in inhuman situations . . .; – the faces of the peasants; as a special group, they live in exile almost everywhere on our continent . . .; the faces of marginalized and overcrowded urban dwellers, whose lack of material goods is matched by the ostentatious display of wealth by other segments of society; – the faces of old people, who are growing more numerous every day, and who are frequently marginalized in a progress-oriented society that totally disregards people not engaged in production.[9]

These faces are not isolated as individual expressions of some 'common' human existence or made objectively real only in God's action; rather, they are the reality of human existence in Latin America.

This human reality, the reality of what it is to be the poor, the despised, the scourged of the earth, is understood, in Latin American liberation theology, through the term 'praxis', which has three distinguishable meanings. First of all, praxis means that human beings are constituted through political-historical reality. Where one lives, the status of socioeconomic class, what kind of power is available, must all be clear considerations for understanding human reality. Secondly, praxis means that human reality is intersubjective, that human beings are not first ahistorical 'I's that express their unique essences in relations to others through language, but that all subjectivity arises out of intersubjective relations between human beings. Finally, praxis as the understanding of human reality means that humans must and can intentionally create history, transforming and shaping reality for the improvement of human flourishing.

This understanding of human reality through praxis is joined by an interpretation, a re-formation, of Christian symbols through the central theme of liberation. The key term 'liberation', like any key term functioning as a material norm in theology, is a tensive metaphor: naming the reign and nature of God, the normative vision of history, the work and person of Christ, the witness and mission of the church.[10] It is with the centrality of this term and the many rich readings of the Bible and Christian tradition, that Latin

American liberation theology is most clearly understood as not merely a form of ethics or social witness, but as a systematic theology, a radically new interpretation and transformation of Christian faith itself. Sin, for instance, in liberation theology is reflected on not merely through individual moral acts or existential separation and despair, but primarily in terms of social structures. Sin results in suffering, whose burden is carried, time and time again, by the poor of history. Sin is radical distortion, not of some private relation with God, but of all reality, especially of the historical-political world that God gives us to live in. Redemption, correlatively, must relate to liberation, though, of course, it cannot be merely identified with any one liberating act; if redemption has to do with the reconciliation of humanity to God and salvation from sins, then it must be related, tensively and expressively but none the less realistically, to our present historical reality. Indeed, among the many readings of Christ in liberation theology – Christ as political rebel, Christ suffering as the scourged of the earth, Christ in solidarity with the poor and oppressed – Christ as liberator, as one who actually effects transformation, as one who brings new ways of being human, is central.

Within the locus of this understanding of human reality and interpretation of Christian symbols, Christianity becomes a praxis of solidarity and liberation; the point of Christianity becomes an activity that is for and of the poor, working for liberation and transformation for all. Christianity represents the witness of freedom: it does not necessarily supply a new political ordering, and it definitely does not offer a new theocratic state; rather it testifies to freedom and liberation, taking sides where God takes sides with the poor and the despised of the earth. Christianity follows God, and as Gustavo Gutierrez has suggested 'The love of God is a gratuitous gift. . . . Loving by preference the poor, doing that, God reveals this gratuity. And by consequence as followers of Jesus Christ, we must also do this preferential option for the poor.'[11] In this way, for Christians, faith and love are not separable, indeed may not be distinguishable, from justice. Christianity must neither conform itself to culture nor be a radical separatist sect: rather, Christianity must discern God's activity amidst the poor and work for radical transformation of the structures of society that all, together, may become new human subjects.

It is best, therefore, to think of Latin American liberation theology as a new way or a new genre of theology based on a specific praxis of faith. Though liberation theology shares some common resources with other theologies, its way of organizing, its criteria for reading scriptures and traditions, its tasks, purpose and intent is specific to Christian praxis amidst the poor. This allows, also, the realization that liberation theologians, while sharing common themes of the option for the poor, God as liberator, and the liberation of theology, make their own individual contributions. Latin American liberation theologians write on issues such as christology and ecclesiology, work on how to use the resources of the social sciences, investigate the relation of popular religion to liberation theology or interpret biblical themes and narratives.

It is, of course, difficult to survey Latin American liberation theologians since liberation theology is a young enterprise, and many of the figures who have written in Spanish or Portuguese have yet to be translated into English. But a brief survey, by alphabetical order, of some figures and their books that are available in English may indicate the range of issues and interests in Latin American liberation theology. In the survey below the theologians mentioned, like most Christians in Latin America, are all Roman Catholic. Latin American liberation theology has arisen primarily in the context of the Roman Catholic Church in Latin America, though there has been a parallel movement in the Protestant churches. After this overview of the major figures and works in liberation theology, we will consider an individual Roman Catholic theologian and then a Protestant theologian for a more in-depth interpretation.

*Hugo Assmann* has taught in his native Brazil, West Germany, and Costa Rica. Assmann's *Theology for a Nomad Church* considers the practical and theoretical nature of theological method in a liberation context. Like other liberation theologians, Assmann's work draws on sociology as a major source for theological reflection and formulates the basis of theological method not through eternal absolutes but through a critical engagement with and interpretation of historical praxis. Also concerned with the nature and method of theological reflection is *Clodovis Boff*, a Brazilian theologian, whose *Theology and Praxis: Epistemological Foundations* serves as the most thorough treatment, at present, of the epistemological presuppositions in liberation theology. Clodovis's brother, *Leonardo Boff*, is well known for his christology, *Jesus Christ Liberator*. Boff's christology is based on the situation of oppression in Latin America and stresses the priority of orthopraxis instead of orthodoxy and the anthropological instead of the ecclesiological element in christology. In recent years, Boff's work has been directed to conversation, and controversy, with the institutional church. His book, *Church: Charism and Power:*

*Liberation Theology and the Institutional Church* seeks not only to address the concerns of the institutional church in relation to liberation theology but to offer a new model of the church. This new model is a pneumatic ecclesiology, recalling the primitive elements of community, cooperation, and charism in Christian life. Boff has authored another book on ecclesiology, entitled *Ecclesiogenesis: the Base Communities Reinvent the Church* in which, drawing on articles written since 1977, he offers a new vision of the church, based in the experience of basic Christian communities. Another theologian who has interpreted the church in the present situation is *José Comblin*, whose book entitled *The Church and the National Security State* attends to the present condition of the Roman Catholic Church in Latin America and offers an interpretation of the present political situation in terms of the failure of developmentalism and the emerging cooperation between oligarchies and multi-national corporations.

If the present and the future of the church is a basic concern for liberation theology, so is interpreting the past. Certainly the history of the church in the Latin American context usually has been neglected, or when addressed, read only from the eyes of the victors. *Enrique Dussel's A History of the Church in Latin America* has made a major contribution to a re-interpretation of the church in Latin America. Dussel, an Argentinian layman in the Roman Catholic Church, also has sought to develop philosophical categories for Latin American liberation theology that focus on 'otherness' and an ethics focused on the liberation of the oppressed. Along with ecclesiology, the Scripture has been a major concern for liberation theologians both as they seek to interpret the concerns of poverty, oppression, and liberation in the Bible and as they reflect on the power of reading the Scriptures as a liberating activity. Books such as *José Miranda's Marx and the Bible: A Critique of the Philosophy of Oppression* and his *Being and the Messiah* suggest a new way of reading the Bible as well as a new interpretation of topics such as sin and redemption in the Bible.

A theologian concerned with the use of Scripture in theology is *Juan Luis Segundo*. Segundo's *The Liberation of Theology* reinterprets the hermeneutic circle in theology, addressing how the Bible is to be interpreted in a manner that does not simply repeat past doctrines, but speaks to and transforms the present historical situation. Uruguay's Segundo is one of the most prolific writers in liberation theology, and one who has had many books translated into English. Segundo also represents many theologians who, in the course of their careers, have 'become' liberation theologians, moving from a form of theological reflection in a European style to reformulating theological reflection in the Latin American situation. In fact, Segundo's series entitled *A Theology for Artisans of a New Humanity*, written as liberation theology began to emerge, can be read as transitional pieces between the older, European model of theology and the concerns and impulses that lie behind liberation theology. This series has five volumes: *The Community Called Church, Grace and The Human Condition, Our Idea of God, The Sacraments Today,* and *Evolution and Guilt.* Segundo's newest series is entitled *Jesus of Nazareth Yesterday and Today* which continues the methodological work of *The Liberation of Theology* in the first volume of this series, entitled *Faith and Ideologies,* and in the next four volumes develops a christology for today. Segundo's work in both reinterpreting theology (what sources are used, what theology is, what genre it follows) and in theological reinterpretations (new meanings and models of ecclesiology, christology, spirituality, sin, redemption, grace) suggests the richness and the breadth of Latin American liberation theology. The work of *Jon Sobrino* of El Salvador indicates the radical reformation of Christianity and of theology that liberation theology represents. Sobrino's *Christology at the Crossroads* offers a christology that combines a re-reading of the historical Jesus (contending that Jesus was on the side of the oppressed) against the background of exploitation, injustice, and oppression in Latin America. Sobrino argues, in this widely read text, that we can come to know Jesus only by following Jesus, which means following Jesus into the struggle against oppression and for liberation. An equally radical treatment of ecclesiology is offered in Sobrino's *The True Church and the Poor*, which begins by tracing the differences between liberation theology and European theology and goes on to consider such ecclesiological issues as the practice of justice as essential to the gospel, the experience of God in the church of the poor, the theological significance of the persecution of the church and evangelization as the mission of the church.

Sobrino, Segundo, the other theologians mentioned in this survey and the many other Latin American liberation theologians left unmentioned here have embarked on a bold, new interpretation of Christian witness in Latin America in the present context. Because of the breadth of issues considered, because of the many different approaches used, because of the reformulation of theology itself, it is important for us to look at two specific theologians and to trace the development of their particular concerns, recourses, issues, and theological methods. We will look, then, at *Gustavo Gutierrez*, a Roman Catholic from Peru, and *José Miguez Bonino*, a United Methodist from Argentina.

## TWO LIBERATION THEOLOGIANS

### Gustavo Gutierrez

Gustavo Gutierrez's work is written from the perspective of the poor; his translated books in English such as *The Theology of Liberation, The Power of the Poor in History, We Drink From Our Own Wells* and *On Job* interpret the Bible, Christian faith, history, and subjectivity through the eyes of the oppressed, the victims of history.[12] Gutierrez, perhaps the most influential of all Latin American liberation theologians, has made his theology the language of God from the perspective of the poor in two somewhat distinguishable stages. In the first stage, the poor were the center of theological reflection based on an argument about the irruption of the poor into history. In this argument Gutierrez offered a philosophy of history as the basis of theological reflection: modern history was characterized by historical praxis relying on individualism and rationalism to create the industrial, progressive first world. But this historical praxis was built upon massive social and economic contradictions, contradictions which again and again rest on the backs of the poor. In this first stage, Gutierrez argues that historical praxis is irrupted by liberating praxis of the poor. This dialectical overturn of history, similar to Marx's reliance on class revolution of the proletariat, occurs, in Gutierrez's work, with a reliance on the symbols of Exodus and Promise, as well as an interpretation of history and politics in light of redemption and liberation.[13] Gutierrez argues that liberation and redemption are related on three levels: particular acts, the project of history, and final redemption. This stage of Gutierrez's theological reflection centers on present possibilities for radical transformation and understands 'history' itself as carrying along this tide. Gutierrez also offers, in this stage, a re-reading of the church and of poverty based on spirituality and an evangelical life. The church is sacrament of God's grace in Gutierrez's theology, and, as a sacrament the church provides a prophetic witness in Latin America. But the church is also the locus of basic Christian communities, wherein, Gutierrez suggests, a spirituality of gratuitousness flourishes: a spirituality based on the presence of

God amidst the poor, combining the scandalous condition of poverty with the gratuitous love of God.

It is this third theme, the gratuitous love of God, that comes to the center of Gutierrez's second stage. Displaced is the objectivization of liberating praxis as an autonomous force to change the world. Now, or so it seems to this author, captivity, suffering, exile are more dominant themes in Gutierrez's theology: what Gutierrez sees from the perspective of the poor is the love and presence of God in their long-suffering struggle to survive. God, faithfulness, and love now become the center of theological reflection instead of a particular philosophy of history.[14] The poor are still the subjects of theology; but they are the real subjects of theology, not because they express or bear a certain, inevitable, historical force but because of God's presence. Gutierrez's argument is worth underscoring at this point: the option for the poor depends not on an interpretation of history but on God's own choice. This second stage is more radical and constructive: more is called into question here about the constitution of modernity and Christianity, more about what it is to be a human subject, more about what it is to experience the love of God, more about what it is to really hear the other of history speak than in the first stage, which can be interpreted as a corrective of a modern philosophy of history.

Throughout his work, Gutierrez forms theology as a rhetorical practice of liberating transformation. Indeed, Gutierrez offers one of the most insightful critiques of modern theology, or what he calls 'progressive theology'. Progressive theology, he argues, worked within the confines of the Enlightenment crisis between reason and belief, a crisis articulated in the question: can one be modern and have the free use of reason and still believe in religion? Progressive theology thus accepted as its subject, a subject it then made as the 'common' subject, the modern bourgeois nonbeliever. Liberation theology, on the other hand, has a quite different subject, a subject of the poor, the oppressed, the victims of history. The questions, visions, stances, and tasks of liberation theology revolve around the poor and God's presence in the poor. It is not merely different from progressive theology, it must also oppose progressive theology, for the bourgeois subject is the subject who represses and oppresses the poor of history.[15] Gustavo Gutierrez has been, for good reason, one of the primary interpreters of liberation theology. Gutierrez's work moves in the direction of a radically new interpretation of Christianity; Gutierrez has taken the basic symbols of Christian experience, and radically reworked them amidst the experience of God's presence in the poor, but, likewise, he has used the classical symbols of Christianity to give voice to the experience of the poor in history. In so doing, Gutierrez has uncovered, for many of us, the presuppositions of power, dominance, and injustice in our basic theological beliefs. What does it mean for modern theology to be so concerned about the nonbelievers in history that it simply ignores the masses of poor? What does it mean for a progressive theology to be so committed to isolating an ahistorical religious dimension that it overlooks historical structures that divide human beings into the rich and the poor, keeping most of God's created subjects as nonpersons in history? Both critically and constructively, Gutierrez offers, by way of a continual journey, a new language of God that denounces sin and announces grace.

## José Miguez Bonino

José Miguez Bonino's work, in books such as *Doing Theology in a Revolutionary Situation*, *Room to be People*, and *Toward a Christian Political Ethics*, exemplifies Latin American liberation theology's understanding of history as the arena of God's action.[16] History has its locus neither in individual historicity nor in the worldly progressive realization of the bourgeoisie, but in the total socio-political-economic context in which humans live and in which God continually acts. Miguez Bonino's work illustrates that history has socio-political determinates based not only on sociological analysis, but based also on theological and scriptural warrants that God acts in history. Indeed, Miguez Bonino suggests that Scripture be understood as a narrative account of God's acts in history and be analogically applied to the present situation. Though God acts in history in different manners and ways at different times, Miguez Bonino suggests, God always acts in love to transform history into the Kingdom of God.

The relation of history to the kingdom is central, according to Miguez Bonino, because in the Scripture this is how God is revealed. We do not relate kingdom to history for our own political ends, but because in the Bible God is constantly transforming history into the kingdom. This important, and tensive, relationship is, unfortunately, frequently misunderstood. There is a tendency to separate the kingdom and history, a position Miguez Bonino characterizes as dualism, which denies the basic biblical thrust of God in history. There is also a tendency merely to reduce the kingdom to history, or better yet a particular time and place in history, the monist solution, which denies the mission of Christianity and threatens to destroy the nonidentity between Christianity and the world. Rather the relation of history and the kingdom must be held to as a process of transformation, a process that might be compared to the resurrection of the body which does not deny or negate but fulfills and perfects.[17] Miguez Bonino also relates history to the Kingdom of God with a future twist; like the Pauline doctrine of works, history takes on its fullness and meaning as it anticipates the Kingdom of God. History, here, has not a merely philosophical meaning nor a materialist one, it is decidedly theological. We act in history because God acts, or better said, God acts in history through love to bring the kingdom, and, in our obedience, we act through Christ's love to bring the kingdom.

It is this praxis of obedience which calls out for theology, since the praxis of obedience must continually interpret God's action in history based on biblical themes and must understand the Bible in light of experiencing God's activity of history. This 'hermeneutical' activity, that is the activity of discerning, interpreting, and appropriating God's activity in history into the praxis of Christian obedience, must begin by realizing its own concreteness: that is, it too is historically bound, and cannot reflect outside of the historical categories and conditions available in a particular historical situation. All theology is therefore situated and political: situated because it is done in a particular historical situation, and political because all reflection, like all other aspects of life, grows out of the full socio-political reality. Yet theologians must not merely mirror the socio-political context; rather, they must position themselves in light of their obedience of Christian praxis, or, as Miguez Bonino says, 'we are situated in reality to be sure – historically, geographically, culturally, and most of all groupwise and classwise – but we can also position ourselves differently in relation to the situation'.[18] Thus theology must learn to dialogue carefully with the social sciences, in order to analyze, critique, and transform the historical situation in light of God's liberating activity.

Miguez Bonino's work demonstrates the centrality of history in Latin American liberation theology, and the socio-political understanding of history. It is important to underscore that socio-political history is central to understanding not only because of sociological arguments, that is, that all knowledge is historically conditioned, but also because of scriptural arguments: history is the arena of God's action, action which is the transformation of history through love. Miguez Bonino's theology, therefore, calls human beings to be responsible for history: responsible both in responding to God's love and responsible for their ever-present involvement in history.

We cannot opt out of history; we always advocate a particular strategy, ethics, position; but we as Christians must position ourselves with God, a God who in our own situations acts with the oppressed of the earth. Miguez Bonino also shows us that liberation theology has a decidedly socio-political cast: it advocates historical transformation, it discerns God's liberating activity, and it uses social sciences for analysis, interpretation, and appropriation.

DEBATE

Latin American liberation theology has been received with a great deal of debate among theologians living in First World countries. Some theologians have responded by rethinking the basic contours and commitments of their own theological and political positions, while others dismiss it as inadequate theological reflection or a form of politics using religion. Among the theologians of the First World countries, the debate about Latin American liberation theology has been centered in three broad areas: Latin American liberation theology's equation of liberation and redemption, its turn to the political as the primary locus of human life, and its theoretical arguments in relation to ethics and social theory.

For many First World theologians the equation of redemption and liberation tempts a kind of temporal messianism, a heralding of the reign of God on the side of one political cause.[19] This is, to many First World theologians, too reminiscent of totalitarian movements. It is also, for many, unbiblical as it poses God on the side of the poor, a claim which many read as God opposed to the rich.[20] Of course, other formulations are varied, some advocating an existentialist theology with implications to move into political realms, while others advocate a more realistic power basis, noting that even Jesus said that the poor will always be with us. To some extent, these arguments also touch a disagreement within liberation theology over how redemption and liberation are related, and correlatively, what is the status of the option for the poor. As we have already seen, Miguez Bonino criticizes some liberation theologians for monist solutions, arguing for a position that distinguishes, while Gutierrez advocates a three-level relation between redemption and liberation. The option for the poor is, as Gutierrez suggested, a statement about God's gratuitousness and not, first of all, a romanticization of the poor. Yet the option for the poor is a judgment against the lifestyles of the rich and against structures supporting the division of the human species into the poor and the rich.

Related to this criticism is often the second, that religion is not simply politics, and that liberation theology has reduced human life to the political realm.[21] For many years Roman Catholic theologians, for instance, distinguished between two realms, one political and one religious, that should be separated without interference. The response of liberation theologians depends upon a broad understanding of the political as the basis of life. Politics now has to do not merely with the managing of the state, but how our lives are organized and expressed, how we as human beings express and fulfill our subjectivity. That is, politics is now intrinsic to the definition of the human subject, not merely a secondary expression. The gospel, then, is not political in offering a particular theory of political management but is political in terms of its promise and demand for the fulfillment of human life. Liberation theologians also respond that theology, like all other forms of thought, is always political, advocating a particular view of life and implying a vision of human flourishing. Thus progressive theology, supposedly removed from the political, advocated a bourgeois existence that ignored, and thus supported, the political status quo.

But even if one grants that in some manner redemption and liberation must be related, and that politics is a necessary dimension of understanding religion, questions can still be asked about liberation theology's theoretical formulations, more specifically, the relative adequacy of its ethical theory and its social theory. Ethicists and theologians in the First World frequently have voiced concern for the lack of ethical concepts and theories to mediate the relation between theological concepts and social reality.[22] Likewise, despite the intrinsic claims in liberation theology to begin in the broadest possible sense of the socio-political, liberation theology has yet to offer a fully adequate social theory of the relation between human consciousness and social structures.[23] Both of these theoretical issues can be addressed and worked out, yet we may assume that liberation theologians will not be able to adopt simply the theories of social change and the concepts of ethical mediation from the First World.

## ACHIEVEMENT AND AGENDA: 'EVEN THE POOR HAVE A RIGHT TO THINK'

The phrase 'even the poor have a right to think' is from Gustavo Gutierrez and suggests the beginning point for even a tentative evaluation of the 'achievements' of liberation theology. For any and all accomplishments must be measured by the intent and promise of this theology, that is, the intent to be a voice of the poor and to speak of God's presence and God's power among the victims of history. Concerns such as liberation theology's methodological rigor or its theoretical sophistication are, of course, important but they are secondary in terms of the voice and the rupturing presence of this theology. Throughout this chapter I, a North American woman, have asked that the reader attempt to hear the integrity of the voice of liberation theology. This is a question of rhetoric: can we suspend the measurement internal to our own theologies long enough to hear and receive others? Rhetoric is not, theologically speaking, 'mere' rhetoric, for it has to do with the persuasiveness of language and how we are constituted as communities and persons in linguistic frameworks which themselves are always maleable, rupturable, changeable. In this light, liberation theology has ruptured much of the discourse, purpose and intent of modern theology even as it has used, intensified, and changed many of its concepts. Freedom, long a concern for the subject of modern theology, becomes intensified in liberation theology to include the historical freedom to become a person having to do with social systems, political rights, economic survival and not merely the freedom of the authentic individual to say yes to God no matter what the historical circumstances. Likewise modern theology's turn to the subject has been used in liberation theology to concentrate on the subject of the poor. And, where modern theology once assumed the bourgeois subject as a given, and God was the ultimate referent for the already assumed subjectivity, Latin American liberation theology establishes the nonpersons of history through the gratuitous action of God. For us, the readers of liberation theology who are not poor, surely the first accomplishment is hearing the voice of the poor, as the irruption of this voice calls our own into question, rupturing our values, beliefs, commitments, language and displaying our control, manipulativeness, power, and repression of others.

This is the accomplishment we receive, but it is not, I trust, the accomplishment liberation theology has for itself. That is, liberation theology's first and foremost commitment is not to convince the rich of the poor, but to speak from the poor for the poor. Therefore, liberation theology must also be understood as a new vision, ordering and interpretation of liberation. Liberation theology has for the poor given voice to new understandings of sin, God, love, grace, Jesus Christ. With the new interpretation of these symbols, liberation theology gives new ways to name the world: the reality of structures, the possibility of the future, the meaning of community, love, and justice, and the fact of human subjectivity.

There is a third accomplishment that is important to mention, having to do with the methodological importance of liberation theology. Latin American liberation theologians, together with black and feminist liberation theologians, have made a convincing case for the situatedness of all knowledge. This achievement has three dimensions: (*a*) the situatedness of all knowledge, (*b*) the inclusion of ideology critique in theology, and (*c*) the argument for the positionality of theology, or, to state it formally, the rhetorical commitments of knowledge. Latin American liberation theologians, such as José Miguez Bonino, have achieved a political and theoretical clarity about how knowledge itself is related to power, class, and ideological interests. This basic insight has led liberation theologians, in a variety of ways, to include ideology critique as intrinsic to the theological task. That is, intrinsic to Christianity and Christian theology is the uncovering of distortions of knowledge, interest, and power in social systems. To be critical, to be able to uncover and reveal the distortions necessitates, of course, also an ability to position oneself and speak constructively, to show a way of being in the world. Indeed, it is in this aspect that the work of Latin American liberation theology continues as the theologians pursue a constructive vision, a world envisioned from the new subjectivity of the poor, a new relation between human consciousness and social structures. The future agenda of liberation theology continues this critical uncovering of the distortions in economic, political, social, linguistic structures; it must, as well, continue pursuing the concreteness of its vision and then begin tracing the possibilities of change and transformation.

### NOTES

1 Gustavo Gutierrez, 'Theology and Spirituality in a Latin American Context', *Harvard Divinity Bulletin*, 14 (June–August 1984).

2 Though a common objection to liberation theology is that it will result in making the poor the rich, and, thus, simply exchange one group of oppressors for another, liberation theologians, from their earliest works on, have advocated a transformation of social structures to rid the world of the massive disparites between the poor and the rich and have offered anthropologies of transformation stressing new ways of being human for all persons.

3 For good introductions to the history of Latin America see: George Pendle, *A History of Latin America* (New York, 1963); Hubert Herring, *A*

*History of Latin America from the Beginnings to the Present* (New York, 1961) and Enrique D. Dussel, *A History of the Church in Latin America: Colonialism to Liberation (1492–1979)* (Grand Rapids, Mich., 1981).

4 See José Comblin, *The Church and the National Security State* (Maryknoll, NY, 1979) and Robert Calvo, 'The Church and the Doctrine of National Security', in *Churches and Politics in Latin America*, ed. Daniel H. Levine (Beverly Hills, Ca, 1979).

5 Joseph Gremillion (ed.), *The Gospel of Peace and Justice: Catholic Social Teaching since Pope John* (Maryknoll, NY, 1976).

6 Representative works by these two theologians are: Jürgen Moltmann, *Theology of Hope: On the Grounds and Implications of a Christian Eschatology* (New York, 1967), *The Crucified God: The Cross of Christ as the Foundation and Criticism of Christian Theology* (New York, 1973); Johann Baptist Metz, *Theology of the World* (New York, 1969) and *Faith in History and Society: Toward a Practical Fundamental Theology* (New York, 1980).

7 For examples of the critical uses of Marxism in liberation theology see: José Miguez Bonino, *Christians and Marxists: The Mutual Challenge to Revolution* (Grand Rapids, Mich., 1976) and Juan Luis Segundo, *Faith and Ideologies*, (Maryknoll, NY, Melbourne, London, 1984).

8 Philip Berryman, *Liberation Theology* (Oak Park, Ill. and New York, 1987), pp. 4–5.

9 John Eagleson and Philip Scharper (eds), *Pueblo and Beyond: Documentation and Commentary* (Maryknoll, NY, 1979), pars 32–9.

10 I use the term tensive metaphor as a way to suggest the multiple meanings and yet systematic center of this theology in the term liberation. This is a metaphorical way of stating Tillich's notion of the material norm of theology. Paul Tillich, *Systematic Theology*, vol. I (Chicago, 1951), pp. 47–50.

11 Gutierrez, 'Theology and Spirituality in a Latin American Context, p. 4.

12 Gustavo Gutierrez, *A Theology of Liberation: History, Politics and Salvation, The Power of the Poor in History: Selected Writings* and *We Drink From Our Own Wells: The Spiritual Journey of a People*.

13 This is developed in Gutierrez, *A Theology of Liberation*.

14 This notion of two stages in Gutierrez's writings should not be taken to mean a major break in Gutierrez's theology, rather, it suggests a certain shifting of the center of his theological reflection from a philosophy of history to an argument about God.

15 See, for instance, the argument about progressive theology in *The Power of the Poor in History*, pp. 178–81 and pp. 213–14.

16 José Miguez Bonino, *Doing Theology in a Revolutionary Situation, Room to be People: An Interpretation of the Message of the Bible for Today's World* (Philadelphia, 1979) and *Toward a Christian Political Ethics*.

17 Miguez Bonino, *Doing Theology*, pp. 136–43.

18 Miguez Bonino, *Toward a Christian Political Ethics*, p. 44.

19 See, for instance, the charge by Dennis McCann that liberation theology 'politicizes' the gospel: 'Practical Theology and Social Action: Or What

Can the 1980s Learn from the 1960s' in *Practical Theology: The Emerging Field in Theology, Church, and World*, ed. Don S. Browning (San Francisco, 1983), pp. 105–25.

20 For instance, the famous 'Ratzinger Letter' (actually 'Instruction on Certain Aspects of the Theology of Liberation') criticizes liberation theology for its faulty biblical hermeneutics, as well as its reductionism and uncritical use of Marxism.

21 Schubert Ogden, for instance, has criticized liberation theologians for equating redemption and emancipation in his *Faith and Freedom: Toward a Theology of Liberation* (Nashville, Tenn., 1979).

22 See, for instance, the criticism of James Gustafson, *Ethics From a Theolocentric Perspective*, vol. I (Chicago, Ill., 1981), p. 73.

23 See, for instance, Rebecca S. Chopp, *The Praxis of Suffering: An Interpretation of Liberation and Political Theologies*, pp. 144–8.

## BIBLIOGRAPHY

### Primary

Alves, Rubem, *Tomorrow's Child: Imagination, Creativity, and the Rebirth of Culture* (New York, 1972).

Assman, Hugo, *Theology for a Nomad Church* (Maryknoll, NY, 1976).

Boff, Clodovis, *Theology and Praxis: Epistemological Foundations* (Maryknoll, NY, 1987).

Boff, Leonardo, *Jesus Christ Liberator* (Maryknoll, NY, 1978).

—, *Church: Charism and Power: Liberation Theology and the Institutional Church* (New York, 1985).

—, *Ecclesiogenesis: The Base Communities Reinvent the Church* (Maryknoll, NY, 1986).

Comblin, Joseph, *The Church and the National Security State* (Maryknoll, NY, 1979).

Dussel, Enrique, D., *Ethics and the Theology of Liberation* (Maryknoll, NY, 1978).

—, *A History of the Church in Latin America: Colonialism to Liberation (1492–1979)* (Grand Rapids., Mich., 1981).

—, *Philosophy of Liberation* (Maryknoll, NY, 1985).

Gutierrez, Gustavo, *A Theology of Liberation: History, Politics and Salvation* (Maryknoll, NY, 1973).

—, *The Power of the Poor in History: Selected Writings* (Maryknoll, NY, 1983).

—, *We Drink From Our Own Wells: The Spiritual Journey of a People* (Maryknoll, NY, Melbourne, 1984).

—, *On Job: God-Talk and the Suffering of the Innocent* (Maryknoll, NY, 1987).

Miguez Bonino, José, *Doing Theology in a Revolutionary Situation* (Philadelphia, 1975).

—, *Toward a Christian Political Ethics* (Philadelphia, 1983).

—, *Faces of Jesus: Latin American Christologies* (Maryknoll, NY, 1984).

Miranda, José, *Marx and the Bible* (Maryknoll, NY, 1974).
Segundo, Juan Luis, *The Community Called Church* (Maryknoll, NY, 1973).
—, *Grace and The Human Condition* (Maryknoll, NY, 1973).
—, *Our Idea of God* (Maryknoll, NY, 1973).
—, *The Sacraments Today* (Maryknoll, NY, 1974).
—, *Evolution and Guilt* (Maryknoll, NY, 1974).
—, *The Liberation of Theology* (Maryknoll, NY, 1976).
—, *Jesus of Nazareth Yesterday and Today*, vol. I, *Faith and Ideologies* (Maryknoll, NY, Melbourne, London, 1982).
Sobrino, Jon, *Christology at the Crossroads: A Latin American Approach* (Maryknoll, NY, 1978).
—, *The True Church and The Poor* (Maryknoll, NY, 1984).

## Secondary

Berryman, Phillip, *Liberation Theology* (Oak Park, Ill., New York, 1987).
Brown, Robert McAfee, *Theology in a New Key: Responding to Liberation Themes* (Philadelphia, 1978).
Chopp, Rebecca S., *The Praxis of Suffering: An Interpretation of Liberation and Political Theologies* (Maryknoll, NY, 1986).
Eagleson, Jon, and Scharper, Philip (eds), *Pueblo and Beyond* (Maryknoll, NY, 1979).
Fabella, Virginia, and Torres, Sergio (eds), *Irruption of the Third World: Challenge to Theology* (Maryknoll, NY, 1983).
Freire, Paulo, *Pedagogy of the Oppressed* (New York, 1970).
Fierro, Alfredo, *The Militant Gospel: A Critical Introduction to Political Theologies* (Maryknoll, NY, 1977).
Gibellini, Rosino (ed.), *Frontiers of Theology in Latin America* (Maryknoll, NY, 1974).
Gottwald, Norman (ed.), *The Bible and Liberation: Political and Social Hermeneutics* (Maryknoll, NY, 1983).
Lamb, Matthew, *Solidarity with Victims: Toward a Theology of Social Transformation* (New York, 1982).
Lernoux, Penny, *The Cry of the People: The Struggle for Human Rights in Latin America – The Catholic Church in Conflict with US Policy* (New York, 1980).
Metz, Johann Baptist, *Theology of the World* (New York, 1969).
—, *Faith in History and Society: Toward a Practical Fundamental Theology* (New York, 1980).
—, *The Emergent Church: The Future of Christianity in a Postbourgeois World* (New York, 1981).
Moltmann, Jürgen, *Theology of Hope: On the Grounds and Implications of a Christian Eschatology* (New York, 1967).
—, *The Crucified God: The Cross of Christ as the Foundation and Criticism of Christian Theology* (New York, 1969).

# 10

# Black Theology

## Patrick A. Kalilombe

The term 'black theology' usually refers to theologies deriving from either the South African or the North American black context. Both these branches of theology are concerned with the present day situation of oppression and discrimination, and address themselves to questions of liberation and political freedom and justice. A distinction is often made between this black theology and 'African theologies' in the independent countries farther north which are considered to be more concerned with questions of culture and to focus more on the past than on the present.[1] However, despite their differences, these three theologies have recently been discovering a common root that binds them together: the experience of being black.

In all of history, Christian and otherwise, being black has never been a neutral, merely racial characteristic. It has usually been a predicament carrying with it concrete and painful consequences in human interactions. In varying degrees, this experience is shared by all black people: Africans in the South as well as in the rest of the continent, and also blacks in North America and in other parts of the world. Any meaningful theology from these situations must necessarily be influenced by this common experience. There is, thus, a point in accepting a wider sense of 'black theology' which would include the South African and North American varieties, as well as the 'African theology' trends.

The significance of this common black-ness as a basis for a specific type of Third World theologies has become clearer since the formation, in 1976, of the Ecumenical Association of Third World Theologians (EATWOT). The theological methodology of EATWOT stresses the importance of contextuality: the need to take into account specific human situations. The Third World theologizing communities of Latin America, Africa, and Asia share common conditions of poverty, exploitation, and powerlessness. They are, as a group, representatives of the 'losers': those on the 'underside of history'.[2] On this common experience of oppression, poverty, and exploitation is based the liberation thrust of all Third World theologies.

And yet black theologies are different from Latin American liberation theologies, as discussions within EATWOT have been demonstrating. Like African and North American types of liberation theology, Latin American theologies are strongly rooted in socio-economic and political questions: but unlike the former, the Latin American brands tend to be more influenced by Marxist analysis, and are mainly concerned with the class struggle in their countries. This type of theology, although one of the best known today, cannot pretend to be the unique model for all Third World theologies: the realities of Latin America are not those of Africa or North America. Africans are more and more aware that 'anthropological poverty' (denial of their culture and very humanity) is more significant for them, while black Americans are particularly conscious of the history of slavery and their experience of being uprooted. The class struggle that concerns Latin Americans is largely irrelevant to these blacks. For them race relations are of greater importance, whether these are a result of slavery, of colonialism or of neo-colonialism.

Therefore the three types, African theology, black theology in South Africa and in North America, have as a common additional Third World element the fact that throughout history the plight of blacks has been related to their blackness. The issue of race cannot be ignored, for their suffering and powerlessness are intrinsically bound up with their race and color.

## NORTH AMERICAN BLACK THEOLOGY

### Historical Development

The roots of black theology in North America are to be found in the experience of slavery. Blacks had been brought across the Atlantic as slaves. They were commodities that could be bought and sold, always dependent, vulnerable to exploitation and abuse, and hardly to be considered human beings. Slavery both created and reinforced the myth of black inferiority; and so widespread and so pervasive was this myth that blacks themselves were constantly in danger of developing a low self-esteem.

When the slaves first arrived, they were forbidden to practice their African religion, but were exposed to the religion of their white masters – Christianity, mostly in its Protestant form. Special missionaries and preachers were employed to teach them Christianity, for the religion they learned was designed to legitimize their state of slavery and to provide a taming influence by promising an escape from their misery into the green pastures of life hereafter. And yet, contrary to their masters' intentions, the Christian message offered the slaves something quite different: the encounter with a God of liberation and equality, with a Christ who understood and sympathized with their plight. Away from their master's watchful eye, in their cabins or in the secret meetings of the woods, they re-interpreted the Scriptures in stories, songs, and dances, giving their own exegesis to the venerable texts. The 'Negro Spirituals' represent an early stage of black theology.[3]

Such an independent appropriation of Christianity was obviously seen as dangerous and subversive by the masters, who then tried to restrict and control the slaves' exposure to the Bible. But this only served to drive the movement underground where an independent type of Christianity, penetrated by African beliefs and customs, developed among the blacks. When, after emancipation, they were able to come into the open, we discover two types of church belonging among the blacks. Some were members of the white-led denominations, often contributing to them a distinctive black flavor. But many others belonged to independent churches, in many cases breakaway groups from the white-led denominations where they had experienced discrimination or had been grudgingly given a second-class membership. In both cases, however, religion has been crucial for black survival, the main source of that astonishing resilience in hope and dignity which has kept the community going on as human beings in the face of tremendous odds. In the Church blacks found a haven where they could recapture and affirm the humanity denied them in everyday life. There they could freely exercize their gifts, could take initiatives, assume positions of leadership, and create a sacred space where the vision of Kingdom of God on earth become credible.

Even after emancipation in 1863, black experience in America has remained difficult. For many blacks freedom hardly meant a change in their situation. They were indeed emancipated, but as a group they have remained poor and powerless. They feel they are treated as second-class citizens by the white-dominated establishment. Although in theory they are considered as part of the American 'melting pot' and called to the same 'American Dream' of progress, affluence and world power, the actual working of socio-economic and political structures is loaded against them. Through practice, and often through unfair legislation, they are kept apart and debarred from free and equal cohabitation with the whites. There were the black belts of the south where blacks were mostly dependent share-croppers and work-hands, and in the north there developed the black ghettos in the decaying inner cores in the industrial centers. Segregation in education keeps blacks confined to poor schools; segregation in jobs and professions reserves for them less significant occupations in which they have little chance of competing with the whites.

To this state of relative poverty and powerlessness two types of response have developed within the black community, which continue the contrasting responses of slavery times: resignation and revolt. One trend, represented in the nineteenth century by Booker T. Washington, avoids confrontation between the races. It continues the traditional response of many blacks: a more or less conscious acceptance of the negative image given them by the white establishment. It promotes harmony and accommodation, seeking to improve the black people's lot through patient and realistic programs of self-help and development, thrift, and industry. The other trend, following in the footsteps of Bishop Henry M. Turner and W. E. B. Dubois, is more combative and suspects accommodation or assimilation as being an acceptance of the black people's submission to white supremacy. It sees social and political equality, and the winning of civil rights, as a prerequisite for black progress. Confrontation with the institutionalized white power structure is unavoidable, and premature accommodation can only weaken the chances of success. This trend continues the tradition of black resistance which has erupted in revolts throughout American history.[4]

## Survey

The conscious development of a distinct black theology is a relatively recent phenomenon. Its origin is usually placed in July 1966 with the declaration 'A Statement by the National Committee of Negro Churchmen'.[5] Three main stimulants have been identified as having led to the need for black theological reflection.[6] The first is the Civil Rights movement of the 1950s and 1960s. The involvement of many black church leaders in the struggle for freedom, alongside Martin Luther King, demanded a fresh confrontation with the message of the gospel. The second was the reaction provoked by a book published in 1964 by the black scholar Joseph R. Washington, Jr, entitled *Black Religion: The Negro and Christianity in the United States.*[7] Washington had said that black religion and the black churches did not have a real Christian theological content because they were separated from the white churches, and only if they became integrated into the mainline Christian tradition would they develop real theology. Such ideas provoked lively discussions about the true nature of black religion. The third and more immediate stimulant was the rise of the Black Power movement. At this time Martin Luther King's nonviolent struggle began to be seen as inadequate, and a more militant, separatist movement began, especially among the youth. Its slogan, 'Black Identity and Black Power', summarizes well its objectives. Confronted with this movement black church leaders were obliged to examine the issue of the relationship between black religion and the quest for identity and power among their people.

Gayraud S. Wilmore distinguishes three stages of development from the 1960s to the present time.[8] Between 1966 and 1970 it developed mainly within the churches, as it was largely black church leaders who responded to the different questions in various meetings and pronouncements. The second stage came in the early 1970s when the discussion of black theology moved from the churches into the universities and seminaries. Black studies had found a place on the curriculum, and black theology became an academic discipline. The influence of the churches decreased, with the result that, as those doing the theology were less accountable to the black community and its current experiences, the theologizing itself became less radical. The third stage, which began in the mid-1970s, saw links being made in various directions. In 1975 the 'Theology in the Americas' project brought black theologians into dialogue with Latin American liberation theology, while at the same time involving other minorities of the United States (Indians, Hispanics, Catholics, women) in the thinking process. Since the inauguration of EATWOT in 1976 American blacks have been participating in its conferences: in Africa, in Asia, in Latin America, and elsewhere. Thus in this third phase black theology is opening up into global concerns, sharing in ecumenical discussions, contributing its own insights as well as receiving challenges and stimulus from other quarters: black feminism and African theology in particular.

Naturally racism is the central theme in black theology, examined not only as a practice of secular society motivated by interests of a political, economic, societal nature, but also in theological terms. It starts off as a critique of traditional theology of both the white churches and the black community. White church theology has at best tended to ignore the uncomfortable topic of racism, and at worst provided a justification for it. Black traditional religious attitudes have let racism off the hook because of an almost exclusive concentration on 'spiritual matters' and on life after death.

In the face of black suffering, the 'theological' and 'christological' issues take on radical urgency. Who is God? On whose side is He? Black theology re-reads the Bible, and there discovers a liberating God, the champion of the oppressed (Exodus, the Prophets). Christ is 'black',[9] not in a facile racist sense, but theologically, since 'in a situation where the colour of a person's skin determines his or her opportunities in life, the gospel is not colour blind'.[10] What, then, does such a God want us to do? Here comes the theme of liberation as a process towards the building up of the 'beloved community' (Martin Luther King's favorite expression). But liberation conjures up a whole series of ethical questions. Being freed from oppression demands struggle, and struggle can be violent or nonviolent. Which is the gospel way, and on what conditions? Liberation is a process for change. Is it to be gradual evolutionary change, or a radical revolution? If racism is a sin, then conversion is called for, and only after such a renunciation of racism and after a change in attitudes can harmony and reconciliation take place in society. Such and many more are black theology's issues, as can be seen from a rapid examination of one of its representative proponents.

*James H. Cone*

Ever since James Cone wrote his *Black Theology and Black Power* (1969) his personality and thinking have been central to black theology. He was among the first to thrust this new type of theology on to the attention of academic scholarship, and has been its most representative exponent in the dialogue with other Third World theologians, especially within EATWOT. Among his major works and numerous articles, *For My People* (1984) is, to date, the most comprehensive survey of his thinking. But *God of the Oppressed* (1975)[11] marks the decisive turning-point, not only of his personal development, but of black theology itself. It is here that one sees the link between theology, the personality of the theologian, and the community from within which that theology is being done.

The book starts with a personal witness: how he was born and grew up in Arkansas, that typical arena of black experience. This early involvement in the black church and community in the American South was followed by academic training in the more liberal North. Subsequently Cone has taught in the South before taking up his present post at Union Theological Seminary in New York. All this was an appropriate background for the theological reflection in the book. The main contention is that 'one's social and historical context decides not only the questions we address to God but also the mode or form of the answers given to the questions' (p. 15). In the first chapters (2–4) the significance of this social context is examined: theology is indeed based on biblical revelation, but even in the Bible social existence gives the concrete shape to divine revelation. The study of Scripture is itself further determined by that same social context, which explains why 'white' theology in America interprets the divine Word differently from 'black' religious thought.

It is important therefore to address seriously the problem of ideology, as H. Richard Niebuhr did in *Christ and Culture* when he explored how human speech about divine revelation is conditioned by cultural and historical relativity. Black Theology results from the interface between God's Word and black experience. Chapters 6–10 take up the main questions. Who is Jesus Christ for us today? What is liberation? How does divine liberation relate to black suffering? In the area of Christian ethics, what relation is there between liberation and violence, between liberation and the reconciliation between Blacks and Whites?

*God of the Oppressed* is primarily an essay in theological methodology; but at that stage in the development of black theology it was a decisive contribution. Before black theology could begin to be taken seriously, the legitimacy of applying the principle of contextuality to black experience had to be established. In this, as in many other areas, James Cone's contribution has been programmatic. A weakness in Cone's early works was his almost exclusive basing of his reflection on the issue of black power, and a relative ignoring of the black church experience at the grass-roots.[12] Although a balance has been established in this respect, it still remains that Cone's works are more for the consumption of fellow intellectuals than a means of dialog with the common black folk. There is also a combative strain which makes the vision of an eventual reconciled black and white community difficult to imagine.

## Debate, Achievement, and Agenda

One area of questioning that North American black theology had to deal with in the early years was that of its relations with African theology.[13] Some African theologians (e.g. J. S. Mbiti and E. Fashole-Luke) refused to recognize that there were real links of kinship between the two theologies. North American theology, because of its roots in slavery, tends to promote separation between black and white, even among Christians. It insists on struggle, seems to condone violence, and is preoccupied with social and political issues. African theology on the other hand is based on culture and religion. It has a distinctively joyful and open spirit, where black theology is negative and narrow. But North Americans criticized African theology for being too much oriented towards the past while ignoring the burning issues of today. Since the foundation of EATWOT this controversy has lost its virulence. Instead, the two theologies now see each other as complementary and mutually challenging prongs of the same struggle.

Within black theology itself there have always been issues and trends confronting one another. Some theologians, for example, are more prone towards reconciliation (e.g. J. Deotis Roberts) while others underline the need for confrontation (e.g. James H. Cone). Should black theology develop primarily as a reaction to white theology with nothing really original from its own resources? Black theology is by no means a monolithic entity. To capture all its richness one should study its various protagonists. Besides G. S. Wilmore and James Cone, there are others like Cecil Cone, G. Eric Lincoln, Cornel West, Charles Long, Vincent Harding, and feminist representatives like Jacquelyn Grant, Delores Williams, or Kelly Brown.

Black theology started as a theological reaction to racism in both church and society, a prophetic voice against the typical 'internal colonization' in the United States. It has extended its arena, through contact with other Third World contexts, to include other manifestations of discrimination, poverty, and oppression. Its main contribution remains its experience in confronting racism at close range and on the home ground of the powerful American establishment whose influence all over the world is a marked feature of our times. The way forward seems to be along the line of mutual enrichment and challenge with the other Third World theologies. As black theology listens to Asia, to South Africa, to the Caribbean, the Pacific, the women, the disabled, etc., its own methodology will be enriched while its agenda is widened and its views challenged or confirmed. Multi-racial Britain could very well become its next partner in dialogue.

## AFRICAN THEOLOGY

### Historical Development

It is difficult to pinpoint exactly when and by whom the expression 'African theology' (*theologia Africana*) was first used, but the movement itself has a long history. Its roots lie in the ideas sown by North American blacks of the nineteenth century, e.g. E. W. Blyden (1893) and W. E. B. Dubois (1890). These early pan-Africanists, reflecting on slavery and colonialism, were concerned mainly with political questions, but they saw that the promotion of black peoples was dependent upon a reaffirmation of African culture and religion.

Moving into Africa, at the turn of the century, such ideas were translated into various forms of ideological resistance, not only to European colonial incursions, but also to the imposition of the white man's Christianity, as is evident in the early rise of independent churches in South Africa and elsewhere.[14]

Thus, as African nationalism took shape between and after the two world wars, there was in the churches also a latent corresponding trend of critique against the way evangelization had taken place. Becoming Christian was often presented as a rejection of the past in favor of adopting Western Christian ways of thinking and behaving. Implicit in this was the conviction that Christianity could not be based on traditional culture and that there was no real continuity between African traditional religions and the Christian message. Thus Christian evangelization was based on the same assumptions as colonialism: a rejection of the African personality and the need to impose Western civilization on Africans. It was against such racist attitudes that African thinkers began to rebel.

There is evidence that already in the years between the wars this movement of cultural and political vindication was growing, especially among young black students in the schools of Europe. In the 1930s a group of Caribbean and African students in Paris, led by such figures as Aimé Césaire (Martinique) and Léopold Senghor (Senegal), launched the famous Négritude movement with its review *Présence Africaine*, an affirmation and rehabilitation of black cultural identity in history, literature, and art. Fr Placide Tempels' *La Philosophie Bantoue*[15] was a seminal work by a European missionary in Africa. There he affirmed that there exists among the Bantu peoples of Africa a coherent thought system, 'a complete positive philosophy of existence, of life, of death and life after death'.[16] He claimed that this philosophy was centered on one value, 'vital force' (*la force vitale*), and then proceeded to show how a whole system of ontology, criteriology, psychology, and ethics derived from this center.

Later critics have rejected Tempels's concordism which artificially forces African thought into scholastic European categories. But the main contention, that the African way of life had a valid philosophy, was not lost on thinking Africans. In 1956 a team of black ecclesiastics studying in European universities published a collection of essays under the title: *Les prêtres noirs s'interrogent.*[17] Following the idea of adaptation in vogue at the time, the writers proclaimed the need to Africanize Christian doctrine, cult, pastoral practice and art, basing them on African culture and religious traditions. These ideas, in line with authoritative Roman Catholic pronouncements, find later support in the Second Vatican Council (1962–5). They represent the standard thinking among Catholic progressive thinkers in the 1960s and 1970s.

In 1960, at the newly founded Catholic Institute of Lovanium in Kinshasa (Zaire), a young student (later to become auxiliary Bishop T. Tshibangu) affirmed the possibility of a 'theology with an African color' based on the specific thought patterns of African culture. For, although divine revelation is one, and the principles of human reasoning are shared universally, there are special African characteristics which make it possible to do theology in an African way. Tshibangu's professor, Canon A. Vanneste, disagreed. For him Christianity and its theology are of universal validity since they are based on divine revelation which is one. It does not make sense, therefore, to speak of an African theology. The most one can concede is that doing theology *in Africa* should take the African experience into consideration, especially in catechesis and pastoral work. But this is not the same as accepting the possibility of an African theology.

Tshibangu's view has clearly won the day, for since the 1960s more and more Africans have joined in the effort to do their own theology. If among Catholics the Second Vatican Council gave impulse to this development, among Protestants the main stimulus has been the All Africa Council of Churches (AACC), founded in 1963.[18] The conferences and consultations which it has been sponsoring have helped many scholars in the churches as well as in the universities and colleges to become acquainted with the movement for African theologizing. In 1977 the Ecumenical Association of African Theologians (EAAT) was started in Accra. It has now become the main forum for the development of African theology.

## Survey

The earlier phase of African theology was mainly apologetic in character. It sought to affirm the validity of African traditional cultures and religions as bases for Christian theology.[19] But even in those years, definite themes and topics had already begun to emerge. Besides rather general works such as Kwesi Dickson's *Theology in Africa*,[20] or John S. Pobee's *Toward an African Theology*,[21] there are now more specific themes, e.g. F. Kabasele et al., *Chemins de la christologie africaine*.[22] In these last years a liberation type of African theology has been developing, the most impressive example of which is possibly Jean-Marc Ela's *The African Cry*.[23]

The main themes in African theology are those aspects of Christian faith and practice which Western culture has either neglected or played down, but which Africans seem to value specially. Such is the importance of community and communion (as against individualism). The value of solidarity and human relationships is affirmed not only among the living (family, clan, tribe), but also with the deceased, especially the ancestors. It goes farther in that life is seen as a constant interaction with the invisible (God, minor deities, and spirits). The whole creation is in fact dealt with as a partner in total existence rather than as an object out there (nature) which humans can exploit at will. There are in this attitude practical implications of an ecological nature. Similarly life is considered holistically as is apparent in traditional conceptions about health and sickness, good and evil. No wonder African theologians find the Old Testament very much alive and near to their way of life, including the propensity to symbolism and ritual.

By its very nature African theology pursues two tasks: a negative and a positive one. Negatively, African theology exposes and refutes several ways of thinking, both cultural and religious, which have underpinned the tendency to despise and do away with traditional cultures and religions. Of these the crudest is the one that claims Africans are sub-human, inferior, or underdeveloped simply because they have not followed the same path of progress as the 'civilized' peoples of the industrialized West. This powerful and deep-rooted myth made slavery and colonialism acceptable, and even conferred on them an aura of benefaction. To this end African theology examines Scripture and takes up the theme of humanity's oneness in spite of its diversity; the theme also of the 'image of God' present in every human being, and the fundamental equality and right to respect that this demands.

It also examines the theme of God's presence and salvific activity among peoples who are not visibly confronted with the historical manifestation of Jesus the Christ. By implication the project of African theology raises the question of what unity of Christian faith means as opposed to uniformity, and how the universality of the one Christian faith is to manifest itself in concrete forms. Many people who reject the whole idea of African or Black theology do so on the ground that there can be only one universal Christian theology which admits of no distinctions of color or race.

But Africa is, in the final analysis, a continent of oral tradition rather than of the written word. Perhaps the most exciting elaboration of African theology is being done in obscure corners where writing plays only a minimal role. Thus what is being lived in the independent churches in celebration, sermon, song, dance, prophecy, dreams, visions, and healing rituals constitutes authentic and original material for African theology. In the same way a new ecclesiology, new interpretations of the gospel message, and new modalities of liberation are being elaborated within the popular circles of the small Christian communities or the revival groups within main-line churches as well as beyond them.[24]

An example of such a theology, so elusive to traditional academic formulation, is Archbishop E. Milingo's ministry of healing and exorcism. What one can read in his writings[25] is but an inadequate expression of a truly theological praxis which has not yet found the kind of verbal form to give it the place it deserves in scientific circles. Among the skills most needed in African academic theologians is that of being sensitive to these theological productions of ordinary people at the grass-roots and being able to locate them, and then translate them into inter-cultural communicable form without betraying their original native quality. How African theologizing is actually done can best be seen through an essay of one of its practitioners.

*John S. Pobee*

Reverend John S. Pobee was born in 1937 in Ghana. A member of the Anglican Church, he studied at Oxford and subsequently taught in his home university of Ghana, Legon. But his acquaintance with different trends of Third World theology has deepened through involvement in Christian ecumenical work, culminating in his post at the World Council of Churches headquarters in Geneva in the department for theological education. He writes extensively on theological topics and has been a fervent promoter of conferences and consultations. His book *Toward an African Theology*,[26] although written in 1979, is the most appropriate place for capturing both his thought and methodology.

The first half of the book, consisting of four chapters, describes the concern of African theology thus: 'to interpret essential Christian faith in authentic African language in the flux and turmoil of our time so that there may be genuine dialogue between the Christian faith and African culture' (p. 22). For Pobee, his native Akan culture is an example of Africa's other cultures. Thus several elements are involved: faith, revelation, reflection. Contrary to some past missionary attitudes, according to which 'non-Christian' cultures are to be destroyed and wiped out (tabula rasa) so that 'Christianity' (i.e., in its Western form) can be put in their place, the right attitude is adaptation, localization or indigenization of Christianity to local cultures. For although Christianity is based on God's special, complete, and definitive revelation in Christ, nevertheless Scripture itself 'affirms that there are revelations of the deity other than the revelation in Jesus Christ' (p. 74). Even if this natural revelation through human cultures is a groping, and is subject to misunderstandings and corruption, there are valid elements in it which Christianity can assume and use in order to bring Christian revelation to the people. With right Christian faith and appropriate reflection, an African theology is therefore not only possible but highly desirable.

The rest of the book gives a series of examples in the application of these principles: christology (Christ as the Akan chief *okyeame*, mouthpiece of the paramount), sin and evil, Christian marriage, and the ethics of power. Typical of African Protestant/Anglican theologians, the method is invariably first to describe the Akan viewpoint, with abundant relevant proverbs, and then to bring in the Scriptures as congruent or critical of the culture. The last example, ethics of power, is evidence against those who accuse the cultural trend of shying away from confrontation with present-day socio-political issues or of simply looking back to a dead past. It is a lucid analysis and condemnation of the misuse of power in modern Africa, using not simply biblical evidence but also what is positive in African traditional culture.

Nevertheless, the limits of African theology are apparent in that even the best 'inculturated' examples make appeal to aspects of Akan culture which, in present-day culture change, might soon lose their power of appeal and usefulness.

## Debate, Achievement, and Agenda

The objection still being made against certain ways of doing cultural African theology is that this theology tends to deal with an artificially reconstructed past culture when it is not sure such a culture has much practical relevance in modern life. Clearly the question here is how one defines culture: as an idealized static collection of items from the past, or as the dynamic ever-evolving way of life of people which is the result of various influences, from the past and from the present, from within and from without. It is a pity that in many writings of African theologians this central notion of culture is not carefully defined or discussed.

African theologians do not speak the same language concerning the question of God's presence and salvific activity in non-Christian religions. While some find no difficulty in accepting the possibility of salvation outside the visible Christian church,[27] others are more cautious. They are sensitive to the dangers of 'syncretism' and what they call 'false universalism of salvation'.[28] In most cases, it seems to depend on what type of Western theological tradition the theologian has inherited. For similar reasons the distinction between 'African theology' and 'African Christian theology' is more meaningful for some than for others. 'African theology' would mean the thinking about God in traditional religion outside Christianity, whether it is considered positively or negatively; while 'African Christian theology' is the confrontation of the Christian faith with the way Africans think, assuming usually that they have been exposed to Christian faith. Here too, unhappily, many African theologians do not discuss fully and explicitly the basic issues implied.

The former type of African theology has probably seen its heyday. As life becomes more and more affected by contact with the wider world, the cultural specifics on which it based most of its reflection will slowly lose their relevance. Nevertheless, the significance of it lay in the values of African culture which it has identified, values which are potential elements of revitalization for world-wide Christianity. The lasting importance of the project of African theology itself lies in its protest against the cultural mutilation of other people's self-consciousness and self-respect, which produces 'anthropological poverty'. It is an achievement of the African theology project to have exposed and refuted any racial superiority complex attempting to justify itself through the Christian Scriptures.

Judging from what the Ecumenical Association of African Theologians has been working on in its recent conferences and consultations, it is permitted to foretell several future trends. There will be less naivete in portraying African traditional cultures and religions: we are more aware today of the wide varieties, contrasts, and complexities. The process of cultural change will be taken more seriously through a more careful analysis of the impact of outside influences, and a more sophisticated use of tools for historical reconstruction. Although the interest in inculturation will continue, more theological work will go into questions of development and liberation. It would seem indeed that the role of women and other marginalized sections of society in setting the theological agenda has been increasing. Africa is becoming more and more patently the scene of endless wars, famine, despotism, refugees, and militarism. The themes of justice, human rights, social and community restructuring will be dominant in theological reflection and praxis.

## SOUTH AFRICAN BLACK THEOLOGY

### Historical Development

Black theology in South Africa has its roots in a long tradition of protest against racial discrimination, appropriation of land, and economic exploitation to which the non-white groups have been subjected in the long history of European settlement in this part of the continent. This is because the Dutch immigrants (forebears of the modern Afrikaners) interpreted their occupation of South Africa and their confrontation with its inhabitants in the light of their Calvinistic faith.

'In obedience to Almighty God and to His Holy Word', so ran the 1942 draft constitution, 'the Afrikaner people recognizes its national calling, manifested in the history of the voortrekkers, as being that of developing South Africa in accordance with the Christian faith.'[29] Such an exegesis of history is based on a peculiar application of the doctrine of predestination. On the South African scene it means that God chose the white people as his own possession and ordained them to subject the heathens (in this case the blacks, the 'kaffirs'–unbelievers) making them into hewers of wood and drawers of water. Color and race became powerful symbols of distinction and apportioning of power and privilege.

In South Africa this blending of religious faith, color symbolism, and down-to-earth socioeconomic and political objectives has been directing the trend of history. The white minority, relying on Christian faith, progressively captured for itself positions of material and cultural superiority over the original black population and, later, other communities of non-European origin. In the name of the same faith a system of relationships emerged which serves to keep the racial groups separate and unequal. This practice of racial segregation became an officially entrenched juridical system (apartheid) when the Afrikaner Nationalist Party came to power in 1948.

The response of the oppressed black population has been expressed on both the secular and the religious levels. In 1912 the African National Congress (ANC) was formed with the intention of protecting the rights of black people and promoting their development. When its nonviolent methods were judged ineffective, the more revolutionary Pan Africanist Congress (PAC) arose in 1958 as a rival branch, with 'Africa for Africans' as its slogan. In recent years the ANC itself has felt pushed to opt for more forceful methods in response to repressions from the state.

Over the years it has become more and more evident that this apartheid system is not the sole responsibility of South Africa. It has links with the world-wide economic system, and is an extreme manifestation of the unjust relationships between the North and the South: between the Center, consisting of the affluent and powerful nations of the East and the West, and the Periphery, consisting of the poor nations in the Third World. In spite of pious words of condemnation directed towards South Africa, most nations are at heart reluctant to dismantle the system because they gain from it.

But since the apartheid system is based primarily on religious belief, black opposition has had to express itself on that level too. Even in the churches, the principle of separate but unequal existence was at work. In many cases Christian denominations have existed in separate congregations according to racial and color differences: white, 'colored', and black. Obviously such distinctions, when justified by God's Word, provoked a re-examination of Christianity itself. Was the God of white people the same as the God Africans acknowledged? Was it the Christ of the gospels that sanctioned discrimination between white and black?

The most impressive of the different reactions against the white people's Christianity has been the well-established and fast-growing movement towards African independent churches. Even if very little elaborate thinking has been produced within these churches, their very existence must be seen as an inchoate black theology.

## Survey

A consistent project for a black theology began to take shape in South Africa during the 1970s. Popular resistance was being met with naked repression, as was the case in the Sharpeville murders of 1960 and the Soweto incidents in 1976. Although the inter-racial Christian Institute, founded in 1963, had drawn the wrath of the regime and was forced to close in 1977,[30] theological reflection could not be stopped. The multi-racial University Christian Movement (UCM), established in 1967, became a forum for social and political reflection. The series of seminars on black theology which it organized in the course of 1971 gave birth to the first important publication of the movement.[31]

In 1969 the all-black South African Students Organization (SASO) was started by Steve Biko as a breakaway from the UCM, initiating the Black Consciousness movement. SASO's 1970 Manifesto on black consciousness stresses the need for South African blacks to reject all value systems seeking to make them foreigners in their own country, to define themselves and not to be defined by others, to become aware of the power they wield as a group, and to involve all oppressed sections in a joint commitment.[32] Predictably this sudden burst of black consciousness and black theology was included in the general proscription of 'subversive movements'. Steve Biko himself died in police custody in 1977.

But black theology itself could not be banished or silenced. It has carried on, especially through such prominent church leaders as Archbishop Desmond Tutu,[33] Bishop Manas Buthelezi and Reverend Allan Boesak.[34] The power of this theology is in its constant link with the leaders' pastoral involvement in the suffering of their people. They speak from personal experience as they too share the lot of their brothers and sisters: vexations, arrests, loss of passport, denigration, even threats of death.

In academic circles, too, there is a growing number of thinkers who brave the dangers involved in creative critical thinking and continue to produce work of theological scholarship: veterans like Gabriel Setiloane, or G. M. Motlhabi, and younger people like Thakatso Mofokeng, Bonganjalo Goba, Simon Maimela, Buti Tlhagale. Since 1976 and 1977 when EATWOT and EAAT were founded, these voices have been joining other Third World theologians in conferences and consultations, offering the challenge of a South African contribution.

Significantly, even the African independent churches and the evangelical denominations, which up to now could be considered as eschewing political involvement, have got down to a more realistic theology, much in line with what black theology has been saying all along.[35] Black theology is thus becoming a type of Christian consensus in face of the South African crisis.

Black Theology hinges on the fundamental theme of color, because the condition of being black or white has become a factor determining relationships between communities and individuals. To be black, or to belong to a given race, straight away determines the whole of life, social, economic, political, as well as religious. Color separates: to some it gives privileged rights and to others it denies even the most elementary ones. But above all, one color (white) grants power and superiority over the other (black).

All this raises fundamental theological questions. Against a long established system of oppression and injustice, is it realistic to put hope in reforms or should people contemplate radical revolution and the elimination of the system itself? But then that implies conflict. In the Christian vision, is there place for creative conflict? Is there such a thing as liberating violence? Christ came to bring reconciliation and love. But what are the requirements for an authentic reconciliation? Since the church is a community of love, what role should it play in a situation of racial discrimination and division?

In the *Kairos Document*[36] most of these questions have been taken up in a short but profound discussion. Theological reflection in South Africa bases itself on the Bible. But in addition to the usual Exodus theme, the more fundamental question of Creation widens the reflection. What does it mean to be made 'in the image of God'? Where do dignity and the rights of the human person come from? Color or ethnic belonging? Then come themes of power, its nature and the reason for its existence, its use and its abuse. What should one do if the very humanity is denied or ridiculed? Has one the duty to struggle to safeguard it? Are God and his Christ on the side of an oppressive group or are they with the poor and oppressed?

South African theology gives great importance to questions of reconciliation, of redemptive suffering, of nonviolence. It insists on the fact that the liberation hoped for is for both blacks and whites. It is a theology deeply rooted in the life of the church and could not be accused of secularism, still less of Marxism. A look at one of the best known South African theologians should help us to see the kind of questions that are usually dealt with.

*Allan Aubrey Boesak*

The choice of Dr Boesak as representative of black theology in South Africa is appropriate for two main reasons. He is a 'colored', that is, of mixed blood: in his very person are manifested the tragedy and the contradictions of the apartheid system. At the same time he is a prominent leader in the Calvinist Dutch Reformed Church, and thus knows from the inside the tradition in which apartheid finds its theological basis.

A South African by birth, he studied in Holland and has intimate knowledge of black theology in the United States. At the assembly of Ottawa in 1982, when the white wing of the Dutch Reformed Church (the NGK) was expelled from the World Reformed Alliance and apartheid was declared a heresy, Boesak was elected President of the World Reformed Alliance. A fitting symbol of creative protest.

In *Black Theology, Black Power*[37] he exposes the 'innocence' of both white and black churches, which 'hides painful truths behind a façade of myths and real or imagined anxieties'.[38] Among whites the myth is that apartheid is based on Christian love: separation and alienation can be tolerated provided the whites can do something *for* the blacks. The blacks innocently accept and internalize the negative image made about them. To demythologize both myths, a biblical analysis of liberation (chapter 1) and power (chapter 2) is necessary.

Liberation starts when the blacks discover that in the specific context of South Africa, Christ cannot be white but black; the Black Messiah; the presence of Yahweh the liberator of the oppressed. His gospel is for the poor; his love for them is in view of eliminating their 'nonhumanity' so that they can begin to love the image of God that is in them. Loving themselves in this way does not mean hating the oppressor, but it means refusing to accept a 'brotherhood' where the one brother is master of the other.

Liberation is not possible without an adequate consideration about power. Oppression and exploitation come from a misuse of power, a usurpation of power-over-others reducing them to dependency. Blacks must protest against such oppression, first by rejecting negative self-images, and then by affirming their God-given power: the Holy Spirit.

In chapter 3, 'Where the Spirit Moves', Boesak examines the meaning and implications of God's Spirit as empowerment. Liberal and nationalistic theologies, as well as black nationalism, are here subjected to criticism. The book ends with a 'Quest for a Black Ethic'. The ethic of black liberation is necessarily situational, in the good sense. Values like hope, reconciliation, love of justice should not be discussed in the air: the total context of South African realities should be taken into account in the search for a truly Christian ethic.

*Black Theology, Black Power* is not an exhaustive or definitive statement of black theology. It can even be accused of being rather one-sided since it offers little in the way of positive and workable suggestions for conversion and change on the side of the white community. But it does offer a helpful model and methodology for confronting theologically the tragic situation in apartheid South Africa. Its great virtue is in not being a recipe for despair. Basically it is a declaration of courageous faith in the possibility of a new South Africa striving towards God's kingdom.

### Debate, Achievement, and Agenda

There was a time when people contrasted South African theology with its insistence on struggle for liberation, and the culture- and tradition-orientated theologies in the North. It is important to understand exactly why South Africans like Manas Buthelezi have expressed suspicion about the zeal to revalorize traditional customs of the past or to insist on maintaining Bantu cultural identity. The danger is not simply that of distracting attention from the real issues of modern life. In the context of South Africa, the apartheid ideology has made so much of national characteristics and has used the idea to keep different ethnic groups separate and divided (cf. the Bantustans). It is dangerous to play into the hands of such divisive and weakening tactics. At the same time, however, scholars like G. Setiloane have pointed out the need for the blacks to discover the basis of their own humanity, for future generations will want to have the assurance of a valuable past on which to build a new, post-apartheid, South Africa.

The two preoccupations need not exclude each other. The present trend is towards a harmonious integration: more and more South Africans are realizing that the blacks will not be able to liberate themselves unless they first regain their cultural and human identity. At the same time theologians of inculturation have learned to give more attention to the present-day problems of post-colonial Africa.

The particular significance of South African black theology lies in that it forces the victims of the worst type of human oppression to fall back on the Word of God as the most promising and creative reaction to their plight. Black theology in South Africa is, on the whole, a truly Christian reflection. It goes beyond mere condemnation of white oppression by stressing that both the oppressed and the oppressor are victims of their fears. It also proposes reconciliation as the final objective, adding, nevertheless, that true reconciliation can only come after genuine conversion from egoistic preoccupation with sectional security and privilege. The basic Christian imperative of 'love chasing away fear' is at its center.

South African black theology is a developing reality: its future shape cannot now be determined in advance. But the main orientations it has taken are a timely challenge to Christian theology generally. Politics and economics can no longer be considered peripheral issues in a world where Christian nations are directly involved in creating wholesale poverty and inhuman suffering through systems of exploitation that attempt to hide safely behind God's Word. This South African theology might become the crucial ingredient in tackling theologically the global issue of North–South relationships.

## NOTES

1 Justin S. Ukpong, *African Theologies Now: A Profile* (Eldoret, Kenya, 1984).
2 Cf. S. Torres and V. Fabella (eds) *The Emergent Gospel: Theology from the Developing World* (London, 1978; original subtitle: 'Theology from the Underside of History').
3 Cf. James H. Cone, *The Spirituals and the Blues*.
4 Lerone Bennett, *Before the Mayflower* (Baltimore, Md, 1966).
5 G. S. Wilmore and James H. Cone (eds), *Black Theology: A Documentary History, 1966–1979*, pp. 23–30.
6 J. H. Cone, *For My People*, pp. 6–11.
7 Boston, 1964.
8 Wilmore and Cone, *Black Theology*, pp. 4–11.
9 Cf. Albert B. Cleage's *The Black Messiah* (New York, 1968).
10 Theo Witvliet, *A Place in the Sun*, p. 73.
11 New York, 1975.
12 Cf. His brother Cecil Wayne Cone's criticism in *The Identity Crisis in Black Theology* (Nashville, Tenn., 1975).
13 Josiah U. Young, *Black and African Theologies: Siblings or Distant Cousins?* (Maryknoll, NY, 1986).

14  Cf. Bengt Sundkler, *Bantu Prophets in South Africa*, 2nd edn (London, Lutterworth, 1961).
15  Paris, 1949.
16  *La Philosophie Bantoue*, p. 14, translated from French.
17  *Black Priests are Asking Themselves*, Paris, 1956.
18  Gwinyai Muzorewa, *The Origins and Development of African Theology* (Maryknoll, NY, 1985).
19  Cf. E. Bolaji Idowu, *African Traditional Religion* (Maryknoll, NY, 1975).
20  London, 1984.
21  Nashville, Tenn., 1979.
22  Paris, 1986.
23  Maryknoll, NY, 1981.
24  Cf. P. A. Kalilombe, 'Doing Theology at the Grassroots: A Challenge for Professional Theologians', *The African Ecclesial Review*, 27 (1985), pp. 148–61; 225–37.
25  Emmanuel Milingo, *The World in Between* (London, 1984).
26  Nashville, Tenn., 1979.
27  Cf. P. A. Kalilombe, 'The Salvific Value of African Religions', in G. H. Anderson and T. F. Stransky (eds), *Mission Trends No. 5*, (New York, 1981), pp. 50–68.
28  For example, Byang H. Kato, *Theological Pitfalls in Africa* (Kisumu, Kenya, 1975).
29  *Vivante Univers*, 1987, p. 8, n. 369 (translation).
30  Peter Walshe, *Church and State in South Africa* (Maryknoll, NY, 1983).
31  Cf. Basil Moore (ed.), *Essays in Black Theology* (Johannesburg, 1972). English editions: *Black Theology: The South African Voice* (London, 1973); *The Challenge of Black Theology in South Africa* (London, 1974).
32  Basil Moore (ed.), *Black Theology* (London, 1973).
33  Desmond Tutu, *Hope and Suffering* (London, 1984).
34  Allan Boesak, *Black and Reformed*.
35  *Evangelical Witness in South Africa: South African Evangelicals critique their own Theology and Practice* by 132 Concerned Evangelicals (Johannesburg, 1986).
36  *Kairos Document: A Theological Comment on the Political Crisis in South Africa*.
37  Allan Aubrey Boesak, *Black Theology, Black Power*.
38  *Farewell to Innocence* is the original (Maryknoll, NY) title of the book.

## BIBLIOGRAPHY

### General

Chenu, Bruno, *Théologies chrétiennes des tiers mondes* (Paris, 1987).
Ferm, Deane William, *Third World Theologies*: 1. *An Introductory Survey*; 2. *A Reader* (Maryknoll, NY, 1986).

Witvliet, Theo, *A Place in the Sun: An Introduction to Liberation Theology in the Third World* (London, 1985).
Young, Josiah U., *Black and African Theologies: Siblings or Distant Cousins?* (Maryknoll, NY, 1986).

## North American Black Theology

Cone, James H. *Black Theology and Black Power* (New York, 1969).
—, *A Black Theology of Liberation* (Philadelphia, 1970).
—, *The Spirituals and the Blues* (New York, 1972).
—, *For My People* (Maryknoll, NY, 1984).
Gardiner, J. and Roberts, Deotis, Sr (eds), *Quest for a Black Theology* (Philadelphia, 1971).
Jones, Major, *Christian Ethics for Black Theology* (Nashville, Tenn., 1974).
Lincoln, C. Eric (ed.), *The Black Experience in Religion* (Garden City, NY, 1974).
Malcolm X, *Malcolm X Speaks* (New York, 1965).
Roberts, J. Deotis, *Liberation and Reconciliation* (Philadelphia, 1971).
Wilmore, Gayraud S., *Black Religion and Black Radicalism* (Garden City, NY, 1972).
Wilmore, G. S. and Cone, James H. (eds), *Black Theology: A Documentary History 1966–1979* (Maryknoll, NY, 1979).

## African Theology

Appiah-Kubi, Kofi and Torres, Sergio (eds), *African Theology en Route* (Maryknoll, NY, 1979).
Imasogie, Osadolor, *Guidelines for Christian Theology in Africa* (Achimota, Ghana, 1983).
Magesa, Laurenti, *The Church and Liberation in Africa* (Eldoret, Kenya, 1976).
Mbiti, John S., *African Religions and Philosophy* (Garden City, NY, 1970).
—, *New Testament Eschatology in an African Background* (London, 1971).
Nyamiti, Charles, *Christ as our Ancestor* (Gweru, Zimbabwe, 1984).
Parratt, John, *A Reader in African Christian Theology* (London, 1987).
Sawyerr, Harry, *Creative Evangelism: Towards a New Christian Encounter with Africa* (London, 1968).
Tshibangu, Tchishiku, *Le propos d'une théologie africaine* (Kinshasa, 1974).

## South African Black Theology

Becken, H. J., *Relevant Theology for Africa* (Durban, 1973).
Biko, Steve, *Black Consciousness and the Quest for a True Humanity* (Durban, 1972).
Boesak, Allan A., *Black Theology, Black Power* (London, Oxford, 1978).

—, *Black and Reformed* (Maryknoll, NY, 1984).

Buthelezi, Manas, *An African Theology or a Black Theology* (Durban, 1972).

de Gruchy, J. W., *The Church Struggle in South Africa* (Grand Rapids, Mich., 1979).

Kairos Document. *A Theological Comment on the Political Crisis in South Africa*, 2nd edn (London, 1986).

Kretzschmar, Louise, *The Voice of Black Theology in South Africa* (Johannesburg, 1986).

Mabona, Anthony, *White Worship and Black People* (Durban, 1972).

Mabuza, W. M., *Christianity and the Black Man in South Africa Today* (Durban, 1972).

Setiloane, Gabriel M., *The Image of God among the Sotho-Tswana* (Rotterdam, 1976).

—,*African Theology: An Introduction* (Johannesburg, 1986).

# 11

# Asian Theology

## Kosuke Koyama

### INTRODUCTION

The aspiration of theological work in Asia has been well expressed by the title of a paper prepared for a consultation on theology and theological education in Indonesia in 1970 – 'Double Wrestle'. The consultation saw theology confronted by two major challenges: study of the Word of God and Christians' social responsibility. This was said against the background of the prevalent theology, mainly imported from the West, which held that the church in Asia should not be involved in social action.

In accordance with the spirit of the Indonesian consultation I want to list six themes through which theology in Asia has expressed itself since 1945, the year of Hiroshima. They are: Christ and (1) revolutionary social changes, (2) massive poverty, (3) ethnic and economic minorities, (4) creative and destructive aspects of cultures, (5) the people of other faiths, and (6) the reality of a divided church. On these subjects a series of books written by the members of the Ecumenical Association of Third World Theologians (EATWOT), and published since 1976, are valuable.[1]

All theological positions and experiences are challenged by the biblical proclamation. Theology in Asia then should not be a mere counter-concept to theology in the West. It must respond primarily to the biblical proclamation of Christ and not to Western theology. This is the basic orientation relevant to what Asian theologians call responsible contextualization of theology.

What is the biblical message that perturbs the core of Asian spirituality? According to Abraham Heschel, the Bible proclaims the God who is impassioned (*pathos*) and rules the world with justice (*ethos*).[2] It is the faith in this God of pathos and ethos that has challenged Asian spirituality in its depth and has inspired theologians in Asia to engage in a process of theological contextualization. This God invites Asians to a new understanding of world and humanity.

Colonial dominance of Asia by the Christian nations of the West began in the early part of the seventeenth century. (The British East India Company was chartered in 1600, the Dutch East India Company in 1602.) Often the Christian West has not behaved ethically towards Asia. An Asian scholar protests:

> [that] European nations had no moral obligations in dealing with Asian peoples (as for example when Britain insisted on the opium trade against the laws of China, though opium smoking was prohibited by law in England itself); this was part of the accepted creed of Europe's relations with Asia.[3]

Asia gradually began to question whether the religion of the West, Christianity, supports or condemns behavior such as that of the West towards Asia. This simple question contains the thrust of the Asian critique of Western colonialism. The accomplishment of Gandhi would have been unlikely apart from the power of this question directed at the Western Christian governments. During the colonial and post-colonial periods, Asia experienced the God of Christianity as the unity of pathos and ethos. Asian theologians today stand in this challenging tradition of theological debate. The four who will be discussed here are: Stanley J. Samartha of India, Choan-Seng Song of Taiwan, Hyun Younghak of Korea, and Kosuke Koyama of Japan.

### STANLEY J. SAMARTHA: THE MYSTERY OF TRUTH

Samartha is a visiting professor at United Theological College and a consultant to the Christian Institute for the Study of Religion and Society, both in Bangalore, India. For ten years he served as the first Director of the Dialogue Program of the World Council of Churches in Geneva. Dr Samartha is an ordained presbyter of the Church of South India. Formerly, he was professor and principal of Serampore College, West Bengal, India.

Samartha's distinctive contribution is in formulating a christology in a multi-religious society such as India. He does this as he endeavors to contextualize Christian theology.

> One must note that putting Jesus Christ in an ochre robe or painting the child Jesus in blue or dressing Mary in a sari does not necessarily make them more at home in India. . . . In India

the task is neither one of Hinduising Christianity nor of Christianising Hinduism. The fundamental question before the Church in India is this: what does it mean to affirm in India today that Jesus Christ is Lord and Saviour?[4]

In these concise words Samartha invites us to the focus of his theological concern: 'to affirm in India today that Jesus Christ is Lord and Saviour'. As this cannot be done simply by 'putting Jesus Christ in an ochre robe', he suggests a methodology of a direct connection between Indian thought and Jesus Christ: 'There is no reason why Semitic thought forms should be the norm for the Church's theological enterprise for all time to come. It is not necessary for Indians to become Jews first before they can catch a glimpse of the fulness of Christ.'[5]

Samartha points out that if Origen made use of the categories of Platonic thought and Aquinas those of Aristotle, Indian theologians must not hesitate to make use of the great philosophical insight of the Vedanta. What is required in India today is 'a spirit of adventure rather than one of conformity'.[6] This theological adventure is described in this way: 'While recognising the distinctiveness of the biblical approach to God and man, it is not necessary to use it as a yardstick to measure other approaches, particularly, in this instance, the advaitic approach to Reality.'[7] The Sanskrit word 'advaita' means 'non-duality' or 'allowing no second'. It means the eradication of 'duality'. God, world, and humanity form a single conception of unity. The great Vedanta philosopher Sankara (?788–820) has expounded the spiritual and philosophical value of the advaita view of the universe. In the perspective of advaita, reality is 'all-inclusive'.[8] For Samartha, however, 'the advaitic approach to Reality' does not take us to theological syncretism. Responsible religious persons reject, according to Samartha, both the 'crusade approach and the fruit-salad approach' to other faiths.[9] They seek rather 'a larger framework in which there is "differentiated inter-relatedness".' There people 'live together in community without in any way ignoring particularities'.[10] The 'differentiated inter-relatedness' expresses the spirit of advaita. The advaita perspective intimates to us Mystery.

It [Mystery] is near yet far, knowable yet unknowable, intimate yet ultimate and, according to one particular Hindu view, cannot even be described as 'one'. It is 'not two' (advaita), indicating thereby that diversity is within the heart of Being itself and therefore may be intrinsic to human nature as well.'[11]

Samartha refrains, however, from calling Jesus Christ an advaitin – one who had realized his identity with the ultimate Brahman.[12] Samartha thinks that making Christ an advaitin may give a fair emphasis on Christ's interiority, but may not give 'sufficient weight to the social, historical dimension of his life and work'.[13] What Samartha is driving home is that in his deep interior spirituality as well as in his 'social, historical dimension', Christ retains his unbound freedom. Here the Indian concept of advaita has done its most useful preparatory job and now it waits for the coming of Christ. In Christ 'history and nature are held together'.[14] The unbound Christ 'can never be identified with any particular cultural situation nor tied down to a particular system of thought'.[15] Thus this Christ presents a stumbling-block to us 'not only in the context of advaita but in every human situation'.[16] It is this Christ who is the incarnation of the Truth of the Truth (*Satyasya Satyam*). The Mystery 'is the transcendent Center that remains always beyond and greater than apprehensions of it or even the sum total of those apprehensions'.[17] Ultimately, humanity is confronted by the Mystery that the unbound Christ reveals. 'Mystery provides the ontological basis for tolerance'.[18] This makes a genuine interreligious dialogue possible. Because of the power of the Mystery, religious dialogue enables us 'to find out both what are the authentic changes which the Gospel demands and the authentic embodiment which the Gospel offers'.[19]

For Samartha there is no human community apart from 'sharing the meaning and mystery of human existence, struggling together in suffering, hope and joy'.[20] The unbound Christ inspires men and women to ask a question 'how in a world of many living faiths and ideologies, men and women can best work together on the basic issues of human life'.[21] To confess that Jesus Christ is unbound in his works of grace in the world is to engage in inter-religious dialogue. Out of dialogue comes a new insight in reading the Bible. An example: 'Just because it [the suffering of Christ] was a "scandal" to the Jews and a "stumbling block" to the Greeks in Paul's time, it is foolish to insist that it ought to be a skandalon to all Hindus and Buddhists.'[22] We are made aware of the Mystery as we 'work together on the basic issues of human life'.

How is the image of the 'distinctiveness'[23] of Christ understood in the world of religious pluralism?[24] The following paragraph expresses Samartha's theological stance.

There are different faiths, there are alternative ways of salvation, there are different hopes about human destiny, there are different affirmations as to what happens in the end. In the last analysis, religions should be recognized as having responded differently to the mystery of the Ultimate. While recognizing the plurality of these answers, Christians believe that in Jesus Christ the Ultimate has become intimate with humanity, that nowhere else is the victory over suffering and death manifested so decisively as in the death and resurrection of Jesus Christ, and that they are called upon to share this good news humbly with their neighbors.[25]

The advaita perspective helps the Indians to see the image of the unbound Christ who intimates the presence of Mystery. Thus Samartha, a faithful and wise son of the great Indian spiritual tradition, wants to convey the pathos of God.

CHOAN-SENG SONG: THE WORD HAS TO ASSUME ASIAN FLESH

Song is Professor of Theology at the Pacific School of Religion in California. He was formerly Principal of Tainan Theological College, in Taiwan, and Associate Director, Commission on Faith and Order of the World Council of Churches in Geneva.

The central theological issue for Song is the meaning of the salvation history embodied in Israel/Church for the Asian peoples.

The people of Israel were singled out, under a divine providence inexplicable to us and even to them, not to present themselves to the rest of the world as the nation through which God's redeeming love would be mediated, but to be a symbol of how God would also deal redemptively with other nations. In the light of the experiences unique to Israel, other nations should learn how their histories can be interpreted redemptively. An Asian nation would have its own experiences of exodus, captivity, rebellion against Heaven, the golden calf. It would have its own long trek in the desert of poverty or dehumanization. What a nation goes through begins to take on redemptive meaning against the background of the history of Israel, symbolically transported out of its original context to a foreign one. An Asian nation will thus be enabled to find its place side by side with Israel in God's salvation. The Old Testament has shown how the history of a nation can be experienced and interpreted redemptively. If this is so, the theology which regards Israel and the Christian Church as the only bearers and dispensers of God's saving love must be called into question.[26]

Song wrote this paragraph in 1976. The focus of the quotation is in the last sentence. Throughout his prolific theological career this theme remains a constant motif. The primary focus of discussion is on the Old Testament (Israel). What is the theological relevance of the story of Israel for Asian peoples? His answer is that Israel is 'a symbol of how God would also deal redemptively with other nations'. Hence the title of the article: 'From Israel to Asia: A Theological Leap'. God would deal with China thus since God has dealt with Israel thus. This is where Song's radical contextualization of theology begins.

Song names his methodology a 'transposition':

> A transposition from the Israel-centered view of history to the view that regards other nations as constructive parts of God's design of history is required for a more realistic perception of God's work in the world. Such new theology of history contains a tacit admission that Israel alone cannot explain world history.[27]

In contrast to the Israel-centered Deuteronomistic theology (i.e. one centered on the historical books of Joshua, Judges, 1 and 2 Samuel, 1 and 2 Kings), Song is deeply moved by the global theology of Second Isaiah.[28] In the episode of God calling Cyrus, the emperor of Persia, for the execution of God's purpose in the world (Isa. 48:15), Song sees a decisive theological breakthrough.

> The relation between God and Cyrus is a far more fundamental kind – it is a relationship of love. It is the intimate bond of love that ties Cyrus to God. It is no easy thing for the Jews in the diaspora to accept this fact into their faith and theology, but they must try. In Cyrus God has shown them another center where people become closely related to God. There will be yet other centers. Their one-center theology must become a multi-center theology. Their one-way system of faith is faced with the possibility of a multi-way system of faith. Second Isaiah proves to be a daring pioneer of faith whose vision of God at work in history is enriched and enlarged by a pagan king whom he calls God's loved one.[29]

It was 'a very big theological blunder' when theologians 'forced God's redemption into the history of a nation and of the Christian Church'.[30] Song's 'Theology from the Womb of Asia' is an example of 'multi-center theology'. Behind such theological assertion is Song's deep commitment to the salvation of Asian humanity: 'As we plunge more deeply into the spirit, the heart, and the soul of our

Asian humanity embodied in religions, cultures, and histories outside the sphere of Christian influence, do we not have to rethink radically the Christian doctrine of election?[31]

In this radical rethinking of the doctrine of election ('transposition'), Song obviously groups together Israel and the Christian church. What is said about Israel can be said to the Christian church. The church, too, is 'a symbol of how God would also deal redemptively with other nations'. Song writes in a compact and critical style: 'One cannot assume the church as the base of theology – as western theology does – when one is doing theology in a multi-religious context or in the context of a political ideology which offers an alternative way of salvation.'[32] For Song, it is not in church but in 'the Word that has assumed Asian flesh' that Asians find their salvation. The following paragraph is important to locate Song theologically.

> In the final analysis, the Word has to assume Asian flesh and plunge into the agony and conflict of the mission of salvation in Asia. This flesh will be broken as it was broken on the cross. But when this Asian flesh assumed by the Word is broken, the saving and healing power of God will be released into the struggle of men and women for meaning, hope and life.[33]

## HYUN YOUNGHAK: THEOLOGY OF THE HAN-RIDDEN GUTS OF THE OPPRESSED

Formerly Professor of Religion and Culture of Ewha Women's University, Seoul, Korea (1946–86), Professor Hyun was Henry Luce Visiting Professor of Ecumenics and World Christianity at Union Theological Seminary, New York in 1982–3.

Hyun Younghak of Korea is a minjung theologian. The Korean word 'minjung' means 'those who are oppressed politically, exploited economically, marginalized sociologically and despised culturally, in Biblical language foreigners, widows, orphans, the poor and "the sinners" and in practical terms poor farmers, exploited industrial workers, urban squatters, beggars, etc'.[34] What then is minjung theology?

> Minjung theology is not of, by, or for the minjung people. It does not intend to 'conscientize' or agitate them. It tries to learn who and what they are both in history and in the current reality through what they see, what they feel, what they perceive, what they think, what they do and how they live, as expressed in

their culture as well as in their 'social biography'. It tries to learn
from them. It tries to trace the Gospel message back beyond 'the
Christian era' when the church became a community of ruling
élites to the earliest church when 'the sinners', those who were
treated as sinners such as prostitutes, collectors and lepers, and
the lowliest ones in the society, were the followers of Jesus.[35]

Hyun recognizes the social fact that he himself, in company with
other minjung theologians (most of them have theological degrees
from the prestigious schools in the West), does not belong to the
class of minjung people, and 'feels guilty' about it. He is confident,
however, that what he is doing is meaningful for his fellow
Christians, intellectuals, and educated people in general.

Associating himself with the minjung, Hyun begins his contextualization of theology. His God is passionate about justice.
Hyun soon discovers that the minjung's 'bodily' perception of the
human reality is 'honest, authentic and truthful'.

Bodily life produces bodily responses to reality in the form of
feeling. This feeling is the total human response to the whole of
reality. It is raw and concrete, not refined or abstract. It is
honest, authentic and truthful. On the other hand, the ruling
class grasps the reality second hand, that is, through reflection. . . .
For the society to be transformed and humanized, the cerebral
elements always have to be faithful to and learn from the
visceral elements, especially in times of radical changes.[36]

Hyun's writings carry the intriguing quality of 'bodiliness' in their
words and concepts. He himself, though not a member of the
minjung class, tries to cross the border from 'second hand' theology.
Bodily history speaks bodily language. It is a language distanced
from that spoken in the traditional circles of theology and ministry.
Hyun describes it thus: 'Obscene and curse words are the language
of the guts that spit out of the twisted guts, the 'han'-ridden guts of
the oppressed and the exploited.'[37]

Hyun realizes that Korean theology has taken shape away from
the concrete reality of people: 'Because of our legalistic and pietistic
preoccupations we have lost sight of our people as they exist in the
concrete world and become indifferent to 'the signs of the times'.[38]
Through the eyes of the minjung Hyun tries to read the signs of the
times. In a number of ways he expresses the minjung's 'bodily' and
therefore 'truthful' perception of reality: 'God saved the Hebrews
physically, liberating them from the slavery in Egypt. There is no
salvation or salvation history apart from the bodily life or the
"secular" history.'[39]

This bodiliness is best seen where Hyun, with fellow Korean professor Suh Nam-dong, combines it with the 'han' of the minjung. The minjung are 'the han-ridden people in the bodily history'.[40] What does the Korean word 'han' mean? 'It is a repressed murmuring, unexpressed in words or actions. It does not change anything. It might arouse a sense of revenge at most. But mostly it would be submission or resignation to fate.'[41] According to the Korean poet Yang Sung-woo, 'the han which has been absorbed into the bones and muscles of the people of the country for 5,000 years is still breathing in the roots of the grass which covers the graves of the dead'.[42] For Hyun the truth of the Christian message resonates through the voice of the han-ridden people, the people who define Hyun's contextualization of theology.

In the concrete life of the han-ridden minjung Hyun sees the depth of humanity. 'The pain in the inner-most part of the deprived helps them to envision and enjoy the deepest and the highest pure joy of the religious nature of human beings.'[43]

The minjung are eschatological people, since they are allowed to experience within this historical time the last laugh with God. 'Minjung looked like a clown', Hyun writes, 'becoming an object of laughter and yet keeping the last laugh for himself with God.'[44] This eschatological quality of the minjung comes from their remarkable freedom from the 'danger of self-righteousness'.[45] The eschatological minjung carry on their shoulders, according to Hyun, the sins of the world.

> It is the sins of the whole human history, the sins of the total social structure and the culture and the sins of the social policy that produce and impose 'han-ridden' life on the minjung. The minjung therefore are the ones who are carrying on their shoulders the sins of the world. They are the scapegoat, the Lamb of God and the Suffering Servant.[46]

## KOSUKE KOYAMA: A PASSIONATE GOD FOR ASIA[47]

Kosuke Koyama was born in Tokyo in 1929. His grandfather had become a Christian through an Englishman, Herbert George Brand. 'One of the few things I heard and I still remember from my grandfather about his conversion to Christianity from Buddhism was that he was impressed by this man who was able to say that Jesus Christ is Lord without ever making derogatory comments upon Japanese culture or Buddhism.'[48] He studied in Japan at Tokyo

Theological Seminary, in the United States at Drew University and Princeton Theological Seminary and in Switzerland at the Ecumenical Institute of the World Council of Churches at Bossey. His master's thesis was on Augustine, his doctorate on Luther. He taught theology in Thailand Theological Seminary (1960–8), was Director of the Association of Theological Schools in South-East Asia (1968–74), and lectured in the University of Otago, New Zealand (1974–9). Since 1980 he has been at Union Theological Seminary in New York where he is Professor of Ecumenics and World Christianity and teaches in the areas of Asian theology, intercultural hermeneutics, ecumenical history and theology, and the theology of religions.

He has been deeply influenced by and theologically concerned with his experience of Japan during and after the Second World War, and his teacher Kitamori's 'theology of the pain of God' has been a constant theme in his own theology. Other concerns have been encounters with members of various religions, especially in Asia; the impact of modernization on Asian societies; the importance of social ethics; the pervasiveness of idolatry; and the interpretation of the Bible in different contexts. His main works have been *Waterbuffalo Theology* (1974), *No Handle on the Cross* (1977), *Three Mile an Hour God* (1978), and *Mount Fuji and Mount Sinai* (1984), together with numerous other books and articles.

The style of Koyama's theology is striking. It is full of freshly coined imagery and pregnant phrases – 'history-gravity' means 'suffering-gravity'; the West as both gun and ointment for the East; taking Christ with 'Aristotelian pepper and Buddhist salt'; the Promised Land as 'a busy, dangerous, unsettling intersection-land' where Asia, Africa, and Europe meet; the danger of Christianity's 'teacher complex'; the contrast of the obvious attractiveness of an air hostess with the 'theological' beauty of some old, wrinkled Russian women; 'the unemployed God who meets us at the periphery'. It is not concerned to develop lengthy analyses or arguments, it subverts or explodes positions that seem to him too neatly systematic and coherent, and it points in many ways to the complexity, variety, and ambiguity of reality. There are few confident overviews in this theology. Rather there is a constant questioning, ethical, and imaginative engagement with particular issues and situations, and the attempt to open them up to a better understanding and future. The approach is dialogical and practical. It proceeds usually in short bursts and in a staccato style which provokes the reader and creates new perceptions and connections. It is a combination of prophetic and wisdom literature suited to the perplexing, agonizing and exciting meeting of ancient and modern, Buddhist and Christian, East and West, rich and poor.

A lively engagement with the Bible runs through all of Koyama's theology. It is not at the level of arguing for a particular status for Scripture or a doctrine of revelation or inspiration. It uses Scripture in a variety of ways, often offering new imaginative insights or making surprising links with modern situations. Its apparent spontaneity and even naivete can be deceptive: it conceals and is disciplined by an acquaintance with modern scholarship and by wide learning in the Christian tradition, especially in patristics, Luther and twentieth-century biblical and ecumenical theology.

Three key themes will serve as an introduction to the content of his thought: God and idolatry, the encounter with Buddhism, and the phenomenon of greed.

On God, one of his favorite texts is Hosea 11:8, 'My mind is turning over inside me, my emotions are agitated all together.' This points to an impassioned God deeply involved in the experience of history. Prophetic theology is the attempt to experience history through the 'painful inner life of God', as made most clear in the crucifixion of Jesus. 'The word of the cross points to God's agitated emotions because of God's love towards us.'[49] A central image is of 'the broken Christ healing the broken world'[50] not by ruling from the center but by going to the periphery and thereby giving a new concept of center symbolism. This then becomes the main criterion in a critique of idolatry, which is seen as the fundamental problem in our world. Idolatry is recognized in many forms: it misuses center symbolism by divorcing it from social ethics and making all serve the selfish interests of the center; it subordinates meaning to efficiency, especially through modern technology; it leads a group on the path of destructive self-glorification; it believes 'might is right'; it boosts the finite to the infinite; it has a god that does not radically criticize his worshippers and who tries to save himself, not others. All this is worked out with reference to contemporary issues, especially the modern history of Japan, and the conclusion is that 'it is the crucified Christ who exposes the subtle essence and manifestation of idolatry'.[51]

The spirituality that accompanies this understanding is best summed up in Koyama's essays 'Towards a Crucified Mind' and 'Three Modes of Christian Presence'.[52] The three modes are:

(a) stumbling presence; can a house unshaken bear witness to the earthquake which is going on?
(b) 'discomforted' presence; can Christians who do not involve

themselves in the great 'discomfort' of the nailed Christ
point to the source of all comfort?
(c) 'unfree' presence; Christians are called to participate in all
situations of life as the Incarnate Lord fully did.[53]

Our second theme, the encounter with Buddhism, has been
worked out by him mainly in relation to Thailand and Japan. He
deliberately makes his approach hard to categorize, as labels such as
inclusive, exclusive, pluralist or syncretistic fail to do justice to the
complexity of interaction, similarity, and mutual illumination or
confrontation. He suggests how the Buddhist philosophy and
lifestyle of detachment can season the Jewish and Christian religion
of God's attachment to humanity. He confronts the tranquillity ideal
with the message of the wrath of God. He stresses the priority of
understanding Buddhists rather than Buddhism. He experiments
with the Hebraization of key Buddhist concepts such as *dukkha*
(suffering, unsatisfactoriness), *anicca* (transitoriness, impermanence)
and *anatta* (no self, no continuing identity). He reflects extensively
on the religious history of Japan, with its interaction of Shintoism,
Confucianism, Buddhism, and Christianity.

Above all he focuses on the contribution Buddhism makes
through its attention to overcoming greed, our third theme. Here
many of his main concerns converge: greed is closely linked to
idolatry, it provides a standpoint for a prophetic critique of modern
industrial society with clear practical implications (especially in his
treatment of Japan), and it leads into his major contribution to the
theology of religions, in *Mount Fuji and Mount Sinai*:

> Both Buddhist and biblical traditions are history oriented since
> they deal with historical human greed. The former speaks about
> history calmly – rationally and mystically – through the
> Conditional Arising, while the latter speaks passionately in the
> image of God who loves the world and history. This observation
> poses a great challenge to Christian theology. The relationship
> between Buddhism and Christianity is not that between 'true
> religion' and 'false religion'. It is to do with two different yet
> intertwined understandings of the history of human greed. God
> 'did not leave himself without witness' (Acts 14:17).[54]

The insistence on the importance of Christianity as a religion
concerned with history is always joined with both a sensitivity to
the ways in which other religions can be seen as 'historical' and also
an appreciation of the contribution of more 'cosmological' religions
to the understanding of reality. And the prophetic thrust is sharpest

in the area of social ethics and politics. The critical awareness of human greed bridges the cosmological and the historical and gives a key to interpreting the modern history of Japan, with its Westernization, imperialism, emperor-worship and post-war democracy and prosperity.

Koyama's theology as a whole is self-consciously Asian and is primarily dedicated to reflecting on the history and contemporary situations of Asia. He sees the appropriate 'personality' of theology in Asia centering on the message of the crucified Jesus. He offers an agenda for Asian theology which he himself sums up at the end of this chapter.[55]

Koyama's achievement is to have attempted a consistently cross-centered and strongly social and ethical theology in relation to the realities of Asia, while drawing extensively on Western Christian theology and himself living for long periods outside Asia. He combines a broad and thorough intellectual background with a style that largely conceals this in a sparkling biblical yet contemporary theology. Some critical questions that need to be pursued are: what, if any, is the place in Asian theology for more systematic, theoretical or analytical approaches? Does this very practical theology need such approaches? Might such a social and political theology benefit from closer engagement with the social sciences and critical history? What is the understanding of the church in his theology? Is his theology deeply connected to any particular Christian community? And finally, what are the problems with a theology that so single-mindedly focuses on the word of the cross and the corresponding suffering of God?

### DEBATE

Theological reflections of our four theologians are relevant to the six areas I mentioned at the beginning of this chapter. Here I would like to focus on four specific subjects that emerged as we considered these theologians.

1 *Evangelism and people of other faiths* Our theologians have suggested that a relativization of the 'Semitic thought form' for Christian theological construction is necessary. They ask does the idea of the Semitic thought form include that of the biblical ethical monotheism itself? In Samartha's words, 'religions should be recognized as having responded differently to the mystery of the Ultimate'. Does the mystery of the Ultimate contain both the Buddhist

Ultimate and the Christian Ultimate? Does the mystery of the Ultimate transcend all thought forms?

2 *Israel and Asia*   How do the Asian Christian theologians understand the remarkable biblical story of Israel? In what way does this specific history have salvational meaning for all humanity? How do the stories of today's Asia and the biblical Israel intersect? What is it that is called 'Asian'? Why does the Bible say simply 'the Word became flesh'? Why does it not say 'the Word became Jewish (Asian, African. . .) flesh'?

3 *Relationship between christology and ethics*   How do we understand a theological insight that the oppressed is the one who 'takes away the sins of the world'? Can christology be subsumed in ethics? How do we keep the two great passages of the Bible (Micah 6:8 and John 1:29) authentically active and meaningful simultaneously?

4 *Universality and apologetics*   All our four theologians are engaged in exploration of the truth of Christ's particularity and universality. They are indicating that this subject must be studied from the perspective of their own history and culture. In short, historically and psychologically, their apologetics does not belong to the apologetic tradition of the Constantine Christendom; it is an apologetics 'from below'. The image of Christ's humility plays a decisive role in their presentation of the universality of the Christian gospel.

### ACHIEVEMENT AND AGENDA

The theological emphases of these Asian theologians point to the biblical image of the God of pathos and ethos. That Christian faith is history-oriented is thus finding expression through Asian languages and thought forms.

The agenda can be summed up under four headings. First, there is the need to continue to understand and assess the experiences of neocolonization and their impact upon the Christian mission in Asia since 1945. In particular, clear distinctions need to be made between faith in Christ and Westernization.

Secondly, church history and tradition need to be reappropriated by Asian Christians. This includes both the task of interpreting and appropriating the Christian past outside Asia – for example, through reflection on the Chalcedonian definition of the person of

Christ against the background of religious challenges faced by the churches in Asia today; and also the reappropriation of the past of Christianity in Asia – for example, the monumental Jesuit missionary work in Asia in the sixteenth and seventeenth centuries carried out by Matthew Ricci, Robert de Nobili and others, which has a great deal to teach about contextualizing Christianity today.

Thirdly, there is the urgent need to work out better forms of the relationship between East and West, North and South. Christian universality must be made concretely meaningful to all humanity. The resources of each area and tradition need to be opened up to others – for example, how might Martin Luther King's 'Letter from the Birmingham City Jail, 1963' contribute to theology in Asia?

Finally, how do we find the meaning for Christians of the great religious traditions of today's Asia, such as Islam, Buddhism, Hinduism, Sikhism, and other religions of China and Japan? They, like Christianity, are undergoing transformations, and the quality of their mutual understanding and interaction will be of vast importance not only to the future of Asia but to the future of all the religions of the world.

## NOTES

1 The Ecumenical Association of Third World Theologians held six consultations between 1976 and 1983 under the themes of (1) The Emergent Gospel, Theology from the Underside of History, 1976; (2) African Theology en Route, 1977; (3) Asia's Struggle for Full Humanity, Towards a Relevant Theology, 1979; (4) The Challenge of Basic Christian Communities, 1980; (5) Irruption of the Third World, 1981; (6) Doing Theology in a Divided World, 1983. A serious limitation of this series is a conspicuous absence of theological voice from the People's Republic of China. I may add that the language used is so elitist that makes it almost incommunicable to the people and the people's theologians of the Third World. Significant chapters in the series are: in (1) 'The Indian Universe of a New Theology', by D. S. Amalorpavadass, pp. 137–56; in (3) 'Towards an Asian Theology of Liberation: Some Religio-Cultural Guidelines', by Aloysius Pieris, pp. 75–95; 'Christian Reflection in a Buddhist Context', by Lynn de Silva, pp. 96–107; 'Asian Theology: An Asian Woman's Perspective', by Henriette Katoppo, pp. 140–51; and in (5) 'Theological Priorities in India Today', by Samuel Rayan, pp. 30–41; 'The Place of Non-Christian Religions and Cultures in the Evolution of Third World Theology', by Aloysius Pieris, pp. 113–39. A few words on the People's Republic of China: the writings of K. H. Ting (Principal of Nanjing Theological Seminary and President of the China Christian

Council), and Luo Zhenfang, Professor of New Testament, Nanjing
Theological Seminary, are significant in expressing theology in the great
social change that has taken place in China since 1949. The first issue of
*Chinese Theological Review* in English appeared in 1985.

2  Abraham Heschel, *The Prophets* (New York, 1962), p. 225.
3  K. M. Panikkar, *Asia and Western Dominance* (London, 1953), p. 35.
4  Stanley Samartha, *The Hindu Response to the Unbound Christ*, pp. 145 ff.
5  Ibid., p. 167.
6  Ibid.
7  Ibid., pp. 175 ff.
8  Ibid., p. 176.
9  Stanley Samartha, (ed.), *Towards World Community*, p. 155.
10  Ibid.
11  J. Hick and P. F. Knitter, *The Myth of Christian Uniqueness* (London, 1987), p. 75.
12  Samartha, *The Hindu Response*, p. 188.
13  Ibid.
14  Ibid. p. 184.
15  Ibid., p. 200.
16  Ibid., p. 194.
17  Hick and Knitter, *The Myth of Christian Uniqueness*, p. 75.
18  Ibid.
19  Stanley Samartha, (ed.), *Living Faiths and the Ecumenical Movement* (Geneva, 1971), p. 8.
20  Stanley Samartha, (ed.), *Faith in the Midst of Faiths*, p. 10.
21  Stanley Samartha, (ed.), *Living Faiths and Ultimate Goals*, p. x.
22  G. H. Anderson and T. F. Stransky (eds), *Christ's Lordship and Religious Pluralism*, (New York, 1981), p. 25.
23  Hick and Knitter, *The Myth of Christian Uniqueness*, p. 81.
24  Ibid.
25  Anderson and Stranskey, *Christ's Lordship and Religious Pluralism*, p. 36.
26  G. H. Anderson and T. F. Stransky (eds), *Mission Trends No. 3* (New York, 1976), p. 216.
27  C. S. Song, *The Compassionate God*, p. 49.
28  Ibid., pp. 47–50.
29  Ibid., p. 64.
30  *Mission Trends No. 3*, p. 217.
31  C. S. Song, *Theology from the Womb of Asia*, p. 60.
32  *Mission Trends No. 3*, p. 220.
33  Ibid., p. 222.
34  *East Asia Journal of Theology*, No. 2 (October 1985), p. 354.
35  Ibid.
36  The Commission on Theological Concerns of the Christian Conference of Asia (ed.), *Minjung Theology*, p. 51.
37  'Theology as Rumormongering' (Lecture given at Union Theological Seminary, New York City, April 1982), p. 7. The meaning of 'han' is discussed in the text below.

38 'Do You Love Me?' (Lecture given at Academy House, Seoul, Korea, June 1981), p. 8.
39 Ibid., p. 2.
40 *East Asia Journal of Theology*, No. 2 (October 1985), p. 359.
41 *Minjung Theology*, p. 25.
42 Ibid., p. 62.
43 *East Asia Journal of Theology* no. 2 (October 1985), p. 212.
44 'Minjung the Suffering Servant' (Lecture given at Union Theological Seminary, New York City, April 1982), p. 10.
45 Ibid.
46 Ibid., p. 4.
47 The section on Kosuke Koyama has been written by the editor [D. F.]
48 Kosuke Koyama, *Mount Fuji and Mount Sinai*, pp. 15–16.
49 Ibid., p. 241.
50 Ibid., p. 243.
51 Ibid., p. 261.
52 Kosuke Koyama, *Waterbuffalo Theology*, pp. 209–38.
53 Ibid., p. 225.
54 Koyama, *Mount Fuji and Mount Sinai*, p. 128.
55 Cf. Koyama, *Waterbuffalo Theology*, pp. 106–14.

## BIBLIOGRAPHY

### Primary

Hyun Younghak, *Minjung Theology* (New York, 1983).
—, 'Cripple's Dance' and 'Minjung Theology and the Religion of Han', in *East Asia Journal of Theology* no. 2 (October 1985).
Kosuke, Koyama, *Pilgrim or Tourist* (Singapore, 1974).
—, *Waterbuffalo Theology* (London, 1974).
—, *No Handle on the Cross* (London, 1977).
—, *Three Mile an Hour God* (London, 1978).
—, *Mount Fuji and Mount Sinai* (London, 1984).
Samartha, Stanley J., *The Hindu Response to the Unbound Christ* (New Delhi, 1974).
—, (ed.), *Living Faiths and Ultimate Goals* (Geneva, 1974).
—, (ed.), *Towards world Community* (Geneva, 1975).
—, (ed.), *Faith in the Midst of Faiths: Reflections on Dialogue in Community* (Geneva, 1977).
Song, Choan-Seng, *Doing Theology Today* (The Christian Literature Society, 1976).
—, *Growing Together into Unity, Texts of the Faith and Order Commission on Concilliar Fellowship* (The Christian Literature Society, 1978).
—, *Third-Eye Theology. Theology in Formation in Asian Settings* (New York, 1979).
—, *The Compassionate God* (New York, 1982).

—, *The Tears of Lady Meng* (New York, 1982).
—, *Tell Us Our Names* (New York, 1984).
—, *Theology from the Womb of Asia* (New York, 1986).

For secondary material, see notes.

# 12

# Feminist Theology

## Ann Loades

### INTRODUCTION: ISSUES AND ORIGINS

Feminist theologians have an argument with their religious tradition
and its value for them in their present culture, and since feminism
minimally defined is a movement which seeks change for the better
in terms of justice for women, a feminist theologian need not be
female by sex; and it is important to notice that not every female
theologian is necessarily a 'feminist theologian'. The major feminist
theologians at the present time are female, however, because a
primary need for women is being expressed in this form of theology,
that is, self-reliance in understanding themselves and their relationship to the God they have found to be theirs although mediated to
them by a religious tradition which causes them profound problems.

Women differ, as do men, by reason of their experiences within
particular social, cultural, and historical situations; by reason of
race, class, and social and psychological factors which construe what
it is to be feminine and masculine in very different ways. Women
none the less claim a unity of experience forged in relation to their
common physiology (as do men), and with that experience interpreted
as one of powerlessness relative to men. Like other feminists,
feminist theologians are preoccupied with forms of thought and
expression which are 'determined by and reflect the needs of the
socially powerful gender group and where, consequently, the needs
and experiences of women are often forgotten, ignored, or at best,
subsumed under categories created by and appropriate to men.'[1]
They are, however, concerned to use gender analysis to examine the
way religious traditions work, the symbolisms they use, the
characteristics of roles within them, the way religious traditions
reflect social assumptions and shape and re-shape those assumptions,

and especially the gender-related way in which we talk about divine reality.

Notwithstanding the important point that God is neither anthropomorphically masculine or feminine, God has been indicated in predominantly masculine terms in Christian theology, arguably with disastrous consequences for women's self-understanding and self-esteem, and at the very high price of neglecting important elements in men's lives too.

Whatever valuable resources for theology are now being recovered by research in forgotten and neglected writing by and about women in the Christian tradition, there is no problem about identifying the doyenne of the present movement in theology. Elizabeth Cady Stanton was a veteran of the nineteenth-century anti-slavery campaign as well as passionately concerned about women's needs and their expression in society. In her eighties, she and a team of colleagues produced a collection of comments on the parts of the Bible which refer to women, and this collection of biblical passages and commentary was published as *The Women's Bible* in 1895 and 1898, and was reissued in a paperback edition in 1985.[2] With all its limitations, it is still worth reading for her perception of the way in which an amalgam of canon and civil law, church and state, priests and legislators, political parties and religious denominations had inculcated in women a fundamental conviction of their inferiority, conveyed to them not least by their alleged incapacity to 'image' God.

As in Elizabeth Cady Stanton's day, it is vain to belittle the influence of the biblical tradition, depending upon how it is used. The political context has changed from that of the anti-slavery campaign and the fight for the vote to the campaign for peace, for instance, but the problem of the use of the Bible in influencing what are deemed to be appropriate possibilities for women in social, ecclesiastical, and educational contexts continues to need the most careful attention, which it receives especially in the United States. So far as feminist theologians are concerned, it is not just the biblical texts, but centuries of habits of exegesis, ecclesiastical practice and tradition which are now ripe for scrutiny, all alike without immunity of any kind. It could be said that whatever seems to propose or be used for what women discern to be a means of 'oppression' in relation to their lives is likely not to carry 'authority' as 'divine revelation' for them, though some still find their resources within the Christian tradition, notwithstanding its ambiguity so far as they are concerned.

SURVEY

Many distinguished women have by now contributed to the discussion of theology, and the present phase of feminist theology may be dated from Valerie Saiving Goldstein's important article of 1960 on 'The Human Situation: a Feminine View', demanding a reconsideration of the categories of sin and redemption to include women's negation of self, learned in societies where women's realization of full self-identity was likely to be characterized as sin or temptation to sin.[3] Some twenty years later Judith Plaskow published her Yale dissertation on *Sex, Sin and Grace*, a critique of the theologies of Reinhold Niebuhr and Paul Tillich[4] which argued 'that in the work of the two theologians, certain aspects of human experience are highlighted and developed while others are regarded as secondary or ignored'. This in itself hardly seems revolutionary; but Judith Plaskow's point was that those human experiences which are developed, judged, and transformed by the work of God in Christ were more likely to be associated with men in our society, while women's experiences were more likely to be regarded as secondary or reinforced by the Christian message. What was thought to be human experience was in fact male experience, so theology was impoverished, and led to support for prevailing definitions of women, which led precisely to the problem identified by Valerie Saiving – the failure to take responsibility for self-actualization.

Judith Plaskow's secondary concern was with the idea that women are 'closer to nature' than men, and with the effect of this stereotype on their lives. She was not saying that the human experiences about which Tillich and Niebuhr wrote were not importai t, or that they were not shared by women, but she was criticizing the universality of their claims. It is not possible to identify and limit 'human' experience by reference only to 'male' experience, as if males are the norm of humanity. Quite apart from the details of her critique of the two theologians, however, although arising from them, there is an important section on 'self-sacrifice' which repays attention. 'Self-sacrifice is a norm addressed to a self constantly tempted to sinful self-assertion.' Women may have no 'self' to sacrifice, and theology may reinforce their servitude. 'It becomes another voice in the chorus of external expectation defining and confining the way women ought to live.' Women's selves need replenishment through the mutuality of their relationships, or they give and give until they are depleted. Women need to hear of a 'grace' which has a dimension 'which corresponds to the sin of failing to take responsibility for becoming a self, of failing to live up to the potentialities of the structures of finite freedom'.

In that twenty-year period between the article and the book, feminist theology had begun to establish itself in the United States, not least because at long last women had gained access to some of the most distinguished divinity schools. For instance, women had been admitted to Harvard Divinity School in 1954, with Letty Russell in the first batch of three to graduate in 1958 and be ordained by the United Presbyterian Church. And as early as 1943, for instance, the first graduate program in theology for women in Roman Catholic theology had opened at St Mary's College, Notre Dame, Indiana, from which there issued in the next twenty-five years women, many of them members of religious orders, with doctorates in theology. All these women, Roman Catholic and Protestant alike, had grown up in a society which told them that anything was possible; that there were always new frontiers to conquer in a society which valued enterprise and the expression of personal opinion; that they had a right to use their voices to determine the direction of the policies under which they lived.[5] And from the early 1960s, religious orders had committed some 10 percent of their effort to work in Latin America, honing the edge of their commitment to gospel values, and helping to overcome residual antagonism between lay and 'religious' women, and between women of different races and cultures.

The Abbott edition of *The Documents of Vatican II* became available in 1965, and still repays careful study for what it does and does not say about women, and for the fuel it provides for women's exasperation with Christian institutions generally, not just with the Roman Catholic Church. One of the few explicit references to women indeed regrets that fundamental personal rights are not universally honored for women, such as the right and freedom to choose a husband, embrace a state of life, or acquire an education or cultural benefits equal to those recognized for men. Paragraph 52 of 'The Church Today', on 'the nobility of marriage and the family', to its credit affirms that if the life of the family is to flower it needs kindly communion of minds and the painstaking cooperation of the parents in the education of their children. But there is no sense of 'cultural construct' in what follows. 'The active presence of the father is highly beneficial to their formation. The children, especially the younger among them, need the care of their mother at home. This domestic role of *hers* [my italics] must be safely preserved, though the legitimate social progress of women should not be underrated on that account.' What is not taken into account here is the *essential* active presence of their father to his children, for both girls and boys, and the evidence already accumulating of the effects on women of their continued restriction to the 'private' as distinct from the public and political realms, not to mention the massive double work burden many of them had carried for a very long time, inside their homes in 'unpaid' work, and outside their homes in necessary paid employment. And in societies where the family is still the economic unit, some 50 percent of the Third World's food is produced by women, including their work at the 'heavy' agricultural labor involved.

In paragraph 60 of 'The Church Today' it is acknowledged that women are now employed in almost every area of life, so that it is deemed appropriate 'that they should be able to assume their full proper role *in accordance with their own nature* (emphasis added). It seems to be understood (given the association of women, rather than men, with nature) that women's nature is both well defined and limiting, though there was also an implicit concession to new possibilities in the need for everyone to 'acknowledge and favour the proper and necessary participation of women in cultural life', to which they may not have contributed. Other possibilities were indicated in the sentence added during the final drafting to paragraph 9 of the document on the laity, in the section on 'the various fields of the apostolate', pointing out the importance of women's participation in the various fields of the church's apostolate. Readers are no doubt meant to be reassured by the footnote which draws attention to the point that this is one of the few places in all the Council documents where special attention is given to the contribution of women to the mission of the church, though it was clearly (to whom?) the mind of the Council that they were included 'and eminently so', whenever the general role of the laity was discussed. The note adds that by the time the Council ended, twelve lay and ten 'religious' women were present as 'auditrices'. Real exasperation was provoked by the closing messages of the council, messages to men (males) regarded in terms of their diversified contributions to society, with women having a message addressed to them alone, and with reference to their sexual states. Women are addressed as girls, wives, mothers and widows, consecrated virgins and women living alone, though with the acknowledgment that they constitute half of the immense human family, and with the claim that the church has 'glorified and liberated' them. Women are associated with 'the protection of the home', with cradles and deaths; mothers are exhorted to 'pass on to your sons and daughters the traditions of your *fathers*'. Women are invited to reconcile men with life, to guard purity, unselfishness and piety, to aid men to retain courage in *their* great undertakings, with women's own concern to be particularly with the peace of the world. They are clearly excluded from the address to 'workers' – 'very loved sons' – with its sense of unease, mistrust and lack of understanding between church and workers.

It was in response to this council that one of the most important books in feminist theology appeared, in 1968 – Mary Daly's *The Church and the Second Sex*. There followed the work of Rosemary Radford Ruether, Elisabeth Schüssler Fiorenza, and in Europe, of Kari-Elisabeth Børrensen and Elisabeth Gössman. Mary Daly's initial article, which led to the invitation to write that first major book, was published in 1965, when she already had a doctorate in theology from Fribourg University in Switzerland, where she was studying philosophy. Mary Daly and Rosemary Radford Ruether were crucial in forming the women's caucus within the American Academy of Religion, at which both delivered important papers in 1971. Rosemary Radford Ruether's was to appear as 'Misogynism and Virginal Feminism in the Fathers of the Church', available with other useful essays in the collection she edited called *Religion and Sexism: Images of Woman in the Jewish and Christian Traditions* (1974). She herself has become the most prolific author of the movement. Mary Daly's much reprinted essay had a deliberately menacing title: 'Theology after the demise of God the Father; a call for the castration of sexist religion'.[6] Mary Daly was to part company with Christianity, however, in the course of writing *Beyond God the Father* (1973), recently re-issued with an 'Original Reintroduction'. One should also read *Gyn/Ecology* (1978) and most recently *Pure Lust* (1984), each of which include devastating attacks on Christianity's core symbolism. Tucked away in a footnote of *Beyond God the Father* is her assessment of Phyllis Trible's paper of 1973 on 'Deptriarchalizing in Biblical Tradition', on which Mary Daly commented that 'It might be interesting to speculate upon the probable length of a "depatriarchalized Bible". Perhaps there would be enough salvageable material to comprise an interesting pamphlet.' Phyllis Trible has gone on to produce two remarkable books in her *God and the Rhetoric of Sexuality* (1978) and *Texts of Terror* (1984), the latter of which would provide Mary Daly with more material even than she has already for her continued attack on life- and women-haters.

There are many critical collections of essays on biblical material which have arisen from feminist theology. Phyllis Trible's work is clearly outstanding in the Old Testament field, and Elisabeth Schüssler Fiorenza's *In Memory of Her* (1983) in the New Testament. It should, however, be clear that these biblical scholars are usually making explicit claims for us to re-think constructively and in a systematic manner our ethics, our ecclesiology, ministry, and our doctrines of God. Their work is conceived with urgent practical needs in view. This characteristic can be found even in the work of the most 'conservative', whether biblical or church historical, reluctant to accept the radical critique of Christianity as irretrievably hostile to women and their needs and the challenges posed by the theology and spirituality which some are now able to find outside the parameters of the Christian tradition. Elisabeth Schüssler Fiorenza is making bold moves in relation to the Christian past by insisting on the recovery of that past as *women's* own past, with Christian origins being appraised as prototype, not as archetype, and so critically open to the possibility of their own transformation. And Rosemary Radford Ruether has been the most consistently innovative of the systematic theologians in looking to the future, from her *Sexism and God-Talk* (1983) to *Womanguides: Readings Towards a Feminist Theology* (1985) and *Women-Church: Theology and Practice of Feminist Liturgical Communities* (1985).

Even church organizations of a multi-national kind have had to take this movement seriously, because they have found that whatever the differences between them in terms of class, race, and educational and economic opportunity, women will not allow themselves to be separated from one another in this struggle. In Europe, the writings of Elisabeth Moltmann-Wendel have been especially helpful, enabling women to find role-models obscured in preaching and exegesis but undoubtedly important in both Bible and tradition. With Jürgen Moltmann-Wendel she was able to make a proposal, 'Becoming human in new community', at the World Council of Churches meeting held in Sheffield, England, in June 1981, a meeting on 'The Community of women and men in the church', the proceedings of which were edited by Constance Parvey.

In Britain there have been two important books published by Elaine Storkey and Mary Hayter, together with the excellent novels of Sarah Maitland to mention only a few representatives of this vigorous movement. At long last, the challenge issued immediately before the Second World War by Dorothy Sayers is being taken up by other women in Britain with access to the kind of educational and social experience which enables them to be articulate about it. Dorothy Sayers had asked, 'Are women human?' and had written on 'The human! not-quite-human' as well as recovering some sense of the living relationship Jesus of Nazareth had with the women in the community of his disciples and the difference that sense makes to the way one lives. Her own theology was not explicitly 'feminist' except in the sense that her creativity as a literary artist provided her with a way of 'modeling'[7] God. At the present time that attempt to re-think our language for God by a woman theologian who is also a representative of feminist systematic theology is best exemplified by Sallie McFague's *Models of God: Theology for an Ecological, Nuclear Age* (1987). This is a theology prompted by feminist ethical concerns, and feminist theologians contribute to the developing fields of feminist ethics, whether Christian or not. In time, it should no longer be astonishing that Kevin Kelly's admirable book about new reproductive technologies, entitled *Life and Love* (1987) should include a chapter on women's views on these matters. Finally, the British contribution to feminist theology has seen two new books, by Daphne Hampson and Ursula King respectively, the one entitled *Theology and Feminism* (1989) and the other, *Women and Spirituality* (1988). Daphne Hampson represents post-Christian feminist theology; Ursula King is uniquely qualified to write from a perspective of Christian theology in dialogue with women in other great religious traditions.

Of the feminist theologians I have mentioned, it is particularly important at this stage to have at least a minimal acquaintance with the work of Mary Daly, Phyllis Trible, Elisabeth Schüssler Fiorenza and Rosemary Radford Ruether, focusing primarily on what they have to say about Christianity's core symbolism and its relationship to women's perception of themselves in the Christian tradition.

## *Mary Daly*

Mary Daly has done more than anyone to clarify the problems women have concerning the central core symbolism of Christianity, and its effects on their self-understanding and their relationship to God. From the beginning, she has been acutely perceptive about the effect on women of false biological and philosophical theories about them, propped by existing social conditions and legislation, and the abuse of the word 'natural' in respect of their lives, like the word 'feminine' employed to keep women within certain bounds and restraints. She rapidly saw through the use of the Pauline 'in Christ there is no male and female' by would-be pacifiers of women (that used to shut them up), since *even if* that is so, the Christ-image is male, and one has to ask what *meaning*-content the passage can actually have in the face of specific and oppressive facts. To those who would argue that 'Jesus was a feminist', the riposte is, 'Fine, wonderful. But even is he wasn't, *I am*'. Daly saw no point in trying to retrieve the purity of the 'original' revelation, as if the past had some sort of prior claim over present experience, necessary to legitimate that experience now, and assuming that there *are* adequate models to be extracted from the past. Women have the option of giving priority to what they find to be valid in their own experience without needing to look to the past for justification.

Mary Daly came to conceive of the women's movement as an 'exodus' community, for those whose sense of transcendence was seeking expressions alternative to those available in Christian institutions. Another key to her thinking is to be found in her argument that religious symbols die when the cultural situation that supported them ceases to give them plausibility. Authentic faith accepts their relativity, and charges fixation on them as idolatrous. That faith displaces prudence as the virtue to be recommended to women, by urging them to existential courage, so that women will not act within a context of the given, but change circumstances, in community with their sisters. *Beyond God the Father* marks the point at which 'patriarchy' comes firmly on to the linguistic map, connecting together the worship of male and masculine identity with particular values, methods of control, struggle for power and physical coercion in every dimension of being – conscious and unconscious, material and spiritual, personal and political. Women in patriarchy have found themselves interpreted as 'other', as inferior, as sources of 'evil', and with grossly unequal access to what serves human well-being.

Mary Daly's attack on patriarchy takes many forms, one of which is to be found in the concluding passages of *Beyond God the Father*, where she draws on Virginia Woolf's *A Room of One's Own* (1929) at the point where the latter decides that men become especially angry with women when women refuse any longer to act as looking glasses for them, reflecting the male as at least twice his natural size. Women, for Mary Daly, now have the exhilarating opportunity of refusing to collaborate with this idolatry; they may *become*, rather than reflect, moving in the current of the Verb, 'the creative drawing power of the Good who is self communicating Be-ing, Who is the Verb from whom, in whom and with whom all true movements move' – one of her modes of referring to the divine. The Looking Glass Society survives, though bent on killing itself off. 'It is still ruled by God the Father who, gazing at his magnified reflections, believes in his superior size. I say "believes", because the reflection now occasionally seems to be diminished and so he has to make a renewed act of faith in himself.'

Other clear examples of her attack on Christianity's core symbolism can be found in her rewarding books; for instance, in *Gyn/Ecology* (p. 38) she writes of the Trinity, excluding female mythic presence from the divine being, denying female reality in the cosmos. Not the least of women's problems is that we can as yet hardly do justice to the feminine in ourselves, let alone in the divine, because we can hardly know what it is to be female and feminine in patriarchal society. As she says in *Pure Lust* (p. 9): 'We do not wish to be redeemed by a god, to be adopted as sons, or to have the spirit of a god's son artificially injected into our hearts, crying "father".' If the symbolism associated with 'Mary' in Christian tradition is deemed to be 'core' symbolism, then her critique of what has been done with that symbolism in Christian tradition also repays detailed attention. Her books may sometimes be exasperatingly difficult to read, but they have the effect of transforming her readers in unexpected ways.

## Phyllis Trible

Phyllis Trible's *God and the Rhetoric of Sexuality* is one way of trying to respond to the position Mary Daly represents. It has never been difficult to find texts indicating women's inferiority, subordination, and abuse in Scripture, but the texts also contain challenges to those, not only in the figures of some of the magnificent women of the Jewish tradition, but, most importantly, in the stories of Genesis chapters 2 and 3, which in turn become the key to unlock the meanings of the Song of Songs; and in some of the metaphors for God, in whose image male and female are made. That theological clue for interpretation comes from within Scripture itself, and Phyllis Trible's methodological clue from rhetorical criticism: 'How the text speaks and what it says belong together in the discovery of what it is.' The second chapter of *God and the Rhetoric of Sexuality* tracks the journey of a single metaphor (womb/compassion) which highlights female imagery for God. A particular example from the 'lexicon of birth' is that of Deuteronomy 32:18 which uses two metaphors for God. One metaphor is that of 'rock', which can relate to the one who bears or the one who begets. The other is that of the labor pains of birth, so in the RSV, 'You were unmindful of the Rock that begot you/and you forgot the God who gave you birth', and *not* the Jerusalem Bible version, 'You forgot the God who fathered you'.

That latter translation is a particular example of the way in which translators interpret Scripture, ignoring such female imagery.

Mayer I. Gruber[8] has not unreasonably criticized Phyllis Trible on the grounds that native speakers of Hebrew would hardly be consciously aware of the etymological relationship of the word for 'womb' and the verb 'to be compassionate', such that references to the compassion of God would be references to the image of God female, and fathers are not by definition as it were necessarily lacking in compassion for their children. Mayer Gruber, however, goes on to reinforce Phyllis Trible's major point about female metaphor for God in his critique of the series of maternal expressions for God to be found in Second and Third Isaiah, not least the extraordinary juxtaposition in Isaiah 42: 13–14 of God as a man of war and as a woman in labor. Scholars (male) have suggested that a warrior is 'active' and a woman in childbirth is 'passive', forgetting, as Gruber points out, that in 'natural childbirth' at least, the woman is active, as God in Isaiah: 'I will scream like a woman in labour/I will inhale, and I will exhale simultaneously.' Mayer Gruber concludes by suggesting that prophets such as Jeremiah and Ezekiel failed to put an end to idolatry in Israel, whereas Second Isaiah could commend God to non-Jews precisely because the prophet could show that a positive-divine value is attached to *both* sexes.

Phyllis Trible's exegesis of Genesis 2 and 3 is also exceptionally interesting in unravelling her theological clue. For both male and female, life originates with God. 'Dust of the earth and rib of the earth creatures are but raw materials for God's creative activity', and their sexual differentiation owes its origin to that creativity. The woman is a 'helper' – a word used for the God who creates and saves – who 'corresponds' in companionship, and it is she who is competent to discuss theology with the serpent. The love story that goes awry is redeemed in the love lyrics of the Song of Songs, with God as it were withdrawing as the lovers rediscover themselves. And in this setting, there is no male dominance, no female subordination, and no stereotyping of either sex, with the story of Ruth and Naomi returning readers to the struggles of daily life, a story 'of women making a new beginning with men'.

### Elisabeth Schüssler Fiorenza

Elisabeth Schüssler Fiorenza's *In Memory of Her* has a remarkably powerful introduction, by way of reconsideration of the story in the second Gospel of the woman who anoints Jesus' head, a prophetic sign-action which despite Jesus' words, 'And truly I say to you, wherever the gospel is preached in the whole world, what she has done will be told in memory of her', did not become part of gospel knowledge. The name and story of the apostle who betrayed Jesus are retold, but not that of this faithful woman. 'Both Christian feminist theology and biblical interpretation are in process of rediscovering that the Christian gospel cannot be proclaimed if the women disciples and what they have done are not remembered.' Elisabeth Schüssler Fiorenza wants both to reconstruct early Christian history as women's history, thus restoring women's stories, and to reclaim this history as the history of women and men. She thinks that Phyllis Trible is in danger of rehabilitating the authority of the biblical text, without seriously addressing the socio-cultural conditions of which the biblical language and text are a manifestation. Rather, 'Androcentric texts and linguistic reality constructions must not be mistaken as trustworthy evidence of human history, culture and religion. The text *may* be the message, but the message *is not* coterminal with human reality and history'.[9]

Elisabeth Schüssler Fiorenza is engaged in as careful an evaluation of the Christian tradition as its most ferocious critics, rejecting, in the name of God, whatever perpetuates violence, alienation and patriarchal subordination, as well as the eradication of women from historical-theological consciousness. Her principles of interpretation want to recover *all* the elements which 'articulate the liberating experiences and visions of the people of God' and which break through patriarchal plausibility structures. For her, revelation is located not in texts but in Christian experience and community, challenging at every point those who relegate women to marginal status in church and theology. Her method importantly makes room for 'an often mixed, confused, inarticulate, and only partially feminist historical consciousness and agency of women' living still *within* the boundaries and mechanisms of what oppresses them, and for the recovery of history as *human* history.[10] The bulk of the book in a way enables its readers to participate in that mixed, confused consciousness and how it can find its resources for change towards mutuality, precisely by paying attention to what happened to the movement initiated by Jesus of Nazareth and the women and men associated with him. Both sexes were indispensable to the early missionary activity of the movement, and its attempt to make its way in a slave-owning society living by certain household codes. Limitation of women's roles, despite the alternative character of what was originally offered to them, gradually restricted what they could do in the religious as well as the social context. Elisabeth

Schüssler Fiorenza's case has to do with her re-presentation of the discipleship and apostolic leadership of women, so that in their appropriation of Jesus' practice of love and service, they too may be seen as 'the image and body of Christ'.

Not the least important section of her book is that on 'The Sophia-God of Jesus and the Discipleship of Women'. She discusses the gracious goodness in the divine indicated by means of Jewish 'wisdom' theology, which arguably used elements of 'goddess' language to speak of God, and made possible Jesus' invitation of women into his discipleship. In that their role could be central, as the story of the anointing of his head by a woman articulates. It is this section of her book that has been taken up into a useful collection edited by Joann Wolski Conn on *Women's Spirituality: Resources for Christian Development* (1986), which also includes an essay by Elizabeth A. Johnson on naming God and one by Bernard Cooke on 'Non-partiarchal Salvation' which help to shift us into the theological agenda.

Elisabeth Schüssler Fiorenza may be claiming far too much for the original community around Jesus, and to be expressing, despite herself, not so much 'remembrance', recoverable notwithstanding the principled 'suspicion' of the feminist critique, but *hope* for new possibilities in Christian tradition. 'Remembering the Past in Creating the Future' is the title of one of the essays in her collection *Bread not Stone* (1984), an important signal that her biblical scholarship is undertaken for the sake of people of today and for tomorrow. There remains the central question of whether Christianity, to remain itself, must be what Rosemary Radford Ruether would call 'a male-identified project of redemption', or whether there has to be a real shift in its fundamental definitions.

## Rosemary Radford Ruether

Rosemary Radford Ruether has been responsible for the production of some twenty-two books, which she has written by herself, co-authored or edited, and at least five hundred articles. Of all the most notable feminist theologians, she has addressed herself to the widest range of 'areas of contradiction'[11] to employ the terminology of Mary Tardiff OP, who is studying her theological method. Rosemary Radford Ruether has written on the question of Christian credibility, with particular attention to ecclesiology and its engagement with church–world conflicts; Jewish–Christian relations ('anti-semitism is the left hand of christology'); politics and religion in

America; and feminism. Feminist issues are integral to each of the preceding areas, and 'sample' essays on each may be found in her *To Change the World: Christology and Cultural Criticism* (1981), with the essay, 'Christology and Feminism: Can a Male Saviour Save Women?' developed in chapter five of *Sexism and God-Talk: Towards a Feminist Theology* (1983).

She, like Elisabeth Schüssler Fiorenza, is prepared to struggle for the future of the Christian tradition, with Rosemary Radford Ruether explicitly advocating as a norm 'both self and other-identified men and women in a mutual discipleship of equals', using liberating historical prototypes translated and recontextualized in the present and the future. For her, Jesus proclaims an iconoclastic reversal of the system of religious status: 'the last shall be first and the first last', that is, the *kenosis* of patriarchy, discarding hierarchical caste privilege. The redeemer is himself one who has been redeemed, and the Christian community continues Christ's identity, so 'we can encounter Christ *in the form of our sister*', as, for instance, in the case of those who saw the martyrdom of Blandina, but without the violence to one another that image has also helped to perpetuate, and believing that, 'Divine Grace keeps faith with us when we have broken faith with her'. Rosemary Radford Ruether's *Womanguides* makes women's speech and presence normative, and *Women-Church* includes not simply possible liturgies for women responding to the failure of Christian institutions to meet their needs but two introductory sections which summarize her enterprise as a theologian, reaching forward to a symbolic universe which can 'heal the splits between "masculine and feminine", between mind and body, between males and females as gender groups, between society and nature, and between races and classes'.[12] Women want to continue to communicate within existing institutions, but cannot cope with what they find there, unless they can find alternative communities which nurture and support them, especially in their denial that existing institutions have a monopoly on truth, salvation, and the mediation of God's Spirit. Theological symbolism or interpretation can no more be finalized than the institutions themselves, and feminists are recommended to 'learn to make creative use of existing institutions without being stifled or controlled by them', with the institutions themselves becoming vehicles for further creativity.

Thinking again about the relationship between nature and grace, creation and redemption, is connected for Rosemary Radford Ruether with specific analysis of which *functions*, as distinct from clerical caste, can allow the needs of a community to be defined and met. Liturgical presidency does not mean that someone 'possesses a power to create redemptive life and mediate it to others, but rather that she or he sums up the redemptive life of the community in its symbolic unity'.[13] Rosemary Radford Ruether's sensitivity to the Jewish heritage of Christian tradition enables her to look afresh at its resources, and to reappropriate the hallowing of nature. 'It is not past human tradition or nature that we reject when we enter messianic community, but rather their corruption.'[14]

## DEBATE

The debate about feminist theology continues between feminist theologians themselves so far as their *methods* and hoped for results are concerned, as has been indicated here. *Contra* David Brown in his recent *Continental Philosophy and Modern Theology* (1988) feminist theologians are acutely aware of the metaphorical character of language about God, and of its reality-depicting functions. If it had been recognized as metaphorical, however, it would be easier to make efforts to modulate that language in liturgy and theology so as to include the feminine in God, with identifiable consequences for women. David Brown is on stronger ground in resisting the re-evaluation of Jesus and Christian beginnings, because he sees it as a way of advocating what the present phase of feminism wants to engage with in present social and political reality; but that engagement is arguably an understandable reaction to the use of Bible and tradition which precisely refuses to directly address women and their interests, as they themselves understand and define them. As David Brown properly indicates, however, critical openness to new knowledge should advance theological knowledge and have ethical consequences. Feminist theologians are among those who inform us that without that advancement, so far as women are concerned, Christianity's case may be terminal, and not only in western post-industrialized societies. It is of course true that 'If there is oppression in a middle-class American home, it is on an altogether different scale from the anguish of the starving slum-dweller', but forms of aggression which spawn themselves from male dominance and female passivity reinforced by religious stereotypes transcend these boundaries, and it is possible to identify them and do something about them. It is unforgivable to trivialize the contribution to theology made, for instance, by Anne E. Carr in her *Transforming Grace: Christian Tradition and Women's Experience* (1988) and in future, nonfeminist theologians should make a serious attempt to appreciate feminist theology of this constructive kind, unless, of course, they are content to maintain unchanged a tradition some elements of which are deeply offensive to those women who want to remain within mainstream 'Christianity'.


## ACHIEVEMENT AND AGENDA

The achievement of the movement has been, over a twenty-year period, to put feminist theology on the map, hopefully in an ineradicable way. The agenda is to get everyone to see that what has passed as 'universal' theology has been partial in its exclusion of women and their insights.[15] The program of a search for a 'universal' theology has been exposed as an attempt to monopolize both theology and salvation. Feminist theology should not make the mistake of recapitulating this error in its turn, but is less likely to do so if it can claim its place in existing institutions where theology is studied, as well as making its own 'spaces' where feminist theology can be developed without the immediate struggle it is bound to encounter.


## NOTES

1 N. Slee, 'Parables and Women's Experience', *Modern Churchman*, 26 (1984), pp. 20–31.
2 E. Cady Stanton, *The Women's Bible* (Edinburgh, 1985).
3 V. Saiving Goldstein, 'The Human Situation: a Feminine View', *Journal of Religion*, 40 (1960), pp. 100–12.
4 J. Plaskow, *Sex, Sin, and Grace: Women's Experience and the Theologies of Reinhold Niehbuhr and Paul Tillich* (Washington, DC, 1980).
5 I. Woodward, 'The Catholic Sisters of the United States: Signs of Contradiction or Signs of the Times?', *Pro Mundi Vita: Dossiers*, 4 (1986).
6 M. Daly, 'Theology after the Demise of God the Father: a Call for the Castration of Sexist Religion', in *Sexist Religion and Women in the Church: No More Silence*, ed. Alice L. Hageman (New York, 1974), pp. 125–43.
7 J. Thurmer, *A Detection of the Trinity* (Exeter, 1984).
8 M. I. Gruber, 'The Motherhood of God in Second Isaiah', *Revue Biblique*, 90 (1983), pp. 351–9.
9 E. Schüssler Fiorenza, *In Memory of Her*, p. 29.
10 Ibid., p. 25.
11 M. Tardiff OP is at the University of St Michael's College, Toronto. Her selected bibliography of Rosemary Radford Ruether's is in *MC*, (the journal of the Modern Churchpeople's Union), xxx: 1 (1988), pp. 50–5.
12 R. Radford Ruether, *Women-Church*, p. 3.
13 Ibid., p. 91.

14 Ibid., p. 108.
15 R. Radford Ruether, 'The Future of Feminist Theology in the Academy', *Journal of the American Academy of Religion*, 53 (1985), pp. 703–16.

## BIBLIOGRAPHY

### Primary

Daly, M., *The Church and the Second Sex* (New York, 1968).
—, *Gyn/Ecology* (New York, 1978).
—, *Pure Lust* (New York, 1984).
Radford Ruether, R., *To Change the World: Christology and Cultural Criticism* (London, 1981).
—, *Sexism and God-Talk: Toward a Feminist Theology* (London, 1983).
—, *Womanguides: Readings Towards a Feminist Theology* (New York, 1985).
—, *Women-Church: Theology and Practice of Feminist Liturgical Communities* (New York, 1985).
Schüssler Fiorenza, E., *In Memory of Her: A Feminist Theological Reconstruction of Christian Origins* (London, 1983).
Trible, P., *God and the Rhetoric of Sexuality* (Philadelphia, 1987).

### Secondary

Bonner, G., 'Augustine's attitude to women and "Amicitia"', in *Homo Spiritalis*, ed. Cornelius Mayer (Wurzburg, 1987).
Børresen, K. E., *Subordination and Equivalence: the Nature and Role of Woman in Augustine and Thomas Aquinas* (Washington, DC, 1981).
Carr, Anne E., *Transforming Grace. Christian Tradition and Women's Experience* (New York, 1988).
Collins, A. Y. (ed.), *Feminist Perspectives on Biblical Scholarship* (Chico, Ca, 1985).
Conn, J. W., *Women's Spirituality: Resources for Christian Development* (New York, 1986).
Hampson, D., *Theology and Feminism* (Oxford, 1989).
Hayter, M., *The New Eve in Christ: The Use and Abuse of the Bible in the Debate about Women in the Church* (London, 1987).
Heine, S., *Women and Early Christianity: Are the Feminist Scholars Right?* (London, 1987).
Hurcombe, L., *Sex and God: Some Varieties of Women's Religious Experience* (London, 1987).
King, U., *Women and Spirituality* (London, 1988).
McFague, S., *Models of God: Theology for an Ecological, Nuclear Age* (London, 1987).

Further bibliography may be found in:
Loades, A., *Searching for Lost Coins: Explorations in Christianity and Feminism*
(London, 1987); and a bibliography of books in this area published
between 1960 and 1985 is being edited by A. O. Dyson.

Part V

# Theology and Religious Diversity

The leading theme through both volumes of *The Modern Theologians* has been the way in which Christian faith, embodied in the Bible, tradition, and forms of life shaped over many centuries, relates to modernity. George Lindbeck takes that as his theme in discussing ecumenical theology with special reference to the period since the Second Vatican Council. He sees a shift from *ressourcement* (renewal by reappropriation of sources), which made the goal of church unity a priority, to *aggiornamento* (renewal that stresses contemporary relevance), which, if it values unity, sees it as a means to other ends. He analyses the success and failure of *ressourcement* both sociologically and theologically, and looks at two of the possible futures. In one the way of renewal through *ressourcement*, as represented by Barth, Rahner, Congar, Balthasar, and others, will be seen as a brief interruption in a long-term process of liberal accommodation to Western culture; in the other there will be a postliberal, postmodern development of classical Christianity. Lindbeck then sketches his postliberal vision of an ecumenical church which has learned to 'inhabit the text' of the Bible and the whole tradition in a classical way; which is not fundamentalist or traditionalist; and which can also do justice to many concerns of *aggiornamento*.

The encounter between religions was part of the early formation of Christianity, but for many centuries most of Christendom was religiously uniform and its relations with other faiths often took the form of polemics, persecution (especially of the Jews) or imperialism. This has now changed for many reasons, such as different power relations, secularization, increased global communication and interaction, population shifts which have brought religious communities into new situations (especially in Britain and the United States), an explosion in the study of religions, and changes in the churches. Many theologians in these volumes have treated the theology of religions at length, notably Tillich (at the end of his life), Küng and Pannenberg in volume I and Kaufman, Tracy and African, Asian, and feminist theologians in volume II. Gavin D'Costa chooses three others – John Hick, George Lindbeck, and Karl Rahner – to mount a debate between positions which are labelled pluralist, exclusivist and inclusivist. He analyses key aspects (theological, philosophical, and phenomenological) of each, then compares them in their treatment of Jesus Christ, the church, mission, and dialogue, before ending with some constructive suggestions. So the final part of this volume concludes with a dialogue between representatives of the three main areas covered by these volumes, Britain, the United States and continental Europe, as they try to come to terms with a global issue.

# 13

# Ecumenical Theology

## George Lindbeck

### INTRODUCTION

For someone like myself, who has been a participant in ecumenical discussions for four decades, the most noteworthy feature of the past twenty years is the growing dissociation of two different ways of being ecumenical. One of these ways is thematic, the other procedural. The first is defined by its theme and goal, the unity of the churches, while the second is a matter of method: it is interdenominational or transconfessional.

Their dissociation is not inevitable. As will be explained in the next section of this paper, the procedural ecumenism of nineteenth-century Protestant interdenominationalism was the seedbed of the thematically-unitive ecumenical movement which came into existence in the first part of the twentieth century. Later, during the mid-century, as the second section notes, they were for the most part mutually supportive. The reason for this, so I shall suggest, was the importance of *ressourcement*, the return to scriptural, patristic, or Reformation sources, for both Protestant and Catholic theology during that time. Since then, however, a change has taken place. Beginning shortly after the end of Vatican II in 1965, the focus shifted to what came to be known during the Council as *aggiornamento*, the 'updating' of the faith. A third and more competitive relationship has developed between the two types of ecumenism. Theology has for the most part become procedurally more ecumenical, but thematically less so. The newer developments cut across confessional boundaries as never before, but they are less concerned about church unity.

Similar developments have occurred in secular disciplines since World War II. Political science and economics, for example, have become thoroughly internationalized, but they are less concerned about uniting the nations. We can take no comfort, however, in the pervasiveness of the trend. In the case of Christianity, it is the future of ecclesial communities and of the theologies which take them seriously which is at stake.

Given the gravity of the problem, I have in the last two sections of this essay gone beyond description to speculation on underlying issues and possible remedies. Despite the present decline of theological interest in the search for church unity, I find myself oddly hopeful. Perhaps there are the beginnings of developments which will help reconcile *ressourcement* and *aggiornamento*, and therefore also procedural and thematically unitive ecumenism. It will be for the reader to decide whether these hopes are warranted.

## SURVEY: TWO TYPES OF ECUMENISM

If church historians such as Winthrop Hudson are correct,[1] one of the enabling conditions for modern ecumenism is the denominational understanding of the church. The seventeenth-century Independents at the Westminster Assembly were perhaps the first fully to formulate it. They argued that divided Christian communities even in a single locality could each be an authentic church with a theological right to separate existence and to recruit members on a voluntary basis. The flowering of this view into 'ecumenical' practice did not occur, however, until the evangelical revivals of the nineteenth century. It was then that Protestants of many different denominations began to join together in large numbers to evangelize, send missionaries abroad, publish and distribute Bibles, educate, establish Sunday Schools, reform society through, for example, abolition and temperance societies, and, somewhat later, form the Student Volunteer Movement and the SCM. These were what we would now think of as thoroughly ecumenical activities, although the word was not then current.

In the course of time, ecclesiastical institutionalism reasserted itself, absorbed many of the transdenominational enterprises into its own structures, and in the process created the bureaucratic pyramids which now organizationally dominate most churches whether their formal polity is episcopal, presbyterial, or congregational. Yet the relative unimportance of denominational differences in the eyes of pietistic and revivalistic Christians, even Lutheran and Anglican ones, made interdenominational cooperation possible.

Thus Protestant evangelicalism, seasoned by theological liberalism, presided at the beginnings of the ecumenical movement, first, in the International Missionary Conference at Edinburgh in 1910, and, second, in the Stockholm Life and Work Conference in 1921. The goal was for the churches to work, live, and (for many) commune together even while agreeing to disagree on many matters of faith and order.

Up until the end of the First World War, it was mostly the Anglicans in the ecumenical movement who argued for more than this, but the increasing desire to include the Orthodox strengthened unitive concerns. These concerns took organizational shape in the Faith and Order Conference at Lausanne in 1927, were integral to the formation of the World Council of Churches at Amsterdam in 1948, have been increasingly reflected in its official statements since the New Delhi Assembly of 1961, and were immensely reinforced by the entrance of the Roman Catholic Church into the ecumenical arena at Vatican II (1962–5).

There is now, at least on paper, a consensus in the organized ecumenical movement that the God-willed unity of the church involves more than interdenominational cooperation and inter-communion between autonomous bodies divided in faith and order. This does not mean that uniformity is desirable. There may be great variations, as even Rome now insists, in practice, worship, organizational structures, and doctrinal formulations, but the differences must be compatible or reconcilable.[2] Thus bilateral discussions between confessional bodies deal at length with the question of reconcilability across the whole range of issues from the Trinity to communion in one kind, and such projects as the World Council's study document, 'Confessing One Faith' (1987) and *Baptism, Eucharist and Ministry* (1982)[3] are at the forefront of the unitive agenda. Also important are questions of governance. Mutual accountability and the capacity, at least *in extremis*, to make decisions in common require some kind of 'ministry of unity', whether that be conciliar patriarchal (as in Eastern Orthodoxy), primatial, or the interlocking of local churches in leadership appointments as in the first centuries. Autonomy (or autocephaly, as the Orthodox put it) may be important, but it cannot be unrestricted. Otherwise mutual accountability and common decision-making would be ineffective, and these are needed for maintaining and nourishing church unity. Such issues are the stock-in-trade of unitive ecumenism. Thus an ecumenical movement which was at first largely procedural and interdenominational has now become in its official pronouncements thematically unitive. This is true not only of the multilateral dialogues conducted under the auspices of the Faith and Order Division of the World Council of Churches and of various national councils, but also of most of the church-sponsored bilateral national and international conversations which have multiplied chiefly since Vatican II.

## THE DISSOCIATION OF THE TYPES

In the wider theological community, however, it is procedural rather than thematic ecumenism which has been gaining ground during most of the time since the Second Vatican Council; and this has as one of its causes, so I shall suggest, a shift from *ressourcement* to *aggiornamento,*

*Ressourcement* seemed to be the wave of the future when theological students of my generation were in seminary in the 1940s and 1950s. It was the way of escape from tired liberalism or oppressive fundamentalism for Protestants and from neoscholasticism for Catholics. It presided at the formation of the World Council of Churches and made possible the changes wrought by Vatican II. Its power was most dramatically evident on the Roman Catholic side. De Lubac, Congar, Rahner, Küng and Ratzinger, to mention some of the better-known conciliar progressives, all joined at that time in seeking renewal first through return to the patristic and biblical roots. This was their way of updating the church, of escaping from the post-Tridentine rigidities which had been intensified by the anti-modernist reactions of the nineteenth and early twentieth centuries. Paradoxically, they triumphed over the conservatives and advanced the cause of modernity by being more traditional than anyone else: they appealed to traditions earlier than the medieval and counter-Reformation ones which the traditionalists favored. Without their mastery of both the spirit and the letter of Scripture and the fathers, it would have been impossible to formulate and defend the reforms of the liturgy, of the understanding of the church and of ecumenism, of the place of the laity, and of religious liberty. Their primary concern was faithfulness to the total catholic heritage and only secondarily adjustment to the contemporary situation, and yet they were the ones who opened the church to ecumenism and to the modern world.

These tradition-minded but not traditionalist renewers of theology were matched on the Protestant side by the neo-orthodox, most notably Karl Barth, with their slogan of 'back to the Bible'. Indeed, Protestant neo-orthodoxy contributed much to Catholic advocates of *ressourcement.* It helped them gain confidence that it is possible to read the Bible in ways that are both faithful to the historic faith and yet also critically historical. It is part of the oral tradition surrounding Vatican II that the Protestant, Oscar Cullmann, was cited more frequently in the discussions outside the aula than any Roman Catholic biblical scholar. The return to the sources was not identical on the two sides: the early fathers were more important for the Catholics, and the Reformers, for the Protestants. Yet scripture was central for both, and both were historical-critical in their methods.

The stress on *ressourcement* and on church unity has receded, however, under the impact of outlooks directed more towards *aggiornamento.* What I have in mind here are not only contextualist, liberationist, and political emphases, but also what may be called 'hermeneutic' approaches (though a leading Catholic practitioner, David Tracy of Chicago, speaks of a 'revised correlational method'). Then, in addition, there are 'interreligious' theologies which attempt to understand Christianity as one of many ways, and perhaps not the unsurpassable one, in which God has revealed himself to humankind. These developments are by no means identical – indeed, sometimes they are in opposition – but for all of them, the visible unification of the historically institutionalized churches is of secondary importance. It is hard from their perspectives to see the relevance of church unity to liberation struggles, or to the search for hermeneutic understanding, or to the promotion of human unity through interreligious dialogue, and this tends to make them indifferent or hostile to the doctrinal and structural concerns of *ressourcement.* Many participants in these movements are personally committed to the unification of the churches, but this often seems to be despite their theologies rather than because of them.

It should not be supposed, however, that these recent theological developments in their Catholic form involve attacks on Vatican II. On the contrary, they appeal for support to the conciliar emphasis on *aggiornamento,* on the signs of the times. This becomes for them the primary theme of the council, and they use it to interpret the other two major conciliar emphases on Scripture and the early church and on continuity with the specifically Roman tradition as it developed after the first centuries. From their perspective, one might say, the central document is not *Dei verbum* with its stress on Scripture, but rather *Gaudium et spes,* the Constitution on the Church in the Modern World.[4] They thus reverse the order of importance which I, like other Protestant observers at the Council, gave to the two documents back in the 1960s. Yet it is hard to say that the Council contradicts them. It nowhere explicitly specifies which emphasis is to be used to interpret the other.

Be that as it may, the shift in primacy from *ressourcement* to *aggiornamento*, from *Dei verbum* (together with the Constitutions on the Church and the Liturgy) to *Gaudium et spes*, is the specifically Roman Catholic way of legitimating a turn from the sources of the faith to the needs of the world which has also characterized much non-Catholic theology in the past twenty years. Liberation theology, for example, despite its Catholic origins, is now as much in favor among Protestants as anywhere. These developments may or may not be justified: that is not the present question. However one evaluates it, a pervasive change in theological orientation has taken place. One of the consequences is that thematic ecumenism attracts less attention than formerly.

The waning of one kind of ecumenism, however, has been more than matched by the waxing of another. The way theologians do their work is more ecumenical than ever before. This increase may have been accelerated by *aggiornamento*, but it also has other causes. Some of these have long been undermining confessional barriers between non-Roman churches, and since Vatican II, they have also greatly affected Roman Catholicism. There has been an efflorescence of interconfessional coalitions, movements, and interest groups. Theologians are less and less restricted by ecclesiastical frontiers. The methods they use, the themes they treat, and the conclusions they reach are increasingly transconfessional. Biblical scholarship in particular has become an almost entirely interdenominational or nondenominational enterprise, and similar developments have also taken place in other areas. Much more than in the past, Roman Catholics pay serious attention to what non-Catholics say even in regard to their own specifically Roman Catholic concerns, and non-Roman Catholics reciprocate. When Protestants read biblical scholars such as Ray Brown, or theologians such as Rahner, Lonergan, Balthasar, and David Tracy, or liberationists such as Gutierrez and Segundo, they do not react to them first of all as members of the Roman communion, but simply as Christians, and they agree or disagree with them in ways which transect ecclesiastical boundaries. We are no longer surprised, as these present volumes illustrate, that Catholic, Protestant, and Orthodox theologians are often closer to each other in basic theological orientation than they are to many members of their own communions.

Yet it would be a mistake to conclude from this that church unity is imminent. Procedural ecumenism and the weakening of distinct ecclesiastical identities which often accompanies it can have the effect of making the unification of the churches less appealing or more difficult. Protestant history in particular is replete with examples. The massive interdenominationalism of nineteenth-century evangelicalism together with its liberal offshoots blurred the lines between the Protestant churches, but by itself contributed nothing to their unity. Organizational separateness has its own momentum. In our own day, the fervent conservative minorities in the mainline churches who support interdenominational and church-independent missionary societies or evangelistic crusades of the Billy Graham type are, as is well known, generally indifferent or hostile to the ecumenical movement. The major reason for their aversion, furthermore, is not that they are parochially Methodist, Anglican, Presbyterian, Lutheran or Baptist, but that the whole question of ecclesial identity and unification is for them a distraction from the one thing necessary, the saving of individual souls.

Anti-unitive interdenominationalism, however, is not simply a conservative-evangelical phenomenon. It is characteristic of Protestants in general. They regard the various denominations as basically interchangeable and move freely from one to another as convenience and congeniality dictate. In the United States, most Protestants, so the surveys indicate, belong to more than one denomination in the course of their lives. One of the chief values of ecumenism for them is that it has legitimated this dissolution of abiding communal loyalties and made church-hopping religiously respectable. There are not a few Roman Catholics who, since Vatican II, are beginning to acquire similar attitudes. Church unity greater than interdenominationalism does not greatly interest them. They are content to stop short with mutual respect, cooperation and intercommunion.[5]

What chiefly concerns us, however, is the reinforcement of this long-standing and originally Protestant popular interdenominationalism by the theological shift to *aggiornamento*. The cleavage between world-oriented and church-oriented factions has been growing during the past two decades within the organized ecumenical movement itself, not least the World Council of Churches. Those who focus on issues of liberation, ecology, peace, justice, poverty, and Third World problems sometimes seem to regard the concern for church unity represented by the World Council's Faith and Order section and by most of the bilateral discussions as a distraction from the one thing needful. To be sure, they are ecumenical, but their ecumenism is at times as antithetic to confessional identities and the unification of the churches as is the overtly anti-ecumenical stance of most conservative evangelicals. As often happens, extremes meet.

The growth of procedural ecumenism which is uninterested in church unity creates, furthermore, odd-seeming reactions. Those who are theologically-committed to church unity sometimes become so disenchanted with church-eroding interdenominationalism that they sound distinctly separatistic. They think that union between churches, whether Protestant or Catholic, which have lost communal identity, loyalty, and self-respect would be a meaningless achievement: what would result would not be a communion, but a bureaucratically organized collection of individuals and interest groups. They argue that when transconfessionalism becomes anti-confessionalism it undermines that sense of ecclesial community and loyalty which is the presupposition of sound ecumenism.

It is concerns such as these which lay behind the strange-sounding appeal for the 'reconfessionalization' of the ecumenical movement which Cardinal Willibrands, head of the Vatican Secretariat for Christian Unity, addressed to the Assembly of the Lutheran World Federation in Budapest in 1984. It is important, he argued, that cooperation across church lines should not destroy communal identities or produce a desire to ignore rather than reconcile the diversities of the historic traditions. Others, however, inspired by pragmatic as well as theological motives, are less nuanced, and are likely to turn into denominational isolationists. Thus, for example, some of the most thoroughly liberal and historically ecumenical denominations in the United States are now departing from their own generations-old practice by making it difficult for candidates for ministry to study in nondenominational seminaries.

These considerations help make understandable the seemingly peculiar way in which the advance of procedurally ecumenical theology is currently accompanied by a decline of the thematic variety. This is not a necessary connection: as we have already seen, there is no intrinsic reason why working ecumenically across confessional boundaries should lead to lack of concern about church unity. Yet in present circumstances, that is what happens. The ecumenical movement, so it is commonly said, is in the doldrums; and this is true, not only popularly and ecclesiastically, but also theologically. The issues which are important for ecclesial unification are far less prominent in the general theological agenda than in the recent past. The excitement once evoked by Vatican II's Decree on Ecumenism, or the bilateral dialogues, or Faith and Order discussions, has vanished from the scene. Theology is becoming simultaneously more and less ecumenical.

To be sure, this does not mean that thematic ecumenism is in danger of dying. Rather, it is flourishing, but in increasingly restricted groups. It has been institutionalized in the church-sponsored multi-lateral and bilateral dialogues, and is as vigorously pursued as ever by some theologians, though fewer in number than before. These theologians do not feel discouraged. They recognize that the Lima document, *Baptism, Eucharist, and Ministry* (1982), is a high point in multi-lateral ecumenism; and, to cite another example somewhat at random, the most recent reports from the United States Lutheran and international Anglican conversations with Roman Catholics on the doctrine of justification (1983 and 1987 respectively) are an advance on any previous work on the subject. In addition, schemes for local or regional church unions continue to be discussed (though the impetus to implement them has markedly declined). Further, there continue to be scholars committed to the search for unity who produce excellent supporting material for the ecumenical endeavors. The joint work on the Reformation by Catholics and Protestants on the occasion of the Augsburg year of 1980 and the Luther year of 1984 (to mention simply enterprises in which I have taken part) is theologically impressive. Thus for those actually engaged in the dialogues, the present situation is not one of ecumenical stagnation, but of steady and sometimes exhilarating progress. Yet the fact remains that, in comparison to the situation twenty or even ten years ago, this progress is now marginal to the main currents of theological thought. Theology, to repeat, is thematically less even though procedurally more ecumenical.

## UNDERLYING ISSUES

In turning now to the underlying reasons for the shift from *ressourcement* to *aggiornamento* and the correlative cooling of ecclesially unitive enthusiasm, it is doubtful that as much weight can be placed on church-political considerations as is done in some quarters. Rome in particular is blamed for the cooling of ecumenical ardor. People have lost interest, it is said, because the Vatican has blocked the implementation of the accords which have already been reached. This analysis seems incomplete. If the Pope stopped temporizing, non-Roman church leaders might well find themselves forced to assume that unwelcome role, not because they are personally opposed to the accords, but because of popular resistance. The churches they head may be full of interdenominational zeal, but interest in church unity generally stops short with the eucharistically and ecclesially pallid intercommunion which most Protestants have long practiced.

Whether or not this is true, it seems clear that only a small part of the shift from *ressourcement* and the problems of church unity to *aggiornamento* and the needs of the world can be accounted for by ecclesiastical policies. Something more fundamental is at work. I shall, in this section, offer some suggestions on what that might be.

One problem with the Protestant neo-orthodox return to the sources, according to Peter Berger, was that its sociological roots were shallow,[6] and something similar can be said of the comparable Catholic movement. *Ressourcement* on both sides of the confessional divide was the product of small and formidably learned theological elites who had mastered modern scholarship yet also learned to live in the world of the sources and to understand modern problems from that perspective. Most of those who followed them, however, did not have the same rootage in Scripture and the pre-modern heritage. They were not so steeped in the thought and the spirituality of the sources that they could, so to speak, absorb modernity into historic Christian outlooks, and thereby view present reality through the spectacles, the lenses, of Scripture and early tradition. Thus it was not so much the approach as the positions of theologies of *ressourcement* which were attractive between the World Wars and into the 1960s. They provided the only alternatives to fundamentalism and traditionalism, on the one hand, and the kind of nineteenth-century liberalism which had been discredited by the naïvety of its view of progress and by its failure in Germany to resist Hitler. Thus Protestants turned to biblical neo-orthodoxy and Catholics to *la nouvelle théologie* even when their primary desire, unbeknownst to themselves, was to update the Christian message rather than to return to its roots. These fellow travelers of theologies of renewal discovered what they really wanted only in the post-conciliar period when newer outlooks began developing whose starting-point was not the sources, but rather the urgent issues of modernity. The enthusiasm which had flowed into *ressourcement* turned quickly to *aggiornamento*, and with it attention shifted away from the search for Christian unity.

Those of us who are old enough to have lived through this transition can verify the psycho-social analysis from our own experience. Gregory Baum, for example, has described himself as undergoing a change which fits this pattern,[7] and much the same could be said of Hans Küng, not to mention any number of Protestants, such as Harvey Cox and Gordon Kaufman,[8] who started out under neo-orthodox influences and later turned to *aggiornamento*. Most theologians of my generation have many friends or acquaintances who illustrate this shift equally well. The pressures of modernity push us all either toward updating the faith or else, in the case of traditionalists, toward immobilism. Both progressive and conservative forces work against *ressourcement*.

Yet there are also internal conceptual problems with the return to the sources which have contributed to its weakness. Its way of reading texts, so it can be argued, has been too exclusively that of modern historical criticism. This has contributed to the elitisim mentioned earlier: the interpretion of Scripture has become the province of specialized scholars rather than a communal enterprise in which all theologians, as well as lay folk, have a part. This does not deny that historical criticism is indispensible in overcoming the rationalistically propositional rigidities of fundamentalists and traditionalists: without it, neither return to the sources nor updating the church is possible. Yet by itself it provides little positive guidance on how to meet new challenges; it excels in ground-clearing operations, not in new construction. The neglect of primarily historical-critical *ressourcement* by the *aggiornamento*-minded has been partly justified, for it gives little help in meeting contemporary challenges.

We shall later speak about possible remedies for this weakness, but first two observations about *aggiornamento* are in order. In the first place, those for whom meeting current needs is primary may be committed to working for the unity of the churches, but if so, their reasons will be instrumental: they will not be interested unless they see how church unity contributes to peace, justice, liberation, and the unification of humanity. Especially if they are Catholics, the description of the church as the sacramental and efficacious sign of the coming unity of all humankind in the first chapter of Vatican II's Constitution on the Church is likely to be a favorite, and they will welcome the growing influence of similar understandings elsewhere, not least in the World Council.[9] Those whose thinking starts with the sources do not necessarily reject such a vision, but will not be likely to understand it as implying that church unity is primarily instrumental to the service of the world. Work for unity is for them a divine imperative which Christians are bound to obey even when they are unable to see clearly what practical effects it might have. Jesus' prayer that his followers be one 'so that the world may believe' (John 17:21) is not conditional on Christians seeing how unity contributes to that end. Thus thematic ecumenism is optional for one group, and necessary for the other.

Yet, in the second place, it would be wrong for those who thus stress *ressourcement* and the reconciliation of the churches simply to bewail the theological movements which have led to their neglect in recent times. Those movements have directed attention both to contemporary problems and to biblical insights which otherwise would have gone unnoticed. Christian engagement with Marxism and feminism, for example, has helped open eyes both to what the world is and what Scripture says. One may think that these insights need to be incorporated into another framework in which faithfulness to the sources rather than present relevance is primary, and yet be grateful for them. For this perspective, recent theological trends are not a defeat for unitive ecumenism, but a challenge which may in the long run contribute to the fullness and faithfulness with which reunited churches find guidance in Scripture and tradition.

## A CONSTRUCTIVE PROPOSAL

If this is to happen, however, there is need for better ways of reading the sources. Familiarity with them does not by itself provide guidance in new situations. When they are approached only with present needs in mind, they are likely simply to echo contemporary clamors rather than also speak with an independent voice. Historical criticism does no better: it tells us, as is often said, what the bible meant, not what it means. Traditionalism and fundamentalism do not even try to meet the problem: they seek unchanging formulations, not the fresh words God utters here and now. For all these approaches, the sources are external to the reader rather than a language one learns to speak, a house or world within which one dwells.

It was not always thus. From the beginnings until well past the Reformation, Scripture was read as a Christ-centered and typologically unified whole with figural applications to all reality. Its world was for believers the truly real one within which they thought and lived both as individuals and communities. It was primarily a means for understanding other things rather than an object for study (though it was also that). Over and over again when change or diversification were required, Scripture shaped consensus among those whose minds, imaginations and behavior were molded by it. Read in the classical fashion, unlike more recent ones, the Bible had consensus-and-community-forming power. It was a followable text with great ecumenical potential (which, to be sure, was by no means always actualized).[10]

The usual supposition that this classic hermeneutics is incompatible with modern science and biblical criticism is the result of confusing it with the two quite different quests: for unchanging doctrine, on the one hand, and for allegorizing pietistic edification, on the other. These interpretive strategies are also ancient, but it was only under the pressure of post-Reformation confessional polemics and early Enlightenment rationalism that they became dominant, and it is they which are opposed to modern scholarship.[11] The earlier stress on narrative, typological and figural meanings has, in contrast, contemporary resonances. It resembles the way many literary critics now read classic texts in order to understand the devices by which they influence the individuals and cultures to which they are familiar.[12]

There is thus no good reason in the present intellectual situation for not once again utilizing this pre-modern way of reading Scripture. After enlarging on this point, I shall, in the second place, comment on the beginnings – admittedly meagre – of this retrieval and, thirdly, ask about its ecumenical potential, its possible role in forming a *consensus fidelium*. (In terms of the categories used in the present volume, these three points together sketch a 'postliberal' view of the present situation and of hopes for the ecumenical future.)

With the loss of Enlightenment confidence in reason and progress, the worlds within which human beings live are increasingly thought of as socially, linguistically, and even textually constructed. Sociology, anthropology, history, philosophy, and literary studies have all contributed to this development. We are aware as never before of the degree to which human beings and their perceptions of reality are socially and culturally determined. Nothing is exempt from this conditioning, not even the natural sciences.

The recent literary emphasis on textuality becomes understandable against this background. Texts, understood as fixed communicative patterns embedded in rites, myths and other oral and representational traditions, are already basic in pre-literate societies. They can be used in different contexts, for different purposes, and with different meanings, and thereby provide frameworks in which individual utterances ('speech acts') are socially significant and effective. This power is enhanced when they take written form, for they can then have a comprehensiveness, complexity, flexibility, and stability which is unattainable in other media (not even modern electronic and cinematographic ones). In short, texts project worlds in which entire communities and cultures can and have lived.

Much contemporary intellectual life can be understood as a search for such habitable texts. Contemporary Marxists and Freudians, for example, now rarely seek to ground their favorite authors' writings scientifically or philosophically. They simply ask that they be followable, that they be construable in such a way as to provide guidance for society, in the one case, and for individual life, in the other. Thus it is that Enlightenment systems which once claimed rational foundations have now turned into foundationless hermeneutical enterprises.

Classic biblical hermeneutics was born in a similar foundationless era when followable texts were in short supply. The Jews had a great advantage: not only did the monotheistic character of their sacred book gave it universal scope and unity, and not only did the long history and diversity of the writings it contained give it extra-ordinarily wide applicability in varying circumstances, but it had directive force and community-building power far superior to the philosophical systems which were its only real rivals. Once Scripture was made applicable to non-Jews by the Christian movement, it proved widely appealing. It was a pre-eminently habitable text in a world needing habitations, and the nations flocked into it.

Ours is again an age when old foundations and legitimating structures have crumbled. Even the defenders of reason think it unreasonable to ask anything more of philosophies and religions, or of the texts which give them richness, comprehensiveness, flexibility, and stability, than that they be followable. There are fewer and fewer intellectual objections to the legitimacy of treating a classic, whether religious or nonreligious, as a perspicuous guide to life and thought. The only question is whether one is interested and can make it work.

There are, to turn to the second point, some developments which suggest that retrieval of the classic hermeneutics is not only possible, but that it is actually beginning. Biblical scholars are increasingly interested in the literary features, social and communal functioning, and canonical unity of the scriptural text. It is, however, for others better qualified than I to comment on these initiatives. Instead, I shall simply mention the names of Karl Barth and Hans Urs von Balthasar. Here are twentieth-century theologians whose use of the Bible is more nearly classical than anything in several centuries and who yet are distinctively modern (e.g., they do not reject historical criticism). Both are wary of translating the Bible into alien conceptualities; both seek, rather, to redescribe the world or worlds in which they live in biblical terms; both treat Scripture as a

Christ-centered and narrationally (or, for von Balthasar, 'dramatically') and typologically unified whole; and in both the reader is referred back to the biblical text itself by exegetical work which is an integral part of the theological program. In short, these two theologians inhabit the same universe of theological discourse as the fathers, medievals and Reformers to a greater degree than do most modern theologians. Disagreements between them are discussable – perhaps even decidable – by reference to the text because they approach Scripture in basically similar ways; whereas in the case of most other theologians, major differences arise from the extra-biblical conceptualities (idealist, Marxist, etc.) by means of which they construe Scripture and are therefore biblically undecidable: indeed, there is sometimes no common conceptuality, scriptural and nonscriptural, in which they can be discussed.

Yet their approaches to Scripture have not been widely adopted. Even Barth's followers (I do not know about von Balthasar's) are for the most part influenced by his theology, not his exegesis. This is understandable, for his exegesis is at times deeply flawed (even if corrigible).[13] What we have in these two authors is only a first, even if important, stage in the work of making the Bible followable in our day, of making it readable classically, and yet not anti-critically. The analogous task in the Graeco-Roman world took hundreds of years, and although it reached a kind of climax in Augustine and the Cappadocians, it could never, given the mutability of that and every world, be definitively completed. We are perhaps at the beginnings of retrieval in theology and biblical scholarship, but no more than that.

The third and most difficult question, however, is whether Christian communities as a whole can again learn to read Scripture classically. That they do so is ecumenically important, for without a biblically-informed *consensus fidelium* it is difficult to see how the diverse confessional traditions can be genuinely reconciled. Communities of interpretation are needed in which pastors, scriptural scholars, theologians, and laity together seek God's guidance in the written word for their communal as well as individual lives. Their reading of Scripture will be within the context of a worship life which, in its basic eucharistic, baptismal, and kerygmatic patterns, accords with that of the first centuries. They may differ in their views of the *de iure divino* status of the threefold pattern of ministry and of the papal institutionalization of the Petrine function, but not on the legitimacy of these forms of ministry as servants of word, sacrament and unity. There will be in these communities a renewed sense that Christians constitute a single people chosen to witness among the nations in all they are, say and do to the salvation that was, that is, and that is to come, and guided by God in his mercy and judgment, and in their faithfulness and unfaithfulness, towards the promised consummation. They will care for their own members, and will also be deeply concerned about Christians everywhere. Openness to receive and responsibility to give help and correction from and to other churches will be embedded in their institutional and organizational fabrics.

This is a dream, a cloud no larger than a hand on the horizon, and yet if it began to be actualized, even if in only a few and scattered places, it would be living proof that Scripture is a unifying and followable text. The news would travel swiftly (it always does in our day), and its influence would mushroom. Public opinion might be widely – perhaps even quickly – affected in all communions, and the transformation of the *sensus fidelium* (which takes longer) might follow in due course.

Not all the problems of how to reshape the church in this age of transition would be solved by such a development. Christians will continue to differ, not only on political questions of peace and justice and of socialism and capitalism, but also on matters of direct ecclesial import such as the ordination of women. Is the tradition against their ordination basically cultural and thus similar to the church's long accommodation to slavery? Retrieval of the classic hermeneutics even in combination with historical criticism does not decide this issue. Yet it changes the context of the debate. Attention focuses, not on entitlements, privileges, and gender, but on the pastoral office itself as God's instrument for the nurturing of his people with word and sacrament. What builds up the church is what counts. Sociologically and historically speaking, it is ultimately the *sensus fidelium* which decides such matters in any case, but to the degree the instinct of the faithful (their connatural knowledge, as Aquinas would say) is scripturally shaped, it not only does but *should* decide.

There is much in the more theologically-oriented ecumenical discussions which points in the direction of these remarks. The life of worship and ministry which is the necessary (not sufficient) context for unifying interpretation is basically that described in the Faith and Order Lima document, *Baptism, Eucharist and Ministry*. Similarly, to cite just one other item, the most recent report of the Lutheran/Roman Catholic International Study Commission marks the beginnings of cooperative thinking on how local interconfessional communities of interpretation (though it does not call them that) might develop which would contribute to the reshaping and renewal rather than the disruption of present church orders.[14]

Yet it must be admitted that this hope for the actualization of the consensus-and-community-building potential of the classic pattern of biblical interpretation in a postmodern setting seems impossibly visionary. The beginnings of talk about it are not accompanied by much in the way of performance. Those circles in which serious Bible reading is most widespread – conservative Protestant, charismatic, Cursillo, base communities – are often fundamentalist and almost always pre-critical in their interpretation. They also need the retrieval of the classic hermeneutics.

On the other hand, there is no reason for discouragement. Scripture permits and perhaps urges us to dream dreams and see visions. Barriers have been erased, retrieval has begun, and we can begin to imagine far more than was possible a mere generation ago, that Roman Catholics, Eastern Orthodox, and heirs of the Reformation will learn to read Scripture together as the Christ-centered guide for themselves and their churches. God's ordering of world and church history has sown the seeds for the rebirth of the power of the written word, and it is for believers to pray, work, and hope against hope that he will bring these seeds to fruition through the Holy Spirit.

## NOTES

1 See W. Hudson, 'Denominationalism as a Basis for Ecumenicity', *Church History*, 24 (1955), pp. 32–50. This essay has been much cited and is reprinted in *Denominationalism*, ed. R. E. Richey (Nashville, Tenn., 1977), pp. 21–42.
2 George Lindbeck, *The Nature of Doctrine: Religion and Theology in a Postliberal Age* (Philadelphia, 1985) proposes a way of understanding church doctrines and a religion such as Christianity which is consistent with this ecumenical program of 'reconciliation without capitulation'.
3 World Council of Churches (Geneva).
4 W. M. Abbott (ed.), *The Documents of Vatican II* (New York, 1966). Another English-language edition is that of Austin Flannery.
5 I have more fully discussed this phenomenon and its implications for ecumenism in 'Non-Theological Factors and Structures of Unity', in *Einheit der Kirche: Neue Entwicklungen und Perspektiven*, ed. G. Gassmann (Frankfurt am Main, 1988), pp. 133–45.
6 He suggests that it was a brief interruption, occasioned by war and the Nazi era, in the long-term theologically liberal accommodation of the churches to the secularization (or, as he might now say, 'dechristianiza-tion') of Western culture. *The Sacred Canopy: Elements of a Sociological Theory of Religion* (Garden City, NY, 1967), p. 165.

7 'Faith and Liberation: Developments since Vatican II', in *Vatican II: Open Questions and New Horizons*, ed. G. M. Fagin, (Wilmington, Del., 1984).

8 I single them out because I know at first hand the kind of theology to which they were exposed when they, like myself, were students at Yale.

9 As expressed, for example, by Günther Gassmann, the present director of Faith and Order, in a discussion of what he hopes for at the next WCC Assembly in Canberra in 1991. See his 'Einheit der Kirche – die Notwendigkeit einer neuen Klaerung,' *Einheit der Kirche*, pp. 13–23, esp. p. 21.

10 I have dealt at length with the theme of this paragraph in the first four sections of a paper, 'Scripture, Community and Consensus', discussed in a colloquy with Cardinal Ratzinger in New York on January 28, 1988, and which will be shortly published in *This World: A Journal of Religion and Public Life*. The remainder of the present chapter is in part extracted from the concluding section of that paper.

11 The story is told in Hans Frei, *The Eclipse of Biblical Narrative* (New Haven, Conn., 1974).

12 The similarities (as well as some of the differences) between modern literary and pre-modern theological interpretation of Scripture are extensively documented in *The Literary Guide to the Bible*, eds Robert Alter and Frank Kermode (Cambridge, Mass., 1987).

13 I have commented briefly on some of the strengths and weaknesses of Barth's exegesis in 'Barth and Textuality', *Theology Today*, XLIII (1986), pp. 361–76.

14 *Facing Unity* (Geneva, Rome, 1985).

## Bibliographical Note

The standard account of the ecumenical movement is provided in the two volumes by R. Rouse and S. C. McNeill (eds), *A History of the Ecumenical Movement (1517–1948)*, vol. 1, 3rd edn (Geneva, 1986) and H. E. Fey (ed.), *A History of the Ecumenical Movement (1948–1968)*, vol. 2, 2nd edn (Geneva, 1986). The latter contains an excellent bibliography covering the period from 1968 to 1985.

The best compendium of the international dialogues is H. Meyer and G. Gassmann (eds), *Growth in Agreement* (Ramsay, NJ, 1984). Much important theological work has also been done by national and regional dialogues, the most prolific of which has been the US *Lutherans and Catholics in Dialogue* (7 vols, various editors; Minneapolis, 1973–85).

Most well-known twentieth-century theologians have published, often extensively, on ecumenism. This is true of all those to whom chapters are devoted in volume I. Yves Congar in particular has written more and more learnedly on Christian unity than any other theologian, and has rightly been called 'the father of Roman Catholic ecumenism' by the long-time head of the World Council, Visser 't Hooft. Among the other authors in

Volume I, Thomas Torrance, Wolfhart Pannenberg, Hans Küng, and Karl Rahner have been especially prolific. Hans Urs von Balthasar's extensive discussions of Reformation and Protestant thought scattered throughout many of his writings are frequently polemical, but yet often ecumenically important, not least because he has, by his own acknowledgement, been deeply influenced by Karl Barth.

Three works, by an Anglican, Roman Catholic and Orthodox respectively, may be singled out (even if somewhat arbitrarily) as representative of recent ecumenical theology:

John Macquarrie, *Christian Unity and Christian Diversity* (London, 1975).
Karl Rahner (with Heinrich Fries), *Unity of the Churches: An Actual Possibility* (Ramsay, NJ, 1984).
John D. Zizioulas, *Being as Communion* (Crestwood, NY, 1985).

# 14

# Theology of Religions

## Gavin D'Costa

### INTRODUCTION

The meeting of religions has produced racism, intolerance, bloodshed, cooperation, hope, love, and equal doses of sympathy and misunderstanding. Religious pluralism raises many practical and theological questions for Christians: should Buddhist meditation groups be allowed the use of church halls; how should religious education be taught; what kind of social and political cooperation is permissible with people of other faiths? There are also fundamental theological issues at stake. If salvation is possible outside Christ/Christianity, what form should mission take? What is the significance of Christ and the meaning of the church? Or if salvation is not possible outside Christ/Christianity, is it credible that a loving God could consign the majority of humankind to perdition, often through no fault of their own? Can Christians learn from these other faiths? Can they be enriched rather than diluted or polluted from this encounter?

I will outline and comment upon three 'types' of Christian response to other religions. These responses are to be found in varying degrees through most of Christian history.[1] There are considerable differences between theologians belonging to the same 'camp', but the validity of distinguishing three, rather than thirteen, types is justified for pedagogic purposes. I shall call these three approaches: *pluralism* (that all religions are equal and valid paths to the one divine reality); *exclusivism* (only those who hear the gospel proclaimed and explicitly confess Christ are saved); and *inclusivism* (that Christ is the normative revelation of God, although salvation is possible through religions other than Christianity). Various presuppositions undergird each approach – which will be explored through discussing three representatives: John Hick (see also chapter 2 above), George Lindbeck (see also chapter 6 above), and

Karl Rahner (see also volume I, chapter 9). I will then discuss some of the central theological issues raised in the debate about other religions, and indicate the agenda for future discussion.

## JOHN HICK'S PLURALISM

John Hick is a Presbyterian and is primarily a philosopher of religion, deeply influenced by Kant, Schleiermacher, and the positivist debates concerning religious language. Hick propounds a number of arguments in favor of pluralism.[2]

### Theological Arguments

Hick argues that the *solus Christus* assumption (that salvation is only through Christ) held by exclusivists is incompatible with the Christian teaching of the *universal salvific will of God* who desires to save all people. There are many millions who have never heard of Christ through no fault of their own, before and after New Testament times – the invincibly ignorant. It is un-Christian to think that God would have 'ordained that men must be saved in such a way that only a small minority can in fact receive this salvation'.[3] Hick therefore proposes a *theocentric* revolution away from a *christocentric* position that has dominated Christian history. Hence, it is God, and not Christianity or Christ, towards whom all religions move, and from whom they gain their salvific efficacy. Hick argues that the doctrine of the incarnation should be understood mythically – as an expression of commitment by Christians, not as an ontological claim that here and here alone God has been fully revealed.[4]

### Phenomenological Arguments

Hick develops his thesis through an inspection of the history of religions. He discerns a *common soteriological structure*, whereby the major religions exhibit a turning from 'self-centredness to Reality-centredness'.[5] This phenomenon reinforces the necessity of a theological paradigm shift from christocentricism to theocentricism.

### Philosophical Arguments

In response to the objection that there are contradictory truth-claims made among the religions, Hick suggests that we are unnecessarily bound by a notion of truth as 'either-or', rather than a holistic notion of truth as 'both-and'. Christians may adopt a complementary model, rather than one of contradiction, whereby different religious insights can be harmonized and viewed as different aspects of the one truth.

### Dialogue

The above arguments cumulatively suggest that Christians can fruitfully view the history of religions as a history of God's activity without making any special claims for Christianity. Christian attitudes to other religions need not be characterized by a desire to convert, or claims to superiority, but a will to learn and grow together towards the truth.[6] Mission should be jointly carried out to the secular world by the religions, rather than towards each other.[7] Hick suggests that exclusivism and inclusivism cannot provide such fruitful conditions for inter-religious dialogue.[8]

A recent shift in Hick's position has come in response to the criticism that his theological revolution is still theocentric and thereby excludes non-theistic religions. Hick makes a Kantian-type distinction to solve the problem. He distinguishes between a *divine noumenal reality* 'which exists independently and outside man's perception of it' which he calls the 'Eternal One', and the *phenomenal* world, 'which is that world as it appears to our human consciousness' and which corresponds to the responses within different religious traditions, both theistic and non-theistic.[9]

### GEORGE LINDBECK'S EXCLUSIVISM

George Lindbeck is a Lutheran theologian deeply committed to Christian ecumenism. He has been strongly influenced by certain theories in sociology, anthropology, philosophy of science, and linguistics (Berger, Geertz, Kuhn, and Wittgenstein, respectively).[10] To understand his position it is important to understand the model of religion with which he works.

Lindbeck suggests there are two dominant ways of understanding religions: 'propositional' and 'experiential-expressivist'. The first construes religions in terms of their cognitive and propositional claims and the latter construes religious language as expressing religious experience – through symbols, gestures, actions and so forth. Lindbeck's own proposal, that of a 'cultural-linguistic' model, inverts the expressivist model. Religions are viewed as analogous to languages. The way in which one experiences the world religiously is determined through the practice of one's inherited religion. 'A religion is above all an external word, a *verbum externum*, that molds and shapes the self and its world, rather than an expression . . . of a preexisting self or preconceptual experience.'[11]

## Theological Arguments

Lindbeck wishes to retain the *solus Christus* as well as the *fides ex auditu* (faith by hearing) tradition – that is, one may only come to salvation through hearing the Word and confessing Christ. This is in keeping with Lindbeck's biblical and Reformation principles. However, within Lindbeck's model of religion this exclusivist position has a number of important ramifications. First, because the cultural-linguistic model allows that different religions may be incommensurable, it also follows that 'there is no damnation – just as there is no salvation – outside the church. One must, in other words, learn the language of faith before one can know enough about its message knowingly to reject it and thus be lost.'[12]

While this seems to heed Hick's problem concerning the invincibly ignorant, it also seems to consign them to limbo – rather than hell, as do many exclusivists![13] However, Lindbeck suggests that non-Christians will have a post-mortem confrontation with Christ (satisfying the *fides ex auditu* principle) and therefore part of the Christian hope is that all people will be saved.[14] Through this strategy, Lindbeck circumvents Hick's criticism concerning the incompatibility of the *solus Christus* with an all-loving God.

## Phenomenological Arguments, Dialogue and Mission

Lindbeck suggests that his approach acknowledges the serious differences betwen religions without trying to explain away their claims through a relativizing process. Hence, in *dialogue*, the other can be acknowledged as truly other rather than trying to fit them into a global schema, as does Hick, often not on their own terms.

Dialogue can also be mutually enriching for it is possible that 'other religions have resources for speaking truths and referring to realities, even highly important realities, of which Christianity as yet knows nothing and by which it could be greatly enriched.'[15] Equally Christians may help their partners 'to purify and enrich their heritages, to make them better speakers of the languages they have'.[16] And of course, by their way of life within the Christian community, as with ancient catechesis, Christians may attract disciples to Christ. In this respect, Lindbeck's proposals counter Hick's claim that exclusivists do not have good theological grounds for dialogue, although in advocating mission it would still fall foul of Hick's strictures.


## KARL RAHNER'S INCLUSIVISM

Karl Rahner (d. 1986) was an influential Roman Catholic theologian whose fundamental outlook (called transcendental Thomism) was based on interpreting Aquinas in the light of Kant, understood through the filter of the early Heidegger and Maréchal.[17] Rahner's theological anthropology shapes his inclusivism. He argues that the precondition of finite (categorial) knowledge is an unconditional openness to being (*vorgriff*), which is an unthematic, pre-reflective awareness of God – who is infinite being. Our transcendental openness to being constitutes the hiddenness of grace. Men and women therefore search through history for a categorial disclosure of this hidden grace. In Jesus' total abandonment to God, his total 'Yes' through his life, death, and resurrection, he is established as the culmination and prime mediator of grace. Therefore the expressly Christian revelation becomes the explicit expression of grace which men and women experience implicitly in the depths of their being.


### *Theological Arguments*

Rahner mediates a path between pluralism and exclusivism. He affirms the *solus Christus* principle (Lindbeck) as well as the notion of the *universal salvific will of God* (Hick). As with Lindbeck, the *solus Christus* has ecclesiological implications – a point that Lindbeck notes is common to Lutherans and Roman Catholics, but not always to Barthians.[18] Christ is historically mediated through the church.

The only way in which these principles can be reconciled according to Rahner is by 'saying that somehow all men must be capable of being members of the Church; and this capacity must not be understood merely in the sense of an abstract . . . possibility, but as a real and historically concrete one'.[19] Rahner develops this comment along the lines of the traditional Catholic teachings regarding the *votum ecclesiae* (a wish to belong to the Church), and the related notion of implicit desire. His application, however, is novel.

Rahner argues that if salvific grace exists outside the visible church (as it does in the history of Israel – and in creation and through conscience), then this grace is both causally related to Christ (always and everwhere – as prime mediator) and his church. Furthermore, given the socio-historical nature of men and women, grace must be mediated historically and socially. The incarnation is paradigmatic in suggesting this. Hence, if and when non-Christians respond to grace, then this grace must be mediated *through* their religion, however imperfectly. Rahner thus coins the term 'anonymous Christian' and 'anonymous Christianity'. The first refers to the source of saving grace that is responded to and the second refers to its dynamic orientation towards its definitive historical and social expression in the church.

### Phenomenological Arguments

Rahner points out that his reflections require to be tested by the historian of religion and those involved in dialogue. Christians may try to discern where and when the movement of grace takes place and to test the hypothesis that men and women constantly search for a mediator.[20]

### Dialogue and Mission

Because God has already been active within the non-Christian partner (*preparatio evangelica*), the Christian can be open to learning about God through the non-Christian religions.[21] Furthermore, the Christian is also free to engage in active social cooperation when appropriate. Contrary to Hick, the inclusivist has a firm theological basis for fruitful dialogue. Given Rahner's notion that grace seeks to objectivize itself, mission is clearly important.

## THE DEBATE

To focus the discussion I shall concentrate on three related issues: *christology, ecclesiology,* and *mission and dialogue.* I believe these three areas (and especially the first) are seminal to the debate about Christian attitudes to other religions. While our three writers have not always explicitly written about each other, they have all criticized the type of view held by the others.

### Solus Christus

*Has Hick gone too far?*

Hick's theocentric revolution is based on a shaky premiss. He rejects the *solus Christus* for he thinks it leads to the a priori damnation of non-Christians. Lindbeck and Rahner show that it need not. Furthermore, when Hick proposes a theocentric revolution away from a christocentric paradigm he is in danger of severing christ-ology from ontology and introducing a 'free floating' reductionist God. The theistic religions all center on revelatory paradigms for their discourse and practice. Hick's theocentric propositionalism pays little attention to the importance of particularity. In fact, the theological basis of the revolution – that of an all-loving God – is undermined if Hick cannot give normative *ontological* status to the revelatory events upon which this axiom is grounded (originally for Hick), that of the revelation of God in Christ. (Clearly the non-theistic religions cannot accept this premiss!). And Lindbeck, more sharply, points out: 'The datum that all religions recommend something which can be called "love" towards that which is taken to be most important ("God") is a banality as uninteresting as the fact that all languages are (or were) spoken. The significant things are the distinctive patterns of story, belief, ritual, and behavior that gives "love" and "God" their specific and sometimes contradictory meanings.'[22] Christology is important precisely because it is *through Jesus* that Christians claim that God has revealed himself in a unique (although not necessarily exclusive) manner. A theocentricism without a christocentricism can only lead towards an abstract common denominator (reductionism) called 'God'.

Hick's problems are multiplied in his later revolution away from theocentricism to 'Reality-centricism'. If the meaning of 'God' lacked specificity in Hick's theocentricism, it is now altogether relativized, for Hick forsees that his solution will not be acceptable to nontheists. He thereby relativizes 'God' as one aspect of the 'Eternal One' that apparently can also be characterized with opposite predicates, as, finally, all these predicates are from the human side. The Kantian noumenal encountered a similar problem in not providing for a correspondence between phenomena and things in themselves. Hick is very close to a transcendental agnosticism (i.e. affirming a transcendence without any qualities).[23] In Hick's attempt to include nontheists he cuts yet another mooring line. It is difficult to imagine any of the semitic religions applauding Hick's most recent developments.

The attraction of Hick's strategy is in trying to circumvent an exclusive linking of God to Christ – a position that Lindbeck holds. His weakness is that his strategy leads to a vacuous notion of 'God' (and eventually 'Reality').[24]

### Has Lindbeck gone far enough?

Lindbeck's retention of the *fides ex auditu* (faith by hearing) controls his employment of the *solus Christus* (Christ alone). The question that can be put to Lindbeck is this: has he sufficiently acknowledged and explained the presence of grace outside the visible Church? While Lindbeck is right to retain the *solus Christus* principle, he surely requires to relate this to God's activity throughout his creation. This difficulty becomes apparent in Lindbeck's comment that non-Christian religions have 'resources for speaking truths and referring to realities' while not specifying whether these realities and truths concern God and can be seen as signs of grace.[25] This latter reading is excluded implicitly when he writes that 'non-Christians can share in the future salvation even though they, unlike those with living Christian faith, have not yet begun to do so'.[26]

There is a further difficulty in Lindbeck's employment of the *solus Christus* principle. Given his cultural-linguistic model, how will people who have never shared Christian language and practice be able to make a decision for or against Christ – as is required by his post-mortem solution? Without being inducted into the Christian paradigm they would be incapable of making such a decision by Lindbeck's own principles.[27]

The strength of Lindbeck's proposals is in his retention of the *solus Christus* principle, but his weakness is in not being able to relate this principle to the activity of God in creation, Israel (before Christ), history, and conscience. However, his stress on the *solus Christus* and *fides ex auditu* as axiomatic principles controlling Christian discourse highlight the difficulties in Rahner's alternative, to which we now turn.

*Has Rahner made Christ invisible?*        visible?

Both Hick and Lindbeck claim that Rahner's notion of the 'anonymous Christian' is imperialist and offensive to non-Christians.[28] Rahner's theory springs from his retention of the *solus Christus* teaching and in this respect it is difficult to square Lindbeck's criticism with his own avowal of the teaching which leads to an equally 'imperialist' post-mortem conclusion. Hick's criticism is also a little unconvincing as his own proposals contain a similar dynamic when he writes that secular 'servants of humanity are involved, without knowing it, in the transition from self-centredness to Reality-centredness'.[29]

There are more substantial criticisms from Lindbeck regarding Rahner's theological anthropology and Christology. He comments that the 'idealist model' emphasizes the prior reality of the experience of Spirit that 'necessarily expresses and fulfills itself in objective cultural and religious forms'.[30] The problem with Rahner's model is that it derives 'external features of a religion from inner experience'. The cultural linguistic model reverses this so that 'it is the inner experiences which are viewed as derivitave'.[31] Developing this point, as has Hans Urs von Balthasar, it may be argued that Rahner neglects the importance of the christoform shape of grace, tending to conform grace to his a priori transcendental anthropology (*vorgriff*).[32] Simply put: does Rahner sever grace from Christ, fitting Jesus as the best and other figures in history as less good expressions of an a priori notion of grace?

This is a complex issue. Rahner does not seem to give enough attention to the *formative* function of the Word (*fides ex auditu*) in eliciting and shaping the response to grace. He stresses continuity and minimizes the discontinuity, the overturning of previous worldviews and the new forms of life enjoined by a christoform pattern of worship and practice – as emphasized by Lindbeck. 'Faith in Christ is not straightforwardly a recognition of the satisfaction of my needs; the form of Christ is always a revelation of our untruth (and thus unreality and unloveliness).'[33] There are two distinct, though related, issues at stake. The first concerns the adequacy of Rahner's transcendental framework and the second his attention to the christoform shape of grace.

In terms of the wider debate, inclusivism is *not* dependent on transcendental Thomism. Having said this, it does seem that Lindbeck and Balthasar rightly highlight the weakness of Rahner's theological anthropology and his consequent lack of attention to the christoform shape of grace. Their criticisms concerning the discontinuity with one's past life brought about by following Christ offers a general critique of the inclusivist-fulfillment christology: that Christ fulfills the aspirations and needs of the world's religions. For example, Rahner's rightful stress on self-giving and trustful love participating in the dynamic of grace is grounded more (although not exclusively) on his transcendental anthropology than on a christological paradigm – or in Lindbeck's words, 'the distinctive patterns of story, belief, ritual, and behavior that give "love" and "God" their specific' and Christian meanings.[34] I am not convinced that this imbalance in Rahner's thought is beyond remedy – but its remedying would make the transcendental framework somewhat redundant. An alternative, to which I shall return later, is to speak of the patterns of self-giving and suffering love (among other patterns) that are found within the world religions and reflect the christoform shape of grace.

Rahner's christology may be problematic, but from the discussion above it will be apparent that the direction of his thought is correct. He rightly retains a christocentric foundation and relates this to grace outside of visible Christianity in a way that Lindbeck fails to, and in a manner which circumvents Hick's relinquishing of the *solus Christus*.

### Extra Ecclesiam Nulla Salus

Both Hick and Lindbeck tend to construe the *extra ecclesiam* axiom (no salvation outside the church) literally, which leads the former to reject it and the latter to maintain it. Their attitudes are related to the *solus Christus* teaching. While exclusivism and pluralism have been found problematic, Lindbeck's cultural-linguistic approach is certainly important in focusing attention on the socially-mediated christoform shape of grace, thereby posing important questions to Rahner's theory of *anonymous Christianity*.

Rahner's invisible church is, according to Lindbeck, unbiblical and also detracts from the importance of explicit confession as a criterion for membership.[35] Rahner *seems* to have conceded that the expression *anonymous Christianity* may be problematic – although he states that his intention in using the term is to denote the dynamic orientation towards the church present in the *anonymous Christian*.[36] Lindbeck retorts: 'There is little evidence that this occurs'; anonymous Christians do not 'have this natural tendency, at least in the present economy of things'.[37] Rahner's argument does not need empirical justification in terms of conversion numbers! His is a theological point. If the fullness of grace is revealed in and through Jesus, then the person who has responded to grace previously (and anonymously) should, if there are no impediments, desire Christian membership in their confrontation with the gospel. The problem with Rahner here, as with his christology, is his emphasis on continuity at the cost of discontinuity. The tragic self-deceit and self-destruction that can cause impediment are not taken as seriously as they should be. (This is not to deny that self-deceit operates within Christianity – a point made by both Rahner and Lindbeck). The discontinuity between explicit and implicit Christianity is obscured in the term anonymous Christianity, although it may appropriately designate elements of continuity regarding the presence of grace.

In this respect Lindbeck's cultural linguistic model of the church is far more satisfactory than Rahner's. However, Rahner's concerns are legitimate: if grace is acknowledged as a possibility outside the visible church, then this grace must be related to the church as the church is intrinsically related to Christ. It is the nature of this relation, the anonymous 'belonging' to the church, that is deeply problematic. A possible way of developing this discussion is to acknowledge that the church _itself_ is not fulfilled until it incorporates all that is good and holy within the non-Christian traditions _within_ its own christological paradigm. (This enlarges and partially reverses the fulfillment-inclusivist model.) This of course has happened throughout Christian history, first and foremost with Judaism but also through its contact with Greek philosophy. Christianity's incarnational dynamism can also be developed in respect to Hinduism, Buddhism and so on, incorporating what may be termed 'fragmentary elements of the Church'.[38] 'Fragmentary', in so much as only their incorporation and _transformation_ within a Christian paradigm makes them truly Christian; but also fragmentary in so much as they are, however imperfectly, related to the mediation of grace. In this case, the _votum ecclesiae_ may not be redundant, but it is also carefully delimited to preserve the biblical and cultural-linguistic integrity and identity of the Christian community.

## MISSION AND DIALOGUE

All three approaches cater for dialogue in which Christians have something to learn and to offer. In some respects, the evaluation of the _solus Christus_ determines the attitude to dialogue and cooperation. All three approaches similarly bring different a priori suppositions to the dialogue – each of which is open to criticism from the other.

Hick, Lindbeck could argue, imposes meaning and definition upon the other thereby stifling genuine dialogue in so much as exclusive revelatory claims, normative ontological definitions, and so on, are disallowed. All such claims are relativized or harmonized as partial expressions of the divine encounter.[39] Hick also a priori disallows mission and in this respect stifles the inner dynamic often present, and necessary within various religions (especially Christianity and Islam). His stipulation against mission can itself hinder dialogue in which the person shares his or her own deepest commitments, hopes and longings. In this respect, Rahner and Lindbeck are to be preferred, while obviously Hick's intention is for dialogue to proceed without the constant suspicion that a partner is *only* there for converting.

Lindbeck could be accused of foreclosing the dialogue in two ways. With his emphasis on the incommensurability of religions – fideism seems to result, despite his protestations.[40] On Lindbeck's terms one cannot engage or learn from another religion until one has adopted it. Hence, it is difficult to make sense of Lindbeck's proposals to purify other heritages by making their adherents 'better speakers of the languages they have'.[41] For a non-Chinese speaker to presume to teach a Chinese speaker how to speak their language better is somewhat presumptious! Secondly, Lindbeck's particular application of the *solus Christus* rules out, a priori, God's self-disclosure in the world's religions. This foreclosure is surely unnecessary and also unhistorical.

Rahner is charged with offending the partner in claiming to know better than they what is going on in the depths of their being. I do not find this criticism convincing (see above), especially as Rahner's theology is not meant for 'presentation' in dialogue, but as an internal Christian reflection. To engage in dialogue with the conviction that God may be present within the non-Christian's religion and life – in a manner that may challenge the Christian's own self-understanding and appreciation of the partner's faith – is surely beneficial. Rahner does not specify the forms that this presence may take. To this end, Rahner's proposals seem the most open-ended and therefore dialogical.

## ACHIEVEMENT AND AGENDA

The modern debate has successfully raised an agenda for theological consideration concerning a range of christological, ecclesiological, and dialogue/mission issues. We have seen aspects of these problems in the discussion above, while others have remained relatively untouched – for example: hermeneutics; indigenization; the particularities and dynamics of the specific encounter of Christianity with Judaism, Hinduism and so on; not to mention the practical difficulties of living, working, and being political in a religiously-pluralist society. To conclude, I would like to highlight some important areas in need of further attention.

### Hermeneutics

I will mention only three issues. The *model of religion* within which one works is central in shaping one's subsequent reflections on religious pluralism. Lindbeck's three basic models help to clarify the underlying presuppositions involved in different approaches. This debate need not be confined to Christian theologians, but theologians should critically examine and justify the models that they employ. This would involve, to give examples, an evaluation of truth-criteria. For instance, Lindbeck and Rahner are christocentric regarding truth (intratextual), while Hick seems to employ criteria from outside the christocentric paradigm (extratextual). Another example would be the hermeneutical rule regarding 'self-definition'. Dialogue cannot be dialogue if the 'other' is not construed in his or her own terms. However, an analysis and appreciation of these terms inevitably involves interpretation. The stipulation concerns attentive listening!

Second, there is also the question of whether a theology of religions should be worked out *systematically*, without the 'other' being interrogatively present and in isolation from the *specific* interface of encounter. For instance, Rosemary Radford Ruether's challenge to christology is generated specifically in the light of Christianity's anti-Judaic history leading to the camps of Treblinka and Auschwitz.[42] Examples could be multiplied. Is it more appropriate to think of specific 'Christian-Jewish', 'Christian-Muslim' theologies of religion, rather than a generalized theology of religions which specifies answers before the encounter? My own inclination would be to argue that both approaches need each other. If the systematic theologian ignores the interface, or vice versa, each will be subsequently impoverished.[43]

Thirdly, there are hermeneutical criteria that affect the basis of reflection. The feminist theologian may well set the agenda for dialogue so as to explore the oppression of women within the religions – raising questions of canonicity (Fiorenza), patriarchal structures (Ruether), and so on. The liberation theologian (increasingly from the traditional mission fields) may well reverse the current hermeneutical procedure in order to start reflection at the point of oppression and pay more attention to the interplay of ethical beliefs within the world religions. They may suggest, as has M. M. Thomas,[44] that Christianity's major contribution to a pluralist world is in dismantling the structures of oppression. The import of the above points towards the collaborative task ahead not only for Christians working together, but also in reflecting and working with their non-Christian neighbors.

## Christology

I have covered a number of christological issues in exploring the debate so I will only highlight a single issue here. Significantly, the *Trinity* is very rarely mentioned in Christian theologies of religion. If christology operates in a trinitarian context, then the employment of the *solus Christus* is greatly enriched through its trinitarian implications. (Rayumando Panikkar is one of the few theologians who has developed a theology of religions in this direction.)[45] One can then look for trinitarian patterns within the world religions (while equally through this process enriching and deepening Christianity's trinitarian understanding). There are, for instance, the cruciform patterns of self-giving love through the Son; the patterns of apophatic silence and encompassing mystery in the Father; and a whole range of interlinking patterns between the latter two through the Spirit. This suggestion could be developed with reference to the *Logos Spermatikos* tradition and to the 'theologies of hope' that emphasize pneumatology.[46]

## Ecclesiology

Through such a trinitarian application of the *solus Christus* the notion of the 'fragmentary elements' of the church may be developed in a number of ways. Through dialogue the Christian will want to embrace and integrate into Christian discourse and action the 'fragmentary elements' of truth, goodness and wisdom found in other religions (indigenization). If dialogue is purely intellectual and remains at the level of comparing doctrines, then spirituality and worship (at the heart of Christianity) are neglected – to its own detriment. A rich area for exploration is the indigenous development of spirituality and liturgical worship arising through Christianity's encounter with new worlds of discourse and practice.[47] It is not accidental that methods of prayer, contemplation, and liturgical practice are in the foreground in Christianity's meeting with the highly-sacramental and meditative forms of Hinduism.

Furthermore, as Moltmann, Thomas, Lindbeck, and Rahner remind us, Christians are called to be signs of hope, signs of Christ, in the world. There is both a receptive and active side to ecclesiology which corresponds to dialogue/indigenization and mission respectively.

At the outset I stated that religious pluralism raises many practical and theological questions for Christianity. Besides the three responses examined in this essay, there is a fourth: conversion away from Christianity! This ultimately is a risk that must be taken. If the reader has gained some sense of the vitality and complexity of the debate – then it will be appreciated that the presence of the world religions presents an engaging and urgent agenda that cannot be ignored by Christians.

## NOTES

I am indebted to Dr Gerard Loughlin for his critical comments on an early draft of this essay.

1 For surveys of theologians adopting these three positions see bibliographical entries under Knitter and D'Costa.
2 The works to which I shall refer are *God and the Universe of Faiths*; *God Has Many Names*; *The Second Christianity*; 'A Philosophy of Religious Pluralism', in *The World's Religious Traditions*, ed. F. Whaling (Edinburgh, 1984), pp. 147–64.
3 John Hick, *God and the Universe of Faiths*, p. 122.
4 John Hick, *God has Many Names*, p. 57.
5 John Hick, *The Second Christianity*, p. 88.
6 Hick, *God has Many Names*, pp. 116–36; 'Philosophy of Religious Pluralism', p. 164.
7 Hick, *The Second Christianity*, p. 88.
8 Hick, *God has Many Names*, pp. 29–36, 117–24.
9 Ibid., p. 105.
10 His main works related to our topic are *The Nature of Doctrine. Religion and Theology in a Postliberal Age*; 'Fides ex auditu and the Salvation of Non-Christians', in *The Gospel and the Ambiguity of the Church*, ed. V. Vajta (Philadelphia, 1974), pp. 92–123; and *The Future of Roman Catholic Theology* (London, 1970).
11 George Lindbeck, *The Nature of Doctrine*, p. 34.
12 Ibid., p. 59.

13 See for example ed. J. Percy, *Facing the Unfinished Task* (Michigan, 1961), p. 9.
14 For a history of this interpretation based on I Peter 3:19, see W. Dalton, *Christ's Proclamation to the Spirits* (Rome, 1965); exclusivists can also be universalists, as was Karl Barth!
15 Hick, *The Second Christianity*, p. 88.
16 Lindbeck, *The Nature of Doctrine*, pp. 61–2.
17 The important works by Rahner on this theme are *Theological Investigations* (London and New York), vol. 5 (1966), ch. 6, vol. 6 (1969), chs 16, 23; vol. 12 (1974), ch. 9; vol. 14 (1976), ch. 17; vol. 16 (1979), ch. 4; vol. 17 (1980), ch. 5; see also DiNoia's essay in this collection, volume I, chapter 9.
18 Lindbeck, '*Fides ex auditu*', pp. 104–5.
19 Rahner, *Theological Investigations*, vol. 6, p. 391.
20 Rahner, ibid., vol. 17, pp. 49–50.
21 Rahner, ibid., vol. 6, p. 40.
22 Lindbeck, *The Nature of Doctrine*, p. 42; and see further my *John Hick's Theology of Religions*, pp. 103–15.
23 See D'Costa, ibid., pp. 170–83 for a development and substantiation of this criticism.
24 This problem with pluralist theologies *in general* is discussed in my *Theology and Religious Pluralism*, pp. 22–51.
25 Lindbeck, *The Nature of Doctrine*, p. 61.
26 Ibid., p. 57.
27 See K. Surin's extended criticism of Lindbeck's post-mortem solution in 'Many Religions and the One True Faith – An Examination of Lindbeck's Chapter Three', *Modern Theology* (January 1988); see also my criticisms of exclusivism *in general* in *Theology and Religious Pluralism*, pp. 52–79.
28 Hick, *God has Many Names*, pp. 27, 68; Lindbeck, *The Nature of Doctrine*, p. 61.
29 Hick, *The Second Christianity*, p. 88.
30 Lindbeck, *The Nature of Doctrine*, p. 35.
31 Ibid., p. 34.
32 See Hans Urs von Balthasar, *The Moment of Christian Witness* (New York, 1969); and see R. Williams' excellent discussion of 'Balthasar and Rahner', in *The Analogy of Beauty*, ed. J. Riches (Edinburgh, 1986), pp. 11–34.
33 Williams, 'Balthasar and Rahner', pp. 31–2.
34 Lindbeck, *The Nature of Doctrine*, p. 42; see Rahner, *Theological Investigations*, vol. 6, ch. 16.
35 Lindbeck, *The Future of Roman Catholic Theology*, pp. 35 ff.
36 Rahner, *Theological Investigations*, vol. 14, p. 281.
37 Lindbeck, *The Future of Roman Catholic Theology*, pp. 53–4.
38 See J. Newman, *An Essay on the Development of Christian Doctrine* (London, 1906); and D'Costa, *Theology and Religious Pluralism*, pp. 10, 17–18, 118–34.
39 See Hick, *The Second Christianity*, pp. 90–1.

40 See D. Tracy, 'Lindbeck's New Program for Theology: A Reflection', *The Thomist*, 49 (1985), pp. 460–72.
41 Lindbeck, *The Nature of Doctrine*, p. 62.
42 See Rosemary Radford Ruether's works in the Bibliography.
43 See A. Camps, *Partners in Dialogue*.
44 M. Thomas, *Risking Christ for Christ's Sake*.
45 R. Panikkar, *The Trinity and the Religious Experience of Man*.
46 See J. Moltmann, *The Church in the Power of the Spirit* (London, 1977), pp. 150–62.
47 See R. Schreiter, *Constructing Local Theologies* (London, 1985).

## BIBLIOGRAPHY

Anderson, G. and Stransky, F. (eds), *Christ's Lordship and Religious Pluralism* (New York, 1981).
Camps, A., *Partners in Dialogue: Christianity and Other World Religions* (New York, 1983).
D'Costa, G., *Theology and Religious Pluralism* (Oxford/New York, 1986).
—, *John Hick's Theology of Religions* (Lanham/New York/London, 1987).
Hick, J., *God and the Universe of Faiths* (London, 1977).
—, *God Has Many Names* (Philadelphia, 1982).
—, *The Second Christianity* (London, 1983).
—, *Problems of Religious Pluralism* (London, 1985).
—, *An Interpretation of Religion* (London/New Haven, Conn., 1988).
Knitter, P., *No Other Name? A Critical Study of Christian Attitudes Towards the World Religions* (London, 1985).
Lindbeck, G., *The Nature of Doctrine: Religion and Theology in a Postliberal Age* (London, 1984).
Panikkar, R., *The Trinity and the Religious Experience of Man* (London, 1973).
Rahner, K., *Spirit in the World* (London, 1968).
—, *Foundations of Christian Faith* (London, 1978).
—, *Theological Investigations* (London and New York), vol. 5 (1966), ch. 6; vol. 6 (1969), chs 16, 23; vol. 12 (1974), ch. 9; vol. 14 (1976), ch. 17; vol. 16 (1979), ch. 4; vol. 17 (1980), ch. 5.
Radford Ruether, R., *Faith and Fratricide: The Theological Roots of Anti-Semitism* (New York, 1974).
—, and McLaughlin, E. (eds), *Women of the Spirit. Female Leadership in Jewish and Christian Traditions* (New York, 1979).
Thomas, M., *Risking Christ for Christ's Sake* (Geneva, 1987).

# Epilogue: Postmodernism and Postscript

## David F. Ford

POSTMODERN THEOLOGY?

The introduction to volume I of *The Modern Theologians* described some of the key features of modernity and the main strategies followed in modern Christian theology. In particular the influence of nineteenth-century thought was discussed and its contribution summarized under three headings: reconceptions of knowledge and rationality; a historical consciousness that tried to do justice to change, novelty, and the differences between periods and cultures, and was allied with new historical methods and criteria; and a variety of new critiques and explanations of religion (or major aspects of it) through philosophy, geology, biology, history, literary criticism, psychology, sociology, politics and economics, and comparative religion. The question raised by 'postmodern' thought[1] is whether the twentieth-century situation in philosophy, the arts, the sciences, and general culture and society (especially in the most developed industrialized countries) has changed so much that it deserves to be seen as a new period beyond modernity.

The discontinuity affirmed by postmodern thinkers deeply affects each of the above three areas. In the area of rationality, they argue that eighteenth- and nineteenth-century conceptions of human subjectivity, reason, and knowledge have broken down beyond retrieval. Kant is often seen as representing in fairly pure form what has to be rejected: an autonomous, self-consciously knowing and acting human 'subject'; an ideal of knowledge and rationality which includes certainty, representation of reality, universality, comprehensiveness and practical imperatives; and an ultimate foundation in the 'unconditioned' or God. Instead of that, the postmodern human subject is seen as 'decentered', inseparably involved with the unconscious, the physical and the irrational, and shaped essentially through particular social relations, language, and culture. Indeed, the notion of a 'common humanity' is seen as illusory. Postmodern concepts of rationality and knowledge emphasize historical and cultural variability, fallibility, the impossibility of getting beyond language to 'reality', the fragmentary and particular nature of all understanding, the pervasive corruption of knowledge by power and domination, the futility of the search for sure foundations, and the need for a pragmatic approach to the whole matter. A specially prominent feature is the 'linguistic turn' which sees human identity as an interplay of various systems of signs and symbols: we inhabit 'texts' of various sorts, their truth is undecidable, they all contain paradoxes and contradictions, and they generate endless interpretations as they are brought into relationship with other texts. There is hostility to theory in favor of more literary or pragmatic forms of discourse, and underlying that is a radical attack on the very notion of truth. The legitimacy of philosophy itself, concerned with such notions as truth, being, and goodness, is rejected and replaced by pragmatism (Richard Rorty), 'deconstruction' (Jacques Derrida), 'paralogy' (Jean-Francois Lyotard) or 'genealogy' (Michel Foucault).

As regards history, postmodern approaches are suspicious of some of the main concepts of history-writing, such as causality, linear continuity, narrative unity, origins, and goals. The rejection of 'representation of reality' means that the boundary between history and fiction is blurred. History is seen as an imaginative reconstruction of the past which has a great deal in common with novel-writing. Claims to objectivity, neutrality or empirical truth are subverted by showing the problematic status of 'facts', the need of the historian always to impose some plot and order on what are taken as facts, and the inevitable bias towards particular cultures, groups, and political interests. Those are the particularities that are emphasized by many postmodern thinkers, and the result is a wide variety of contextualized approaches which include irreconcilable contradictions, alternative accounts, discontinuities and ruptures. At the very least, the conventional and literary nature of history-writing is exposed, and its assumptions about itself and 'reality' are opened up to radical questioning.[2]

In the area of alternative explanations of religion, postmodern thought has tried to undermine precisely those overall interpretations of reality which have given many nineteenth- and twentieth-century critiques of religion their confidence and impact. Marx, Freud, the natural and social sciences, and philosophy are all subjected to special criticism for their tendency to offer total explanations. It is rarely done in the interests of Christianity, but the approach works in favor of what has been marginalized or explained away by the dominant bodies of knowledge.

It is not, however, only in such difficult and intellectual areas that the idea of postmodernity finds its support. The context of that thinking is a late twentieth-century world which has been profoundly traumatized. Edith Wyschogrod has summed this up as 'the death event'. That is shorthand for the new, vast scale, speed and technological efficiency of 'man-made mass death' in our century, beginning with the First World War and continuing through the Soviet concentration camps, the Holocaust, the Second World War, Hiroshima and Nagasaki, and the continuing threat of nuclear and ecological destruction.[3] This has been the outcome of typically modern developments in science and technology, political, social and economic organization, and forms of 'progress' which have also had other devastating global consequences. It is the crisis represented by 'the death event' that leads many to see the end of modernity, to suspect its confidence, ideas and achievements, and to try to find a chastened, fragmentary, and practical way through to something better.

Yet many others, who take just as seriously the problems about modern rationality, history, and explanatory schemes, and who also want to do justice to the traumatic events of the twentieth century, still would not accept the designation 'postmodern'.[4] This is because they understand the present as a late stage of modernity, still involved with its critical problems, still indebted to its considerable achievements, and now challenged to go through a transformation which could bring a wiser maturity. This has been the approach which has so far had most influence on theologians, especially through such thinkers as Jürgen Habermas, Hans-Georg Gadamer, Paul Ricoeur and Alasdair MacIntyre. 'Late modernity' would for them be a better description of our more self-critical stage.

How does all this relate to theology? At several points in these volumes the issue of postmodernity has been raised. In volume I, Robert Jenson suggested Barth might be the only truly postmodern theologian because he refused to accept the general suppositions of the Enlightenment and constructed a theology that was consistently particular in its rethinking of reality in terms of Jesus Christ. In the present volume, Daniel Hardy recovers an English tradition which, in its concern for common practice and particularity, is in line with postmodern emphases. Kenneth Surin has indicated the lines which a postmodern critique of process theology might follow, rejecting the 'structures of intelligibility and plausibility constitutive of "modernity"', and, more specifically, seeing the whole concept of 'theism' as an inadequate seventeenth- and eighteenth-century theoretical construction. William Placher concludes that the post-liberal approach might be the most appropriate way for theology to join in a general intellectual debate that includes such postmodern philosophers as Rorty, Derrida, and Foucault. And George Lindbeck proposes a postliberal future for Christianity in the wake of what he sees as the collapse of modern rationalist attempts to rule out 'the legitimacy of trusting a classic, whether religious or nonreligious, as a perspicuous guide to life and thought'.

There are some common threads through those remarks when taken in context. One is the welcome given to postmodernity's undermining of types of rationality and historical authority that have often attempted to dominate and dictate to theology. Another is the emphasis on particularity: theology is free to engage deeply with the specificity of Christianity in its narratives, social forms, behavior, and affirmations of faith. As Daniel Hardy says in chapter 2 of this second volume, a major tendency in philosophical and theological approaches to religion has been towards greater abstraction and generality: no longer treating Christianity but religion; even no longer focusing on religion but on more general matters such as beliefs, symbols or the transcendent. Postmodern approaches reverse that. A third thread is the status given to texts (both written and 'inscribed' in traditions, behavior, and institutions), and the recognition of their pervasive, formative influence. A fourth is the resonance found between the trauma of this century and the centrality of the cross in Christianity. Yet all those threads could also find affinities in 'late modern' thinkers who do not see so sharp a discontinuity with modernity. There is also a notable absence of the darker, nihilistic side of postmodernity in relation to truth, goodness, and history, and a reserve no doubt related to the fact that most postmodernisms are also 'post-theological'.

Most of the references to postmodernity mentioned occur in relation to Barth or theologians broadly sympathetic to him. These are often seen as 'neo-orthodox' or 'neo-conservative', and it is interesting that there is a similar ambiguity in response to postmodern thinkers: some see them as going through and beyond modernity, while others see them giving up the gains and worthwhile struggles of modernity. Predictably, theologians who differ sharply from Barth and the postliberals, and often see them as reactionary, also take up the postmodern themes in a very different way. David Tracy, in responding to a situation which he accepts as postmodern, follows a method of critical correlation more like

Tillich's.[5] Mark Taylor takes deconstruction to lead to the 'death of God', 'the end of history' and a completely nonreferential, pragmatic interpretation of the Bible and other Christian codes.[6] The journal *Semeia* has been a forum for radical exercizes in applying postmodern literary methods to the Bible. And others with more political interests take advantage of the postmodern affirmation of the marginal and the suppressed.

Unsurprisingly, therefore, it is possible to see the emergence of postmodern or late modern versions of most types of modern theology. So the typology outlined in the introduction to volume I can help to map these developments too.

## POSTSCRIPT

The Christian theologies studied in these volumes have been those which offer fairly comprehensive statements of Christian faith at its cutting edge of engagement with contemporary situations. They tend to come somewhere in between, on the one hand, purely confessional theologies, and, on the other hand, an approach through 'neutral' religious studies or philosophy of religion or through some way of thinking that rejects Christianity. It is a type of theology that is 'civilized' in the sense that its concern for the identity, truth, and relevance of Christianity encourages its involvement with the cultures of which it is a part.

The Christian tradition to which these modern theologians belong is that begun in the first centuries of Christianity when the church arose within the sophisticated Hellenistic civilization of the Roman Empire. The mainstream response was to attempt both to confront and learn from that civilization, and the results of the engagement are still controversial. There have been variations on that theme ever since, and there has also been repeated and fruitful interaction with classical Greek and Roman roots – vitally important not only in the patristic period but also in the Middle Ages, Renaissance, Reformation, and modernity.

Most of the theologians in these volumes, both those writing and those written about, have been formed within that tradition which has interwoven Christianity and Western civilization. Now, as is clear from the challenges of liberation and non-Western theologies, theologies of religions and post- or late modern thought, the relation of Christianity to civilization has new dimensions of complexity and controversy. As Christianity becomes more global in its understanding of itself and the world, a transformation seems to be happening that is at least as fundamental as that undergone at other pivotal periods, such as the transition to a largely non-Jewish church in the early years, or the rise of Western European Christianity and its later global repercussions. The present transformation, like the earlier ones, calls for new theological work which will be rooted in and address church, academy, and society. *The Modern Theologians* reflects something of the critical and constructive vigor that has gone into Christian theology so far this century and which shows every sign of continuing.

As the first reader and editor of these volumes, I would add two concluding reflections on doing this sort of theology.

The first is that if I were to choose one thread running through these theologies it would be their search for wisdom. It is a wisdom which makes great demands in terms of knowledge and skills; but beyond that it requires a wrestling with deep and mysterious questions, the slow process of thinking, discernment and commitment, and a willingness to be controversial. It is inevitably a social matter, deeply and essentially indebted to past and present partners; and it is more fundamental than any division between theory and practice. It is both Christian and civilized, and may relate these two in a variety of ways, but it is always concerned to do justice to the issues in which the central Christian affirmations have been concentrated, such as God, creation, humanity, Jesus Christ, salvation, the church, and the future.

The final remark is about the social side of theology. The 'inside story' of modern theology, which surfaces in most chapters, is that of the fascinating network of relations between teachers, students, colleagues, friends, fellow-disciples, and opponents. Such relationships, usually in pairs and small groups, are perhaps the primary places for the genesis of wisdom. These volumes are deeply rooted in them, and they will have fulfilled a large part of their purpose if they can make a contribution to the flourishing of such networks in the future.

## NOTES

1 For a good introduction to and selection of extracts from postmodern thinkers and some of those who differ from them, see *After Philosophy. End or Transformation?*, eds. Kenneth Baynes, James Bohman and Thomas McCarthy.
2 For a discussion of the debate, see Linda Hutcheon, *A Poetics of Postmodernism. History, Theory, Fiction.*

3 Edith Wyschogrod, *Spirit in Ashes. Hegel, Heidegger and Man-made Mass Death* (New Haven, Conn., and London, 1985).
4 This side of the debate is well represented by Karl-Otto Apel, Jürgen Habermas, Hans-Georg Gadamer, Paul Ricoeur, Alasdair MacIntyre, Hans Blumenberg, and Charles Taylor in *After Philosophy* eds. Kenneth Baynes et al.
5 See especially David Tracy, *Plurality and Ambiguity. Hermeneutics, Religion, Hope.*
6 Mark C. Taylor, *Erring: A Post-Modern A/theology.*

### BIBLIOGRAPHY

Baynes, Kenneth, Bohman, James, and McCarthy, Thomas, *After Philosophy. End or Transformation?* (Cambridge, Mass., and London, 1988).
Bernstein, R. (ed.), *Habermas and Modernity* (Cambridge, Mass., 1985).
Hutcheon, Linda, *A Poetics of Postmodernism. History, Theory, Fiction* (New York and London, 1988).
MacIntyre, Alasdair, *Whose Justice? Which Rationality?* (London, 1988).
Rajchman, J. and West, C. (eds), *Post-Analytic Philosophy* (New York, 1985).
Taylor, Mark C., *Erring: A Post-Modern A/theology* (Chicago, 1984).
Tracy, David, *Plurality and Ambiguity. Hermeneutics, Religion, Hope* (San Francisco, 1987).
Wright, T. R., *Theology and Literature* (Oxford, 1988).

# List of Dates

| | |
|---|---|
| 1848 | P.T. Forsyth b. |
| 1861 | A.N. Whitehead b. |
| 1863 | *Emancipation of slaves, United States of America* |
| 1871 | S.N. Bulgakov b. |
| 1884 | C.H. Dodd b. |
| 1892 | Reinhold Niebuhr b. |
| 1893 | G.V. Florovsky b. |
| 1894 | H. Richard Niebuhr b. |
| 1895 | *'The Women's Bible' published* |
| 1897 | C. Hartshorne b. |
| | N. Sykes b. |
| 1900 | H. Butterfield b. |
| 1903 | G.C. Berkouwer b. |
| | V.N. Lossky b. |
| 1904 | K. Rahner b. |
| 1908 | H. Thielicke b. |
| 1912 | G.W.H. Lampe b. |
| 1913 | C.F.H. Henry b. |
| | D.M. MacKinnon b. |
| 1914–1918 | *First World War, Russian Revolution* |
| 1919 | J. Macquarrie b. |
| 1920 | S. Samartha b. |
| 1921 | D.E. Nineham b. |
| | P.T. Forsyth d. |
| 1922 | H.W. Frei b. |
| | J.H. Hick b. |
| 1925 | J.B. Cobb b. |
| | G. Kaufman b. |
| 1927 | *Faith and Order Conference, Lausanne* |
| | G. Lindbeck b. |

| | |
|---|---|
| 1928 | M. Daly b. |
| | S. Ogden b. |
| 1929 | E. Farley b. |
| | K. Koyama b. |
| | C.S. Song b. |
| | M.F. Wiles b. |
| 1934 | D. Cupitt b. |
| 1936 | R. Radford-Ruether b. |
| 1937 | J. Pobee b. |
| 1938 | J. Cone b. |
| | E. Schüssler Fiorenza b. |
| 1939–1945 | *Second World War, The Holocaust, Atomic bombs on Japan* |
| 1939 | D. Tracy b. |
| 1940 | S. Hauerwas b. |
| 1944 | S.N. Bulgakov d. |
| 1946 | A.A. Boesak b. |
| 1947 | *India and Pakistan independent* |
| | A.N. Whitehead d. |
| 1948 | *Nationalist Party in power in South Africa, State of Israel founded, World Council of Churches formed* |
| 1949 | *People's Republic of China founded* |
| 1958 | V.N. Lossky d. |
| 1961 | N. Sykes d. |
| 1962–1965 | *Second Vatican Council* |
| 1962 | H. Richard Niebuhr d. |
| 1963 | *All-Africa Council of Churches formed, Civil Rights movement in USA* |
| 1968 | *Meeting of Latin American Bishops at Medellin* |
| 1971 | Reinhold Niebuhr d. |
| 1973 | C. H. Dodd d. |
| 1976 | *Ecumenical Association of Third World Theologians formed* |
| 1977 | *Ecumenical Association of African Theologians formed* |
| 1979 | H. Butterfield d. |
| | G.V. Florovsky d. |
| 1980 | G.W.H. Lampe d. |
| 1981–1989 | *Ronald Reagan President, USA* |
| 1984 | K. Rahner d. |
| 1986 | H. Thielicke d. |
| 1988 | H. Frei d. |

# Glossary

| | |
|---|---|
| a priori | Latin phrase referring to thought or knowledge which arises from a concept or principle, or which precedes empirical verification, or occurs independently of experience. |
| absolution | Act of releasing a penitent from sins. |
| absolutism | Position which makes one element, text, person, ideology, or reality supreme or absolute in relation to everything; or, an understanding of the absolute (ultimate reality) as existing independently or unconditionally. |
| advaita | Non-dualist school of thought, one of the principal forms of the Hindu Vedanta, denying the ultimate reality of everything but the impersonal Brahman. |
| agapic | Having the quality of *agape*, a Greek word for 'love' used in the New Testament to describe the love of God expressed in Jesus Christ and required between human beings and God, and among human beings. |
| *aggiornamento* | Italian word for renewal, bringing up to date (especially used with reference to the reforms of the Second Vatican Council). |
| agnosticism | Belief that it is not possible to know whether or not something is true; often in theology referring to the belief that no one truly knows or can know whether or not God exists. |
| androcentric | Male-centred; understanding or implying that the masculine is superior or primary in relation to the feminine. |
| Anglican | Name given to the churches and the members of the churches stemming from Henry VIII's schism from the Roman Catholic Church in 1534 and now members of the Anglican Communion. |
| animistic | Relating to animism, religious belief and practice involving a complex pantheon of spiritual beings and seeing natural objects as having spiritual life and values. |

| | |
|---|---|
| anthropology | Study of the nature of human being; or, the scientific study of humankind. |
| anthropomorphism | Ascribing human attributes and characteristics to God. |
| anti-metaphysical | In opposition to a metaphysical understanding of reality; rejecting or lacking interest in overall, general accounts of reality. |
| anti-semitism | Term for prejudice against and hostility towards Semites, usually meaning Jews. |
| apocalyptic | Literally, the unveiling of what is covered or hidden; a genre of literature concerning the last things and the end of the world; more widely, revelatory literature concerned with eschatology, often containing dreams, allegories, and elaborate symbolism. |
| apologetics | Branch of theology concerned with defence of orthodox doctrine in face of opposition. |
| apophatic | Relating to what is beyond expression in speech; more specifically, relating to the method of negative theology, which stresses the transcendence by God of all human language and categories, and prefers forms of reference which say what God is not. |
| Aristotelian | Relating to the philosopher Aristotle (384–322 BC), or his thought, or that of his followers. |
| asceticism | Practice of the denial and overcoming of many human desires and tendencies as part of a spirituality. |
| aseity | The quality of God as completely self-sufficient and independent of all other beings, having his being from himself alone. |
| Athanasian creed | Fifth-century creed, wrongly ascribed to Athanasius of Alexandria (c.296–373), which expresses the doctrines of the incarnation and Trinity. |
| atheism | Belief that God does not exist, that there is no God. |
| atonement | Literally, at-one-ment; the work of Jesus Christ on the cross reconciling the world to God; the doctrine of the salvific work of Christ. |
| Augustinian | Of or relating to Augustine of Hippo (354–430), bishop, theologian and saint. |
| autonomy | State of being self-directing, independent. |
| biblical criticism | Use of techniques applicable to other forms of literature to study the Bible, usually focusing on original meaning and context, authorship, form, style and historical reliability. |
| biblical theology | Theology conceived from and with constant reference to the Bible, especially applied to a movement producing such theology mainly in 1940s and 1950s. |
| black theology | Theological movement expressing the Gospel in relation to black people, their history, experiences, and cultures. |

| | |
|---|---|
| cabbalistic | Relating to Cabbalism, or the Kabbalah, the name for various streams of Jewish mysticism and spirituality. |
| Calvinism | Type of Christianity or theology associated with the Protestant Reformation leader John Calvin (1509–64) and his followers. |
| Cappadocian fathers | Group of church leaders and theologians from Cappadocia (in modern Turkey), especially Gregory of Nazianzus (329–89), Basil of Caesarea (330–79) and Gregory of Nyssa (330–95). Their theology, especially about Jesus Christ, the Holy Spirit, and the Trinity, was supported by the Council of Constantinople (381). |
| Cartesian | Referring to the philosophy of René Descartes (1596–1650), often indicating the separation of subject from object, knower from known, and affirming that the individual thinking self is the best starting point for philosophy. |
| catechesis | Term for the oral teaching or instruction given to those preparing to become full members of a church. |
| Chalcedonian | Relating to the Council of Chalcedon (AD 451) and especially to its definition of the person of Jesus Christ which affirmed his full divinity and full humanity. |
| charismatic | Relating to the gifts of the Holy Spirit, such as prophecy, healing, words of wisdom, discernment of spirits, speaking in tongues, interpretation of tongues; also refers to a Christian movement (sometimes called Neopentecostalism) beginning in the 1960s, which encourages the exercise of gifts of the Holy Spirit. |
| christocentric | Centred on Christ. |
| christology | Branch of theology concerned with the doctrine of the person and work of Jesus Christ. |
| classic theism | Understanding of God as absolute, unchanging and transcending the world, which reached its classical expression in the Middle Ages. |
| classical | Related to the standard accepted formulation of something, or to what became the paradigm for what followed; more specifically, referring to the period, civilization, and thought of ancient Greece and Rome. |
| cognition | Intellectual knowledge; the act of knowing. |
| conciliar | Relating to the councils of the church, e.g. Nicea, Trent, Vatican II. |
| confessional | Referring to a theological position based on a particular confession or statement of faith (usually one of the Reformation statements); or, more widely, referring to a stance or position adopted from the inside as distinct from phenomenology or observation from the outside. |
| Congregationalist | Referring to Congregationalism and the Congregational Churches, a Protestant denomination in which ultimate |

powers in matters of church polity lie with each local congregation.

consubstantiality — Possession of the same substance or being; from a Latin translation of the Greek word *homoousios*, which was incorporated into the creed at the Council of Nicea (AD 5) in order to designate the relationship of Jesus Christ to God.

contextual — Relating to context, the particular setting of something in history, culture, or other respects.

contingent — Relating to contingency, the fortuitous character, or non-necessity, of an event or existing being.

continuum — Structure which is continuous, the parts of which are interrelated rather than separate components.

correlation — Literally, one-to-one correspondence; in theology since Tillich, the relating of questions and issues of modernity with answers or symbols from the tradition.

cosmology — Study or comprehensive understanding of the cosmos or universe.

covenant — Agreement; in the Bible, an agreement initiated by God between God and His people.

crisis theology — See dialectical theology

criteriology — Study or discussion of criteria, the standards applied to something to judge it, usually regarding its truth or value.

crypto-Apollinarian — Term for theological positions leaning towards the understanding of the incarnation associated with Apollinarius (310–90), which denied that Jesus was either fully God or fully human, or was both, and affirmed that he was a mixture of the two.

cultural-linguistic — Term referring to an understanding which sees religion best described by the analogy of a culture or language, a system of meaning with its own rules that have to be learnt and which offers an idiom through which to experience, act, and understand in relation to all reality.

deconstruction — Method of description and analysis which stresses the arbitrariness, manipulation, or bias in the composing of texts or the construction of modes of thinking, speech, or behavior, and the appropriateness of exposing this by 'deconstruction'.

deductive — Relating to deduction, a method of reasoning in which the conclusion is the logical and necessary consequence of the premises.

deism — Understanding of God as creator, but denying continuing divine participation or intervention in the created order.

| | |
|---|---|
| demythologization | Process of interpreting traditional texts considered mythological (in the sense that they express their meaning in terms of an outmoded worldview), with the aim of showing that their continuing existential or practical relevance can be grasped despite their mythological expression. |
| denominational | Referring to the variety of religious bodies, or denominations, within Christianity which are self-governing and doctrinally autonomous. |
| determinism | Understanding of cause and effect seeing necessity and inevitability in all historical events; theologically, it is sometimes held to be a consequence of the doctrine of the sovereignty of God. |
| deuteronomic theology | Theological development of the Jewish Torah as seen in the Book of Deuteronomy. |
| dialectic | Method of reasoning in which the conclusion emerges from the tension between two opposing positions; or, a force seen as operating in history, moving it through conflict towards some form of culmination. |
| dialectic (Hegelian) | The rational process of reality, uniting the movement of the object (the 'in-itself') and the movement of the subject (the 'for-itself') in the movement of the whole (the 'in-and-for-itself'), oriented towards the uniting of all in absolute spirit. |
| dialectical materialism | Marxist theory of history in which material forces are determinative and progress happens by continual conflict and resolution of conflict in further stages, heading for the classless society. |
| dialectical theology | Theology of the period after the First World War (initiated mainly by Barth's *Epistle to the Romans*), which radically negated (above all by reference to the crucifixion) all human ways of knowing and relating to God, and stressed the corresponding need for God's initiative in revelation; also known as crisis theology because of its stress on God's judgment (Greek *krisis*) on church and world. |
| diaspora | Dispersal of the Jewish people around the Mediterranean world after 586 BC; more widely, any dispersion of a group from its original location. |
| ditheism | Belief in the existence of two gods, usually one good and the other evil, struggling for supremacy. |
| dogmatics | Coherent presentation of the Christian faith through its doctrines. |
| dualism | View of the world which holds that there are two ultimately distinct principles or spheres, such as good and evil or matter and spirit. |
| ecclesial | Relating to the church. |

| | |
|---|---|
| ecclesiology | Understanding or doctrine of the church. |
| ecumenical | Relating to ecumenism (from a Greek word meaning the whole inhabited world); in Christianity, the movement for worldwide unity among Christian churches; or, relating to any worldwide movement of integration. |
| ecumenics | Study of ecumenism. |
| *ekstasis* | Greek term for 'standing outside oneself', or being in a state in which one's normal consciousness or capacities are enhanced, often in relation to the divine. |
| election | Doctrine that God chooses people for salvation (and, within some traditions, for damnation). |
| empirical | Approach to knowledge based upon what can be derived from sense experience. |
| empiricism | Understanding of sense experience as the source and test of all knowledge. |
| episcopalian | Relating to episcopalism or episcopalianism, a form of church government in which ultimate authority resides with a body of bishops rather than with one leader or with the general membership; more specifically, a term for Anglicans and the Anglican Church in Scotland, the USA, and some other countries. |
| epistemology | Study of human knowing, regarding its bases, forms, criteria. |
| Erasmian humanism | Renaissance humanism of a moderate, conciliatory and scholarly nature, concerned with church reform based on New Testament principles, associated with Erasmus of Rotterdam (*c.*1466–1536). |
| eschatology | Understanding or doctrine of the eschaton, or ultimate destiny of the world. |
| eschaton | Consummation or end time of world history, traditionally known as the Last Day or Day of Judgment. |
| essentialism | Understanding of objects from their essence. |
| ethical naturalism | Ethical position grounded in natural or biological principles. |
| ethical realism | Theory of ethics affirming the objective reality of values; or, an approach to morality which stresses the ambiguities and imperfection of people and societies, and the limited possibilities of improvement. |
| eucharist | Sacrament or celebration of the Lord's Supper (from a Greek word for thanksgiving). |
| evangelical | Relating to the New Testament Gospel or to the concern for preaching it; also, a term for the Protestant church in Germany and Switzerland; also, a term for a diverse movement, spanning many Protestant churches and groups, with special concern for the final authority of Scripture, evangelism, and personal salvation and holiness. |

| | |
|---|---|
| exclusivism | Belief that God will not grant salvation to those outside the Christian church, or outside faith in Christ. |
| exegesis | Detailed and methodical interpretation of a text. |
| existentialism | Movement of thought, most influential in philosophy, theology, literature, and psychotherapy, which focuses on individual existence and subjectivity, affirms that existence precedes essence (especially in the sense that a person's decisions and responses to contingent events, rather than his or her supposed essential nature, constitute who that person essentially is), upholds the freedom of the will and its irreducibility to anything else, wrestles with the darker aspects of the human predicament such as anxiety, dread, inauthenticity, meaninglessness, alienation, guilt, anticipation of death and despair, and is suspicious of generalization, abstraction, rational overview, systematization, claims to objective knowledge regarding human existence, and fixed ethical principles. |
| Exodus | Second book of the Bible, so called after the departure (exodus) of the Israelite people escaping from oppression in Egypt. |
| exorcism | Act of driving out an evil spirit. |
| experiential-expressivist | Relating to experiential expressivism, an understanding of religion as originating in inner experience of the transcendent, the various outward aspects of religion being attempts to express this. |
| extra-textual | Referring to the location of the meaning or reference of a text outside or independent of the text itself. |
| fatalism | Belief in the unalterable determination of events in advance, human freedom having no significant role. |
| feminism | Movement concerned with the dignity, rights, and liberation of women and the implications of this for humanity. |
| feminist theology | Theology sharing the concerns of feminism, in Christianity especially focusing on the critique of the tradition as patriarchal and on reconceiving it in non-patriarchal terms. |
| fideism | Position that faith is the central and irreducible basis of all theological reflection and knowledge; often used pejoratively of a position which appeals to faith and denies the need or possibility of rational justification. |
| *filioque* | Latin word meaning 'and from the Son' added by the Western Church to the Nicene Creed to indicate that the Holy Spirit proceeds not only from the Father, but also from the Son. |
| finite | Limited, especially to the natural order; unable to transcend certain boundaries. |

| | |
|---|---|
| finitude | State of being finite. |
| form criticism | Approach to a text which focuses upon its constituent units and their particular functions for the original audience or readers. |
| foundationalism | Approach to philosophy or theology which affirms certain truths as the bases and criteria for all other truths. |
| functionalism | Understanding of an object or discipline in the light of its purpose or function. |
| fundamental theology | Branch of theology which tries to ground as comprehensively as possible the whole enterprise of theology, usually with extensive consideration of the contributions of philosophy and other disciplines. |
| fundamentalism | In Christianity, a varied movement usually affirming a set of basic beliefs by reference to the authority of a literally interpreted, inerrant Bible. |
| Hegelianism | Thought and system associated with the philosopher G. W. F. Hegel (1770–1831) and his followers. |
| Hellenism | Greek culture and ideas influential in non-Greek areas in the period after Alexander the Great (356–323 BC). |
| hermeneutics | Study of interpretation and meaning. |
| Hermetism | Tradition of thought associated with the mysterious figure, Hermes Trismegistos, and especially with a collection of texts of a generally Gnostic character attributed to him and produced in Alexandria between the first and third centuries AD, whose rediscovery in the Renaissance was influential in relation to later esoteric philosophy, magic, and various types of cosmology and mystical spirituality. |
| heterodox | Other than the accepted opinion in matters of faith and doctrine; opposite of orthodox. |
| historical-critical method | Approach to a text which seeks to determine its meaning in the light of what it would have meant in its earliest form and context, and to understand beliefs, institutions, and practices in terms of how they were produced by historical conditions and events. |
| humanism | Movement, originating in the Renaissance, to understand human life without recourse to higher (divine) authority; more widely, a worldview cultivating respect for humanity and confidence in its possibilities. |
| hypostases, divine | Members of the Trinity. |
| hypostasis | Greek word originally meaning 'substance'; it came, in relation to Jesus Christ and the Trinity, to mean individual reality, the subject of attributes, or person (in the sense of a member of the Trinity). |

| | |
|---|---|
| iconoclasm | Literally, the breaking of images; more widely, disrespect for or attack on established beliefs, ideas, or practices. |
| idealism | Philosophical tradition originating in Plato which understands the mind, ideas, or spirit as fundamental to reality. The forms of idealism most influential on modern Christian theology have been Kant's transcendental idealism and the absolute idealism of Fichte, Schelling, and especially Hegel. |
| ideology | Structure of concepts and beliefs governing the action and understanding of a group of people; often used pejoratively to describe beliefs and ideas which are rationalizations justifying vested interests or an oppressive system or practice. |
| idolatry | Literally, worship of idols; more widely, false worship, worship of, or treating as ultimate, anything less than or other than God. |
| immanent | Relating to immanence, indwelling presence, usually referring to God's presence in the world; or, referring to the Trinity, the understanding of God's being 'in himself' through his internal relations, rather than in relation to the world and humanity, as in the economic Trinity. |
| incarnation | Literally, becoming flesh; the event of God becoming a human being. |
| inclusivism, religious | Position that one religion includes what is true and salvific in other religions. |
| indigenization | Inculturation or expression in local terms of what comes from elsewhere. |
| individualism | Attitude or position favoring the rights, value, or salvation primarily of persons, understood as autonomous and not essentially social. |
| infallibility | Inerrancy, being incapable of making a mistake; more specifically, the Roman Catholic dogma that pronouncements of the Pope made *ex cathedra* are without error. |
| infinite | Unlimited, inexhaustible, without boundaries. |
| interiority | A person's subjectivity, especially the capacity for self-consciousness, reflective judgment, and decision. |
| intra-textual | Referring to the location of the meaning or reference of a text within itself, without reference to or justification by what is outside it. |
| Irenaean theodicy | Understanding of evil in relation to God in line with the theology of Irenaeus, Bishop of Lyons (*c*.130–*c*.200). |
| justification | Being pronounced or made righteous; the act of God, through the death and resurrection of Jesus Christ, bringing about reconciliation between himself and human beings. |

| | |
|---|---|
| justification by faith | Justification understood as a free, unconditional gift of God received in faith. |
| Kantian | Relating to the philosophy of Immanuel Kant (1724–1804) and his followers. |
| kenotic christology | Understanding of the incarnation of Jesus as involving the self-emptying (Greek, *kenosis*), or laying down of certain divine attributes (e.g., glory, omnipotence), in order to become fully human. |
| kerygma | From Greek word for a herald's message, a term used for the proclamation of the New Testament church about Jesus. |
| liberalism | In theology, a movement attempting to open theology to modern experience, worldviews, and criteria, and especially to the contributions of other academic disciplines; more specifically, nineteenth-century liberal theology tended to stress religious experience, historical consciousness, and the need for freedom from traditional dogma and frameworks in recovering Christianity. |
| liberation theology | Theology originating in Latin America in the 1960s in contexts of political and economic oppression, which seeks to apply the Christian faith from the standpoint of the needs of the poor and exploited. |
| liturgy | Communal worship of God (from a Greek word meaning action of the people); more narrowly, a term for the varied aspects of prescribed public worship. |
| logos | Greek for 'word'; more widely, the rational or ordering principle in something or in reality as a whole; in christology, used to refer to Jesus Christ as the Word of God, God's self-disclosure. |
| Lutheran | Referring to churches, traditions, or theologies stemming from the Reformation tradition begun by Martin Luther (1483–1546). |
| Marian | Referring to Mary, the mother of Jesus. |
| Marxism | Thought or movement stemming from Karl Marx (1818–83). |
| materialist | Relating to materialism, a philosophical position with special emphasis on matter as the only constituent of the world and on the denial of the spiritual realm. |
| Mennonites | Protestant denomination founded by Menno Simons (1496–1561), stressing believers' baptism, congregational autonomy, pacifism, and nonparticipation in public office. |
| messianism | Hope for the coming of a messiah or savior who will liberate from oppression. |

| | |
|---|---|
| metaphysics | Study of reality in general; the science of being, existence, and knowing, aiming to encompass and understand the basic constituents of reality. |
| Methodist | Member of, or relating to, the Protestant denomination founded by John Wesley (1703–91). |
| methodology | Reflection on the systematic approach to a topic or field. |
| monarchial | Relating to monarchia, from a Greek word meaning 'one origin' or 'one rule'; referring in trinitarian theology to the Father as the source of the Son and Spirit; sometimes interpreted heretically to mean that Jesus was not divine, or was divine in a secondary sense. |
| monarchianism, dynamic | A second- and third-century heresy maintaining that Jesus was God only in the sense that a power of influence (Greek, *dunamis*) from the Father rested on His human person. |
| monism | Position that one regulative principle governs the universe; also, a position that all reality is one, or is to be explained in terms of one fundamental constituent. |
| monotheism | Belief in only one God as ultimate reality. |
| mysticism | Strand in many religions stressing the knowledge of God or the transcendent through experience, often in the form of immediate intuition or other direct communication or sense of union, and often denying the possibility of adequate linguistic communication of such experience; often contrasted knowledge of God through indirect means such as reasoning, scripture, or tradition. |
| myth | In theology, usually understood as an expression of religious meaning through story or symbol, often using a premodern worldview. |
| natural religion | Unrevealed religion; religion arrived at through human reasoning about the world and human existence. |
| natural theology | Theology attempting to know God and God's relationship to the world through nature and human reasoning without divine revelation. |
| naturalism | Position affirming that the world can be understood (especially through the natural sciences) without reference to any explanatory factor beyond the natural order, which is usually understood in a materialist way. |
| negative theology | Way of knowing God through negation and silence, indicating his transcendence of all thought and expression. |
| Neo-Calvinist | Relating to a new or modern interpretation of Calvinism. |
| neo-conservatism | Term for the theology of Barth and his followers, interchangeable with neo-orthodoxy; or, a movement in contemporary Protestantism, often fundamentalist and politically right-wing. |

| | |
|---|---|
| neo-Marxism | New or modern version of Marxism, usually referring to revisions of Marxism relating it to recent developments in capitalist countries. |
| neo-orthodox | Relating to neo-orthodoxy, a term applied to the Protestant theological movement associated with Barth, Emil Brunner, and Reinhold Niebuhr, referring to their attempt to counter the 'unorthodox' liberal nineteenth-century theology by regrounding theology on the principles of Reformation Protestantism. |
| Neoplatonism | Religious philosophy of Plotinus (*c.*AD 205–69) and his followers, which owed most to Plato and offered a rational spirituality aimed at union with the One or the absolute which unites all reality. |
| neo-scholasticism | Nineteenth- and twentieth-century Roman Catholic movement which revived the theology and philosophy of Thomas Aquinas and made it the norm against which all other theology and philosophy are judged. |
| Nicene Creed | Creed formulated at the Council of Nicea (AD 325), noted especially for its affirmation that Jesus Christ is of one substance, essence, or being (Greek, *homoousios*) with God the Father. |
| nihilism | Belief that all reduces ultimately to nothing, or that existence makes no sense and is purposeless. |
| nonconformist | Relating or belonging to nonconformity, the refusal to conform to the doctrines, polity, or discipline of any established church; originally referring to those Presbyterians, Congregationalists, Quakers, Baptists, and Methodists who refused to conform to the discipline and practice of the Church of England. |
| nontheistic religion | Religion that does not include belief in God or gods. |
| noumenal | Relating to a noumenon, an object of intellectual intuition. |
| numinous | Term applied to those elements in the experience of the holy which are mysterious, awe-inspiring, and fascinating. |
| omnipotence | Possession of all or infinite power. |
| omniscience | Possession of complete knowledge of all things. |
| ontology | Branch of philosophy concerned with the study of being, of reality in its most fundamental and comprehensive forms. |
| orthodoxy | Right belief in and adherence to the essential doctrines of a faith as officially defined; or, conventional or traditional belief. |
| orthopraxis | Right belief combined with right practice, a term specially used in Latin American liberation theology, |

often in contrast with an orthodoxy seen as uninterested in the practical and political content of faith.

| | |
|---|---|
| Palamism | Teaching associated with Gregory Palamas (*c*.1269–1359), especially concerning the form of mystical prayer called hesychasm and the distinction between the divine essence and the divine operations or energies. |
| panentheism | Understanding of the world as existing in God yet without negating the transcendence of God; often also holding that the world and God are mutually dependent upon each other for their fulfillment. |
| pantheism | Understanding that identifies God and the world as one, either without qualification, or with the world as a divine emanation, body, development, appearance, or modality. |
| paradigm | Model, pattern, ideal type, or basic set of ideas serving to integrate or explain reality. |
| paralogy | Postmodern approach to the analysis of discourse, associated with Jean-François Lyotard, which undermines established language use by indicating differences and contradictions, and by constant innovation and experimentation, and which is especially subversive of totalities, general truths and 'metanarratives', stressing instead the pluralism, contingency, and local character of all discourse. |
| parousia | Expected appearance of Jesus Christ (the 'second coming') before the consummation of history in the eschaton or Last Judgment. |
| particularity | What is specific, definite, and distinctive; often implying the primacy of reference to contingent, historical reality over general or abstract statements. |
| patriarchy | Literally, rule by fathers; more widely, a male-dominated authority structure. |
| patripassianism | Belief that God the Father suffered and died in the death of God the Son. |
| patristic | Referring to the fathers of the church and their period, usually covering the first five centuries AD. |
| Pelagian | Relating to the fifth-century English monk, Pelagius, and his teaching that human beings are autonomously able to do good and contribute to their own salvation, thus denying the doctrine of original sin. |
| personalistic | Relating to personalism, a philosophical movement beginning in the nineteenth-century, stressing the human personality as the ultimate value and key notion in understanding reality. |
| petrine | Relating to the apostle Peter; more widely, relating to the type of church authority represented by the Roman Catholic Church, whose papacy is traced to Peter. |

| | |
|---|---|
| phenomenal | Relating to appearances, or to what appears to the human observer. |
| phenomenology | Philosophical movement aiming to ground philosophy in a descriptive and scientific method, which understands religious and other phenomena in nonreductionist terms as they reveal themselves to consciousness, and seeks the distinctive laws of human consciousness, especially emphasizing its intentional character. |
| philosophical theology | Branch of theology that relates theological and philosophical thought, usually concentrating on areas of mutual concern. |
| pietism | Originally, a seventeenth- and eighteenth-century Protestant movement reacting against the rationalism and rigidity of traditional Lutheran orthodoxy with an emphasis on the personal, devotional, and practical aspects of Christianity; more widely, a type of faith combining deep feeling, stress on personal salvation and holiness, and lack of concern for theological elaboration. |
| Platonism | Thought of the Greek philosopher Plato (*c*.427–347 BC), and of the various philosophical and theological traditions stemming from him. |
| plerosis | Greek word meaning completeness or fulfillment. |
| pluralism | Situation or understanding which embraces a diversity of contrasting cultures, values, ideas, religions or other major elements seen as independently valid. |
| pneumatic ecclesiology | Understanding or doctrine of the church as created and sustained by the Holy Spirit. |
| pneumatology | Branch of theology dealing with the doctrine of the Holy Spirit. |
| polemic | Confrontational, controversial statement directly challenging an opposing position. |
| positivism | In the nineteenth century, a movement associated with Auguste Comte (1798–1857), which saw history in terms of inevitable progress culminating in the 'positive' stage of scientific knowledge, technology, and an atheist religion of reason and humanity; in the twentieth century, logical positivism has been a philosophical movement stressing empirical verification, natural scientific method, and the rejection of metaphysics. |
| postliberal theology | Theology affirming Christian orthodoxy and claiming to take account of modern liberal critiques and theologies so that it is not preliberal (as is much conservative and traditional theology), but postliberal. |
| postmodernism | Position regarding the present intellectual and cultural situation, especially in advanced capitalist societies, as in discontinuity with modernity and representing a new stage beyond it. |

| | |
|---|---|
| pragmaticism | In philosophy, a synonym for pragmatism, a position stressing knowledge derived from experience and experiment and used to solve practical problems, with truth tested by its practical utility and consequences. |
| praxis | Greek term for action, practical ability or practice, used in Marxism and adopted by Latin American liberation theology to denote a combination of action and reflection aimed at transforming an oppressive situation. |
| predestination | Doctrine of the eternal decision and knowledge of God with respect to the destiny of human beings as regards salvation or damnation (sometimes called the doctrine of election and rejection). |
| Presbyterianism | Reformed church tradition, particularly influenced by Calvinism, in which authority is centred upon elders. |
| prevenience | Literally, coming before or first; usually referring to a quality of God or God's grace as having the initiative in relation to human action, and being its prior cause or condition. |
| primatial | Relating to the role of leader or primate among the bishops of a church or communion of churches. |
| process theism | Understanding of God in process theology, stressing God's dipolarity, capacity to be affected by creation, and persuasive rather than absolute power. |
| process theology | Theological movement, following the philosophy of A. N. Whitehead (1861–1947), which emphasizes notions of movement and becoming (process), rather than being or substance, and which affirms divine participation in process. |
| prolegomena | Work of a preliminary, introductory nature, preparing for fuller treatment. |
| propositionalism | Method of asserting or proposing statements that are capable of being judged true or false. |
| rationalism | Position in philosophy emphasizing reason as the primary source of knowledge, prior or superior to, and independent of, sense perceptions, often testing truth by criteria of coherence and logical consistency; more widely, used pejoratively of positions whose appeal to reason is seen as narrow, reductionist and unable to do justice to the subject matter. |
| rationality | That which is characterized by conformity with reason, adhering to qualities of thought such as intelligibility, consistency, coherence, order, logical structure, completeness, testability, and simplicity. |
| realism | Philosophical position (in opposition to nominalism) affirming that a universal category (e.g., animal) may have a reality outside its individual manifestations (e.g., lion, cow) and independently of human consciousness; |

|  | or, a philosophical position (in opposition to idealism) affirming that reality exists independently of the human knower, that it requires the human mind to correspond to it, and that what is known about a thing exists in the thing known and would exist without the knower. |
| --- | --- |
| realism, sociological | Approach which focuses on the way people in groups actually behave and on how social structures actually function. |
| realism, theological | In the twentieth century, usually referring to a position (contrasting with theological idealism or liberalism) which stresses the reality and initiative of God in revelation and the need for human knowing to correspond to that; also, a position in ethics and politics which stresses the imperfection of the world and the limits of human attempts to improve it. |
| realized eschatology | Understanding that the eschaton has been actualized in history, especially associated with C. H. Dodd's position that the eschaton was present in the life and death of Jesus. |
| reconciliation | Reestablishment of a state of harmony or good relationship between God and humanity or amongst human beings; often used interchangeably with redemption, atonement, or salvation. |
| redemption | Literally, buying back; a financial metaphor (relating originally to ransom payments and slave-buying) for atonement, reconciliation, or salvation; the act or process by which liberation from bondage (described variously in Christian theology as sin, death, the law, the devil, the world) takes place. |
| reductionism | Explanation of complex data in inappropriately simple terms; in theology, often referring to the attempt to explain beliefs referring to, e.g., God, in terms that do not assume the reality of God, e.g., in psychological, sociological, philosophical, or other terms. |
| Reformation | Movement for the reform of the Roman Catholic Church, beginning in the sixteenth century, resulting in the formation of independent Protestant churches. |
| reincarnation | Return to existence in another form, referring to the belief that human life is one stage in a cycle of existence to be carried on beyond death in a different form. |
| relativism | Position holding the impossibility of attaining final, eternal truth or values, and stressing diversity among individuals, groups, cultures, and periods; sometimes also ruling out the comparison of truth claims and values. |
| religious socialism | Movement, especially strong in continental Europe after the Russian Revolution (1917), uniting socialism with Christianity and especially with the expectation of the Kingdom of God. |

| | |
|---|---|
| *ressourcement* | French word for return to original sources in order to inform modern understanding. |
| revelation | Disclosure of what was previously unknown; in theology, usually the disclosure to human beings by God of his nature, salvation, or will. |
| revisionist | Relating to revisionism, the questioning and reconceiving of the core of a tradition. |
| Ritschlianism | Theology associated with the German Albrecht Ritschl (1822–89), which was especially concerned with justification, ethics, and the Christian community, and suspicious of metaphysics and religious experience. |
| romanticism | Movement, especially in literature, art, philosophy, and theology, which rejected Enlightenment rationalism, autonomy, and duty-centred ethics in favor of a stress on feeling, artistic sensitivity and genius, community, and an ethics that took account of nature, desire and passion; more specifically, a movement in late eighteenth- and early nineteenth-century Germany whose leading figures were Goethe, Schlegel, and, in theology, Schleiermacher. |
| sacrament | Action, ceremony, or celebration in which created things become channels and symbols of God's activity and promises (in Roman Catholicism: baptism, eucharist, confirmation, matrimony, holy orders, penance, and extreme unction; in Protestantism, usually: baptism and eucharist); more widely used to refer to the ways in which God and salvation are communicated through action and material reality. |
| salvation history | Those events which the Bible narrates as revealing God's action for the salvation of the world. |
| scholastic theology, scholasticism | Education, methods, and theology of the thirteenth-century Christian thinkers often called the Medieval schoolmen, and of their followers in later times, notable especially for their application of logic to theology and their systematic attempts to reconcile faith and reason. |
| sectarianism | Position associated with a sect, a religious or other group claiming exclusive possession of some truth or way of salvation, and tending to stress boundaries, division and oppositions in relation to other groups – usually used pejoratively. |
| secularism | Position advocating the elimination of religious influence in the state, social institutions, and the understanding of reality as a whole. |
| Semitic | Relating to the racial grouping common to most peoples in the Middle East, but particularly referring to Jews. |
| social gospel | Teaching emphasizing the material and socio-political implications of the Christian message. |

| | |
|---|---|
| sophiology | Study of wisdom (Greek, *sophia*); or, a theology or philosophy whose central concept is wisdom. |
| soteriology | Branch of theology concerned with the doctrine of salvation (or reconciliation, atonement, or redemption). |
| stoicism | School of philosophy founded at Athens by Zeno (335–263 BC); a form of materialist pantheism which sees God as the energy pervading and sustaining the natural world and as the rationality or *logos* which orders it, and which emphasizes living in conformity with this natural order; best known for teaching detachment from desires and passions in the interests of self-sufficiency and imperturbability. |
| subjectivism | Approach to knowledge focusing on the knowing subject rather than the object to be known, emphasizing the contribution to knowledge of the knower's mental constitution and states and denying the possibility of affirming truth objectively; or, an approach to aesthetics and ethics emphasizing values as reflections of the feelings, attitudes, and responses of the individual and as having no independent or objective validity. |
| supernatural | Relating to that which is conceived to be beyond the natural order, or beyond nature unaided by grace. |
| syncretism | Combination of varied or opposing ideas, doctrines, or practices, especially in the realm of religious and philosophical thought. |
| synoptic | Referring to the Gospels of Matthew, Mark, and Luke. |
| systematic theology/ systematics | Type of theology seeking to give a rationally ordered, comprehensive account of the doctrines of a religion and their interrelationships. |
| talmudic | Relating to the Talmud, a body of commentary and elaboration on parts of the Mishnah (the Jewish legal and theological system completed *c*.AD 200). |
| theism | Belief in, or set of beliefs about, God. |
| theocentric | God-centred; revolving around the reality of God. |
| theocracy | Literally, rule by God; an institution or society which is governed by its religious authorities. |
| theos | Greek word for 'God'. |
| Thomist | Relating to the theology of, and the schools of thought stemming from, Thomas Aquinas (1226–74). |
| traditionalism | Position appealing to past forms of a religion, culture, or other form of belief, understanding or behavior; more specifically, a reaction to modernity holding that religious knowledge cannot be derived from human reason or experience but only through faith in divine revelation communicated through tradition. |

| | |
|---|---|
| transcendent | Existing, going or leading beyond; of God, referring to his being beyond all created reality; of self, going beyond one's present state, often by knowing, willing or some other mode of consciousness. |
| transcendental philosophy | Usually referring to the philosophy of Kant and his followers. |
| transcendental theology | Theology concerned to explore the fundamental conditions of theological knowledge, beyond any particular instances of such knowledge. |
| transcendental Thomism | Movement in twentieth-century theology (e.g., Maréchal, Rahner, Lonergan) concerned to marry the theology and philosophy of Thomas Aquinas with the philosophy of Kant and post-Kantian philosophers, and especially focusing on the knowing and willing human subject. |
| Trinity | Christian understanding of the Godhead as three in one: the Father, the Son, and the Holy Spirit. |
| triune | Being three in one. |
| universalism | Understanding of the all-encompassing nature of salvation, including the belief that ultimately all will be saved. |
| utilitarianism | Approach to ethics focusing on the consequences of human action and aiming at the assessment and achievement of the greatest good for the greatest number. |
| Vedanta | Sacred writings of the Hindu religion. |
| voluntarism | Understanding of human action focusing on the role of the will in determining action and behavior and stressing human freedom. |

# Index

Absolute, God as 49–50, 105–6
advaita 219–21
Afanasiev, Nikolai 166–7
Africa, independent churches 208–9, 210
African theologies 192, 194, 200, 201–7, 254
agency
  divine 94, 98
  of man 97–8
agency, correspondence of 32
*aggiornamento* 253, 255–6, 258–61, 263–5
agnosticism 161–2, 281
Alexander, Samuel 35
All Africa Council of Churches 202
Anderson, Ray 129, 130, 131–50
Andrewes, Lancelot 17
Anglican-Roman Catholic International Commission 23
Anglicanism
  and ecumenical theology 256–7
  and patristic theology 20–1
  and reformed tradition 24, 30
  and teaching of theology 4, 17
Anselm of Canterbury, St 9, 119
anthropology, theological
  in liberation theology 176–7, 179
  in Macquarrie 51, 52–3
  in Metz 175
  in Rahner 278, 282–3
  in Reinhold Niebuhr 77, 79–80
  in Russian Orthodoxy 155
anthropomorphism 60, 62, 162, 236
*apatheia*, axiom of 109
  *see also* patripassianism

apocalyptic, and political theology 175
Apollinarianism 159, 160
apologetics 5–6
  in Asian theology 230
  of Henry 143, 145, 146
  in postliberalism 117–19
Aquinas, St Thomas
  cognitivism 124
  ethics 85
  theism 110
Arius 19, 20
Arminius, Jacob 135
aseity 107
Asian theology 217–31, 254
Assmann, Hugo 179
atonement
  in Forsyth 9
  in Henry 145
  in Lampe 18
  moral influence theory 9
Auerbach, Erich 115
Augustine, St 81
authority
  in English tradition 30–2, 61, 65
  in evangelical theology 144–5
  in Orthodoxy 154, 158, 160, 163
  *see also* scriptures, authority of
autonomy
  of churches 257
  in Cupitt 62–3
  in Reformed theology 135–6
axioms, middle 78
Ayer, A. J. 37

Balthasar, Hans Urs von 49, 159, 260, 268–9, 282

baptism, Lampe on 18
Barth, Karl 3, 7, 8, 14, 50, 79, 84, 98, 118, 136, 268–9, 293–4
  influence 18, 115, 139, 146, 164, 258
basic communities 175, 176, 180, 182–3
Baum, Gregory 264
Bavinck, Herman 134, 135–6, 147
Bennett, John C. 78, 84, 87
Berdyaev, Nikolai 160
Berger, Peter 115, 264, 276
Berkouwer, G. C. 129, 134, 135–8, 146–7
  on correlation of faith and revelation 136–7, 145
  influences on 135–6
  on Scripture 136
  *see also* epistemology; faith; Holy Spirit; revelation
Bible, historical-critical studies 7–8, 16–17, 259, 265–8, 270–1
Biko, Steve 209
black theology 73, 171–2, 193–213
  North America 194–201
  South African 207–13
Bloesch, Donald 147
Blyden, E. W. 201
Boesak, Allan 172, 209, 211–12
Boff, Clodovis 179
Boff, Leonardo 179–80
Böhme, Jacob 153
Bolotov, V. 162
Bonino, José Miguez 171, 184–6, 189
Børrensen, Kari-Elizabeth 240
Boyer de Sainte Suzanne, R. de 161
Bradley, F. H. 48, 49
Brand, Herbert George 225
Brightman, Edgar 144
Britain, theology in 1–2, 3–28, 30–69, 293
  critical orthodoxy 11, 12, 15, 17–19
  persistence and change 34–40
  *see also* practice, common
Brown, David 249
Brown, Kelly 200
Brown, Ray 260
Buckley, James J. 73, 89–101
Buddhism
  and Christianity 109, 228
  in Cupitt 63
Bulgakov, S. N. 129, 156–9, 160, 162, 164, 165, 168, 169
  on human nature 156–8

Bultmann, Rudolf 3, 14, 90, 94
  influence 48, 50–1, 139
Buthelezi, Manas 209, 212
Butler, B. C. 43
Butterfield, Herbert
  on history 1, 23, 25–6
  on Old Testament 26
  theology of crisis 27

Cabbalism 159
Calhoun, Robert Lowrie 77, 84, 87
Calvin, Calvinism 50, 131, 207
Carnell, Edward John 142
Carr, Anne E. 249
Césaire, Aimé 201
Childs, Brevard 116
China, theology in 231 n. 1
Chopp, Rebecca S. 171, 173–91
Christian, William 96, 116
Christianity, anonymous 279, 282, 283–4
christocentrism 55, 58, 98, 158, 275, 280, 283, 286
christology
  in African theology 205
  in Asian theology 230
  in black theology 198
  in Bulgakov 158–9, 160
  in Dodd 6, 11
  in ecumenical theology 280–4, 287
  in evangelical theology 10
  in Farley 92, 98
  in Florovsky 165
  in Forsyth 8, 9–11
  in Frei 118–19
  in Hick 59, 275, 283
  'high'/'low' 15, 16–17
  in Kaufman 93, 98
  kenotic 9–11, 158–9, 160
  in Lampe 19–20
  of liberation theology 178, 179, 181
  in Macquarrie 53
  in Moule 6, 15
  in Nineham 6
  in Ogden 93, 94, 98
  plerotic 10–11
  in Samartha 218–21
  in Thielicke 146
  in Tracy 92–3, 98
church, *see* ecclesiology
church and state 23–4, 27, 66 n. 10, 154

Clark, Gordon 144, 147
Clément, Olivier 160, 167–8
Cobb, John B. 74, 103, 108–9
  on creative transformation 109
Collingwood, R. G. 164
Comblin, José 180
Cone, Cecil Wayne 200, 213 n. 12
Cone, James H. 172, 198–9, 200
confirmation, Lampe on 18
Congar, Yves 161, 258, 268
contextuality 149, 194, 199, 217–19,
  222, 224–5, 231, 292
Cooke, Bernard 247
correlation method 91, 94–6, 98, 259,
  294–5
cosmology, in Soloviev 154–5
Cox, Harvey 265
creeds
  in Lampe 17, 19–20
  in Thielicke 146
  in Wiles 20
Creighton, Mandell 24
Cullmann, Oscar 259
culture
  African 194, 201–2, 205–6, 207, 212
  influence of 38, 61, 91, 178
  religion as 120
Cupitt, Don 2, 59–65 67 n. 11
  on faith as response to contingency
  60, 64–5
  on function of religion 62, 63, 64–5
  see also ethics; freedom; God, doctrines of; incarnation
Cyril of Alexandria 166

Daly, Mary 172, 240, 242–4
Daniélou, Jean 161
D'Costa, Gavin 254, 274–90
de Gandillac 161
De Lubac, Henri 161, 258
deconstruction 93, 125, 292, 295
Deism 35, 60
Derrida, Jacques 125, 292, 294
Descartes, René 110, 135, 139, 153
determinism 82, 155, 160, 164, 267
Dewey, John 80
Dickson, Kwesi 203
Dilthey, Wilhelm 164
ditheism 107
Dodd, C. H. 11–15
  crisis theology 13, 14, 27

  on Fourth Gospel 14
  on Paul 13
  *see also* christology; eschatology;
  history; revelation
dualism, nature-hypostasis 157, 159
Dubois, W. E. B. 196, 201
Dumitriu, Petru 168
Dussel, Enrique 180

ecclesiology
  in Bulgakov 158–9
  in Butterfield 6
  in ecumenical theology 256–7, 265,
  270, 283–4, 287–8
  in Florovsky 166
  in Forsyth 10
  in Hauerwas 122–3, 125
  in liberation theology 180–1, 182–3
  in Lindbeck 125
  in Lossky 163
  in Macquarrie 53
  in Rahner 278–9
  in Russian Orthodoxy 154, 158–9
  in Song 223
  in Sykes 6, 24
  in Thiemann 125
Ecumenical Association of African
  Theologians (EAAT) 203, 207, 209
Ecumenical Association of Third World
  Theologies (EATWOT) 193–4, 197,
  198, 200, 209, 217
ecumenical theology 109, 203, 253,
  255–72
  dialogue and mission 284–5, 286
  as procedural/interdenominational
  255–63, 265
  as thematic 255–8, 260, 263–6
ecumenism 156, 159, 167, 168
Ela, Jean-Marc 203
election 223
Eliade, Mircea 116, 166
empiricism 57
episcopacy, in Anglicanism 24
epistemology
  in Berkouwer 136–7
  in Florovsky 164–5
  in Henry 142, 144–5, 146–7
  in Hick 55
  in Kuyper 135–6
  of liberation theology 179

and revelation 123
in Wiles 21
equality, racial 86
eschatology
in Asian theology 225
in Hick 57
and political theology 175
realized, in Dodd 12–13, 16
ethicism, social 86
ethics
in Asian theology 230
in black theology 198, 199, 212
in British theology 42
in Cupitt 61–4
in feminist theology 242
in Forsyth 9, 10
in Hauerwas 121–2
of Jesus 75–6, 82
in liberation theology 187
in MacKinnon 43–4
modern Protestant 85–6
natural law tradition 85
in Thielicke 139, 148
eucharist, in Orthodoxy 158, 165–6
evangelical theology 129–30, 131–50
identifying 132–4
and mission 132, 148–9
Evdokimov, Pavel 166
evil
in Hartshorne 107
in Hick 57, 58
in MacKinnon 46, 48
exclusivism 274, 275, 276–8, 283; see
also religions, theology of
existentialism 90, 94, 139, 186
and British theology 27, 48, 50–2, 54
experience
in evangelical theology 133, 136–8,
144–5, 147
in Hick 55
and language 120–1
in liberation theology 173–4
of women 237, 243
expressivism, experiential 120–1, 121–
2, 277

faith
in Berkouwer 136–8
in Farley 93, 95
in Forsyth 8

in Henry 143–5
in Hick 55–6, 58
in Macquarrie 49, 52, 53
in Reinhold Niebuhr 80
in Thielicke 140, 146
faiths, world, and Christianity 253–4
Farley, Edward 73, 89, 91
on intersubjectivity 92, 93
as mediating theologian 90
and Tracy 95
on truth of Christianity 91, 95–6
see also christology; faith; God, doctrines of
Farmer, H. H. 35
Farrer, Austin 38
Fashole-Luke, E. 200
feminist theology 73, 125, 172, 235–50,
254, 286
fideism 115, 126 n. 2, 285
Florensky, Pavel 157
Florovsky, G. V. 129, 163–6, 167, 169
Ford, David F. 291–7
form criticism 14, 16, 23
Forsyth, P. T. 1, 6–11, 13, 25, 27
on biblical criticism 7–8
on holiness 8–9
on mode of being 11
on priestly religion 10
on sacrifice 9–10
theology of crisis 27
see also christology; ecclesiology;
faith; Holy Spirit; incarnation
Foucault, Michel 125, 292, 294
foundationalism 123–4
freedom
in Bulgakov 157
and Christian Realists 78
in Cupitt 60, 62–3
in Florovsky 165, 166
in Hick 56–7, 59
in liberation theology 178, 188
in process theology 105
in revisionist theology 97
Frei, Hans 74, 124–5
on Bible as narrative 117–18
on identity of Christ 118–19
see also resurrection
functionalism of Christian teaching
125–6
fundamentalism 89, 131, 134, 141–3,
146, 148, 258, 264–6, 271

Gadamer, Hans-Georg 125, 165, 168, 293
Gassmann, Günther 272 n. 9
Geertz, Clifford 115, 276
genealogy 292
generalism in theology 35–8, 41, 49, 52–3, 54
*Geschichte* 8
Gilson, Etienne 161
Goba, Bonganjalo 209
God, doctrines of
   in black theology 198
   in Bonino 185–6
   in Bulgakov 157–8
   in Cupitt 60–1, 62–5
   in Farley 92, 97
   and feminine imagery 159
   in feminist theology 236, 242–5
   in Frei 119
   in Hartshorne 106–8
   in Henry 143–5
   in Hick 56–8, 275, 280–1
   in Kaufman 92, 93–4, 97
   in Koyama 227
   in liberation theology 178, 183, 185–6, 188
   in Lossky 162–3
   in MacKinnon 47–8
   in Macquarrie 49–50, 50–1, 53
   monarchical 92
   in Ogden 92, 97
   in Thielicke 146
   in Thiemann 124
   in Tracy 92, 97
   in Whitehead 103–5, 106, 107, 110
   *see also* theism
Gössman, Elisabeth 240
grace, in Forsyth 7–8
Grant, Jacquelyn 200
Greece, Orthodoxy 167
Gruber, Mayer I. 245
Gustafson, James 86, 191 n. 22
Gutierrez, Gustavo 171, 173, 182–4, 187, 260
   on love of God 178, 183, 186

Habermas, Jürgen 293
Hampson, Daphne 242
Hanson, N. R. 59, 69 n. 76
Harding, Vincent 200

Hardy, Daniel 1–2, 30–69, 293, 294
Harnack, Adolf von 11, 13
Hartshorne, Charles 74, 94, 103, 106–8
   on divine perfection 106–7
   on existence of God 107–8
Hauerwas, Stanley 74, 86, 121–3, 124
   on Christian community 121, 122–3
   on stories 122
Hayter, Mary 241
Hegel, G. W. F. 90
   influence on Russian Orthodoxy 152–3, 156–7, 165
Heidegger, Martin 48, 50, 167, 168
Henry, Carl F. H. 73, 129, 134, 141–5, 146–8
   on conversion 145
   on role of theology 144
   *see also* epistemology; faith; God, doctrines of; Holy Spirit; revelation; salvation
hermeneutics 66, 259, 268, 270–1
   of ecumenical theology 286–7
   of liberation theology 180, 185
   of Lossky 160
   in Macquarrie 52
   in Thielicke 146
   in Tracy 95, 96
hermetism 153, 157
Heschel, Abraham 217
Hick, John H. 2, 21, 54–9, 67 n. 11
   on encounter 55, 59
   on experience 58
   life 54–5
   on New Testament 58
   pluralism 274, 275–6
   as polarizing 56
   on quality 56
   on significance 55
   and world religions 58–9, 254, 274–6, 277–8, 280–1, 282–3, 285–6
   *see also* epistemology; eschatology; faith; freedom; God, doctrines of; incarnation; revelation; salvation
Hilary of Poitiers 166
*Historie* 89
history
   in Asian theology 228–31
   in Dodd 1, 12–14, 16, 23
   ecclesiastical 22–4
   in feminist theology 246
   generalization in 37–8

in Kaufman 93
in liberation theology 180, 182–6, 188
in MacKinnon 45
in Macquarrie 50
in Nineham 15–16
and philosophy 30–1, 34, 37–8, 41, 46, 54
in postmodernism 292
of religions 14, 275–6
in Russian Orthodoxy 155, 164–5
salvation history 8, 221–2, 224, 230
theology through 6, 7–8, 27–8, 40
Hobbes, Thomas 81
Holmer, Paul 126 n. 2
Holy Spirit
  in Berkouwer 136, 137
  in Boesak 211–12
  in Forsyth 8
  in Henry 145
  in Lampe 19
  in Lossky 162
  in Thielicke 140
Hooker, Richard 30–2, 36, 61
Horton, Walter Marshall 76, 77, 87
Hudson, Winthrop 256
Hyun Younghak 172, 218, 223–5

idealism
  English 48
  German 35, 152–3, 155, 157, 163–4, 175
ideology, and theology 189, 199
idolatry, critique 227, 228
immanentism 64–5
incarnation
  in Cupitt 60, 64, 69 n. 82
  in Forsyth 10–11
  in Hick 58, 275
  in Lampe 18–20
  in MacKinnon 45, 47–8
  in Macquarrie 53
  in *Myth of God Incarnate* 22
  in Rahner 279
  in Soloviev 154
  in Thielicke 139–40
inclusivism 274, 276, 278–9, 282–3; *see also* religions, theology of
infallibility
  of Bible 7–8, 20, 54, 146–7
  papal 23

intellectualism 161–2
interdenominationalism 255–7, 260–2, 264

Jenson, Robert 293
Jesus, historical 13–14, 16, 45, 48, 51, 181
  'New Quest' 14
Johnson, Elizabeth A. 247
Jung, C. G. 166
justice 80–1, 84, 86–7, 94
  in Asian theology 224
  in liberation theology 178, 181
justification, in Thielicke 139–40

Kabasele, F. 203
*Kairos Document* 210
Kalilombe, Patrick 171–2, 193–215
Kant, Immanuel 3, 35, 36, 44, 46, 55, 57, 275, 291
Kantzer, Kenneth 142
Karsavin, L. P. 162
Kaufman, Gordon 73, 89, 254, 265
  on human nature 92
  as mediating theologian 90
  on modernity 95, 96
  on theological method 93–4
  on truth of Christianity 91, 95–6
  *see also* history
Kelly, Kevin 242
Kelsey, David 116–17, 124
*kenosis, see* christology, kenotic
Khomyakov, Alexei Stepanovich 129, 154, 155
Khrapovitsky, Antonii 166
Kierkegaard, Søren 7, 126 n. 2, 162–3
King, Martin Luther 197, 198, 231
King, Ursula 242
kingdom of God
  in black theology 195
  in liberation theology 184–5
Kireevsky, Ivan Vasilievich 129, 153–4, 155, 160
Kitamori 226
knowledge, as situated 189
Koyama, Kosuke 172, 216–33
Krivoshein, Basil 162
Kuhn, Thomas 115, 276
Küng, Hans 5, 254, 258, 265
Kuyper, Abraham 134, 135–6, 147

Ladd, George E. 142
Lampe, G. W. H.
  on doctrines and dogmas 18–19
  on history in theology 1, 17–20, 22
  *see also* christology; Holy Spirit;
    incarnation; Trinity
language
  religion as 120
  religious 21–2, 37, 51, 124
    in Cupitt 60
    and feminist theology 249
    and Hellenistic influence 165
    in Hick 57
    and religious experience 120–1, 277,
      281–2, 283–4
Lessing, G. E. 35
liberalism 89–101; *see also* Protestantism, American liberal; theology,
  liberal
liberation 177–8, 182, 186–7, 198, 210–
  12
liberation theology 90, 94, 173–89, 194,
  197, 260, 286–7
  influences on 171, 174–5
Lightfoot, R. H. 16
Lincoln, G. Eric 200
Lindbeck, George 74, 115, 117, 125–6,
  253, 255–72, 294
  on doctrines 119–21, 124
  on ecumenical theology 254, 271 n.
    2, 276–8, 280, 281, 282–6, 288
  *see also* salvation
Lindsell, Harold 146
Loades, Ann 172, 235–51
Locke, John 36, 110, 118
Logos
  in Bavinck 135, 136
  in Cobb 109
  personification of 19
Lonergan, Bernard 90, 260
Long, Charles 200
Loomer, Bernard M. 103
Lossky, V. N. 129, 159–63, 166, 167
  on doctrine of 'energies' 162
  on *filioque* clause 162
  on negative theology 161–2
  on person and nature 160–1
  *see also* ecclesiology; God, doctrines
    of; hermeneutics; Holy Spirit;
    Trinity
Lovin, Robin 73, 75–87

Luo Zhenfang 231 n. 1
Luther, Martin 8, 25, 81, 140
Lutheranism 131, 146
Lyotard, Jean-François 292

McCann, Dennis 190 n. 19
McFague, Sally 242
Macintosh, D. C. 77
MacIntyre, Alasdair 125, 293
MacKinnon, Donald 2
  life 42–3
  on the transcendent 44–6
  *see also* ethics; God, doctrines of;
    history; incarnation; resurrection;
    revelation
Mackintosh, Hugh Ross 3
Macquarrie, John 2, 90
  as Anglican 49
  existentialism 50–2
  life 48–50
  on New Testament 50
  *see also* christology; ecclesiology;
    faith; God, doctrines of; hermen-
    eutics; history; incarnation; re-
    velation; transcendence; Trinity
*magisterium* 66 n. 7
Maimela, Simon 209
Maitland, Sarah 241
Manson, T. W. 23
Mar Gregorios, Paulos 168
Marsden, George 132, 133
Marxism
  influence 77–8, 175
  and liberation theology 171, 175–6,
    194
  and Orthodoxy 156–7
Mascall, E. L. 38, 161
Mbiti, J. S. 200
Meeks, Wayne 116
messianism 186
metaphysics, theistic 108, 110
Metz, Johannes Baptist 109, 175
Meyendorff, John 167
Milingo, E. 204
minjung theology 223–5
Miranda, José 180
Mitchell, Basil 67 n. 14
Mofokeng, Thakatso 209
Moltmann, Jürgen 109, 168, 175, 241,
  288
Moltmann-Wendel, Elisabeth 241

monarchianism, modalist 21
monism 107, 160, 162, 182, 186
Moore, G. E. 37
Motlhabi, G. M. 209
Moule, C. F. D.
  on history in theology 1, 15, 22
  on Paul 15
  *see also* christology; resurrection
mysticism 153
myth, in Macquarrie 50
*Myth of God Incarnate, The* 1, 21–2

narrative 74, 98, 117–19, 123–4, 124–5, 267
National Association of Evangelicals 133, 142
naturalism, ethical 44
neo-Marxism 90
neo-orthodoxy 90, 93, 258–9, 264–5, 294
Neoplatonism 152
New Testament studies 1, 5, 8, 23; *see also* Dodd, C. H.; Moule, C. F. D.
Nicaea, council 22
• Niebuhr, H. Richard 73, 81–4, 115
  on radical monotheism 83–4, 237
  on sectarian groups 82
  and theocentric relativism 79, 82–3, 199
  and theological realism 77, 81–4, 87
Niebuhr, Reinhold 73, 79–81
  on human nature 77, 79–80, 82, 85
  on justice 80–1, 84–5
  *Moral Man and Immoral Society* 77, 79
  *The Nature and Destiny of Man* 80
  as theological realist 77–8, 81, 84, 87
  *see also* faith
Nineham, Dennis
  on history in theology 1, 15–16, 22
  *see also* christology
noncontradiction, law of 144

objectivism 95
objectivity, in Cupitt 60
Ogden, Schubert 73–4, 89, 118, 191 n. 21
  on human experience 108
  as mediating theologian 90
  on method of correlation 91, 94, 95–6

on the self 92
  *see also* God, doctrines of
Okenga, Harold J. 142
Oldham, J. H. 78
Oman, John 35
ontology
  in MacKinnon 45
  in Macquarrie 51–3, 54
Orthodox theology 129–30, 152–69
orthodoxy
  critical, *see* Britain, theology in
  of evangelical theology 131, 133, 134, 147, 149

Palamas, Gregory 162
panentheism 53, 106, 159
Panikkar, Rayumando 287
Pannenberg, Wolfhart 118, 254
Pannikar, K. M. 218
pantheism 106, 107, 155, 157, 159
paralogy 292
particularity 12, 46, 52, 65, 96, 148–9, 280, 294
Parvey, Constance 241
Pascal, Blaise 154
patripassianism 21
personalism 146
phenomenology 41, 67 n. 11, 90, 93, 96
philosophy
  in British theology 3, 30–1, 34, 37–8, 40–1, 46–7, 49, 65
  moral 86
philosophy, of religions 96
pietism 89, 136, 153
Placher, William 74, 115–27, 294
Plaskow, Judith 237
Plato, influence on doctrines 19–20, 35
pluralism 275–6, 283–4
  *see also* religions, theology of
Pobee, John S. 172, 203, 204–6
politics, in liberation theology 186–7
poor
  and black theology 194–6, 211
  and liberation theology 173–84, 186–9
Popper, Karl 59
positivism, logical 44, 57, 62, 275
postliberalism 74, 115–27, 168, 253, 267, 294
postmodernism 64, 65, 74, 110–11, 168, 253, 291–5

power
  in black theology 211
  in morality 86
practice, common
  in English theology 31–2, 32–4, 61, 65, 293
  *see also* ethics
pragmatism, American 80, 292
praxis 99 n. 23, 149
  in African theology 204, 207
  in liberation theology 171, 176–9, 182, 185
predestination 207–8
presuppositionalism 144
prevenience of God 123
Price, H. H. 54
priesthood of all believers 10
process theology 73–4, 103–12, 293–4
Proclus 152
proofs, of existence of God, ontological 107, 119
propositionalism 119–20, 124, 265, 277, 280
Protestantism
  American liberal 75–6, 79, 84
  and ecumenism 258–61, 264
  and evangelical theology 131–2
Pseudo-Dionysius 152, 161

racism 194, 198, 200, 201, 207–8
Radford Ruether, Rosemary 172, 240–1, 242, 247–9, 286
Rahner, Karl 3, 90, 260
  on ecumenism 254, 258, 280, 282–6, 288
  influence 49, 51
Ramm, Bernard 146
Ramsey, Paul 86
rationality
  in English theology 31–2, 33–4, 36–8, 46–7, 65
  in Henry 144–5
  in postmodern thought 291–2
Ratzinger, Cardinal 258
'Ratzinger Letter' 191 n. 20
Rauschenbusch, Walter 75
realism 35, 38, 56, 59, 62, 66
  Christian 76, 81, 85, 86
  ethical 46–7
  theological, in American theology 73, 75–9, 81–7

reason, as contingent 37
redemption, in liberation theology 178, 182, 186–7
reduction 155, 280
reincarnation, in Hick 57
relativism
  historical 37, 73, 82, 199
  religious 69 n. 82, 143
  theocentric 73, 79, 82–3, 105, 280–1
religions, theology of 274–88
*ressourcement* 253, 255–6, 258–60, 263–6
resurrection
  in Frei 119, 124
  in MacKinnon 45
  in Moule 15
revelation
  in African theology 205
  in Berkouwer 136–7, 145
  in black theology 199
  in Dodd 14
  in evangelical theology 147, 148
  in feminist theology 246
  in Florovsky 164
  in Henry 143, 144–6, 147
  in Hick 58
  in MacKinnon 47
  in Macquarrie 52
  natural 205
  in Reformed theology 135–6
  and revisionism 96
  in Russian Orthodoxy 155
  in Thielicke 139–40, 145–6
  in Thiemann 123–4
  unity of 14
revisionism 89–101, 111
Ricoeur, Paul 293
Ritschl, Albrecht 7, 9, 139
Roberts, J. Deotis 200
Robertson Smith, William 7
Roman Catholic Church, and ecumenism 258–61, 263–4
Romanides, John 167
Rorty, Richard 123, 125, 292, 294
Russell, Bertrand 37
Russell, Letty 238
Russia, Orthodox theology in 152–3
Ryle, Gilbert 115, 119

sacraments 6
  in Macquarrie 53
Saiving Goldstein, Valerie 237

salvation
  in African theology 206
  in ecumenical theology 275, 277, 279, 280–4
  in evangelical theology 132, 133, 137, 145, 148
  in Henry 145
  in Hick 58, 275, 283
  in Lindbeck 120
  in political theology 175
Samartha, Stanley J. 172, 218–21, 229
sanctification, in Thielicke 139–40
Sankara 219
Sayers, Dorothy 241–2
Schelling, Friedrich, influence on Russian Orthodoxy 152–3
Schillebeeckx, Edward 90
Schleiermacher, Friedrich 20, 55, 89–90, 139, 146, 154, 275
Schmemann, Alexander 167
scholasticism, *see* Thomism
Schüssler Fiorenza, Elizabeth 172, 240–1, 242, 24. 7, 248, 286
Schweitzer, Albert 13, 16
science and theology 35
Scotland, and teaching of theology 4–5, 7, 40
scriptures
  in Asian theology 217–18, 227
  authority of 116–17, 123, 132, 133, 136–8, 145–8, 295
  in black theology 199, 204–5
  in ecumenical theology 266–71
  in English theology 32, 33, 41, 65
  in feminist theology 236, 240–1, 244–5, 246
  in liberation theology 180, 184–5
sectarianism, sociological 125
Segundo, Juan Luis 180–1, 260
Sellars, Wilfred 123
Senghor, Léopold 201
Setiloane, Gabriel 209, 212
Sherburne, Donald 110
sin
  in feminist theology 237
  in Forsyth 9
  in liberation theology 178
Smart, Ninian 67 n. 11
*sobornost'* 154–5, 158–9, 163, 166
Sobrino, Jon 181

Social Gospel movement 75–6, 79, 82, 87
social theory, in liberation theology 187
socialism, religious 76, 77–8
society, and theology 33–4, 39–40, 41, 43, 65–6, 175–6, 178, 295–6
  in American theology 75, 77–9, 80–1, 84–5, 125
sociology, and liberation theology 179, 185
sociology of religion 86
Soelle, Dorothée 109
solidarity
  in African theology 203
  in liberation theology 175, 178
Soloviev, Vladimir Sergeevich 129, 154–5, 156–7, 160, 169
Song, Choan-Seng 172, 218, 221–3
Sophia
  in feminist theology 247
  in Russian Orthodoxy 154–5, 157–9, 164
Staniloae, Dumitru 162, 168
Stanton, Elizabeth Cady 236
Storkey, Elaine 241
subjectivism 51, 95, 162
Suh Nam-dong 225
Surin, Kenneth 73–4, 103–12, 289 n. 27, 293–4
Sykes, Norman, on history 1, 22–5, 27
Sykes, S. W. 1, 3–28
symbolism, core 227, 240, 242–4

Tardiff, Mary 24
Taylor, A. E. 35, 42
Taylor, Mark 295
Tempels, Placide 201–2
Temple, William 35, 78
Tennants, F. R. 35
Tenney, Merrill 142
texts, religious 116, 117–19, 267–70, 292, 294
theism
  classical 92, 104–5, 110, 111
  evangelical 143, 144, 145, 146
  neoclassical, process 97, 103, 104–6, 108–11, 293–4
  ontological 51

theocentrism 55, 58, 86, 275, 275–6, 280–1
theodicy, in Hick 57
theology
  biblical 5
  confessional 35, 66 n. 10, 295
  crisis 76, 79, 84–5
  dialectical, and British theology 27
  dogmatic 5, 17–18
  ecumenical 23, 27
  liberal 89–90, 111, 141–2, 264
    opposition to 7, 14, 27, 134, 139
  liberation 28
  mediating, *see* revisionism
  modern 5
  negative 161–2
  *nouvelle théologie* 264
  patristic 17–22, 160–1, 163–6, 168–9
  philosophical 5–6, 30–69, 51–3
  political 73, 175–6
  symbolic 52–4
  systematic 5–6, 42, 49, 94–5, 141
  teaching of 4–5, 7, 12, 16, 17–18, 27–8, 33, 34–5, 40, 116
  *see also* African theologies; Asian theology; black theology; ecumenical theology; feminist theology; Orthodox theology; process theology; religions, theology of
Thielicke, Helmut 129, 134, 138–40, 145–6, 147–8
  on human person 139
  on proclamation 138–9
  *see also* christology; ethics; faith; God, doctrines of; hermeneutics; Holy Spirit; incarnation; justification; revelation; Trinity
Thiemann, Ronald 74, 96, 123–4, 125
  on prevenience 123–4
  on promise 124
Thomas, M. M. 287, 288
Thomism 160–2
Tillich, Paul 14, 77, 90, 116, 190 n. 10, 237, 254, 285
Ting, K. H. 231 n. 1
Tlhagale, Buti 209
Torrance, Thomas 3, 5
Toulmin, S. 94
Tracy, David 73, 89, 254, 260
  as mediating theologian 90

on method of correlation 91, 94–6, 259, 294–5
  on modernity 95
  on the self 91–2
  *see also* God, doctrines of; hermeneutics
tradition
  in English theology 32, 33, 65
  in Russian Orthodoxy 155, 163, 168
traditionalism 264–6
transcendence
  in MacKinnon 44–6
  in Macquarrie 452–3
Trible, Phyllis 172, 240–1, 242, 244–6
Trinity
  in Bulgakov 157, 158
  in ecumenical theology 287
  in feminist theology 244
  in Lampe 6, 18–20, 21
  in Lossky 161–2
  in Macquarrie 53
  in *Myth of God Incarnate* 22
  and procession of Holy Spirit 19
  in Thielicke 139
  in Wiles 6, 20–1
triumphalism 47
Troeltsch, Ernst 73, 82
truth, of Christian theology 91, 95–8, 124, 276
Tshibangu, T. 202
Turner, Henry M. 196
Tutu, Desmond 209

United States of America 73–4, 90, 103, 167
  evangelical theology 129, 134, 141–8
  teaching of theology in 116, 141, 148
  *see also* black theology; feminist theology; Henry, Carl

Vanneste, A. 202
Vatican II 171, 175, 202, 238–40, 255, 257–60, 262
Vedanta, and Christianity 219
Vidler, Alec, *Soundings* 18
voluntarism 162, 166

Wahl, Jean 163
Ward, Keith 110
Ware, Kallistos 168
Washington, Booker T. 196

Washington, Joseph R. 197
Weber, Max 82
Weiss, Johannes 13, 16
Welker, Michael 110
West, Cornel 200
Whitehead, Alfred North 35, 74, 94, 108
  on concept of God 103–5, 107, 110
Wieman, Henry Nelson 103
Wiles, Maurice
  on history in theology 1, 20–2
  *see also* epistemology; Trinity
Williams, Delores 200
Williams, Rowan 129–30, 152–69
Willibrands, Willi 262
Wilmore, Gayraud S. 197, 200
Wittgenstein, L. 37, 115, 124, 126 n. 2, 168, 276
Wobbermin, Georg 8
Wolski Conn, Joann 247
women, ordination 270
Wood, Charles 124
World Council of Churches 257–8, 261–2, 265
Wyschogrod, Edith 293

Yale University 74, 115–17
Yang Sung-woo 225
Yannaras, Christos 167, 168
Yoder, John Howard 125

Zizioulas, John 167, 168

*Index by Meg Davies*